PandoraHearts

Jun Mochizuki

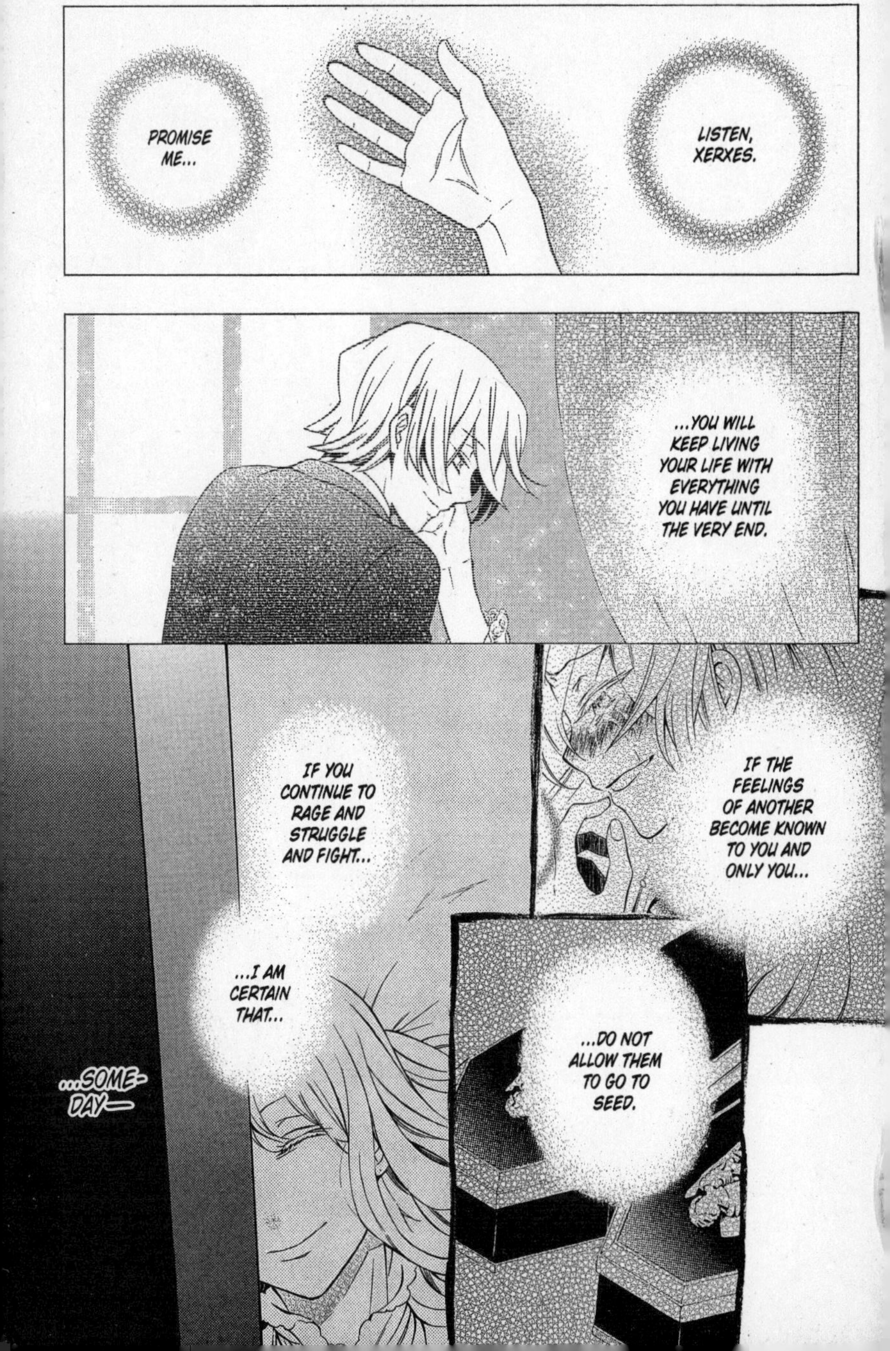
LISTEN, XERXES.
PROMISE ME...
...YOU WILL KEEP LIVING YOUR LIFE WITH EVERYTHING YOU HAVE UNTIL THE VERY END.
IF THE FEELINGS OF ANOTHER BECOME KNOWN TO YOU AND ONLY YOU...
...DO NOT ALLOW THEM TO GO TO SEED.
IF YOU CONTINUE TO RAGE AND STRUGGLE AND FIGHT...
...I AM CERTAIN THAT...
...SOME-DAY—

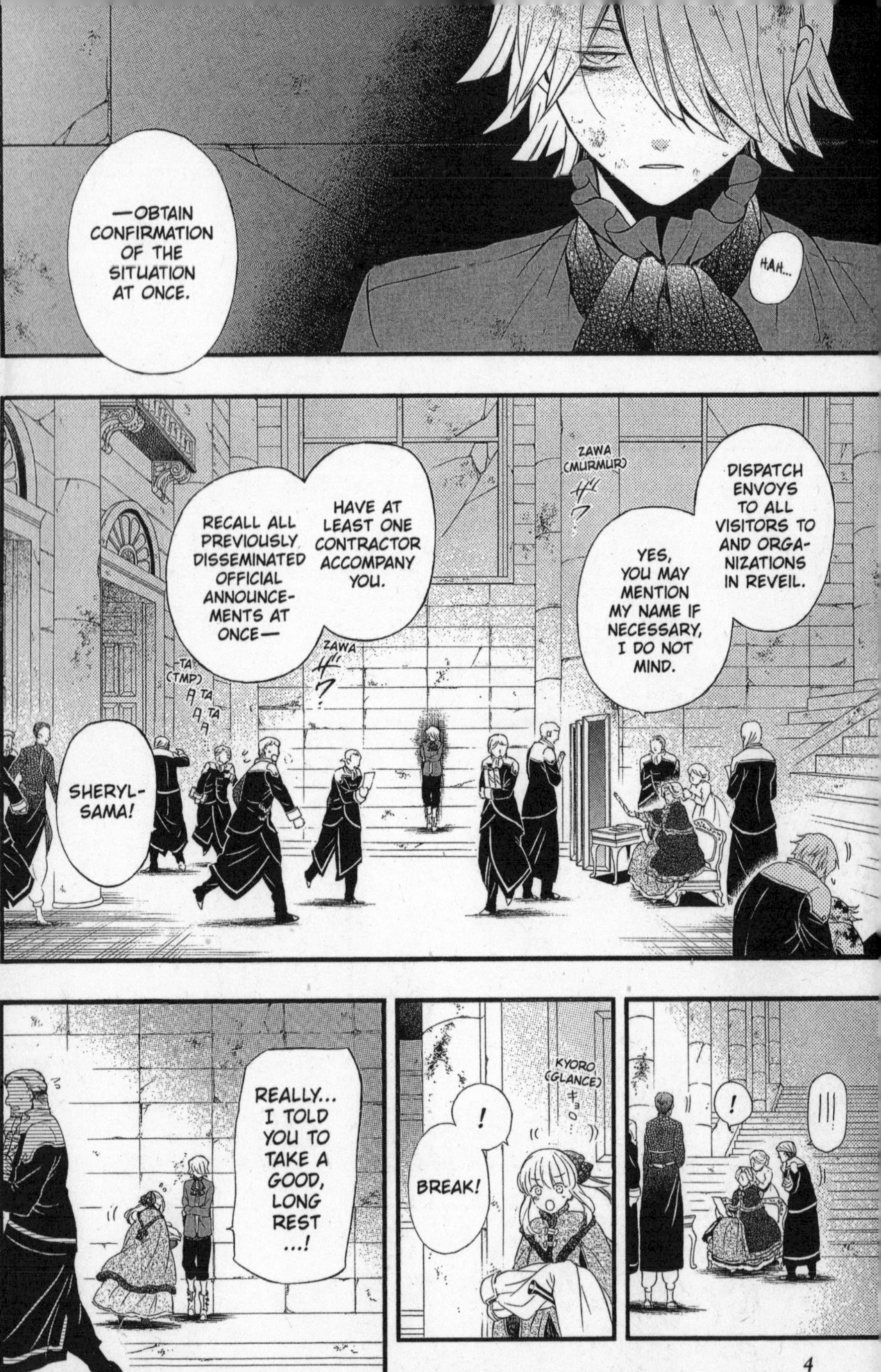
HAH...
—OBTAIN CONFIRMATION OF THE SITUATION AT ONCE.
DISPATCH ENVOYS TO ALL VISITORS TO AND ORGANIZATIONS IN REVEIL.
ZAWA (MURMUR)
YES, YOU MAY MENTION MY NAME IF NECESSARY, I DO NOT MIND.
HAVE AT LEAST ONE CONTRACTOR ACCOMPANY YOU.
RECALL ALL PREVIOUSLY DISSEMINATED OFFICIAL ANNOUNCEMENTS AT ONCE—
ZAWA
TA (TMP) TA TA
SHERYL-SAMA!
!!!
!
KYORO (GLANCE)
!
BREAK!
REALLY... I TOLD YOU TO TAKE A GOOD, LONG REST ...!

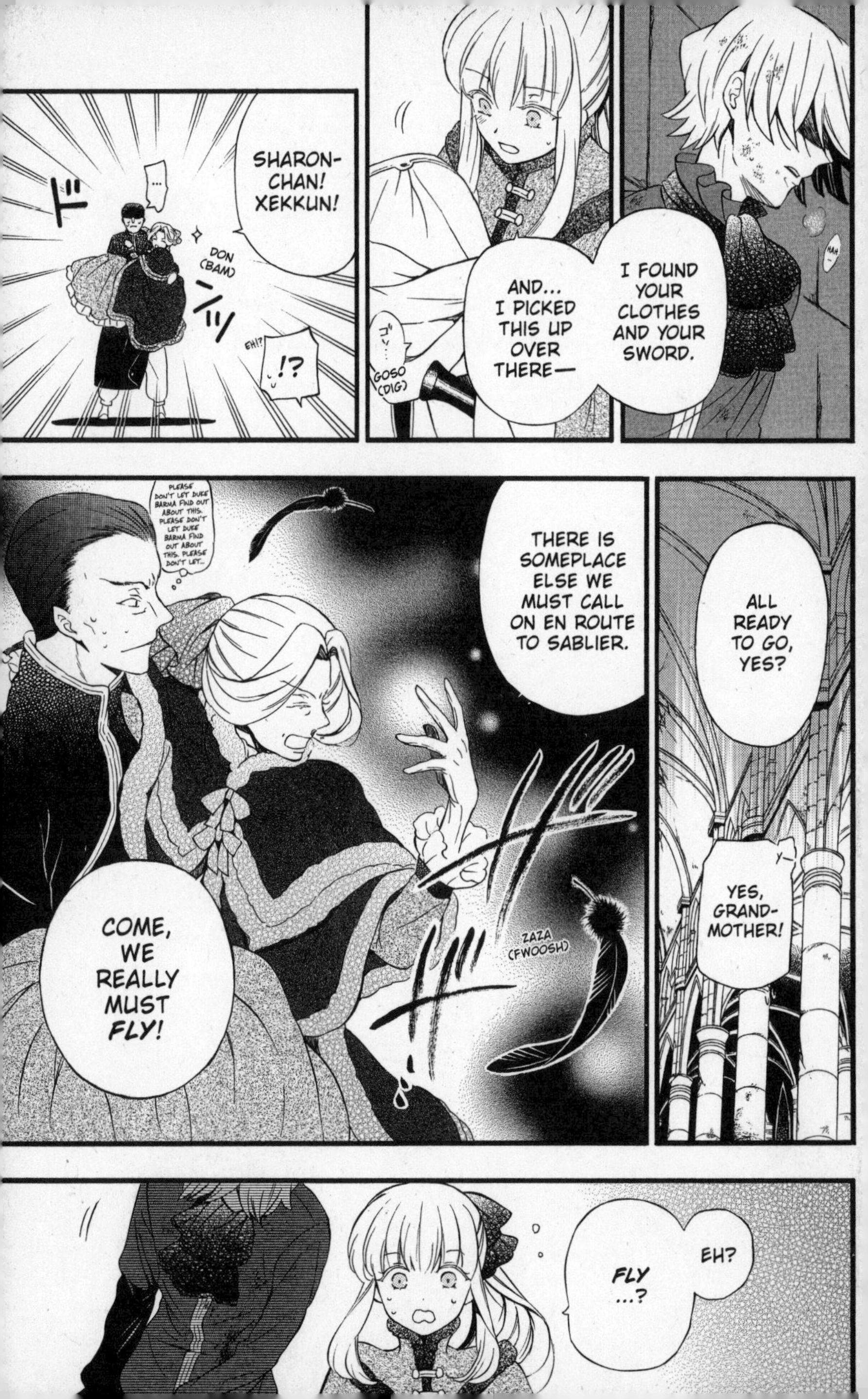
HAH—
I FOUND YOUR CLOTHES AND YOUR SWORD.
AND... I PICKED THIS UP OVER THERE—
GOSO (DIG)
SHARON-CHAN! XEKKUN!
...
DON (BAM)
EH!?
!?
ALL READY TO GO, YES?
Y—
YES, GRAND-MOTHER!
THERE IS SOMEPLACE ELSE WE MUST CALL ON EN ROUTE TO SABLIER.
PLEASE DON'T LET DUKE BARMA FIND OUT ABOUT THIS. PLEASE DON'T LET DUKE BARMA FIND OUT ABOUT THIS. PLEASE DON'T LET...
COME, WE REALLY MUST FLY!
ZAZA (FWOOSH)
EH?
FLY ...?

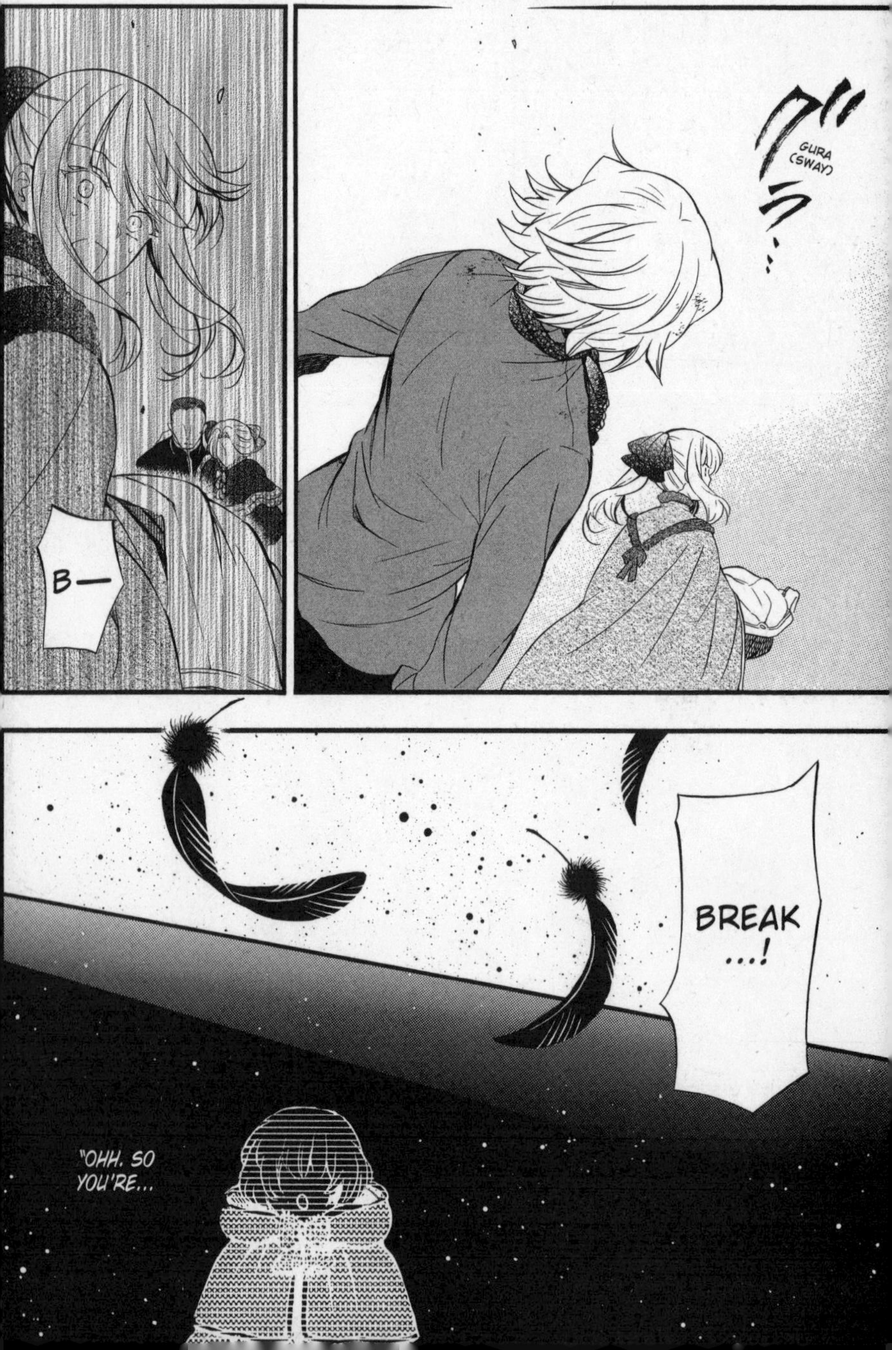
GURA (SWAY)
B—
BREAK ...!
"OHH. SO YOU'RE...

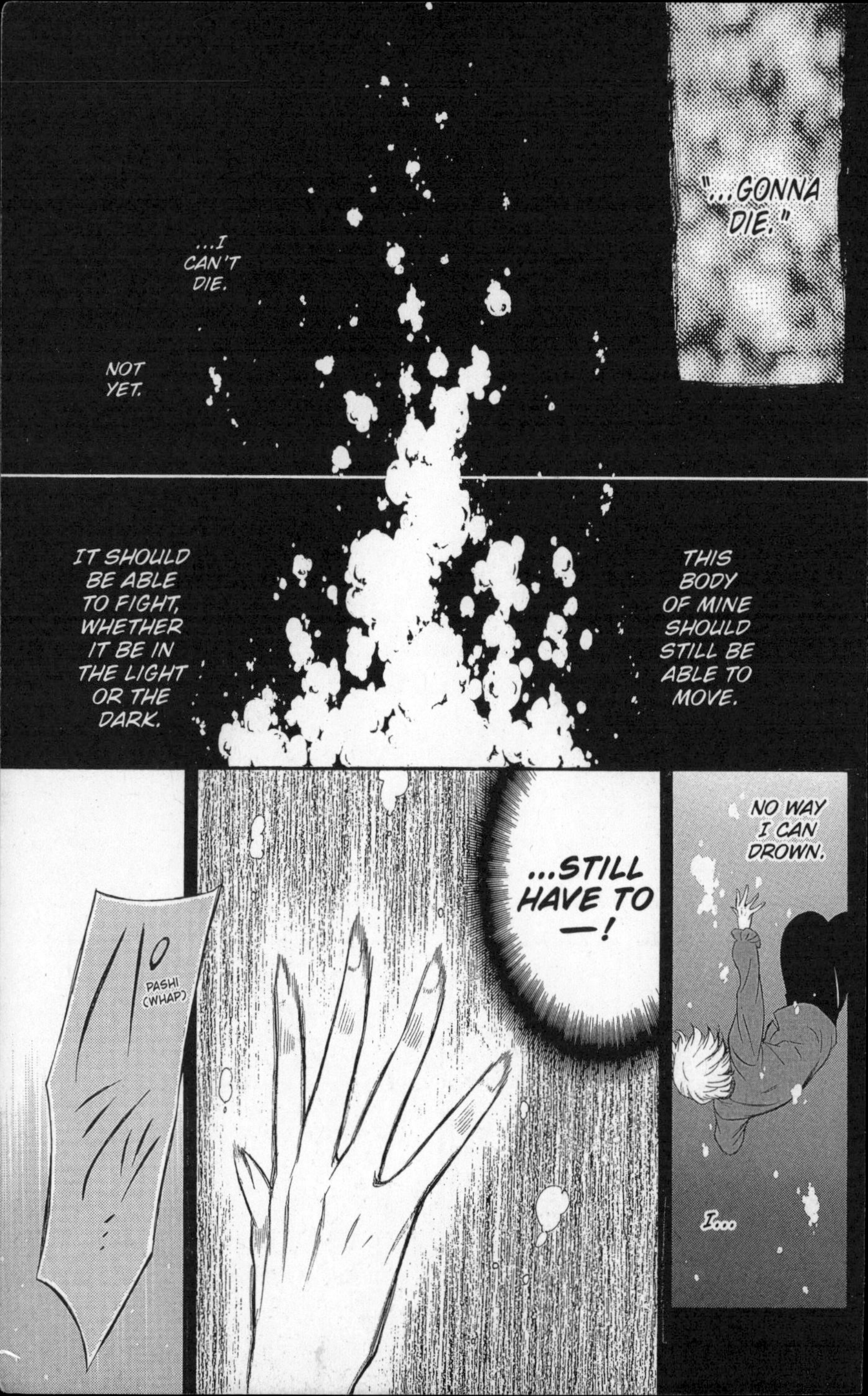
"...GONNA DIE."
...I CAN'T DIE.
NOT YET.
THIS BODY OF MINE SHOULD STILL BE ABLE TO MOVE.
IT SHOULD BE ABLE TO FIGHT, WHETHER IT BE IN THE LIGHT OR THE DARK.
NO WAY I CAN DROWN.
I...
...STILL HAVE TO—!
PASHI (WHAP)

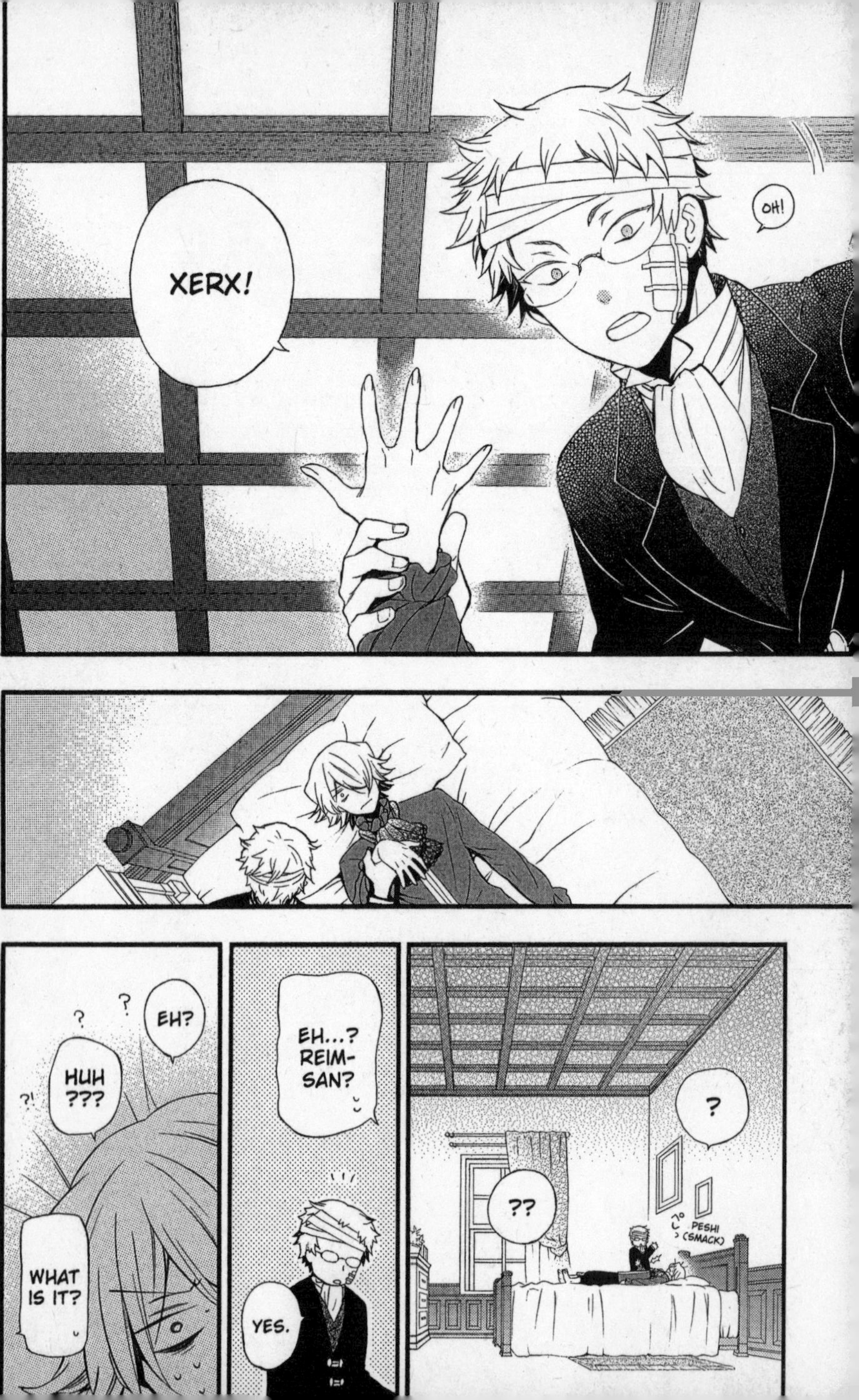
OH!
XERX!
?
PESHI (SMACK)
??
EH...? REIM-SAN?
YES.
EH?
HUH ???
WHAT IS IT?

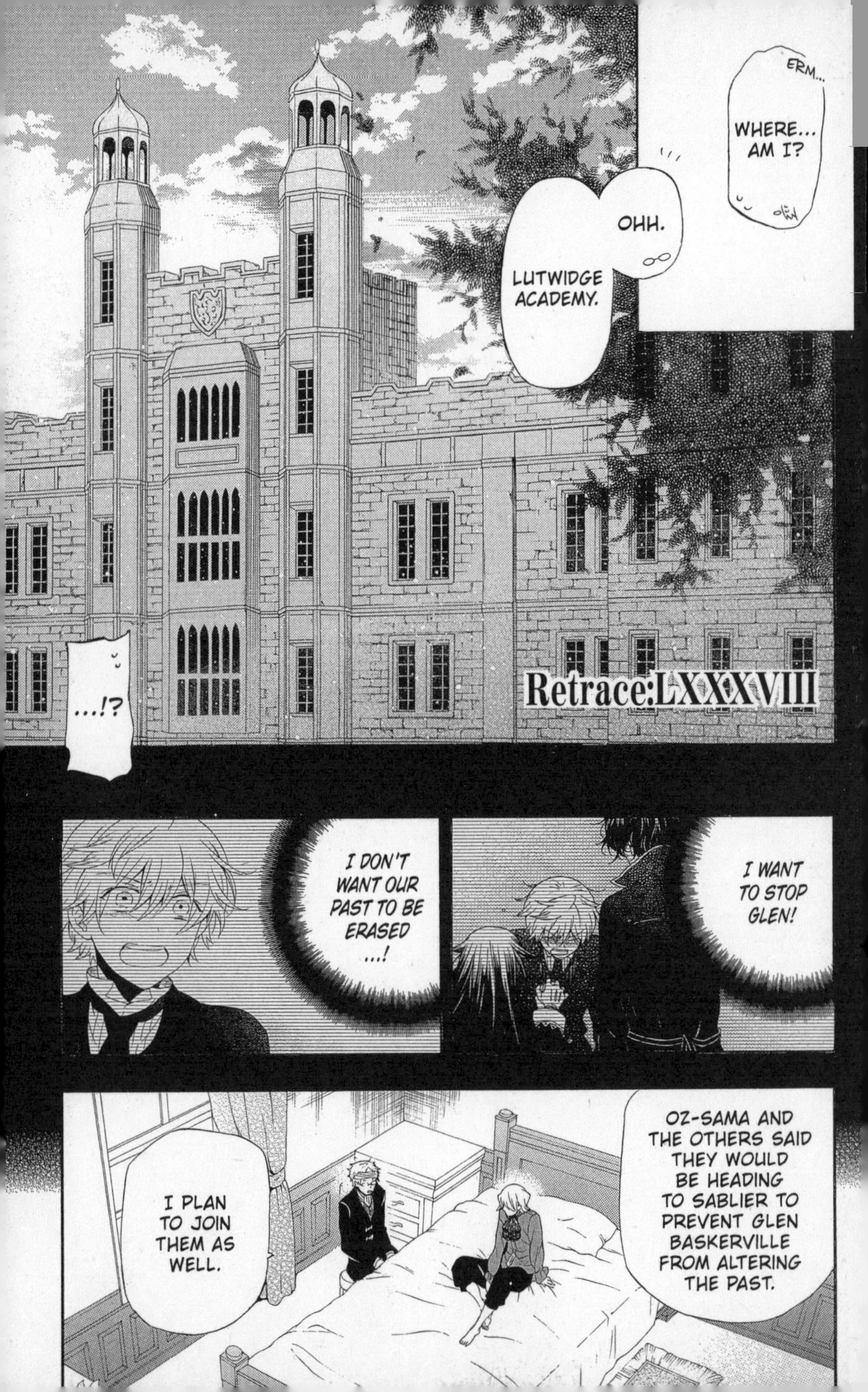
ERM...
WHERE... AM I?
OHH.
LUTWIDGE ACADEMY.
Retrace:LXXXVIII
...!?
I WANT TO STOP GLEN!
I DON'T WANT OUR PAST TO BE ERASED ...!
OZ-SAMA AND THE OTHERS SAID THEY WOULD BE HEADING TO SABLIER TO PREVENT GLEN BASKERVILLE FROM ALTERING THE PAST.
I PLAN TO JOIN THEM AS WELL.

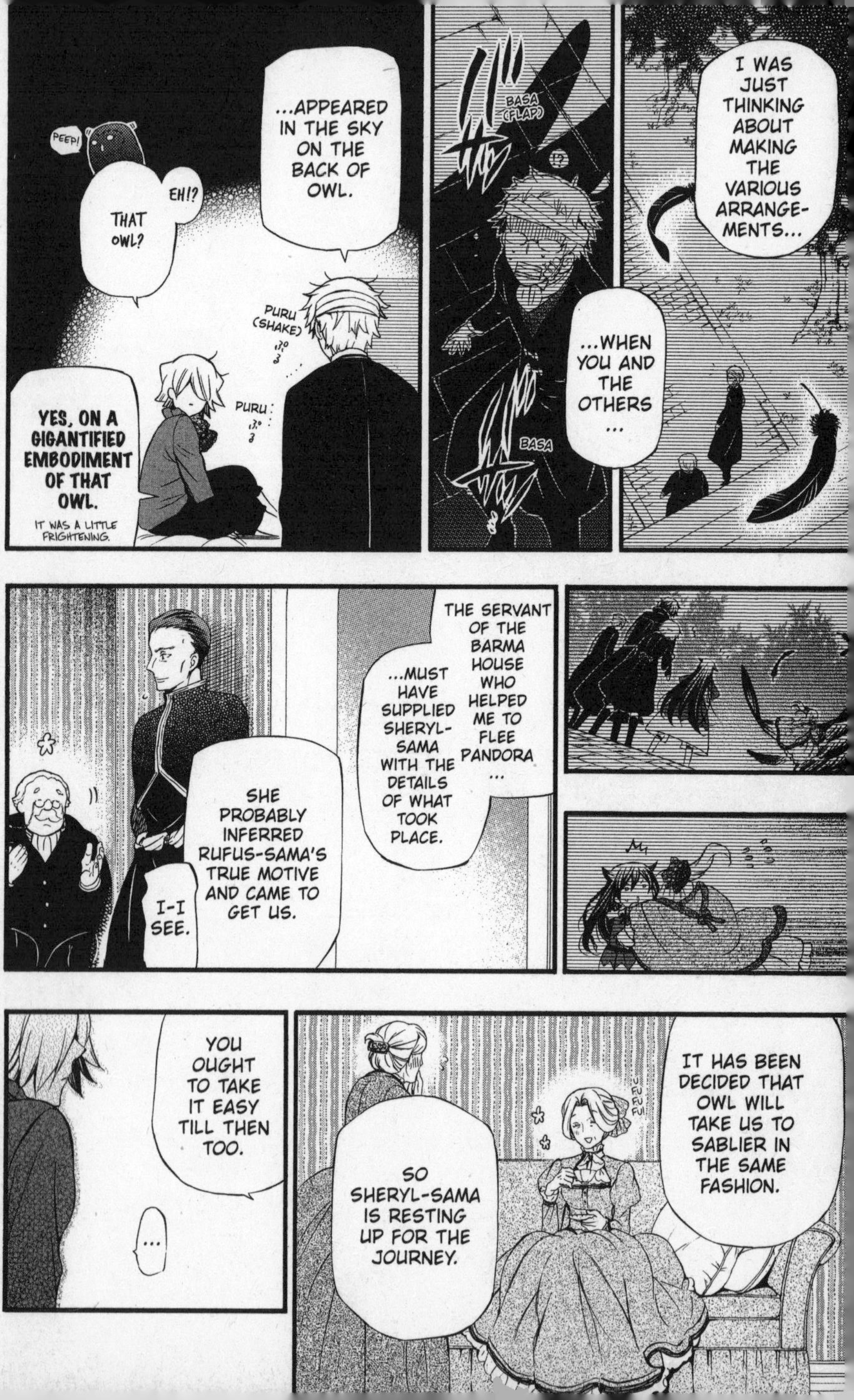
I WAS JUST THINKING ABOUT MAKING THE VARIOUS ARRANGE-MENTS...
...WHEN YOU AND THE OTHERS...
BASA (FLAP)
!?
BASA
...APPEARED IN THE SKY ON THE BACK OF OWL.
EH!?
THAT OWL?
PEEP!
PURU (SHAKE)
PURU
YES, ON A GIGANTIFIED EMBODIMENT OF THAT OWL.
IT WAS A LITTLE FRIGHTENING.
THE SERVANT OF THE BARMA HOUSE WHO HELPED ME TO FLEE PANDORA...
...MUST HAVE SUPPLIED SHERYL-SAMA WITH THE DETAILS OF WHAT TOOK PLACE.
SHE PROBABLY INFERRED RUFUS-SAMA'S TRUE MOTIVE AND CAME TO GET US.
I-I SEE.
IT HAS BEEN DECIDED THAT OWL WILL TAKE US TO SABLIER IN THE SAME FASHION.
UFUFUFU
SO SHERYL-SAMA IS RESTING UP FOR THE JOURNEY.
YOU OUGHT TO TAKE IT EASY TILL THEN TOO.
...

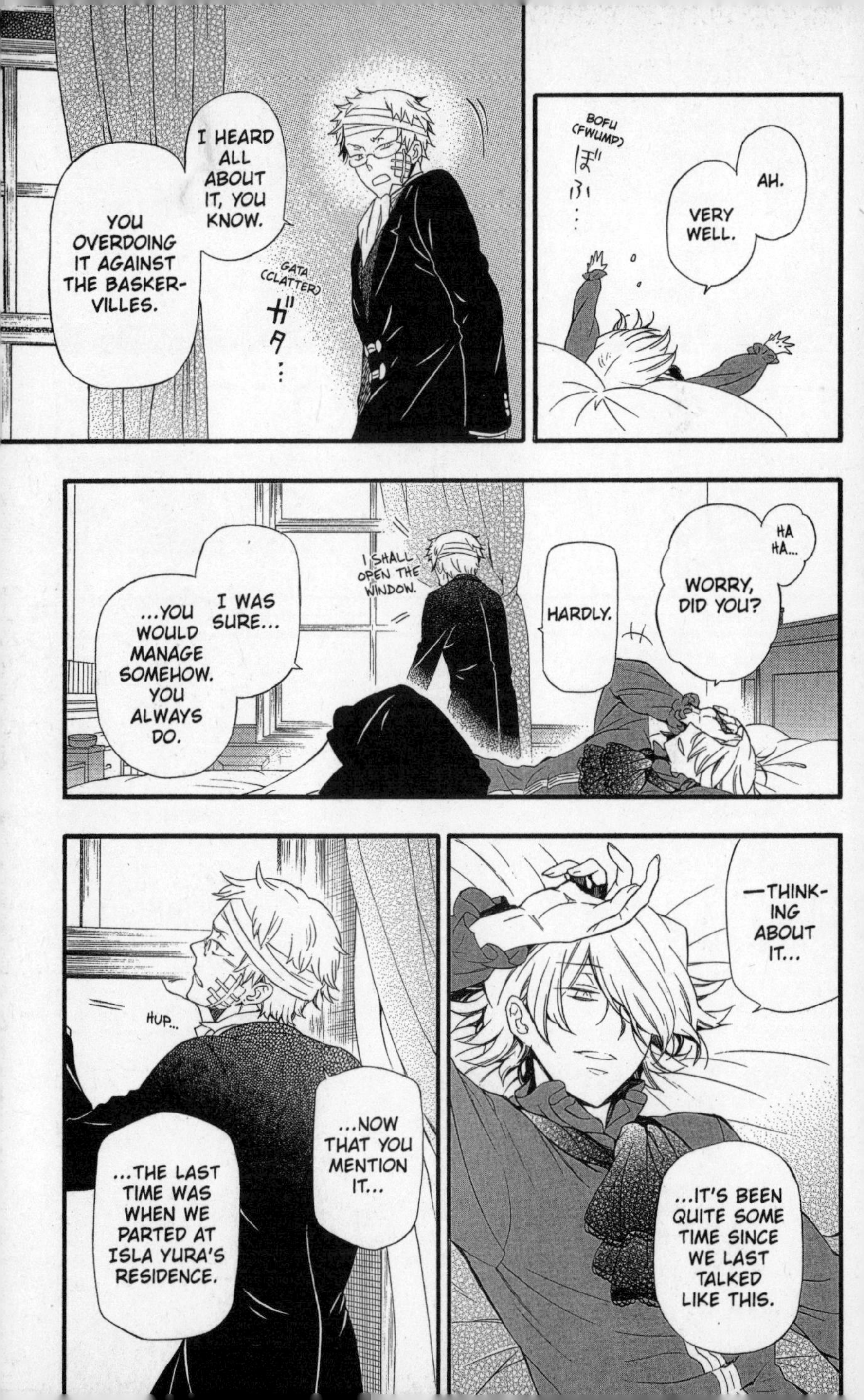
AH. VERY WELL.
BOFU (FWUMP) ぼふ…
I HEARD ALL ABOUT IT, YOU KNOW.
YOU OVERDOING IT AGAINST THE BASKER-VILLES.
GATA (CLATTER) ガタ…
HA HA...
WORRY, DID YOU?
HARDLY.
I SHALL OPEN THE WINDOW.
I WAS SURE...
...YOU WOULD MANAGE SOMEHOW. YOU ALWAYS DO.
—THINK-ING ABOUT IT...
...IT'S BEEN QUITE SOME TIME SINCE WE LAST TALKED LIKE THIS.
...NOW THAT YOU MENTION IT...
HUP...
...THE LAST TIME WAS WHEN WE PARTED AT ISLA YURA'S RESIDENCE.

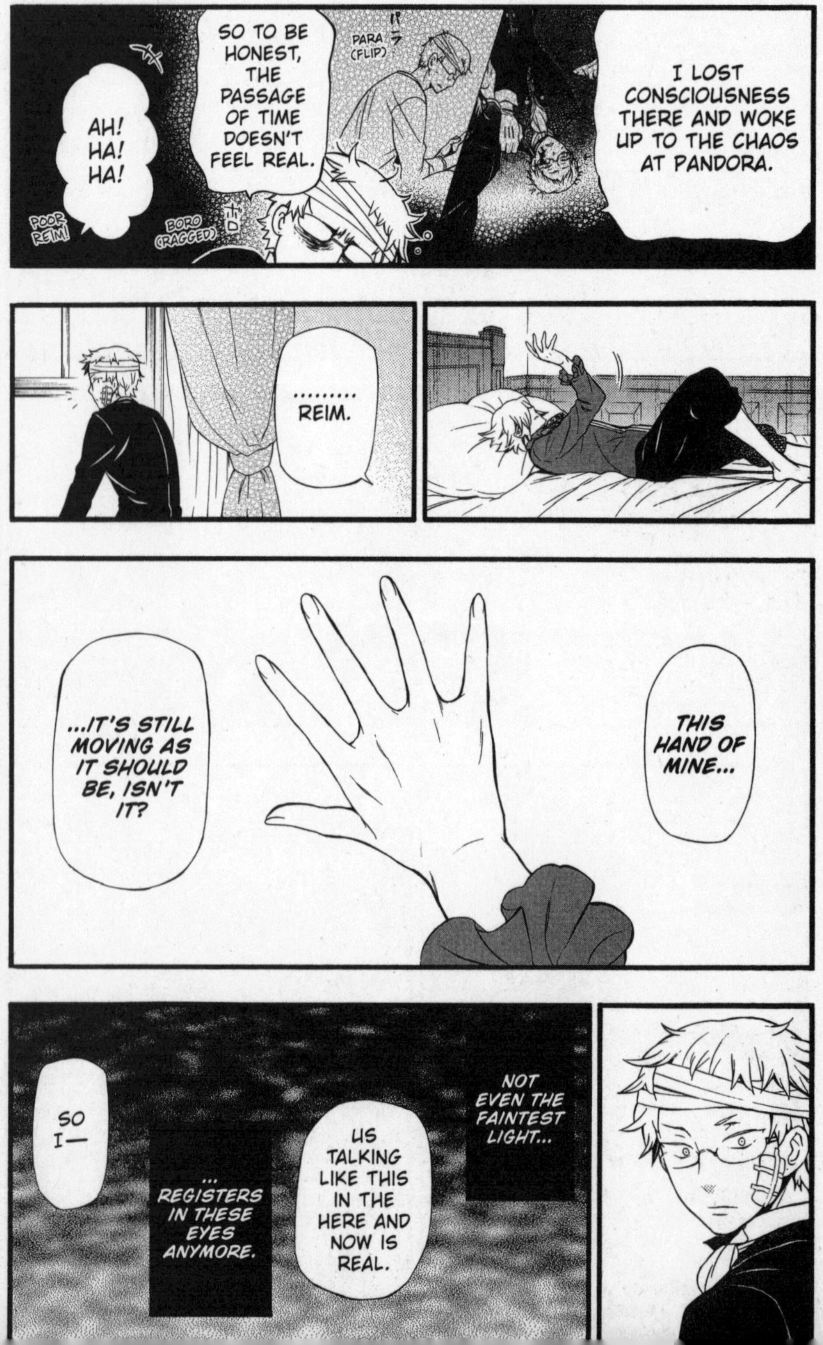
I LOST CONSCIOUSNESS THERE AND WOKE UP TO THE CHAOS AT PANDORA.
PARA (FLIP)
SO TO BE HONEST, THE PASSAGE OF TIME DOESN'T FEEL REAL.
BORO (RAGGED)
AH! HA! HA!
POOR REIM!
.... REIM.
THIS HAND OF MINE...
...IT'S STILL MOVING AS IT SHOULD BE, ISN'T IT?
NOT EVEN THE FAINTEST LIGHT...
US TALKING LIKE THIS IN THE HERE AND NOW IS REAL.
...REGISTERS IN THESE EYES ANYMORE.
SO I—

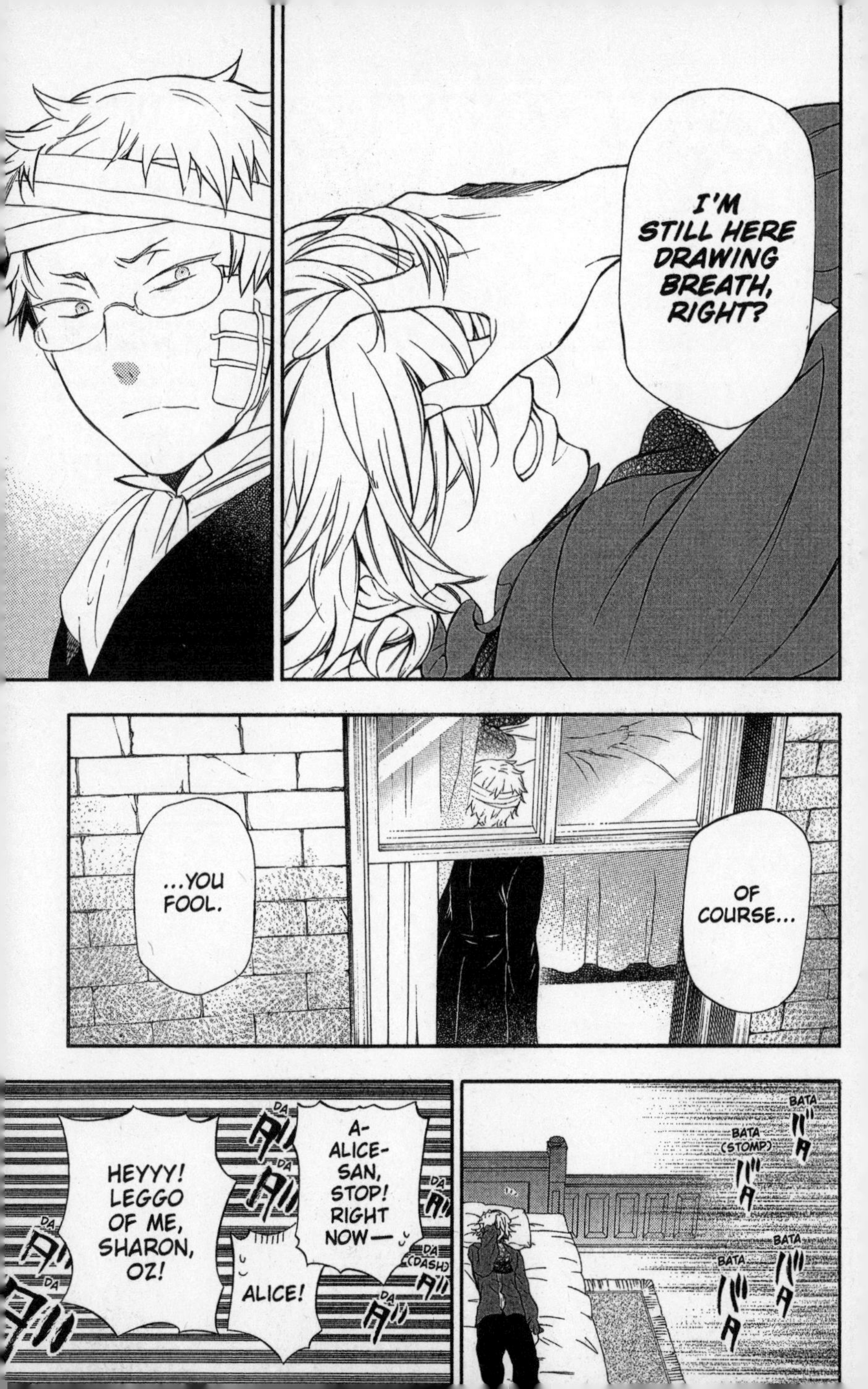

I'M STILL HERE DRAWING BREATH, RIGHT?
OF COURSE...
...YOU FOOL.
BATA
BATA (STOMP)
BATA
BATA
A-ALICE-SAN, STOP! RIGHT NOW—
DA
DA
DA
DA (DASH)
DA
HEYYY! LEGGO OF ME, SHARON, OZ!
DA
DA
ALICE!

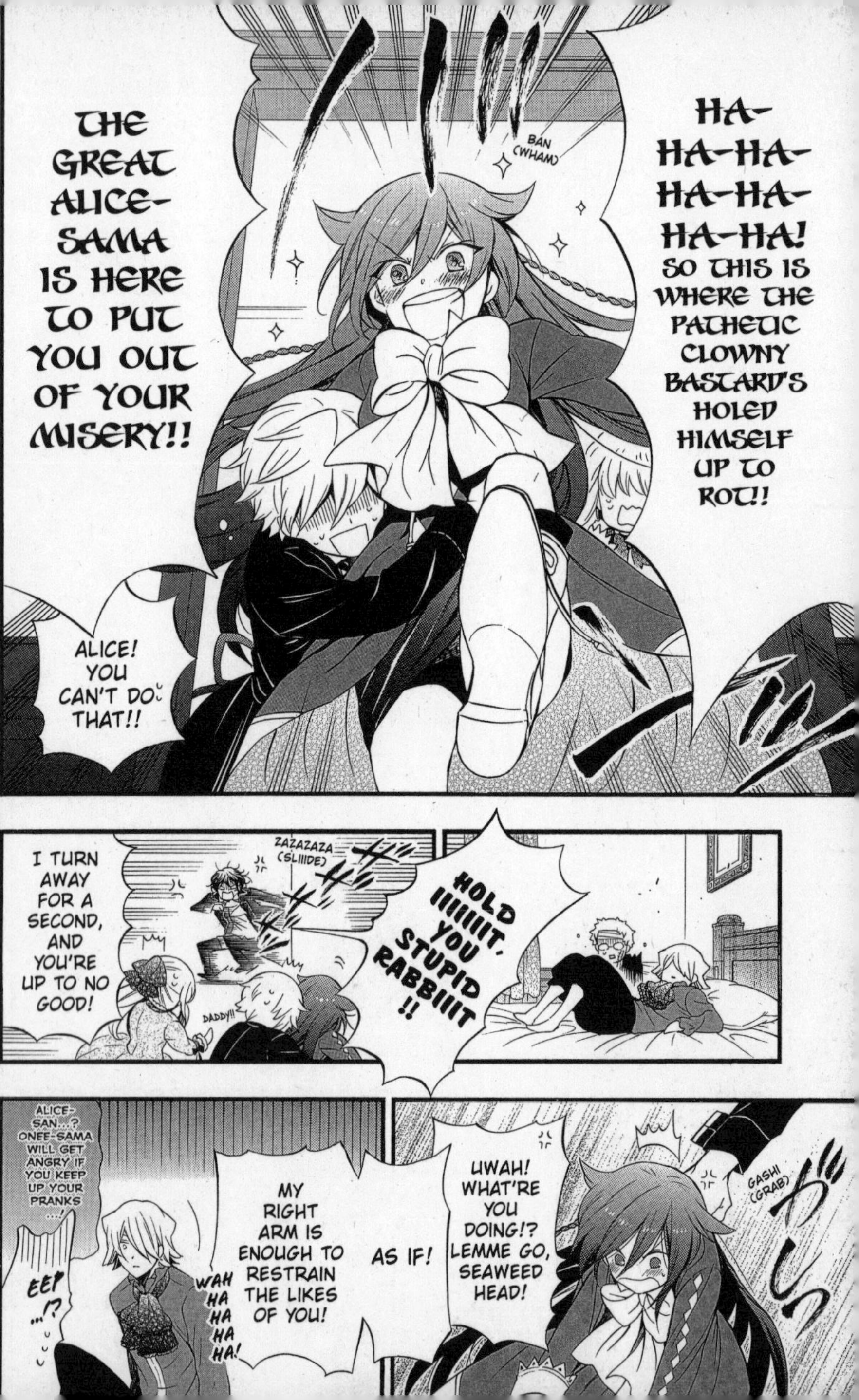
HA-HA-HA-HA-HA-HA-HA! SO THIS IS WHERE THE PATHETIC CLOWNY BASTARD'S HOLED HIMSELF UP TO ROT!!
BAN (WHAM)
THE GREAT ALICE-SAMA IS HERE TO PUT YOU OUT OF YOUR MISERY!!
ALICE! YOU CAN'T DO THAT!!
HOLD IIIIIIT, YOU STUPID RABBIIIT!!
ZAZAZAZA (SLIIIDE)
I TURN AWAY FOR A SECOND, AND YOU'RE UP TO NO GOOD!
DADDY!!
GASHI (GRAB)
UWAH! WHAT'RE YOU DOING!? LEMME GO, SEAWEED HEAD!
AS IF!
MY RIGHT ARM IS ENOUGH TO RESTRAIN THE LIKES OF YOU!
WAH HA HA HA HA!
ALICE-SAN...? ONEE-SAMA WILL GET ANGRY IF YOU KEEP UP YOUR PRANKS...!
EEP...!?

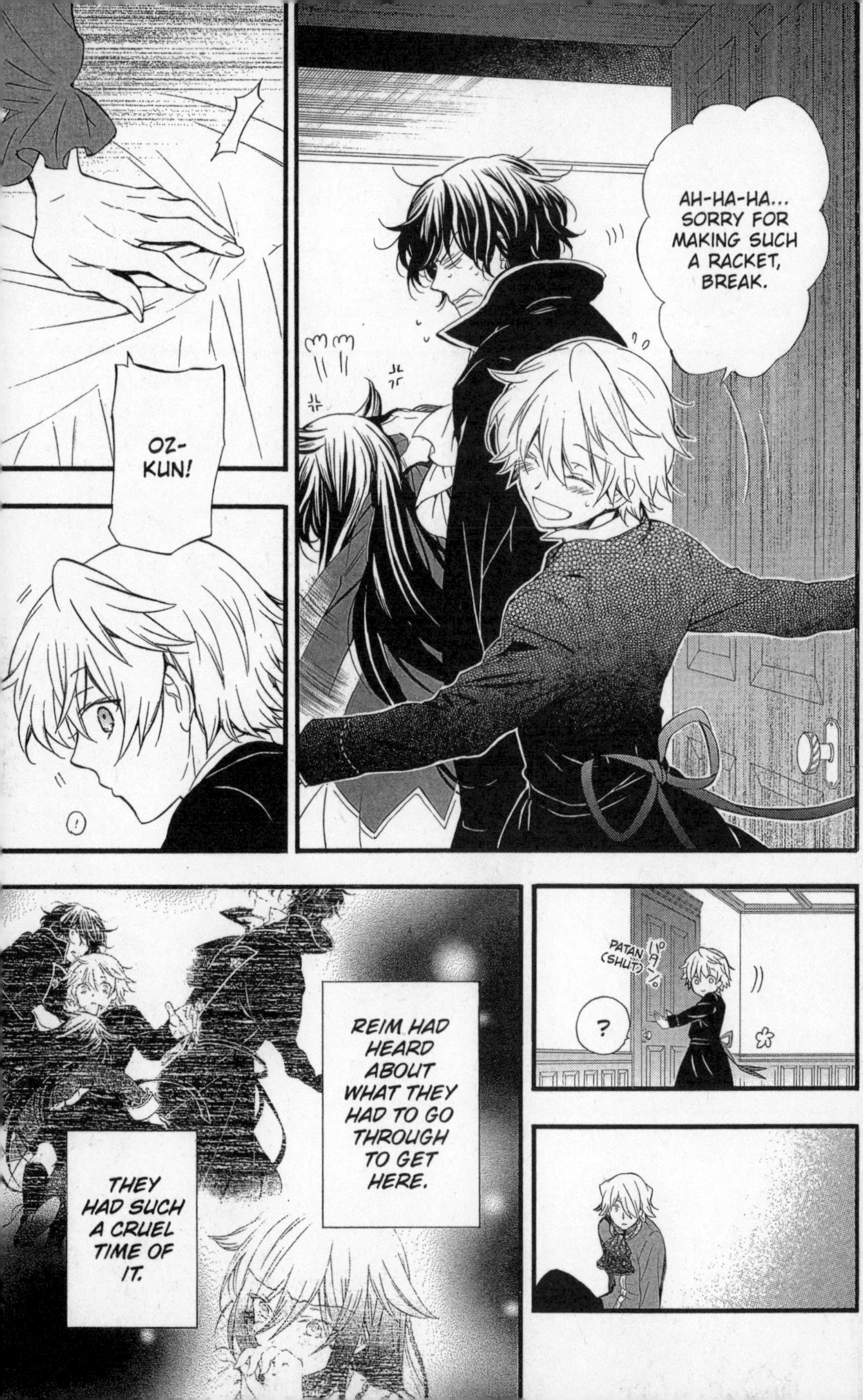
AH-HA-HA... SORRY FOR MAKING SUCH A RACKET, BREAK.
OZ-KUN!
PATAN (SHUT)
?
REIM HAD HEARD ABOUT WHAT THEY HAD TO GO THROUGH TO GET HERE.
THEY HAD SUCH A CRUEL TIME OF IT.

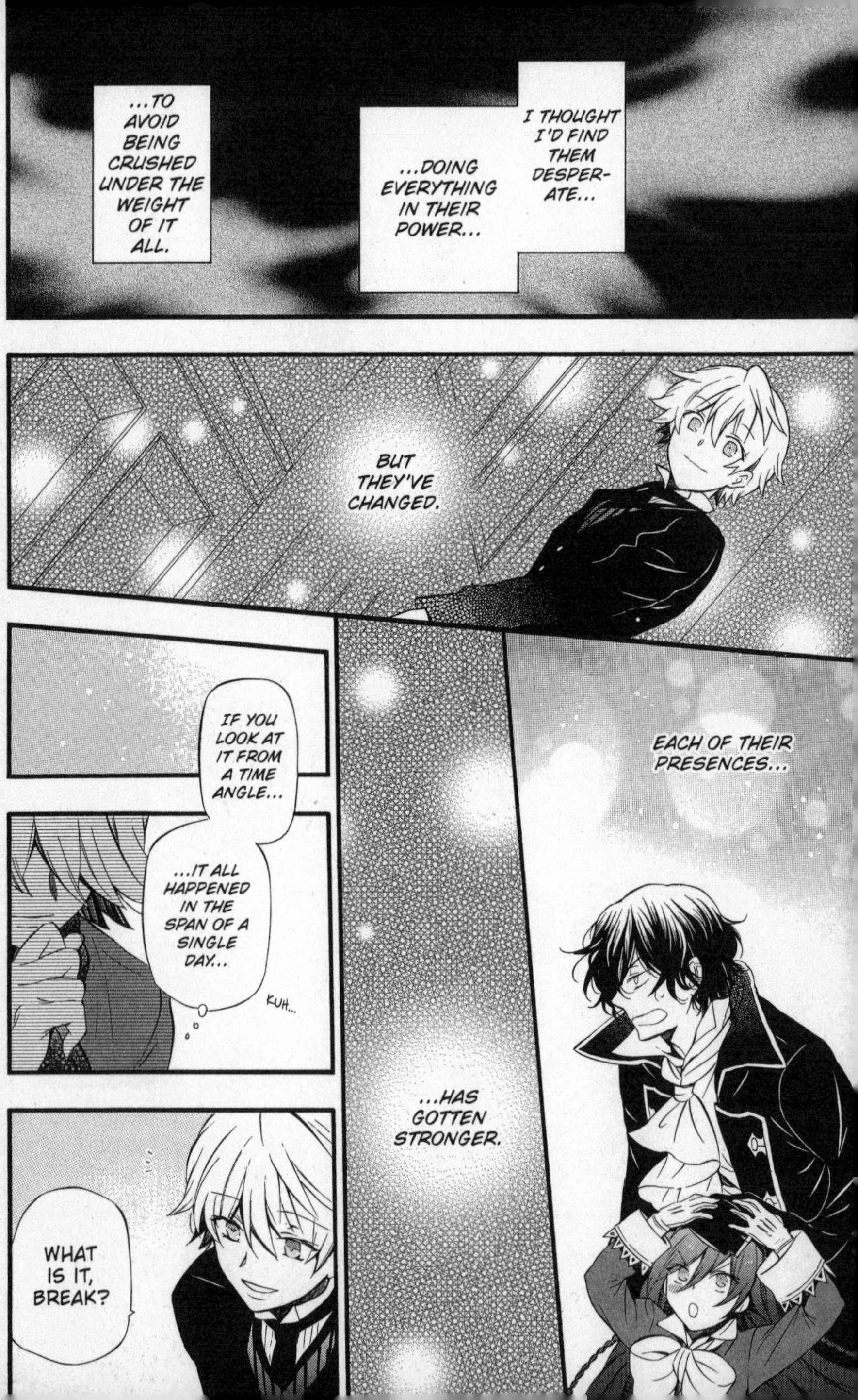
I THOUGHT I'D FIND THEM DESPERATE...
...DOING EVERYTHING IN THEIR POWER...
...TO AVOID BEING CRUSHED UNDER THE WEIGHT OF IT ALL.
BUT THEY'VE CHANGED.
EACH OF THEIR PRESENCES...
...HAS GOTTEN STRONGER.
IF YOU LOOK AT IT FROM A TIME ANGLE...
...IT ALL HAPPENED IN THE SPAN OF A SINGLE DAY...
KUH...
WHAT IS IT, BREAK?

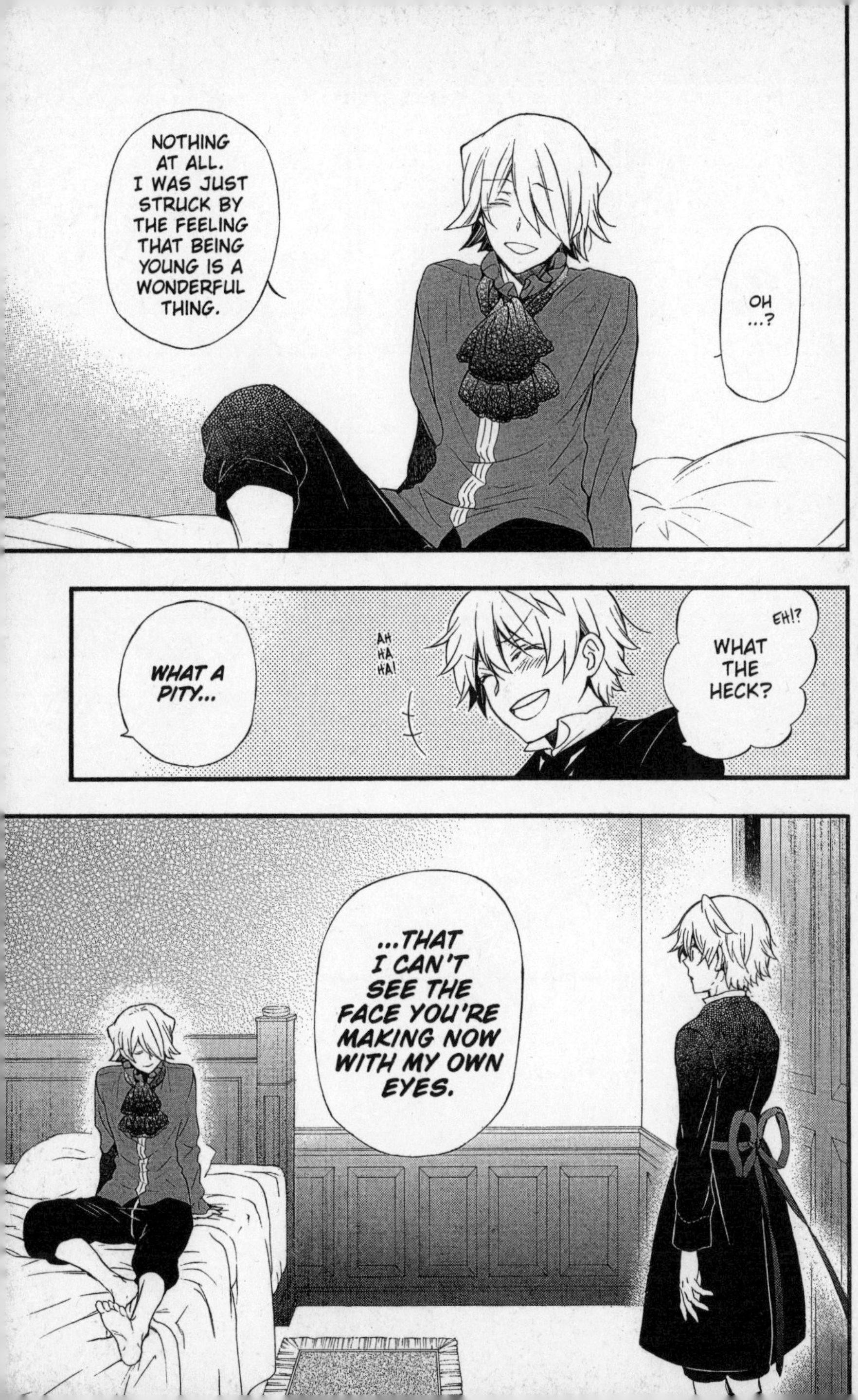
OH ...?
NOTHING AT ALL. I WAS JUST STRUCK BY THE FEELING THAT BEING YOUNG IS A WONDERFUL THING.
EH!?
WHAT THE HECK?
AH HA HA!
WHAT A PITY...
...THAT I CAN'T SEE THE FACE YOU'RE MAKING NOW WITH MY OWN EYES.

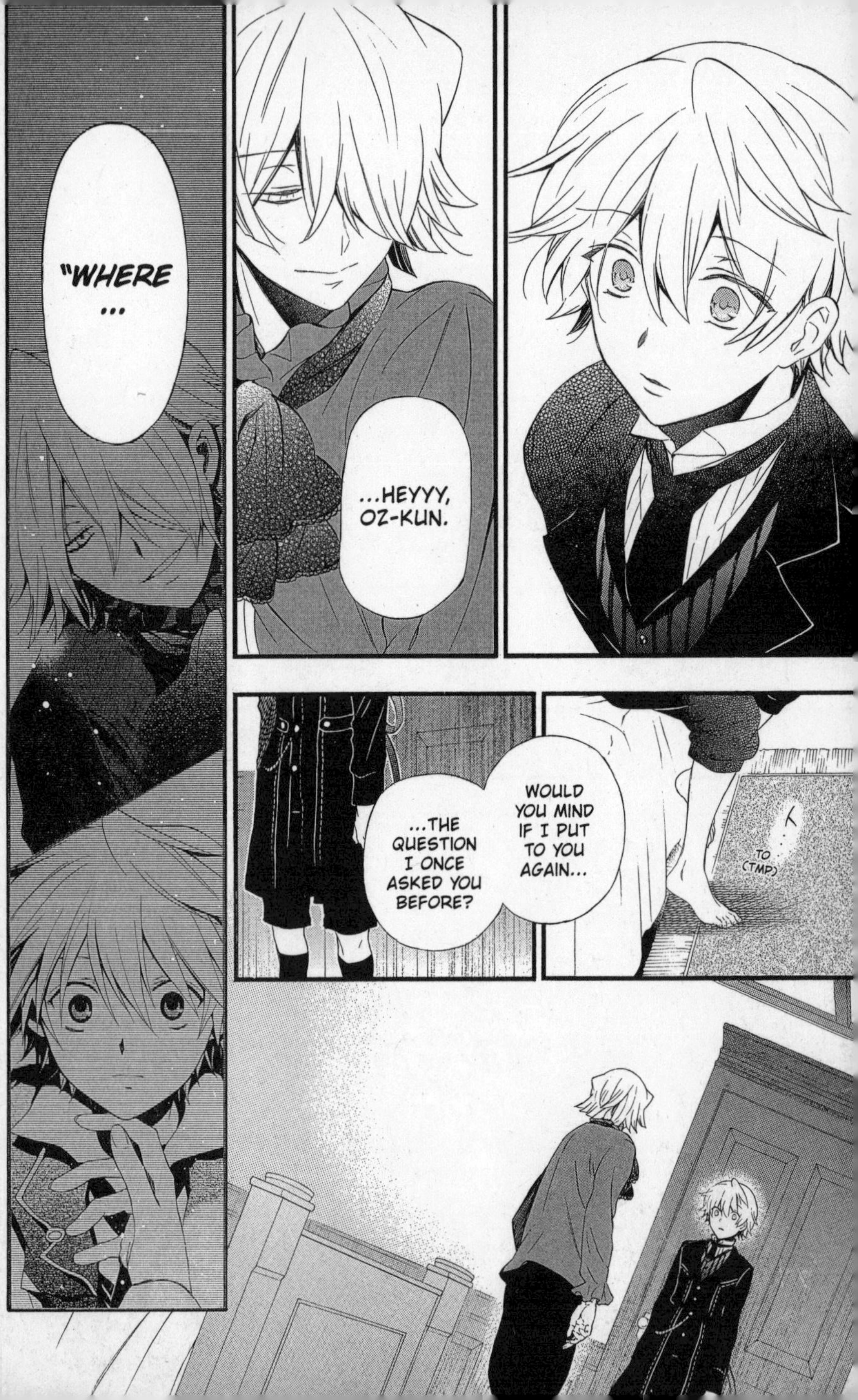
...HEYYY, OZ-KUN.
WOULD YOU MIND IF I PUT TO YOU AGAIN...
TO (TMP)
...THE QUESTION I ONCE ASKED YOU BEFORE?
"WHERE ...

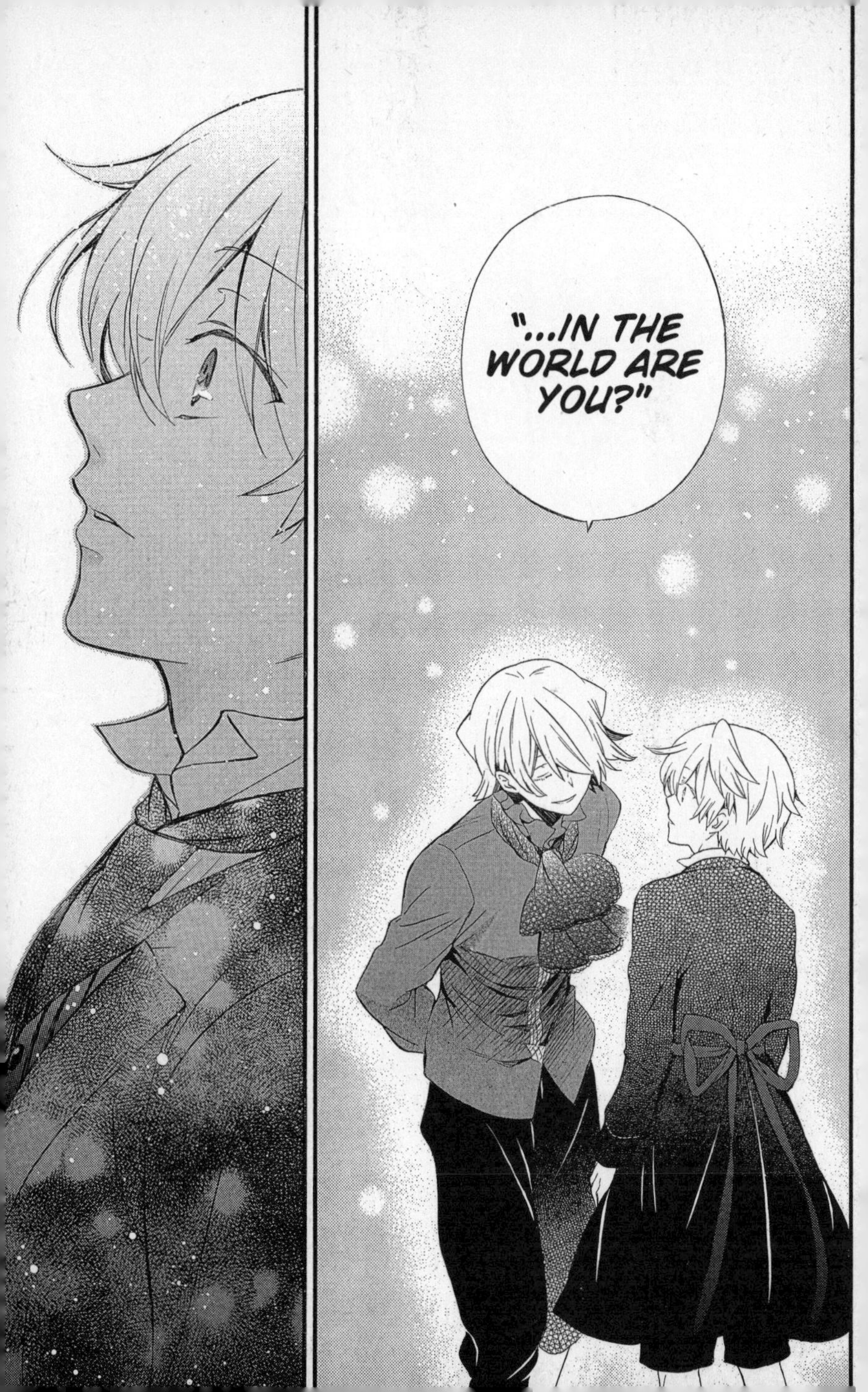
"...IN THE WORLD ARE YOU?"

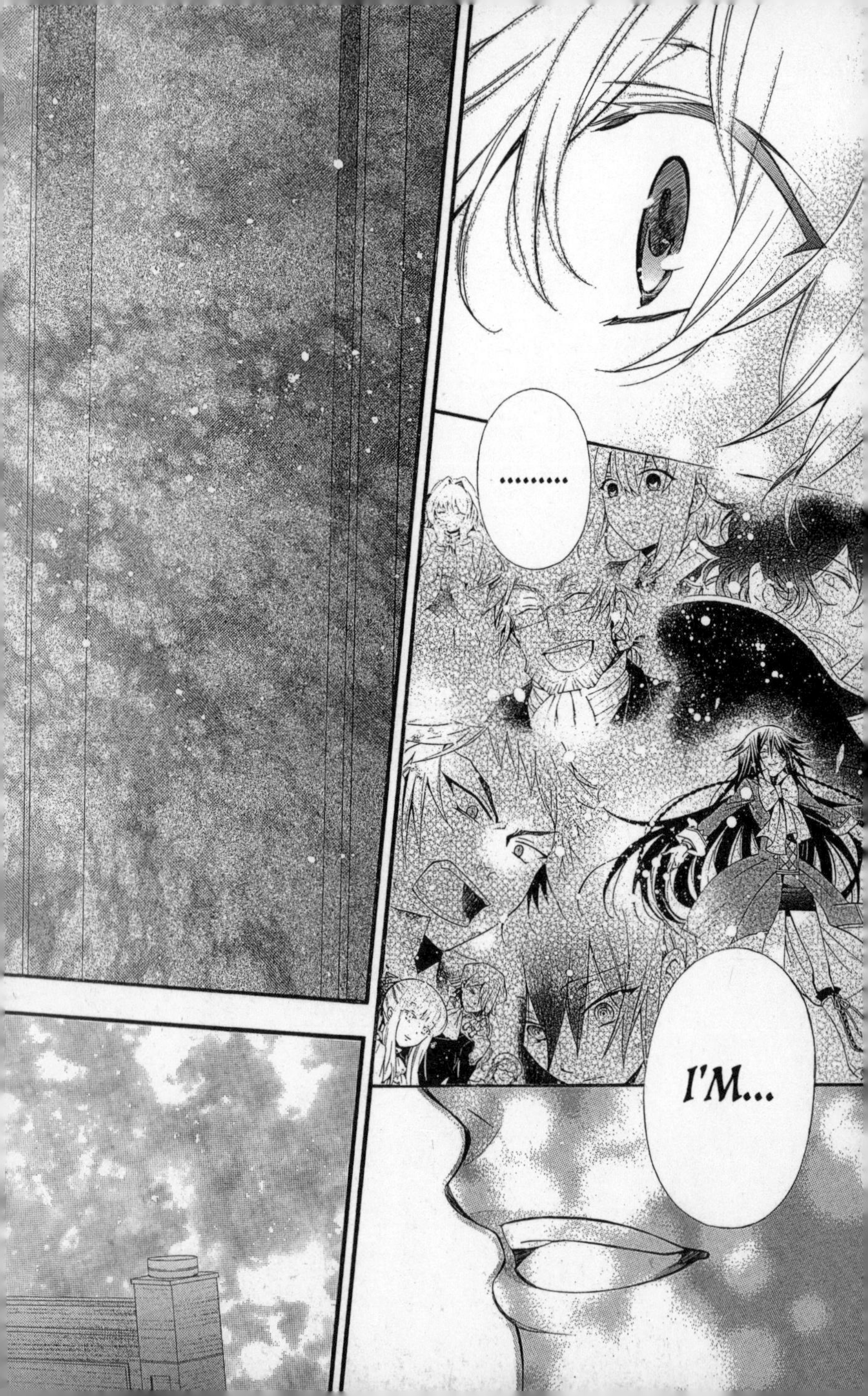
....
I'M...

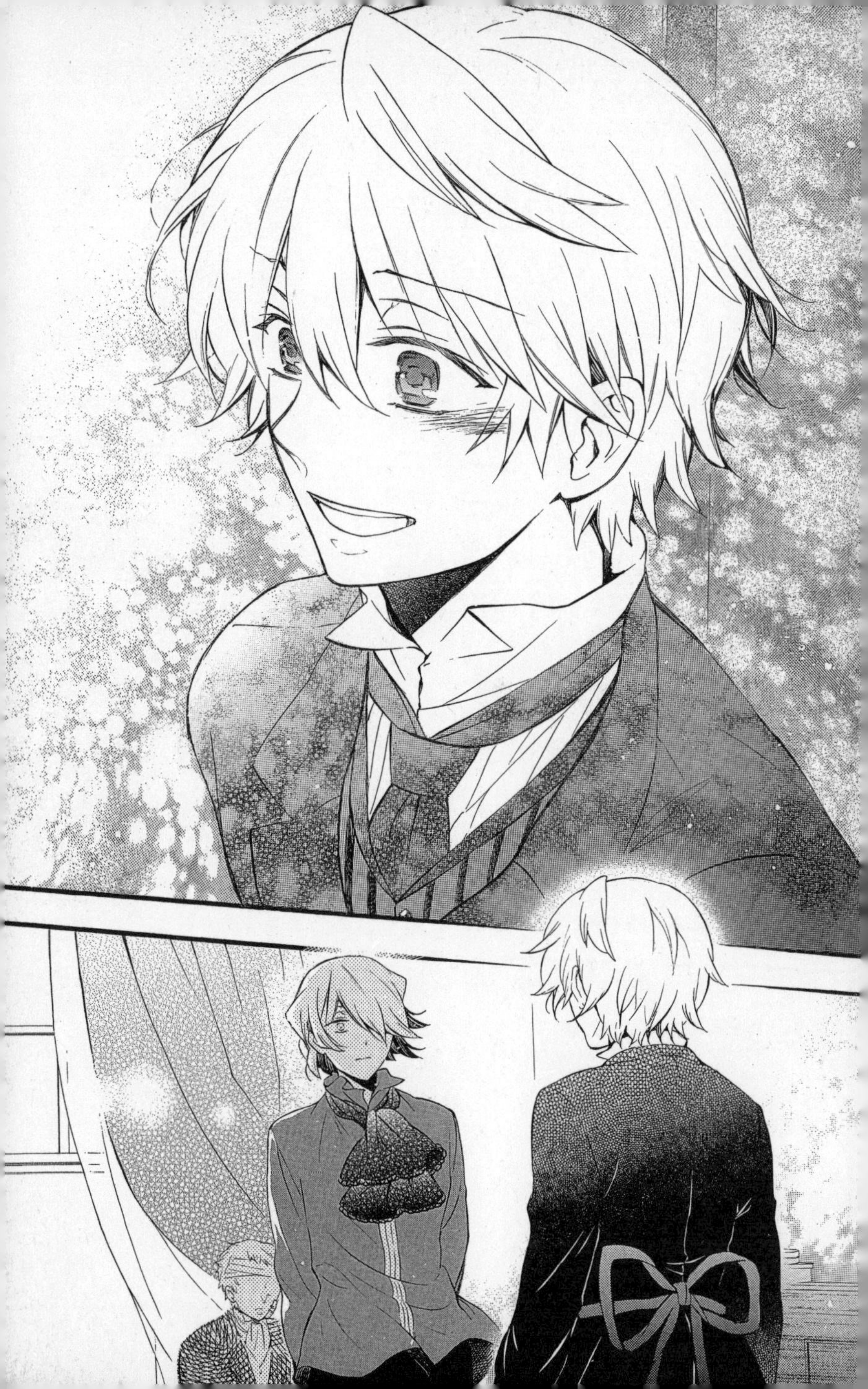

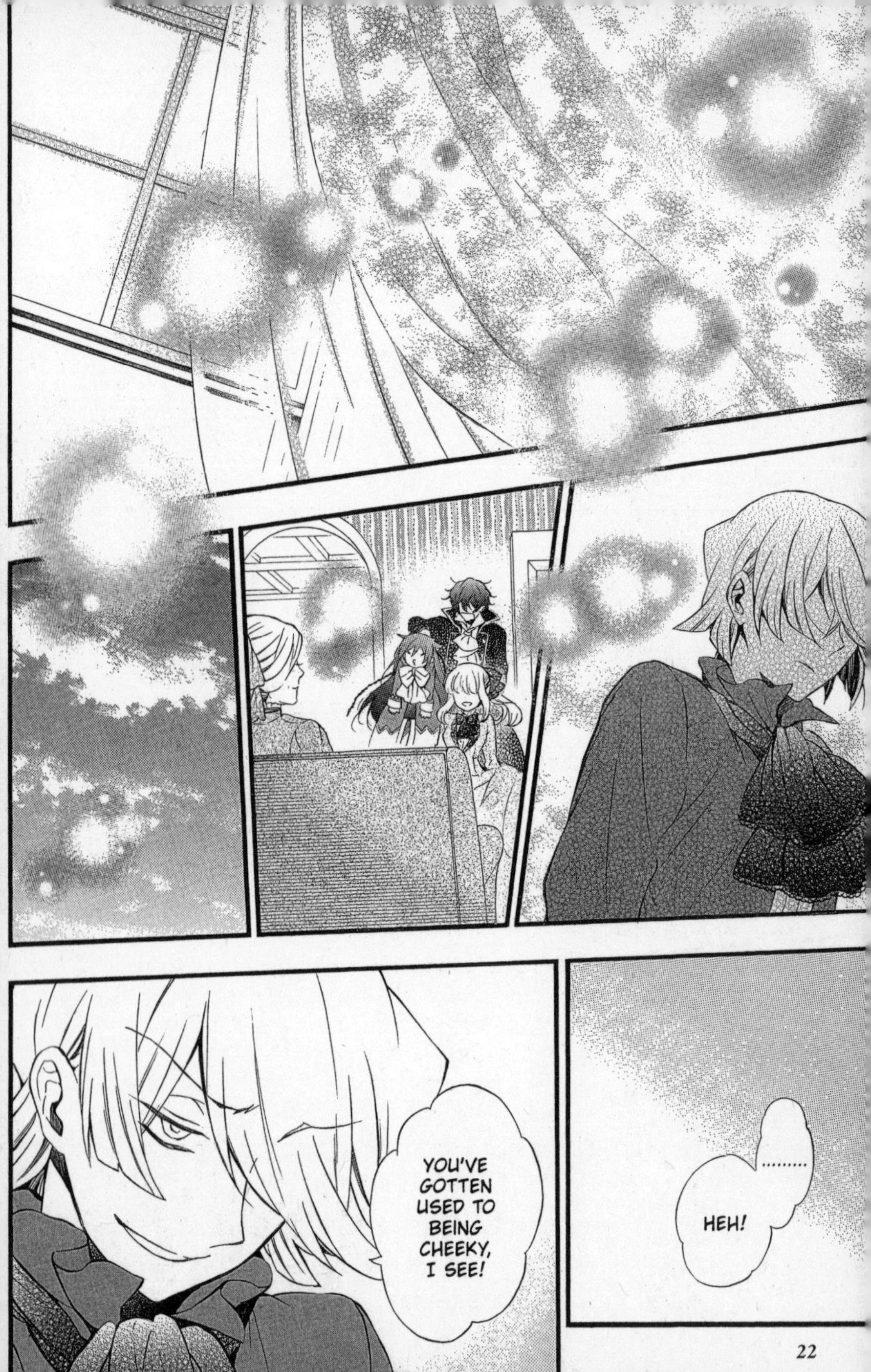
....
HEH!
YOU'VE GOTTEN USED TO BEING CHEEKY, I SEE!

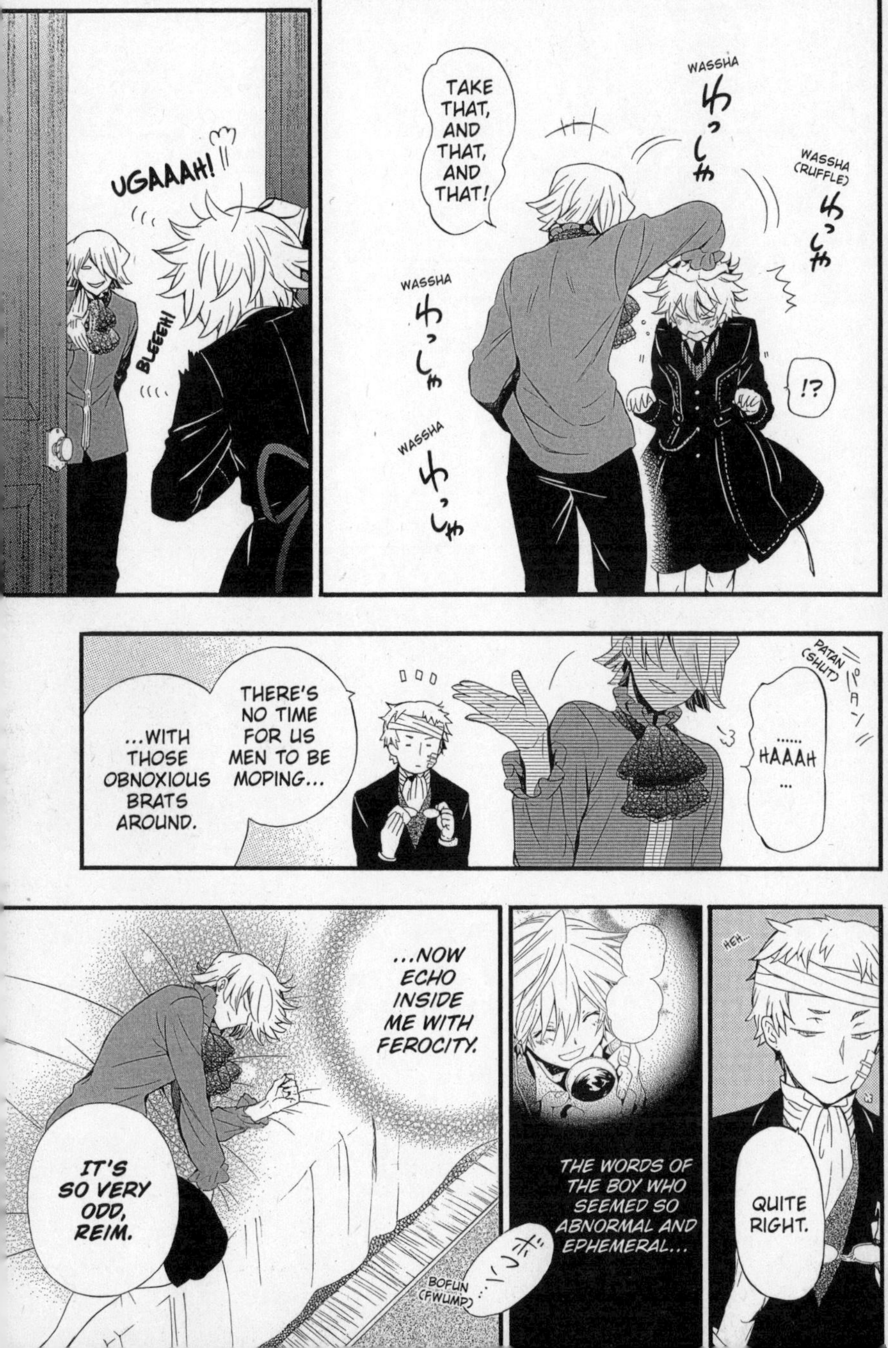
WASSHA
WASSHA (RUFFLE)
TAKE THAT, AND THAT, AND THAT!
WASSHA
!?
WASSHA
UGAAAH!
BLEEEH!
PATAN (SHUT)
......HAAAH...
THERE'S NO TIME FOR US MEN TO BE MOPING...
...WITH THOSE OBNOXIOUS BRATS AROUND.
HEH...
QUITE RIGHT.
THE WORDS OF THE BOY WHO SEEMED SO ABNORMAL AND EPHEMERAL...
...NOW ECHO INSIDE ME WITH FEROCITY.
BOFUN (FWUMP)
IT'S SO VERY ODD, REIM.

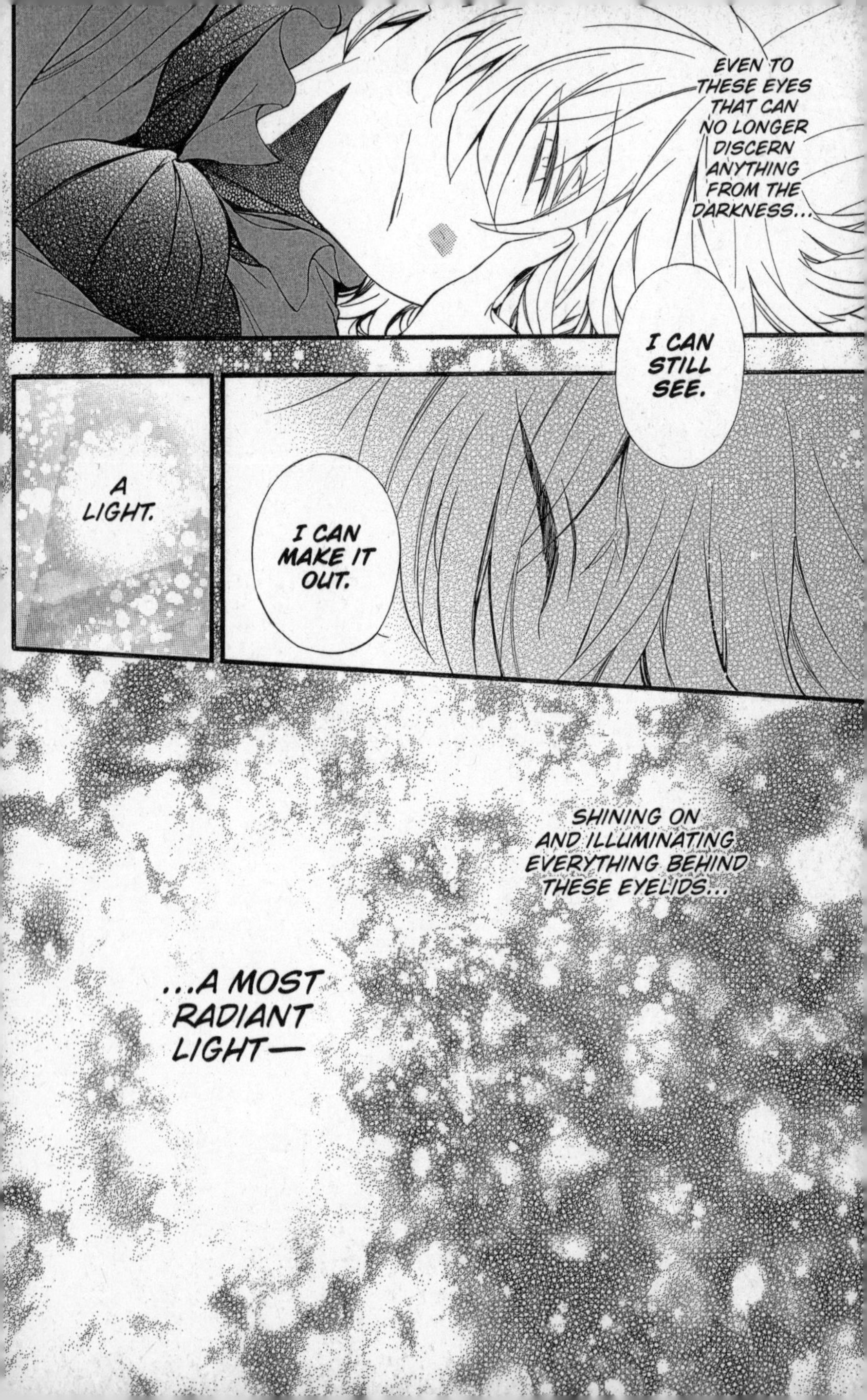
EVEN TO THESE EYES THAT CAN NO LONGER DISCERN ANYTHING FROM THE DARKNESS...
I CAN STILL SEE.
I CAN MAKE IT OUT.
A LIGHT.
SHINING ON AND ILLUMINATING EVERYTHING BEHIND THESE EYELIDS...
...A MOST RADIANT LIGHT—

Retrace:LXXXVIII Answer

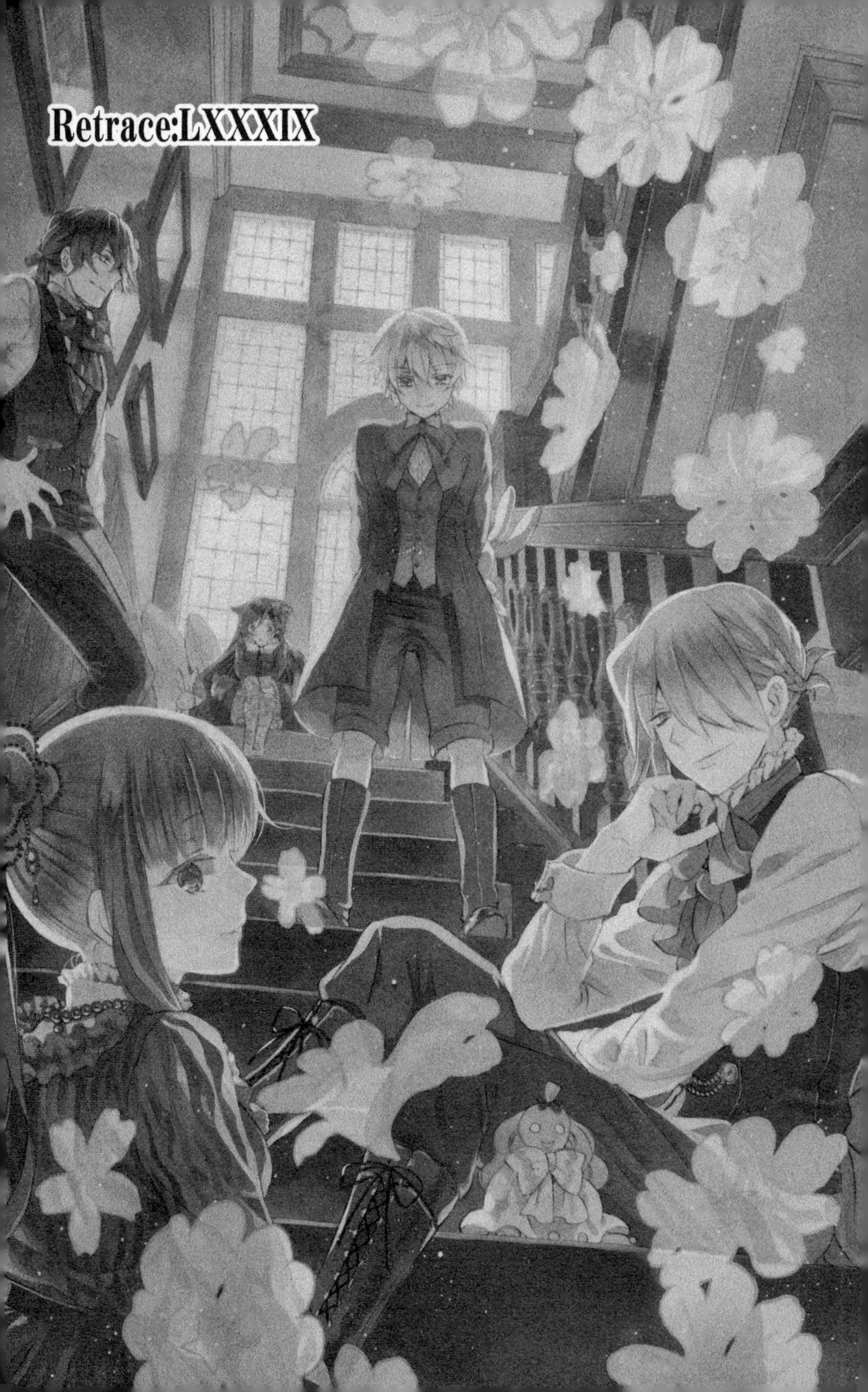
Retrace:LXXXIX

BONUS: I LIKE ALICE THE WAY SHE IS! (SAYS OZ)

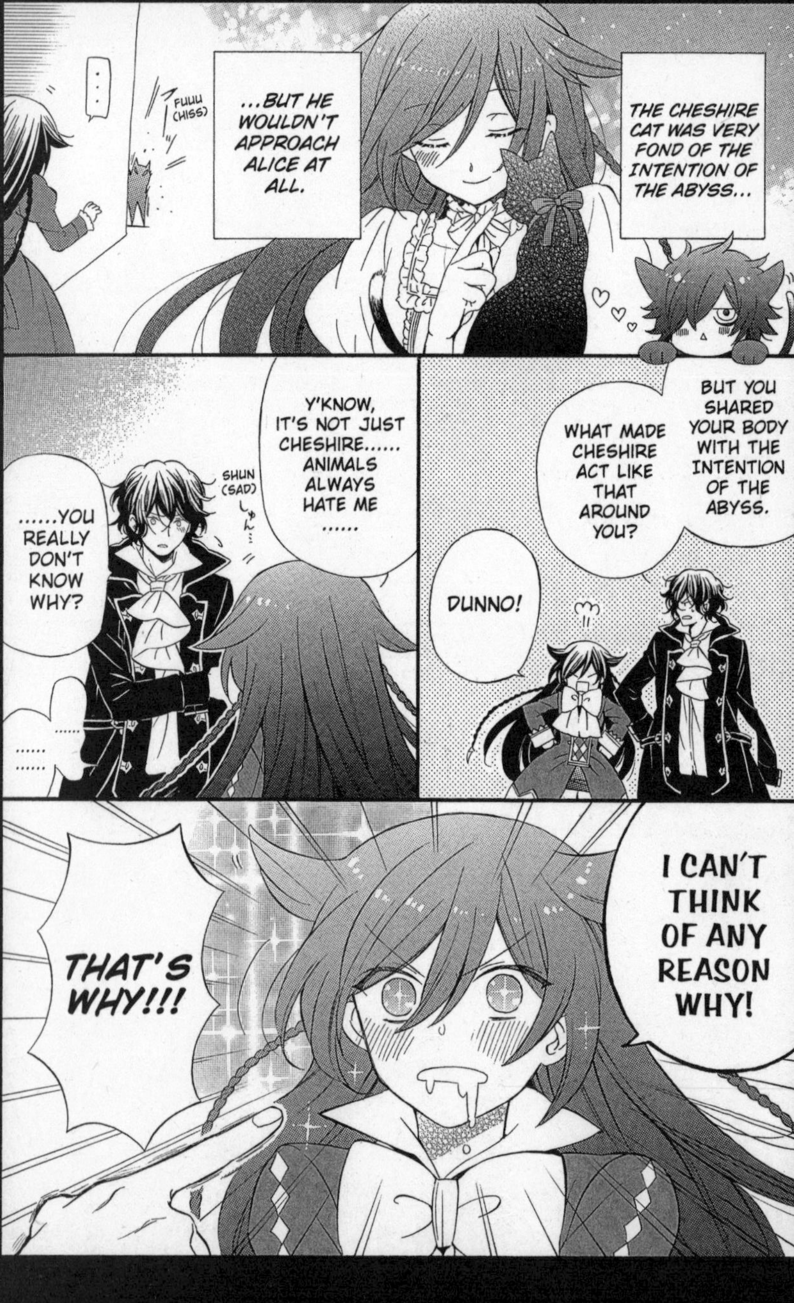
THE CHESHIRE CAT WAS VERY FOND OF THE INTENTION OF THE ABYSS...
...BUT HE WOULDN'T APPROACH ALICE AT ALL.
FUUU (HISS)
...
BUT YOU SHARED YOUR BODY WITH THE INTENTION OF THE ABYSS.
WHAT MADE CHESHIRE ACT LIKE THAT AROUND YOU?
DUNNO!
Y'KNOW, IT'S NOT JUST CHESHIRE...... ANIMALS ALWAYS HATE ME ......
SHUN (SAD)
しゅん…
......YOU REALLY DON'T KNOW WHY?
....
I CAN'T THINK OF ANY REASON WHY!
THAT'S WHY!!!

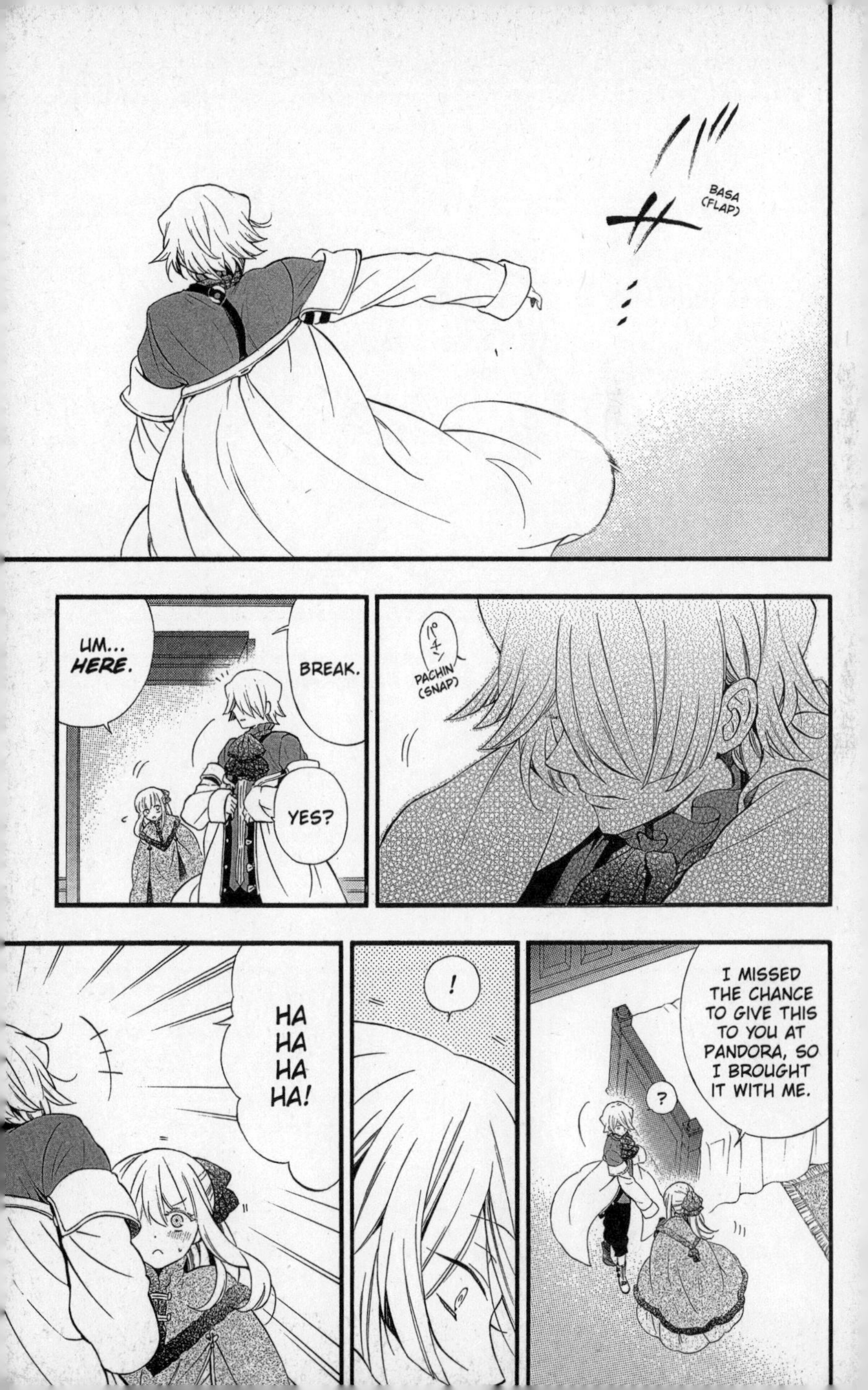
BASA (FLAP)
パチン
PACHIN (SNAP)
BREAK.
UM... HERE.
YES?
I MISSED THE CHANCE TO GIVE THIS TO YOU AT PANDORA, SO I BROUGHT IT WITH ME.
?
!
HA HA HA HA!

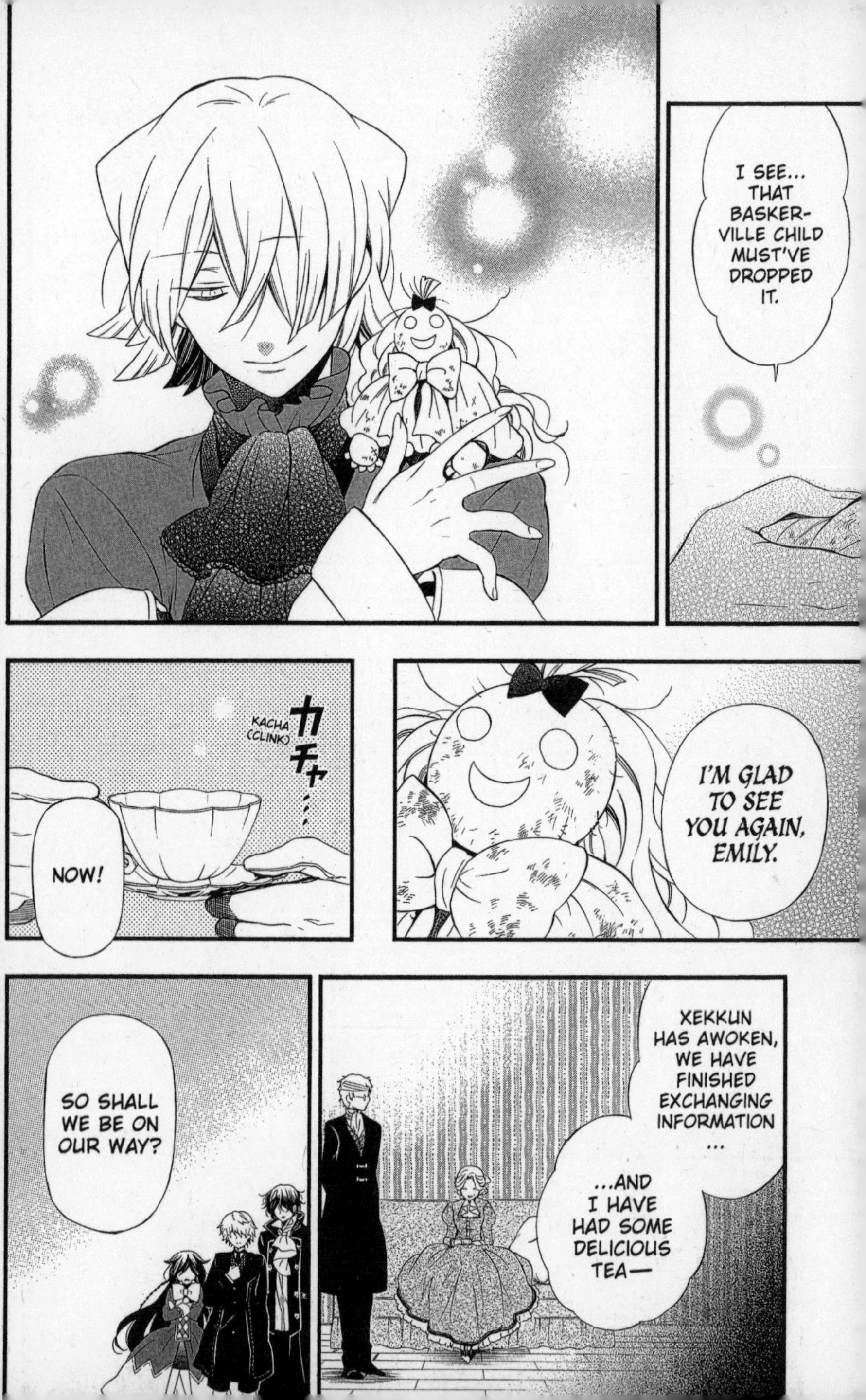
I SEE... THAT BASKER-VILLE CHILD MUST'VE DROPPED IT.
I'M GLAD TO SEE YOU AGAIN, EMILY.
KACHA (CLINK)
カチャ...
NOW!
XEKKUN HAS AWOKEN, WE HAVE FINISHED EXCHANGING INFORMATION ...
...AND I HAVE HAD SOME DELICIOUS TEA—
SO SHALL WE BE ON OUR WAY?

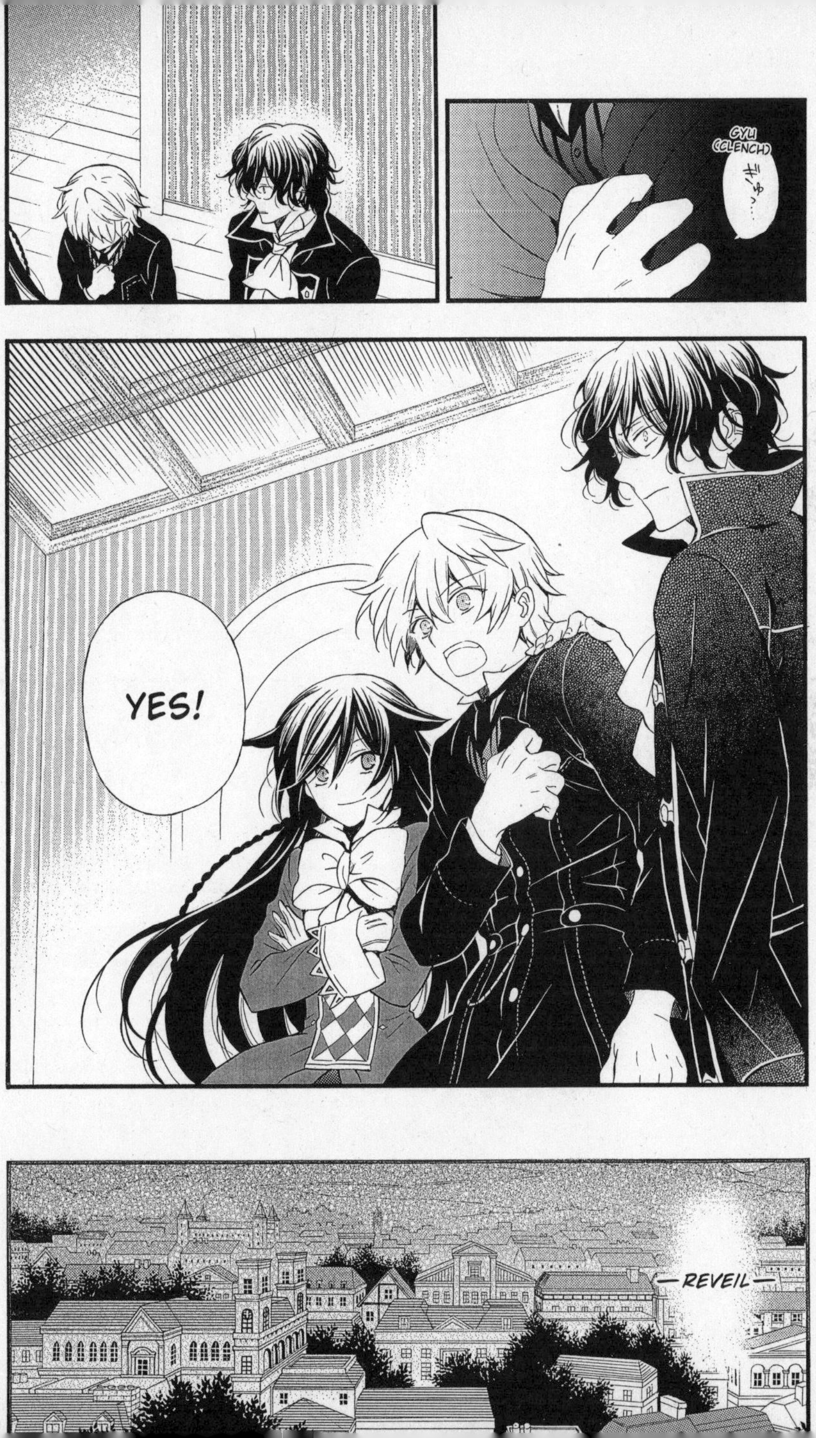
GYU (CLENCH)
ぎゅっ…
YES!
—REVEIL—

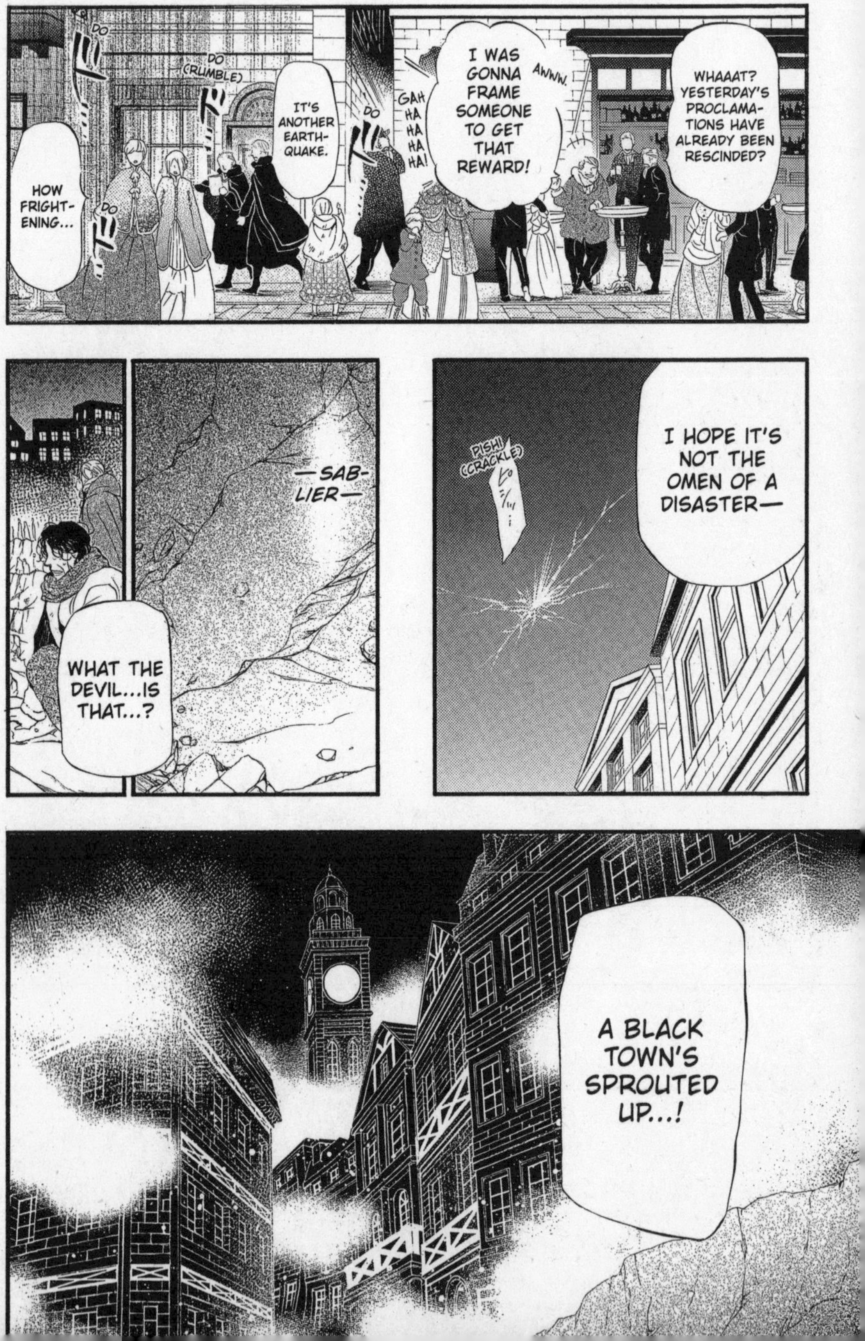
WHAAAT? YESTERDAY'S PROCLAMATIONS HAVE ALREADY BEEN RESCINDED?
AWWW.
I WAS GONNA FRAME SOMEONE TO GET THAT REWARD!
GAH HA HA HA HA!
DO
IT'S ANOTHER EARTHQUAKE.
DO (RUMBLE)
DO
DO
HOW FRIGHTENING...
I HOPE IT'S NOT THE OMEN OF A DISASTER—
PISHI (CRACKLE)
—SABLIER—
WHAT THE DEVIL...IS THAT...?
A BLACK TOWN'S SPROUTED UP...!

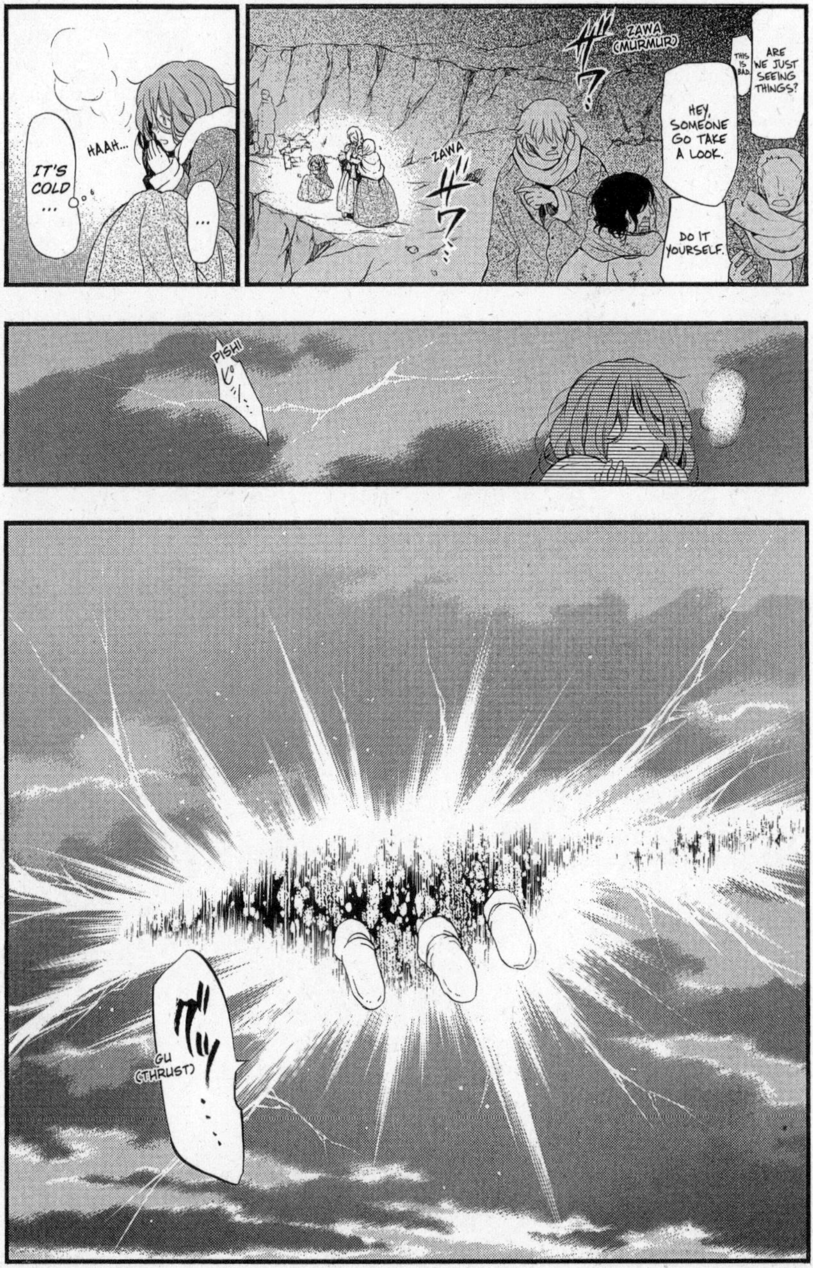
ARE WE JUST SEEING THINGS?
THIS IS BAD.
ZAWA (MURMUR)
HEY, SOMEONE GO TAKE A LOOK.
DO IT YOURSELF.
ZAWA
HAAH...
...
IT'S COLD ...
PISHI
GU (THRUST)
...

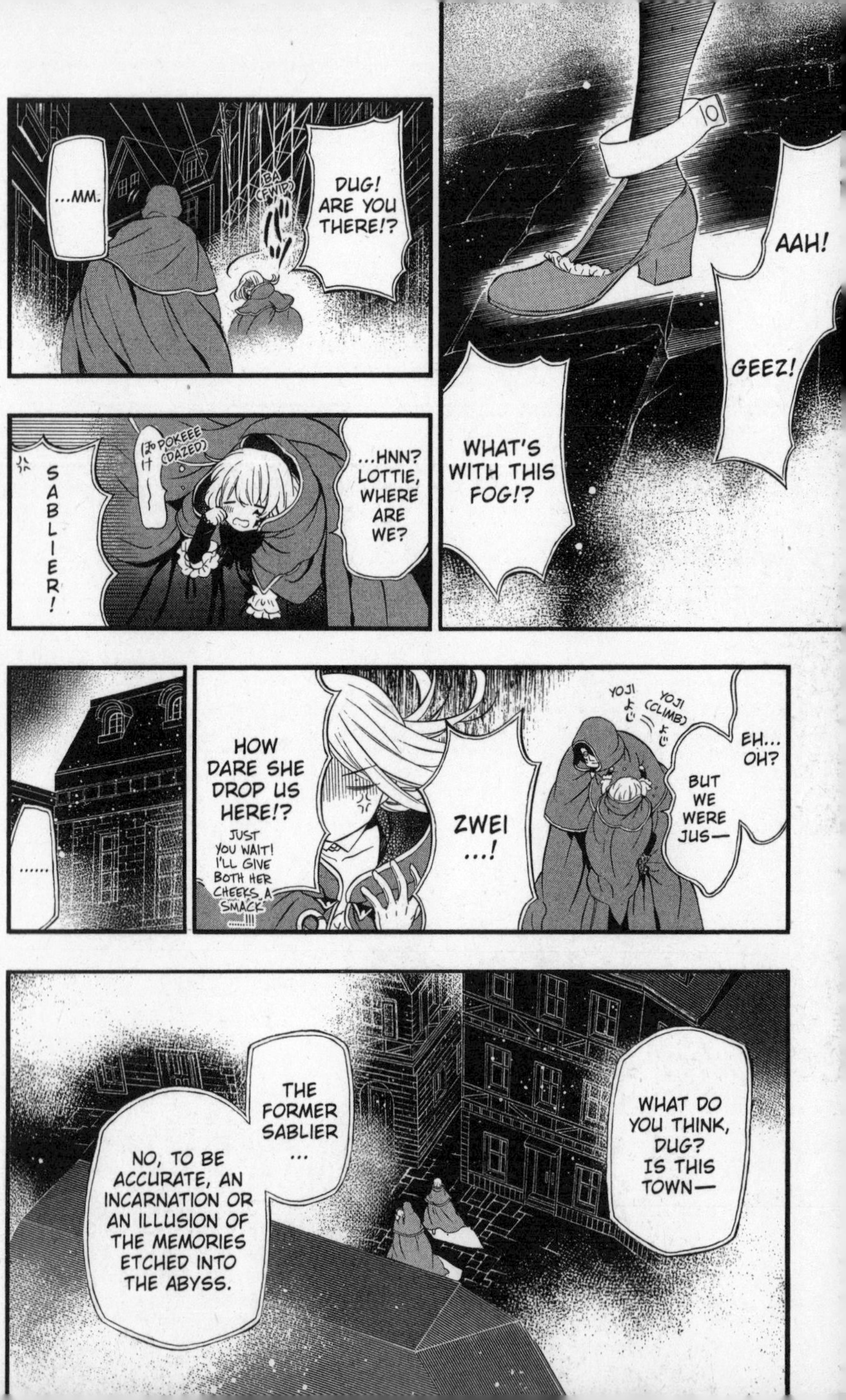
AAH!
GEEZ!
WHAT'S WITH THIS FOG!?
DUG! ARE YOU THERE!?
BA (FWIP)
...MM.
...HNN? LOTTIE, WHERE ARE WE?
ぽけ POKEEE (DAZED)
SABLIER!
EH... OH?
BUT WE WERE JUS—
YOJI よじ YOJI (CLIMB) よじ
ZWEI ...!
HOW DARE SHE DROP US HERE!?
JUST YOU WAIT! I'LL GIVE BOTH HER CHEEKS A SMACK ......!!!
......
WHAT DO YOU THINK, DUG? IS THIS TOWN—
THE FORMER SABLIER ...
NO, TO BE ACCURATE, AN INCARNATION OR AN ILLUSION OF THE MEMORIES ETCHED INTO THE ABYSS.

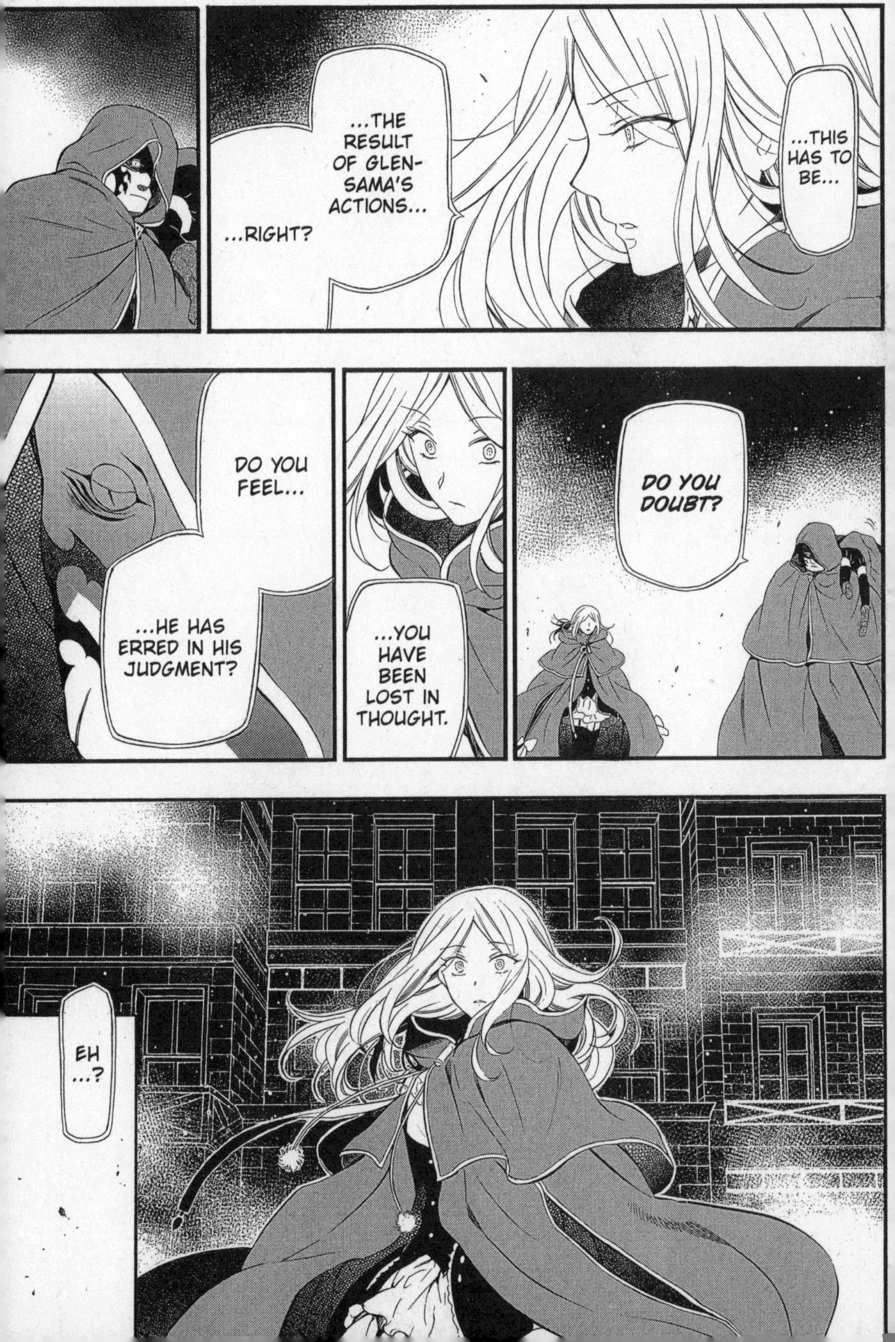
...THIS HAS TO BE...
...THE RESULT OF GLEN-SAMA'S ACTIONS...
...RIGHT?
DO YOU DOUBT?
...YOU HAVE BEEN LOST IN THOUGHT.
DO YOU FEEL...
...HE HAS ERRED IN HIS JUDGMENT?
EH ...?

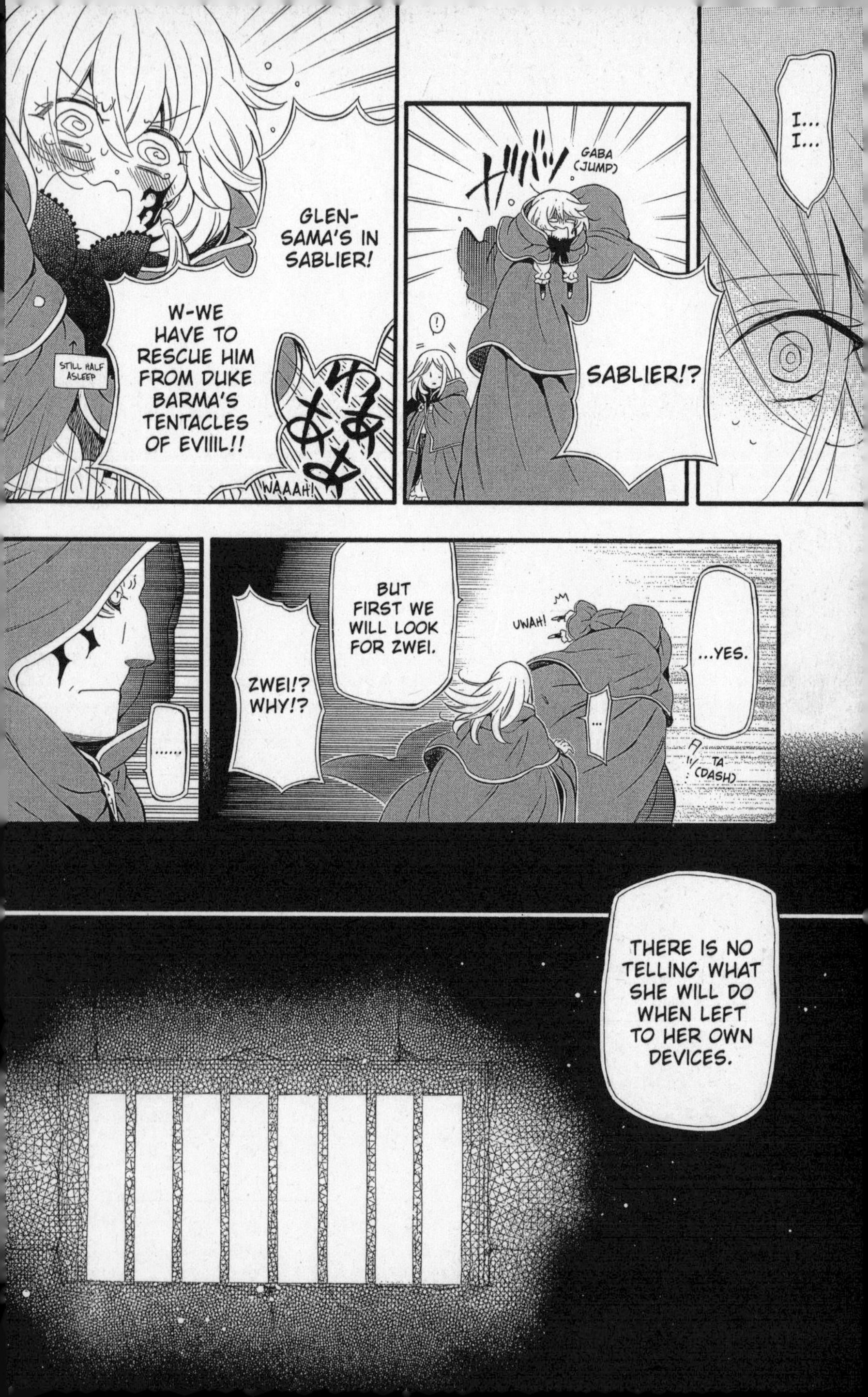
I... I...
GABA (JUMP)
SABLIER!?
!
GLEN-SAMA'S IN SABLIER!
W-WE HAVE TO RESCUE HIM FROM DUKE BARMA'S TENTACLES OF EVIIIL!!
STILL HALF ASLEEP
WAAAH!
...YES.
UWAH!
BUT FIRST WE WILL LOOK FOR ZWEI.
...
TA (DASH)
ZWEI!? WHY!?
......
THERE IS NO TELLING WHAT SHE WILL DO WHEN LEFT TO HER OWN DEVICES.

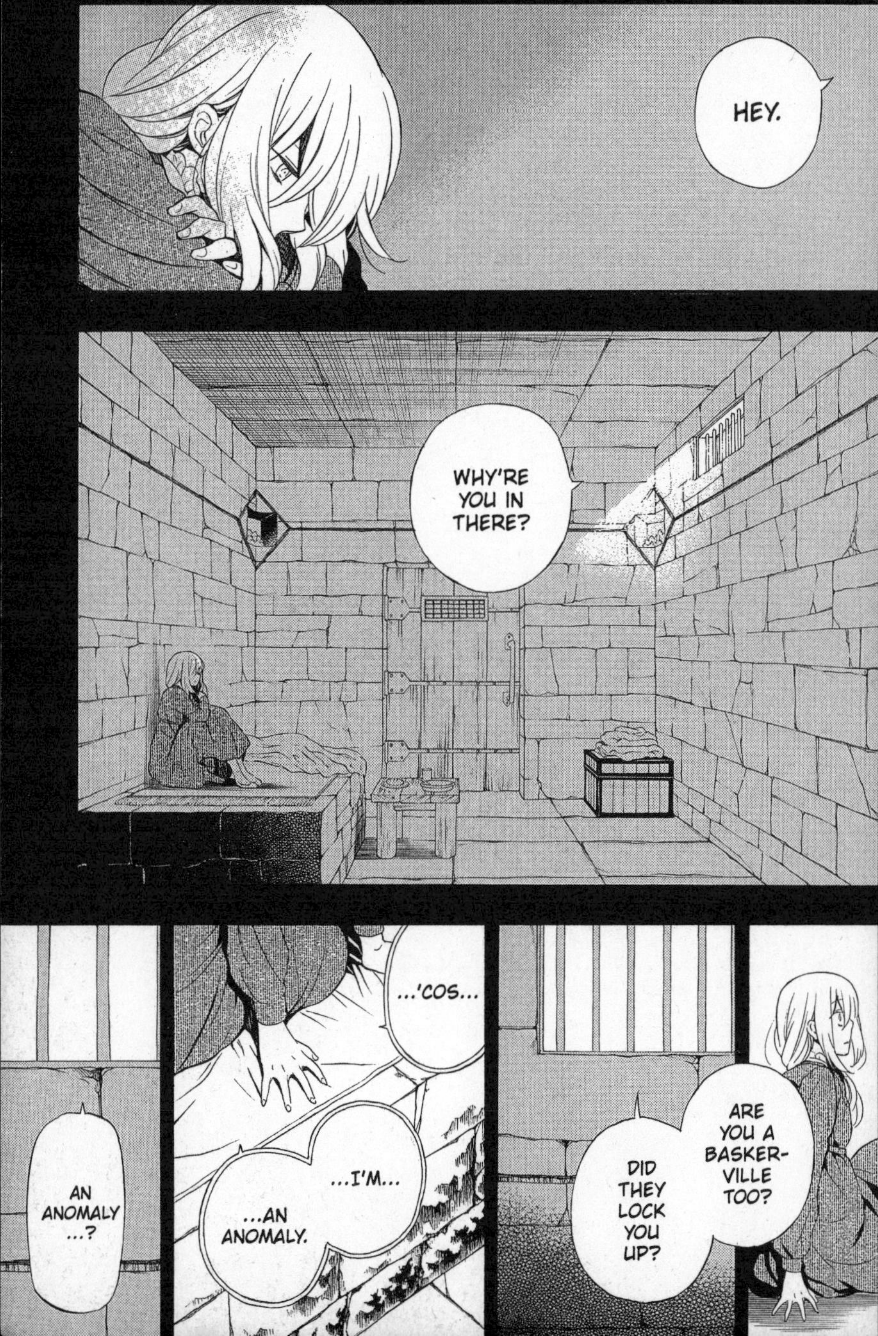
HEY.
WHY'RE YOU IN THERE?
ARE YOU A BASKER-VILLE TOO?
DID THEY LOCK YOU UP?
...'COS...
...I'M...
...AN ANOMALY.
AN ANOMALY ...?

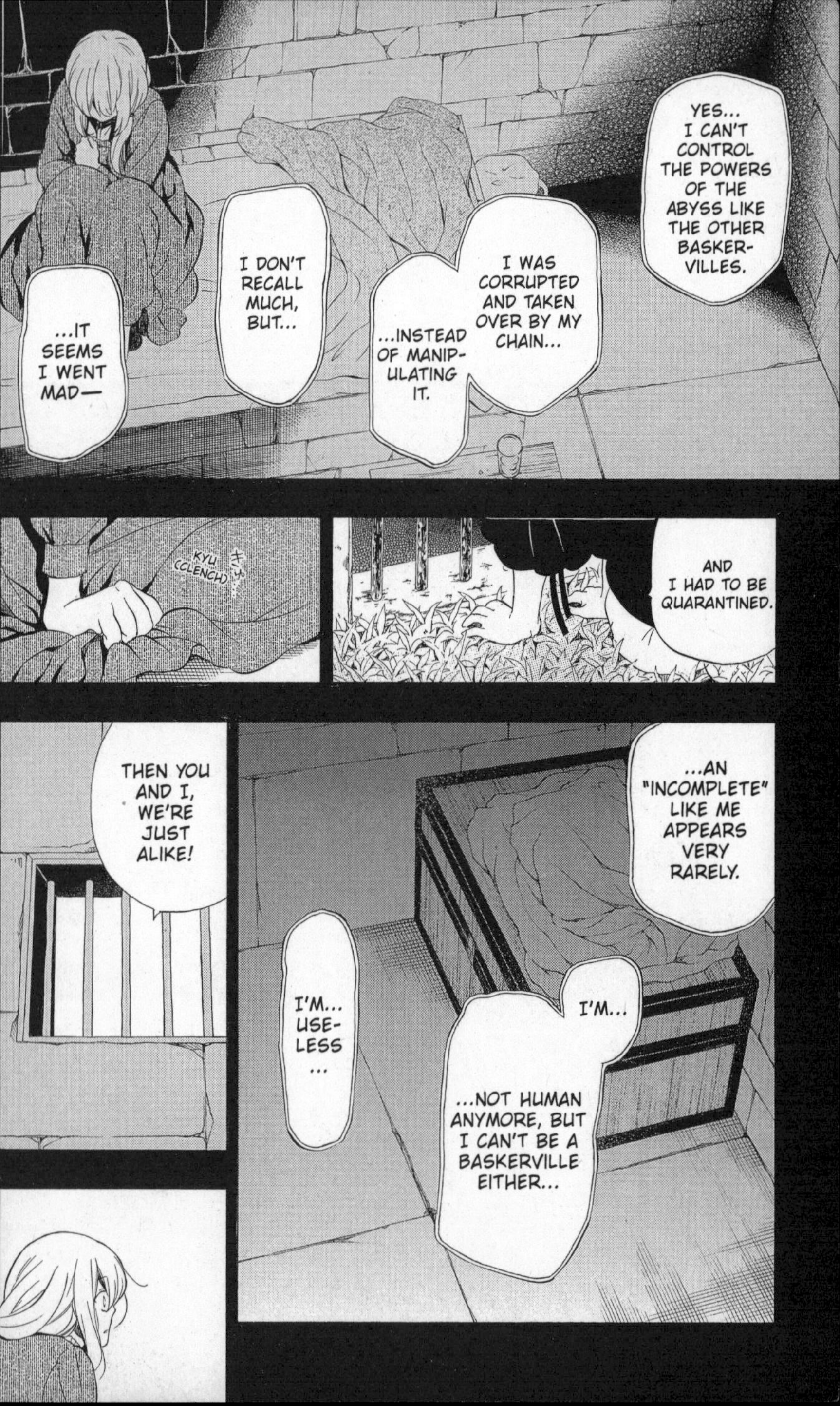
YES... I CAN'T CONTROL THE POWERS OF THE ABYSS LIKE THE OTHER BASKER-VILLES.
I WAS CORRUPTED AND TAKEN OVER BY MY CHAIN...
...INSTEAD OF MANIP-ULATING IT.
I DON'T RECALL MUCH, BUT...
...IT SEEMS I WENT MAD—
AND I HAD TO BE QUARANTINED.
KYU (CLENCH)
...AN "INCOMPLETE" LIKE ME APPEARS VERY RARELY.
I'M...
...NOT HUMAN ANYMORE, BUT I CAN'T BE A BASKERVILLE EITHER...
I'M... USE-LESS...
THEN YOU AND I, WE'RE JUST ALIKE!

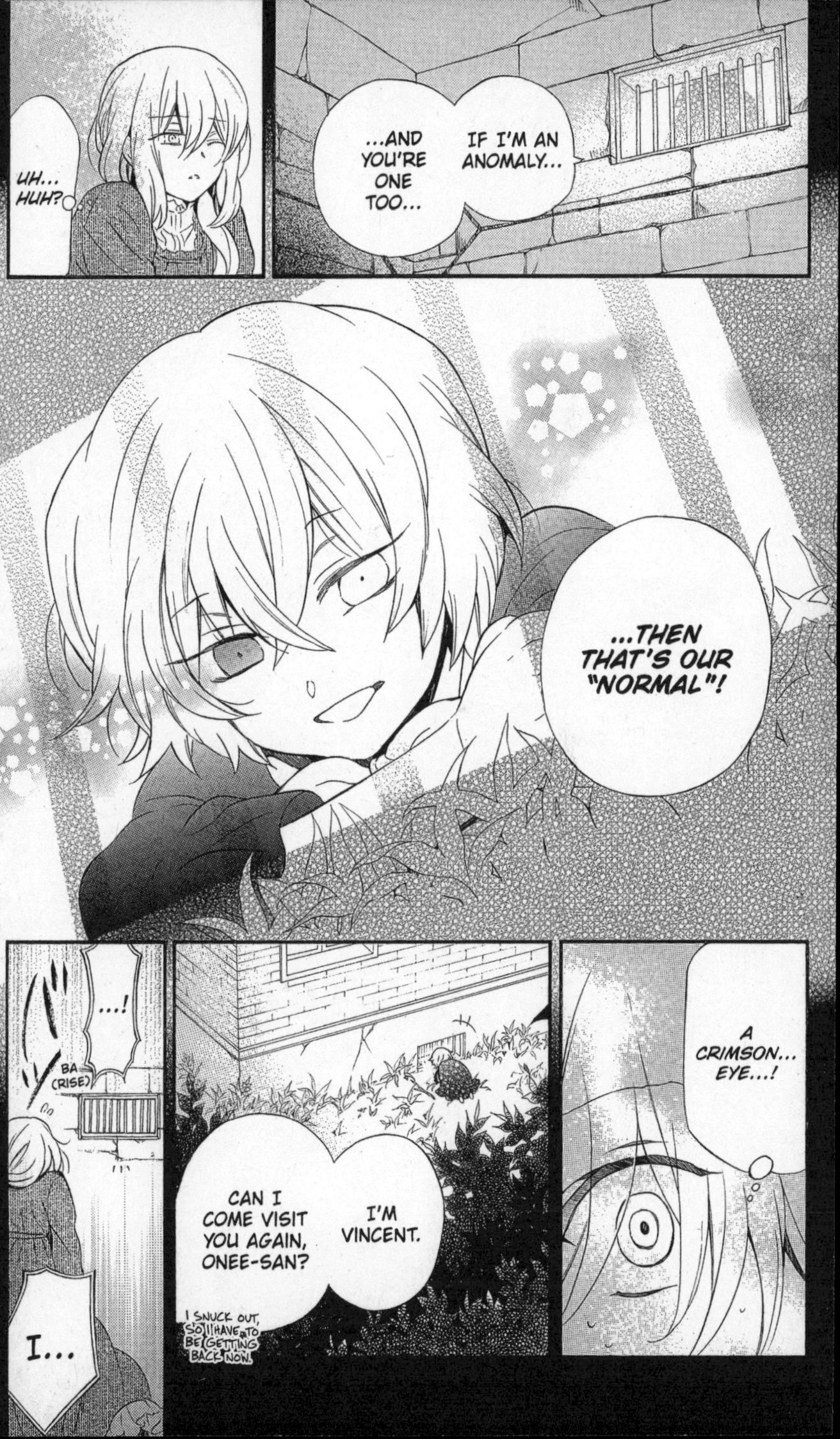
IF I'M AN ANOMALY...
...AND YOU'RE ONE TOO...
UH... HUH?
...THEN THAT'S OUR "NORMAL"!
A CRIMSON... EYE...!
I'M VINCENT.
CAN I COME VISIT YOU AGAIN, ONEE-SAN?
I SNUCK OUT, SO I HAVE TO BE GETTING BACK NOW.
...!
BA (RISE)
I...

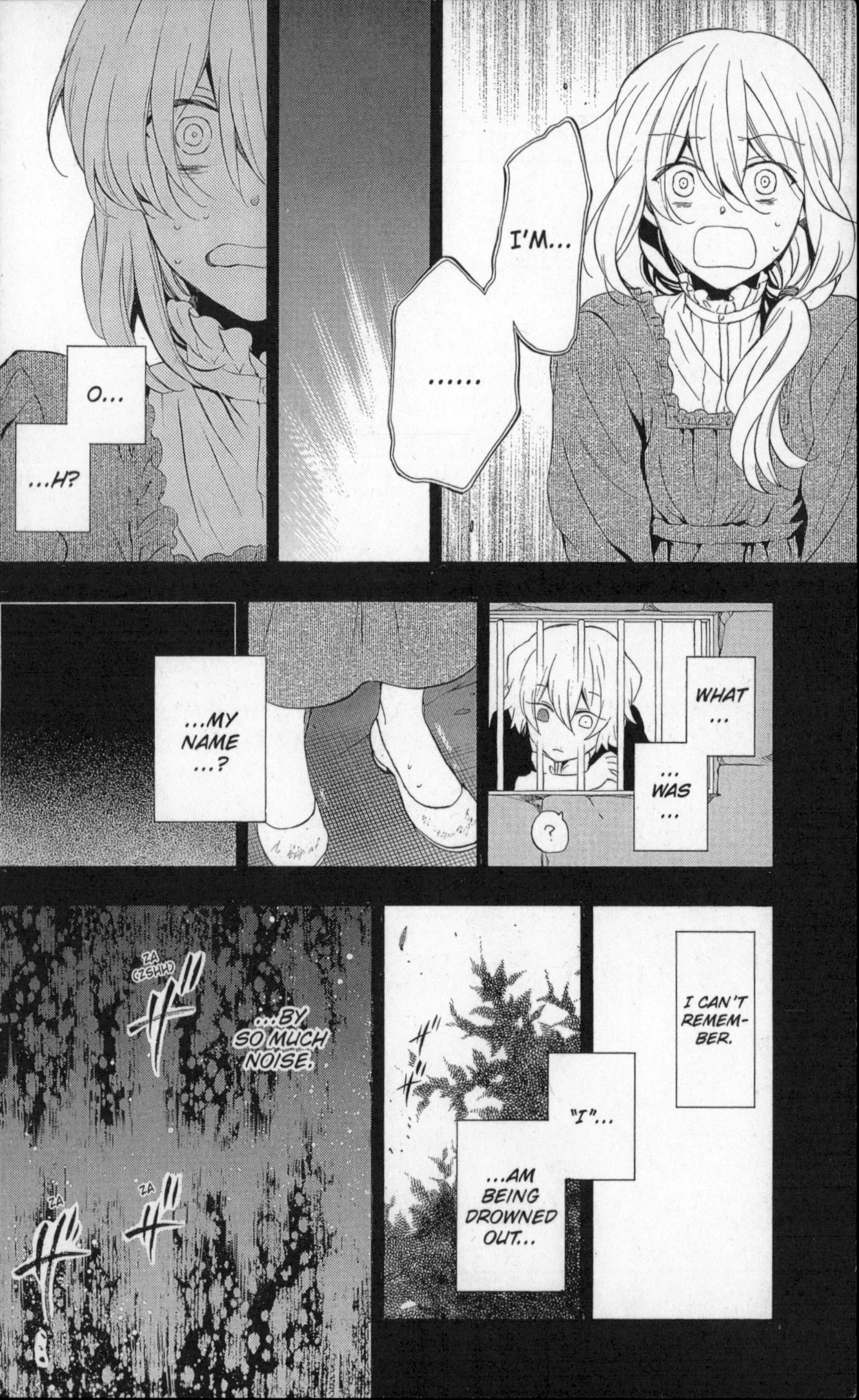
I'M...
......
O...
...H?
WHAT...
...WAS...
?
...MY NAME...?
I CAN'T REMEMBER.
"I"...
...AM BEING DROWNED OUT...
ZA (ZSHH)
...BY SO MUCH NOISE.
ZA
ZA

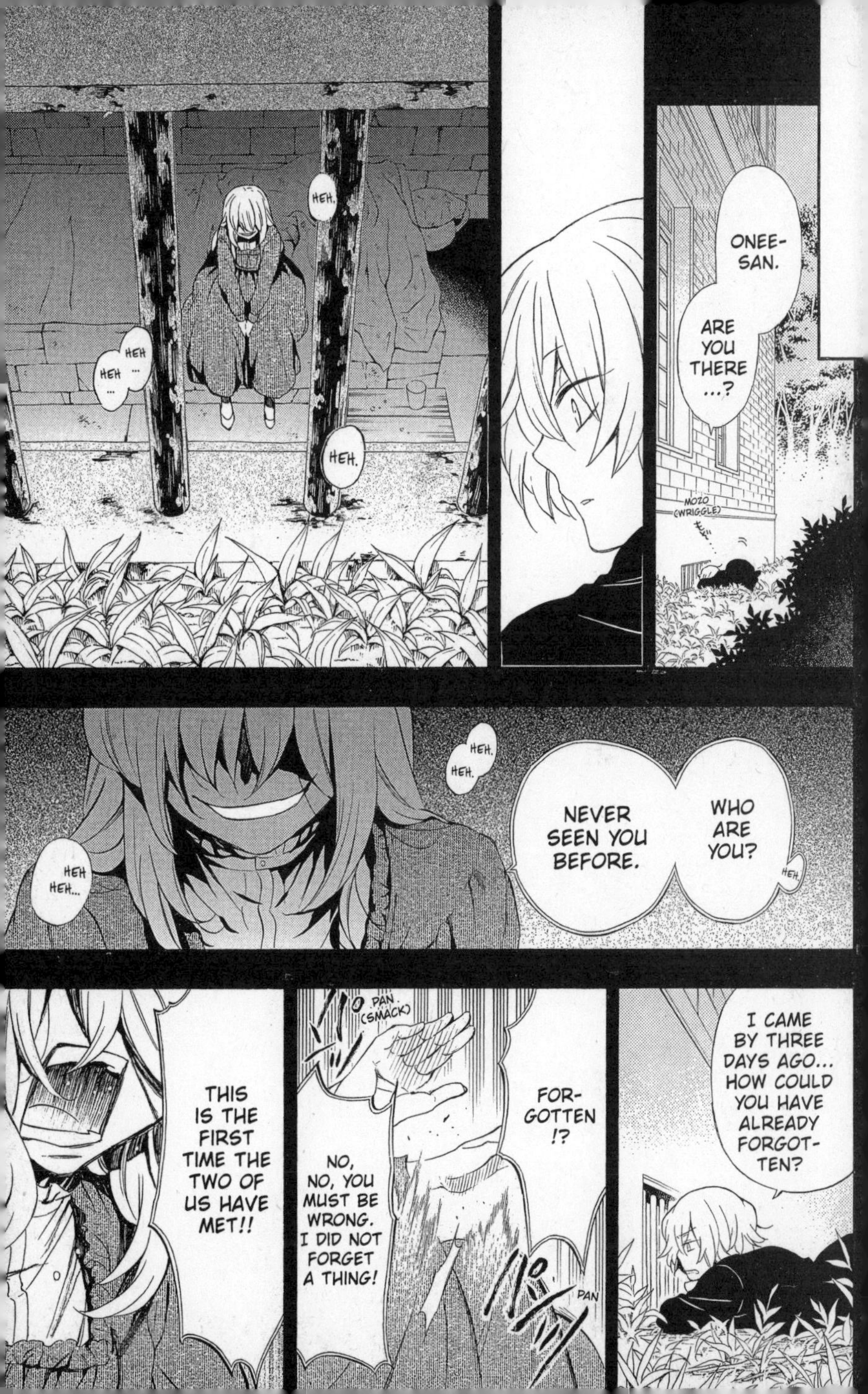
ONEE-SAN.
ARE YOU THERE ...?
MOZO (WRIGGLE)
HEH.
HEH ... HEH ...
HEH.
WHO ARE YOU?
NEVER SEEN YOU BEFORE.
HEH.
HEH. HEH.
HEH HEH...
I CAME BY THREE DAYS AGO... HOW COULD YOU HAVE ALREADY FORGOT-TEN?
FOR-GOTTEN !?
PAN (SMACK)
PAN
NO, NO, YOU MUST BE WRONG. I DID NOT FORGET A THING!
THIS IS THE FIRST TIME THE TWO OF US HAVE MET!!

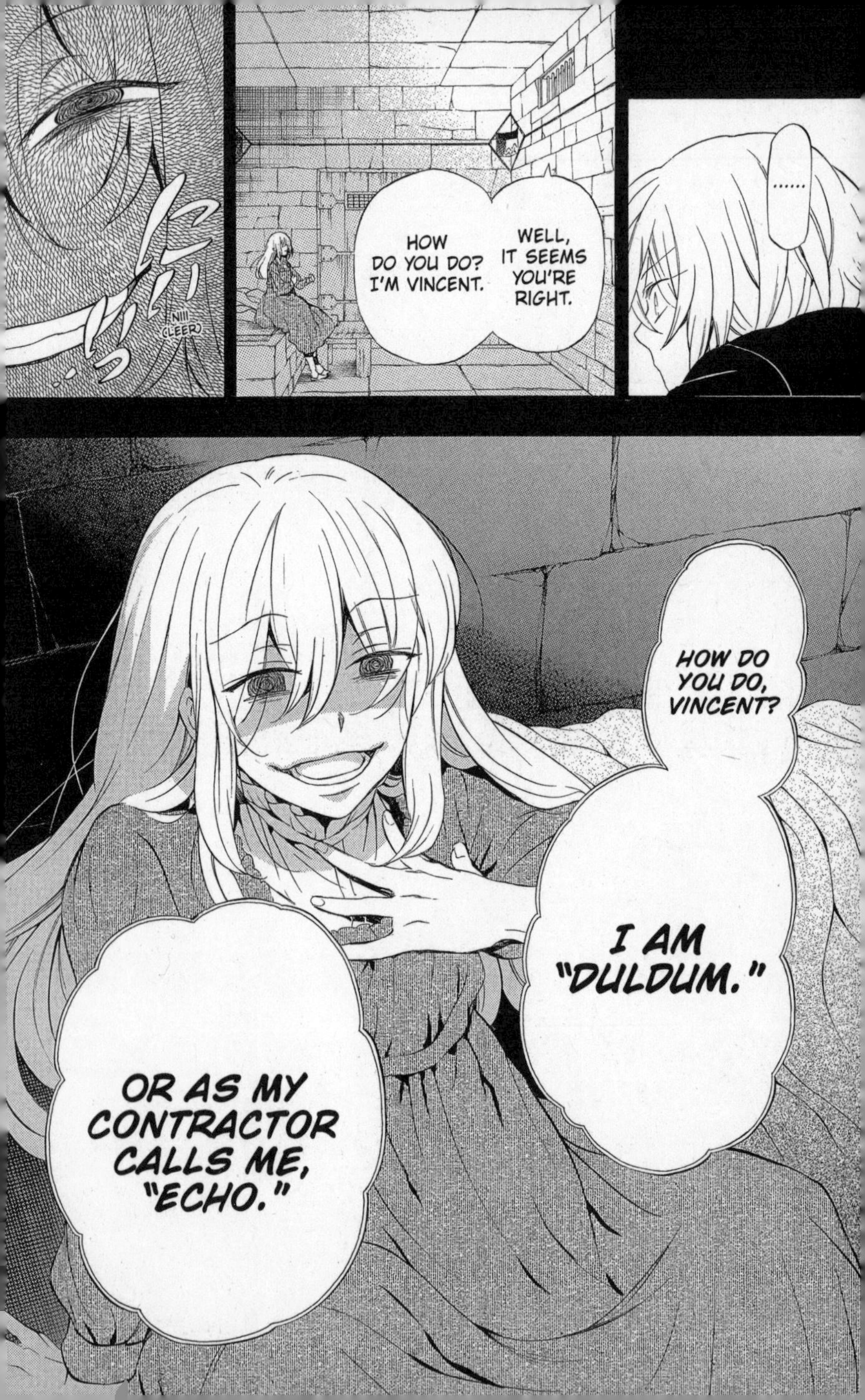
......
WELL, IT SEEMS YOU'RE RIGHT.
HOW DO YOU DO? I'M VINCENT.
NIII CLEER
HOW DO YOU DO, VINCENT?
I AM "DULDUM."
OR AS MY CONTRACTOR CALLS ME, "ECHO."

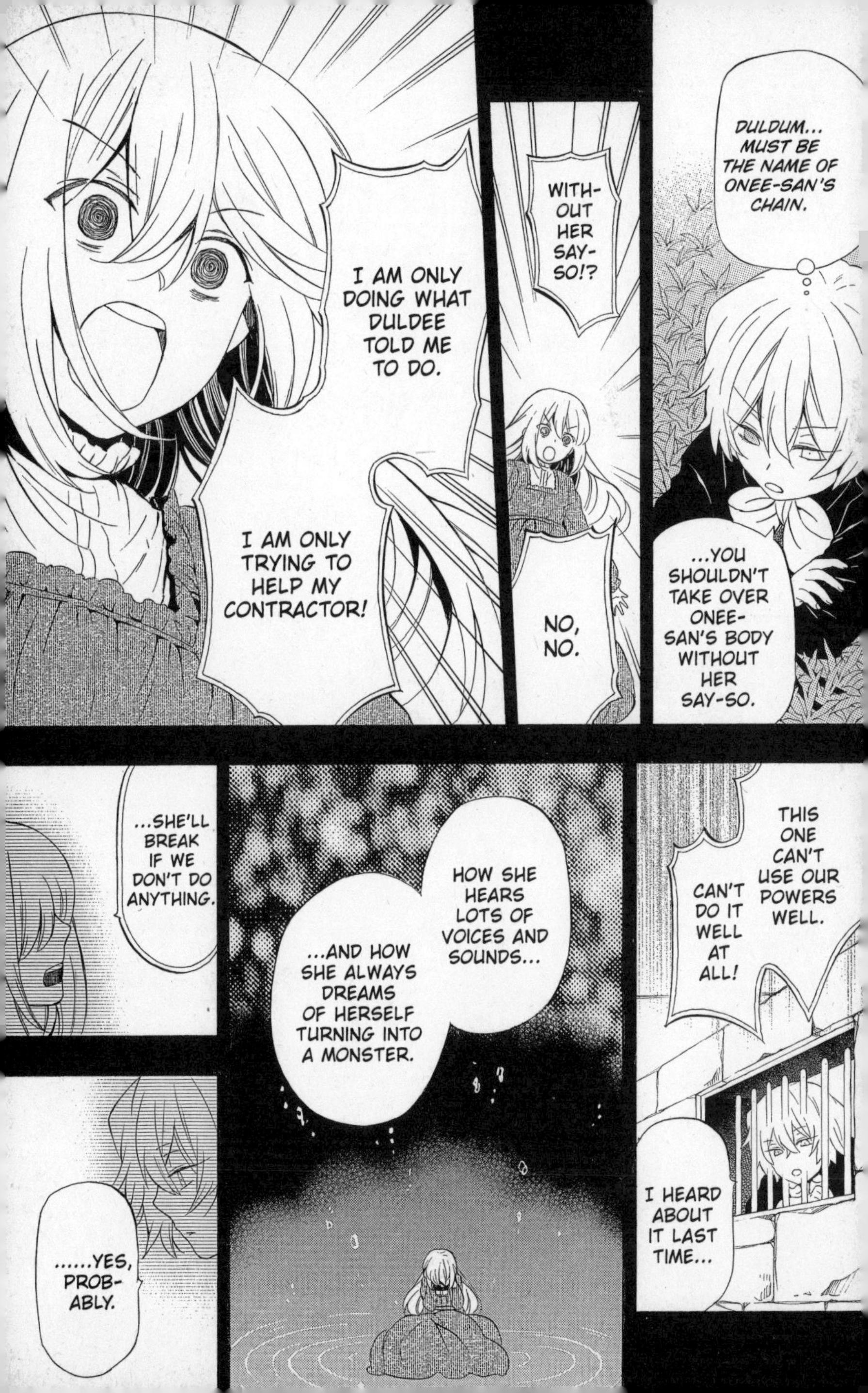
DULDUM... MUST BE THE NAME OF ONEE-SAN'S CHAIN.
...YOU SHOULDN'T TAKE OVER ONEE-SAN'S BODY WITHOUT HER SAY-SO.
WITH-OUT HER SAY-SO!?
NO, NO.
I AM ONLY DOING WHAT DULDEE TOLD ME TO DO.
I AM ONLY TRYING TO HELP MY CONTRACTOR!
THIS ONE CAN'T USE OUR POWERS WELL.
CAN'T DO IT WELL AT ALL!
I HEARD ABOUT IT LAST TIME...
HOW SHE HEARS LOTS OF VOICES AND SOUNDS...
...AND HOW SHE ALWAYS DREAMS OF HERSELF TURNING INTO A MONSTER.
...SHE'LL BREAK IF WE DON'T DO ANYTHING.
......YES, PROB-ABLY.

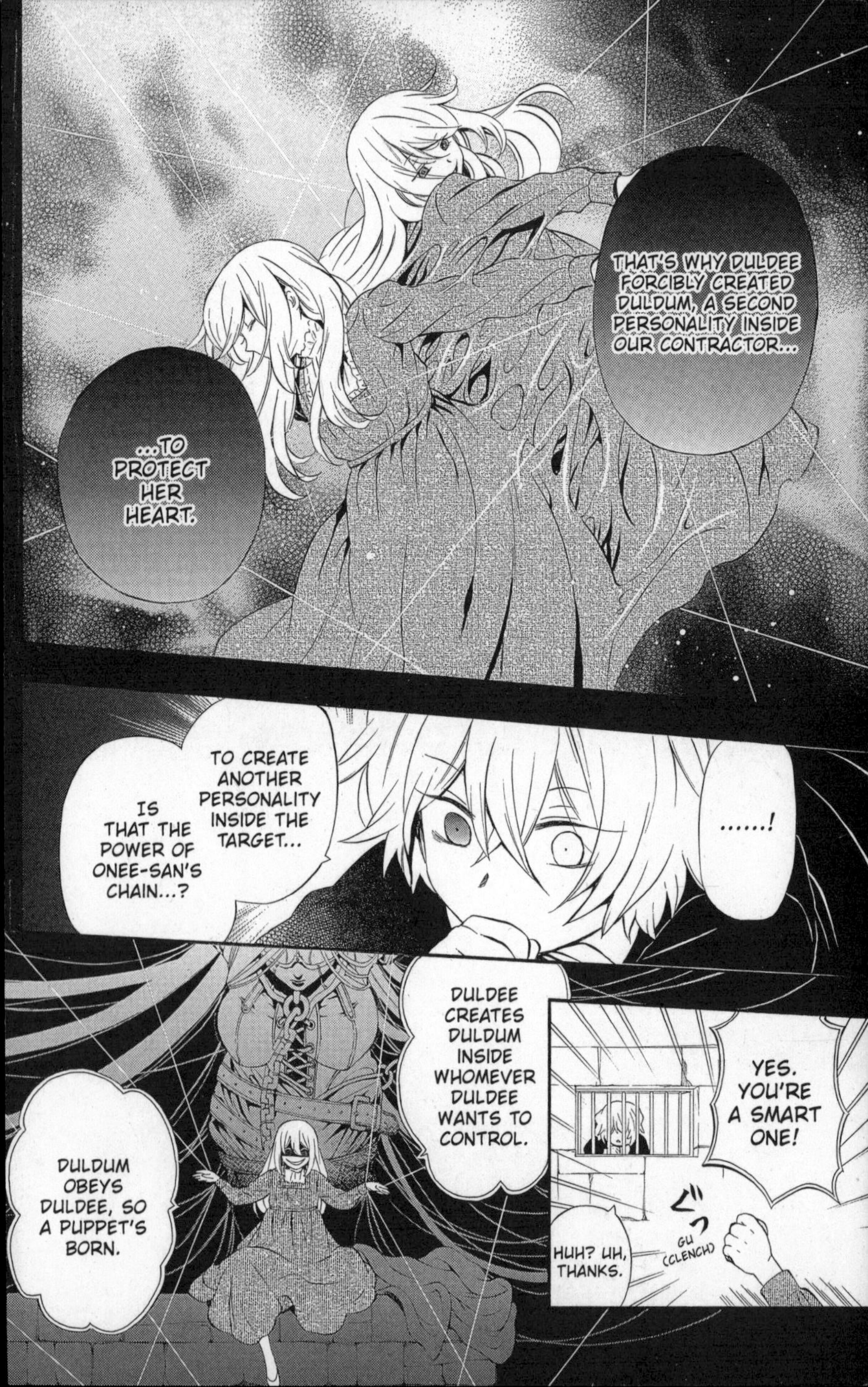
THAT'S WHY DULDEE FORCIBLY CREATED DULDUM, A SECOND PERSONALITY INSIDE OUR CONTRACTOR...
...TO PROTECT HER HEART.
......!
TO CREATE ANOTHER PERSONALITY INSIDE THE TARGET...
IS THAT THE POWER OF ONEE-SAN'S CHAIN...?
YES. YOU'RE A SMART ONE!
ぐっ
GU (CLENCH)
HUH? UH, THANKS.
DULDEE CREATES DULDUM INSIDE WHOMEVER DULDEE WANTS TO CONTROL.
DULDUM OBEYS DULDEE, SO A PUPPET'S BORN.

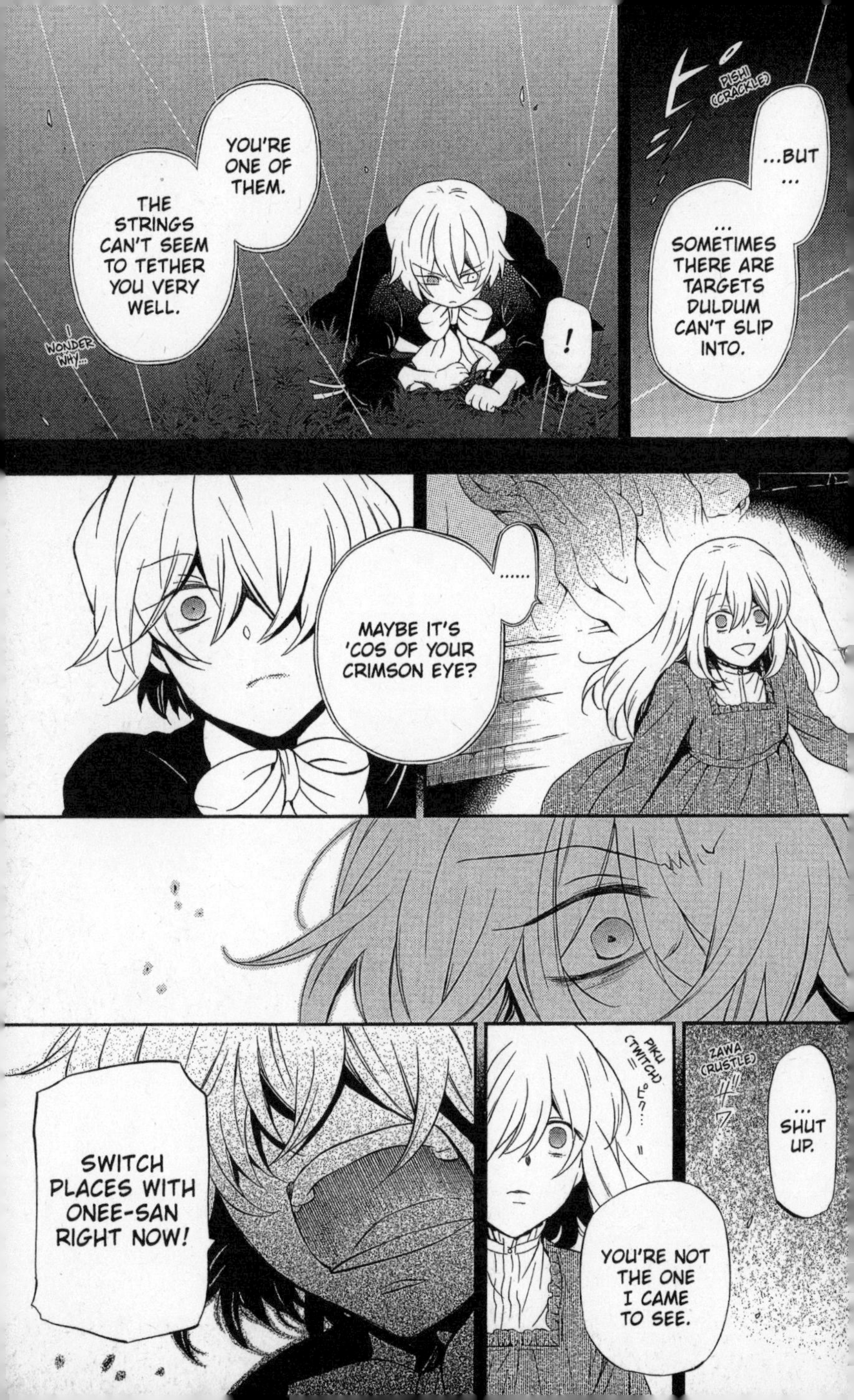
PISHI (CRACKLE)
...BUT ... ... SOMETIMES THERE ARE TARGETS DULDUM CAN'T SLIP INTO.
YOU'RE ONE OF THEM.
THE STRINGS CAN'T SEEM TO TETHER YOU VERY WELL.
I WONDER WHY...
!
......
MAYBE IT'S 'COS OF YOUR CRIMSON EYE?
ZAWA (RUSTLE)
... SHUT UP.
PIKU (TWITCH)
YOU'RE NOT THE ONE I CAME TO SEE.
SWITCH PLACES WITH ONEE-SAN RIGHT NOW!

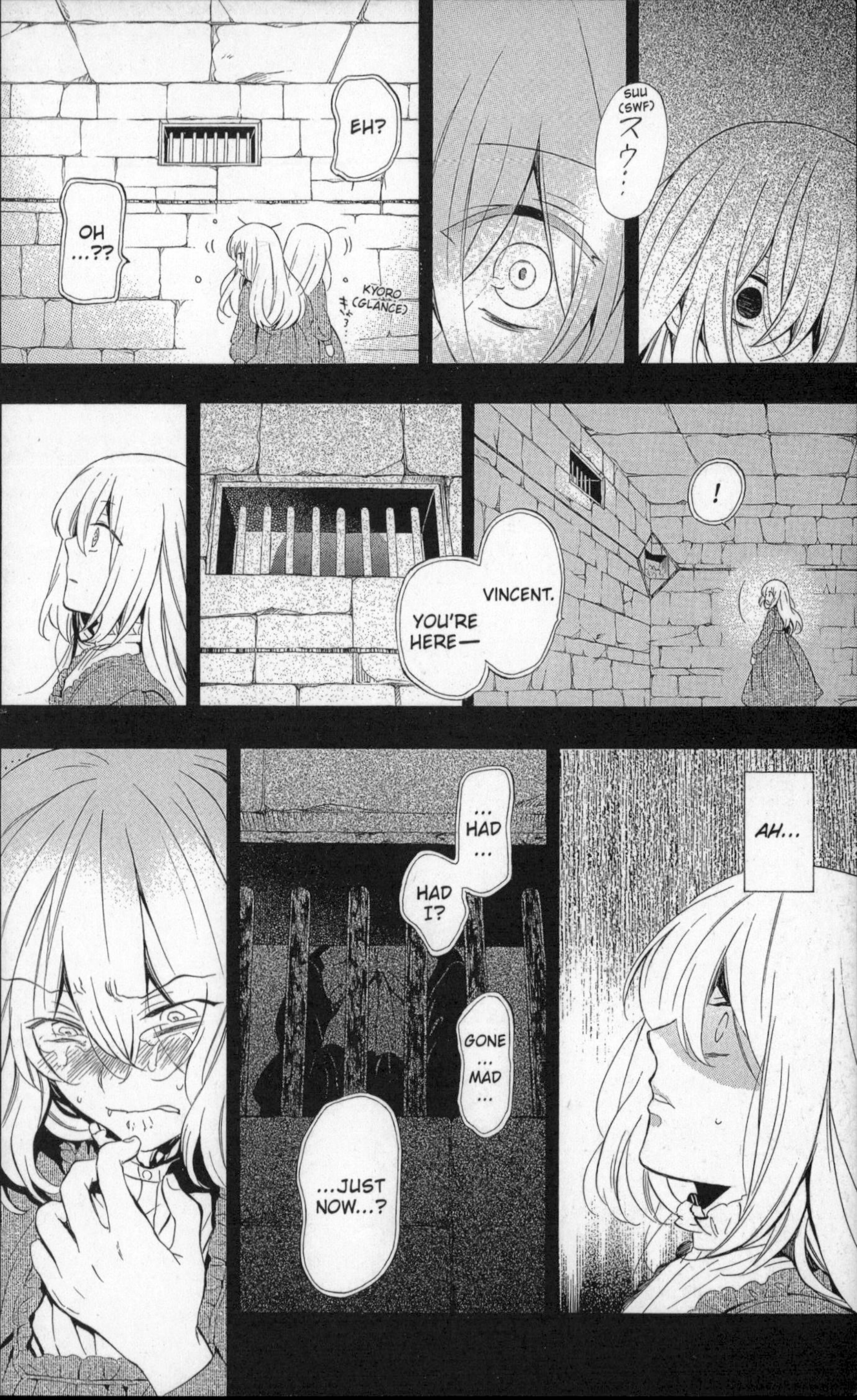
SUU (SWF) スゥ…
EH?
OH …??
KYORO (GLANCE)
!
VINCENT. YOU'RE HERE—
AH…
…HAD… HAD I?
GONE… MAD…
…JUST NOW…?

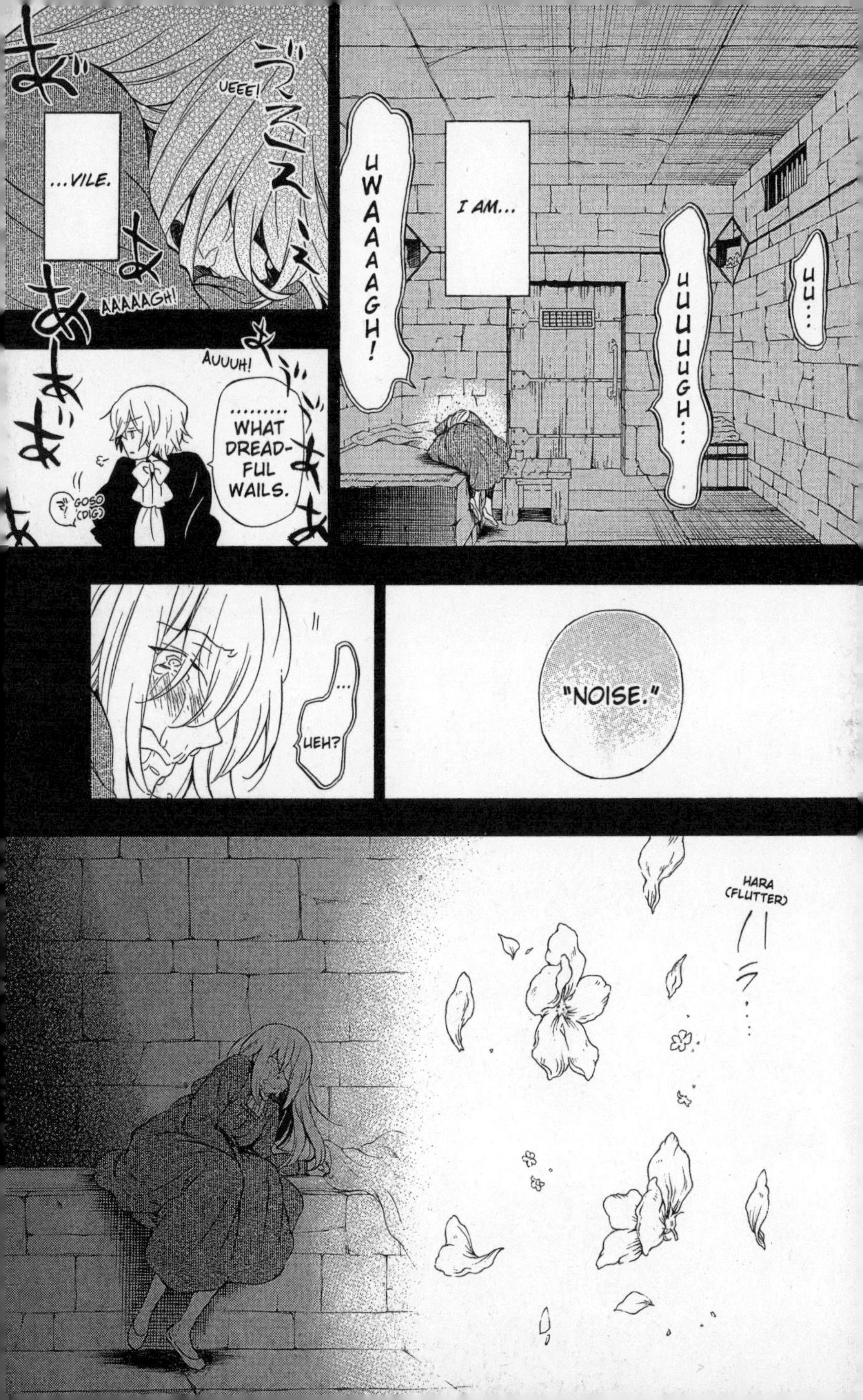
UU...
UUUUUUGH...
I AM...
UWAAAAAGH!
UEEE!
...VILE.
AAAAAGH!
AUUUH!
.... WHAT DREAD-FUL WAILS.
GOSO (DIG)
"NOISE."
... UEH?
HARA (FLUTTER)

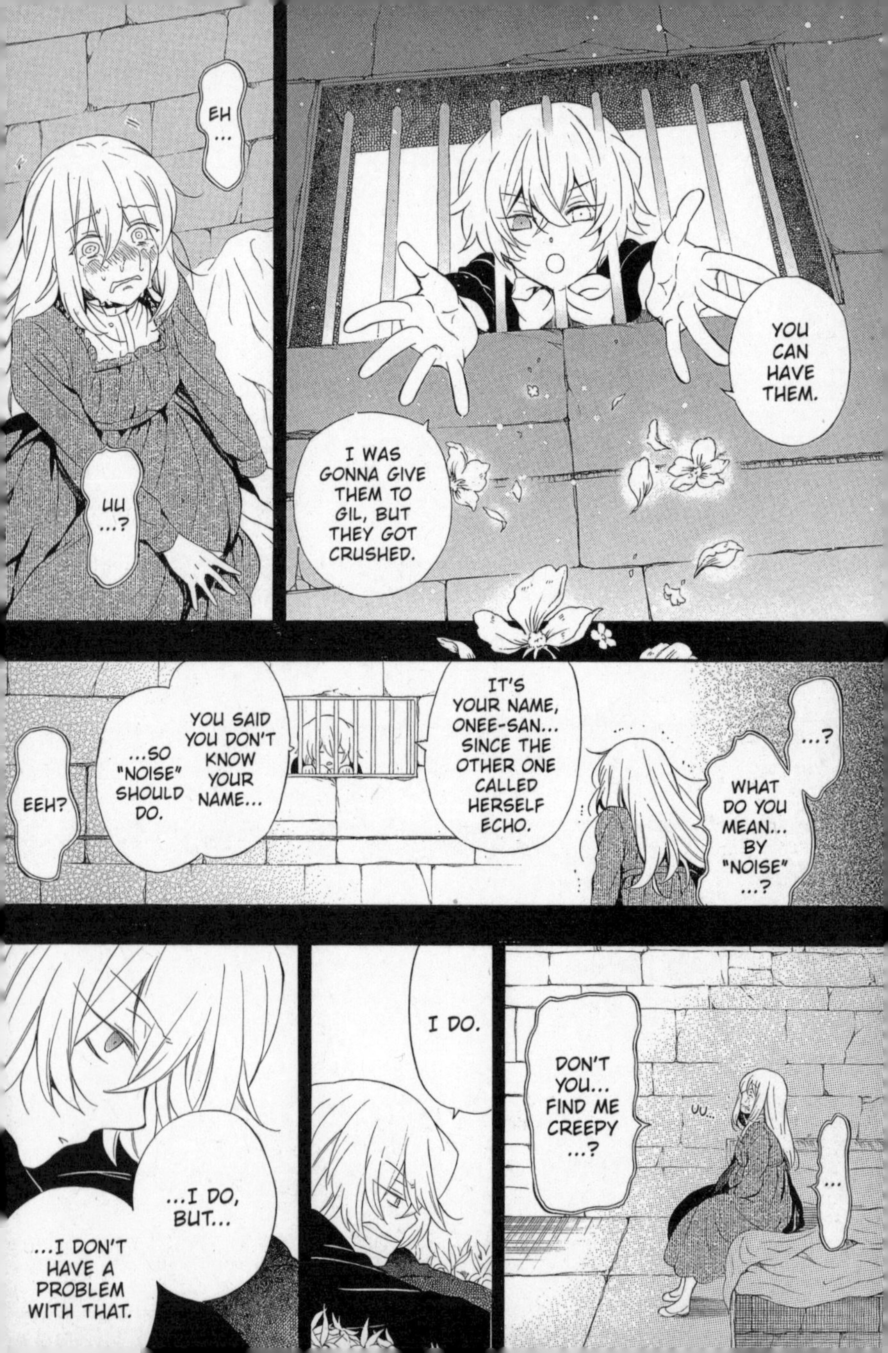

YOU CAN HAVE THEM.
I WAS GONNA GIVE THEM TO GIL, BUT THEY GOT CRUSHED.
EH ...
UU ...?
...?
WHAT DO YOU MEAN... BY "NOISE" ...?
IT'S YOUR NAME, ONEE-SAN... SINCE THE OTHER ONE CALLED HERSELF ECHO.
YOU SAID YOU DON'T KNOW YOUR NAME...
...SO "NOISE" SHOULD DO.
EEH?
DON'T YOU... FIND ME CREEPY ...?
UU...
...
I DO.
...I DO, BUT...
...I DON'T HAVE A PROBLEM WITH THAT.

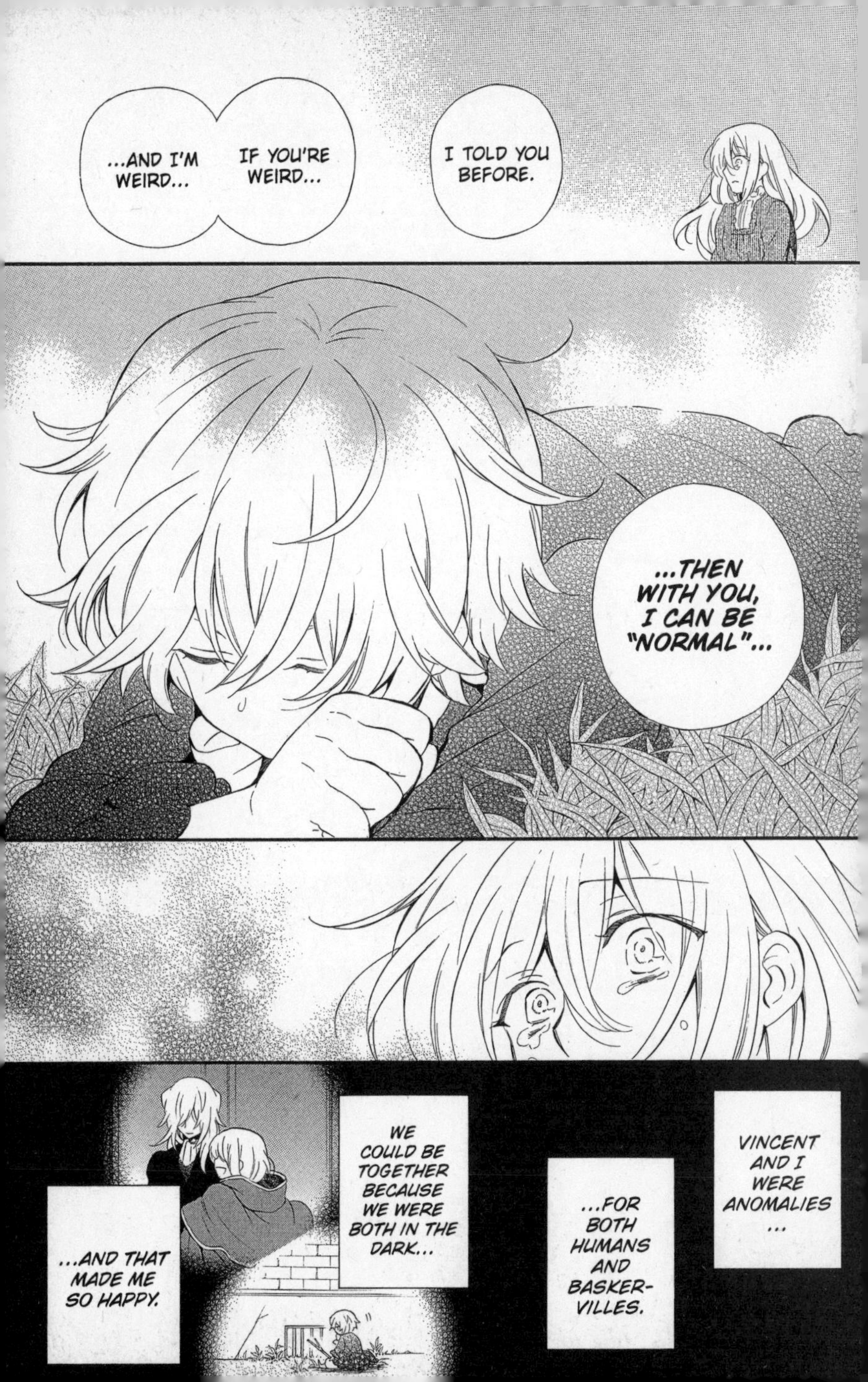
I TOLD YOU BEFORE.
IF YOU'RE WEIRD...
...AND I'M WEIRD...
...THEN WITH YOU, I CAN BE "NORMAL"...
VINCENT AND I WERE ANOMALIES ...
...FOR BOTH HUMANS AND BASKER-VILLES.
WE COULD BE TOGETHER BECAUSE WE WERE BOTH IN THE DARK...
...AND THAT MADE ME SO HAPPY.

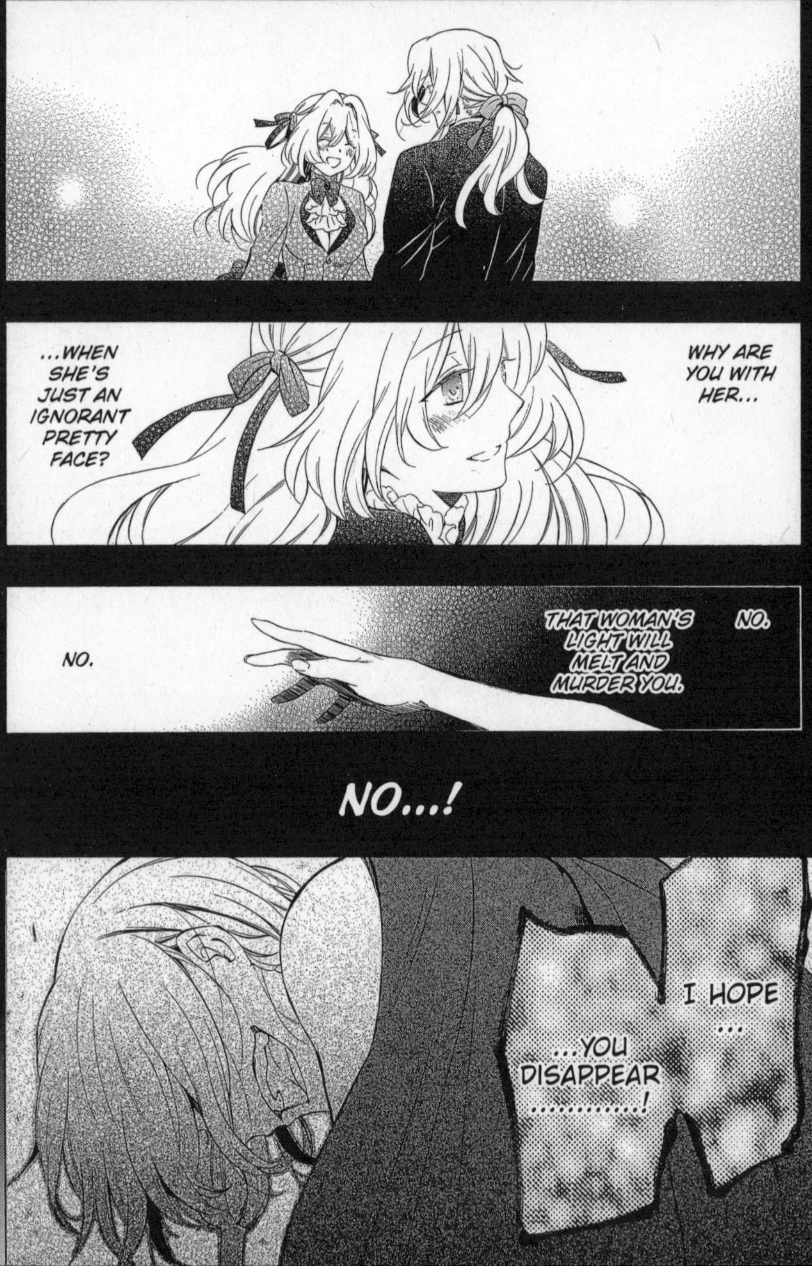
WHY ARE YOU WITH HER...
...WHEN SHE'S JUST AN IGNORANT PRETTY FACE?
NO.
THAT WOMAN'S LIGHT WILL MELT AND MURDER YOU.
NO.
NO...!
I HOPE ...
...YOU DISAPPEAR ....!

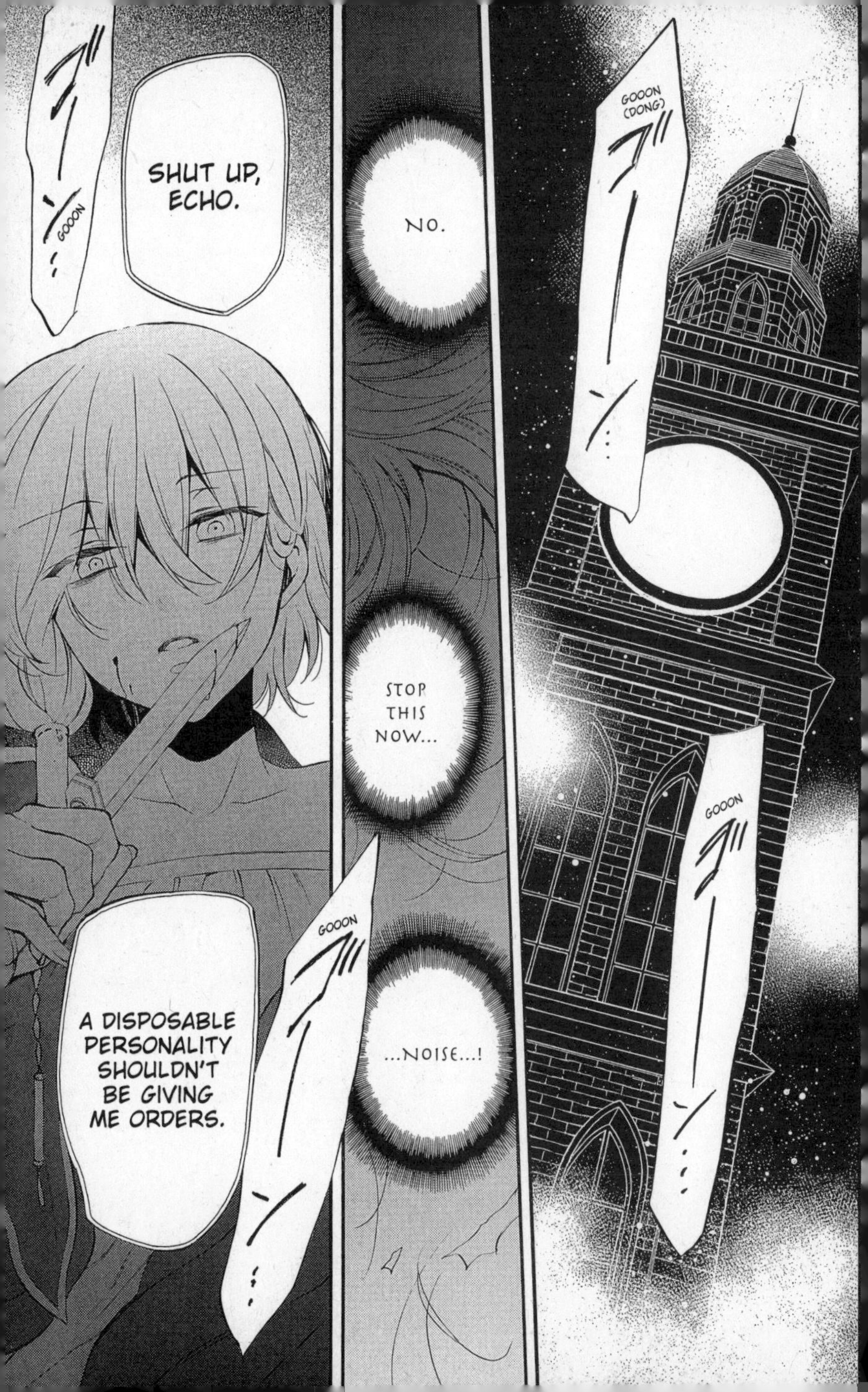
GOOON (DONG)
GOOON
NO.
STOP THIS NOW...
...NOISE...!
GOOON
SHUT UP, ECHO.
GOOON
A DISPOSABLE PERSONALITY SHOULDN'T BE GIVING ME ORDERS.

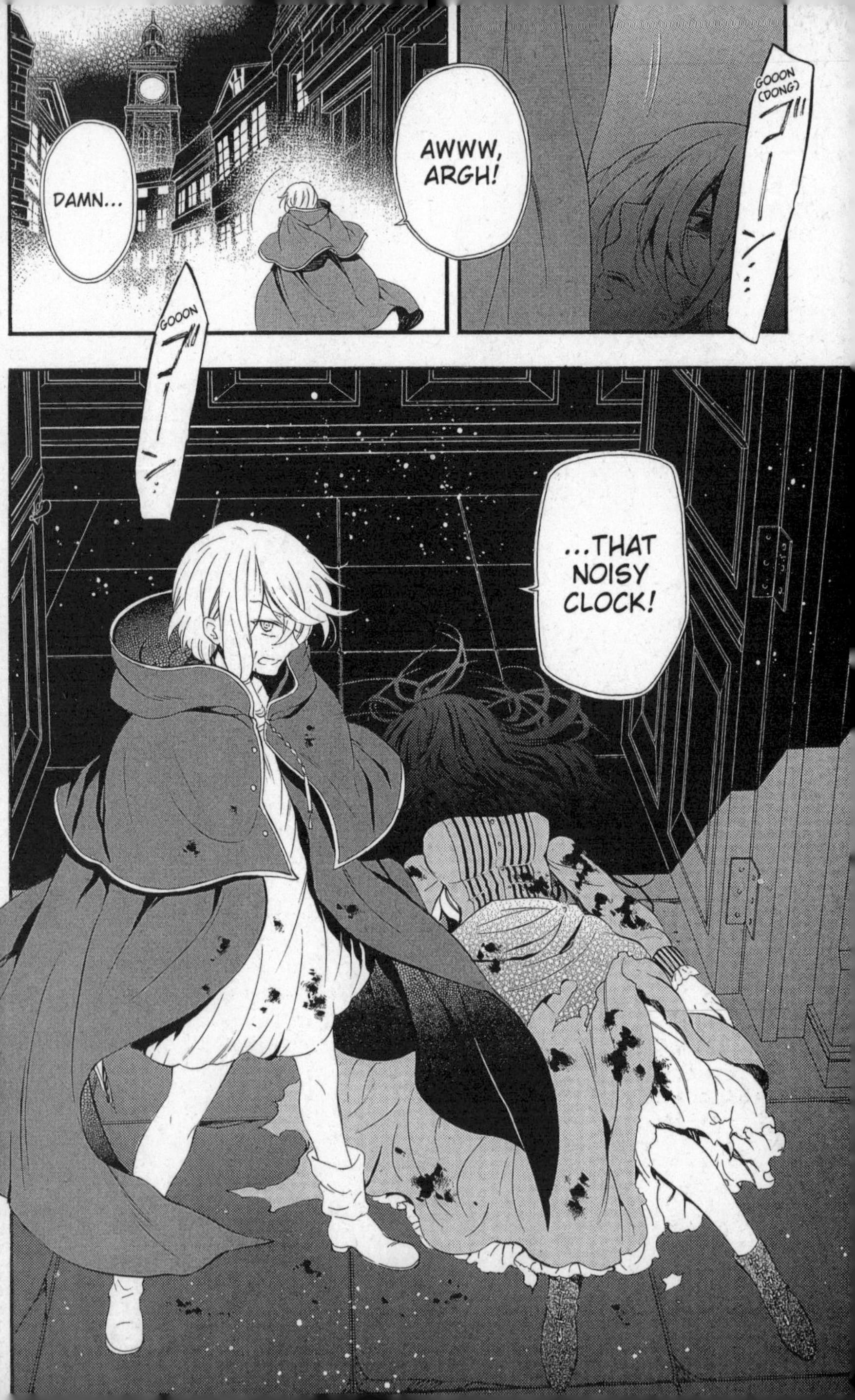
GOOON (DONG)
ゴーン…
AWWW, ARGH!
DAMN...
GOOON
ゴーン
...THAT NOISY CLOCK!

Retrace:LXXXIX Staccato Drop

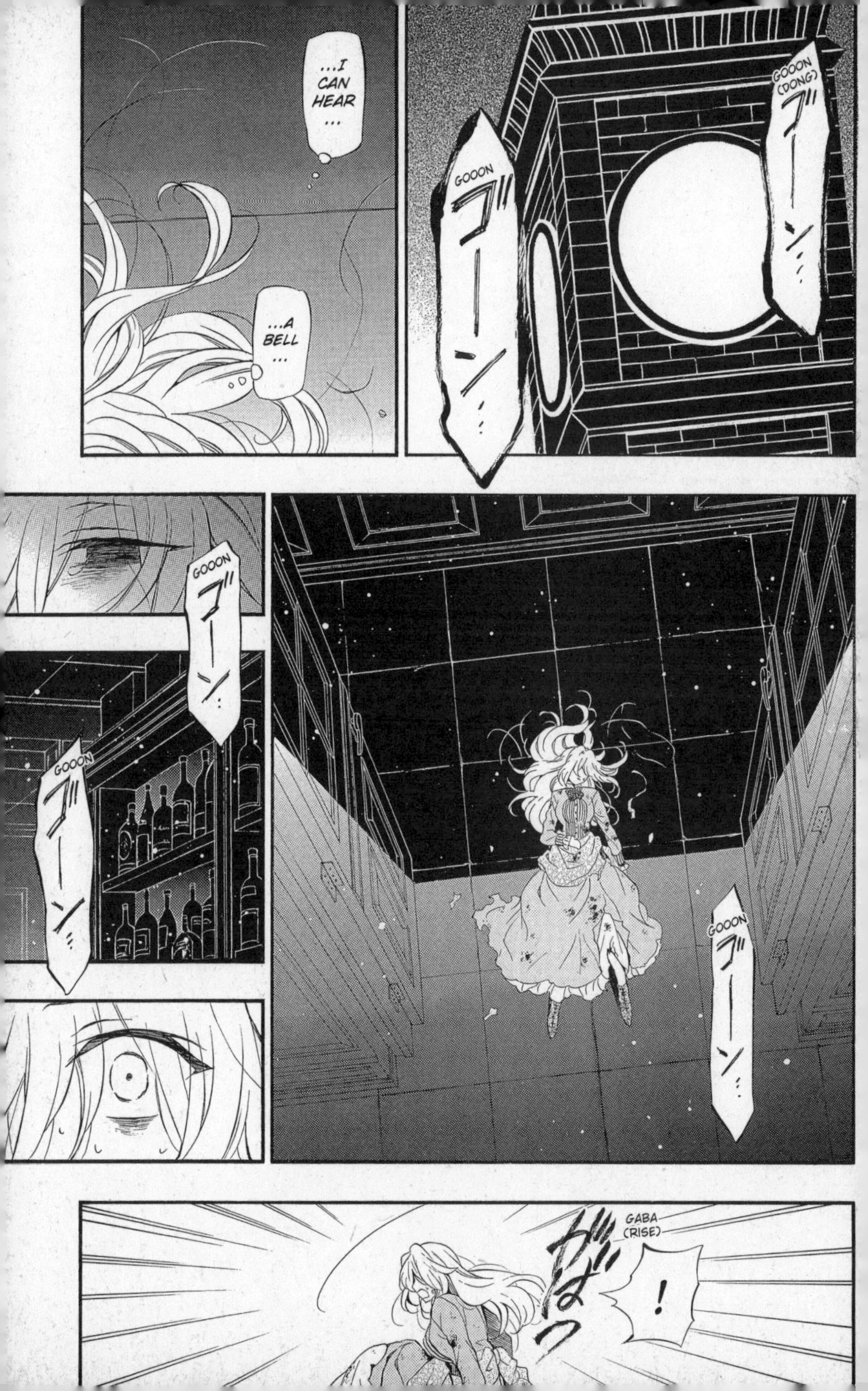
GOOON (DONG)
GOOON
...I CAN HEAR...
...A BELL...
GOOON
GOOON
GOOON
GABA (RISE)
!

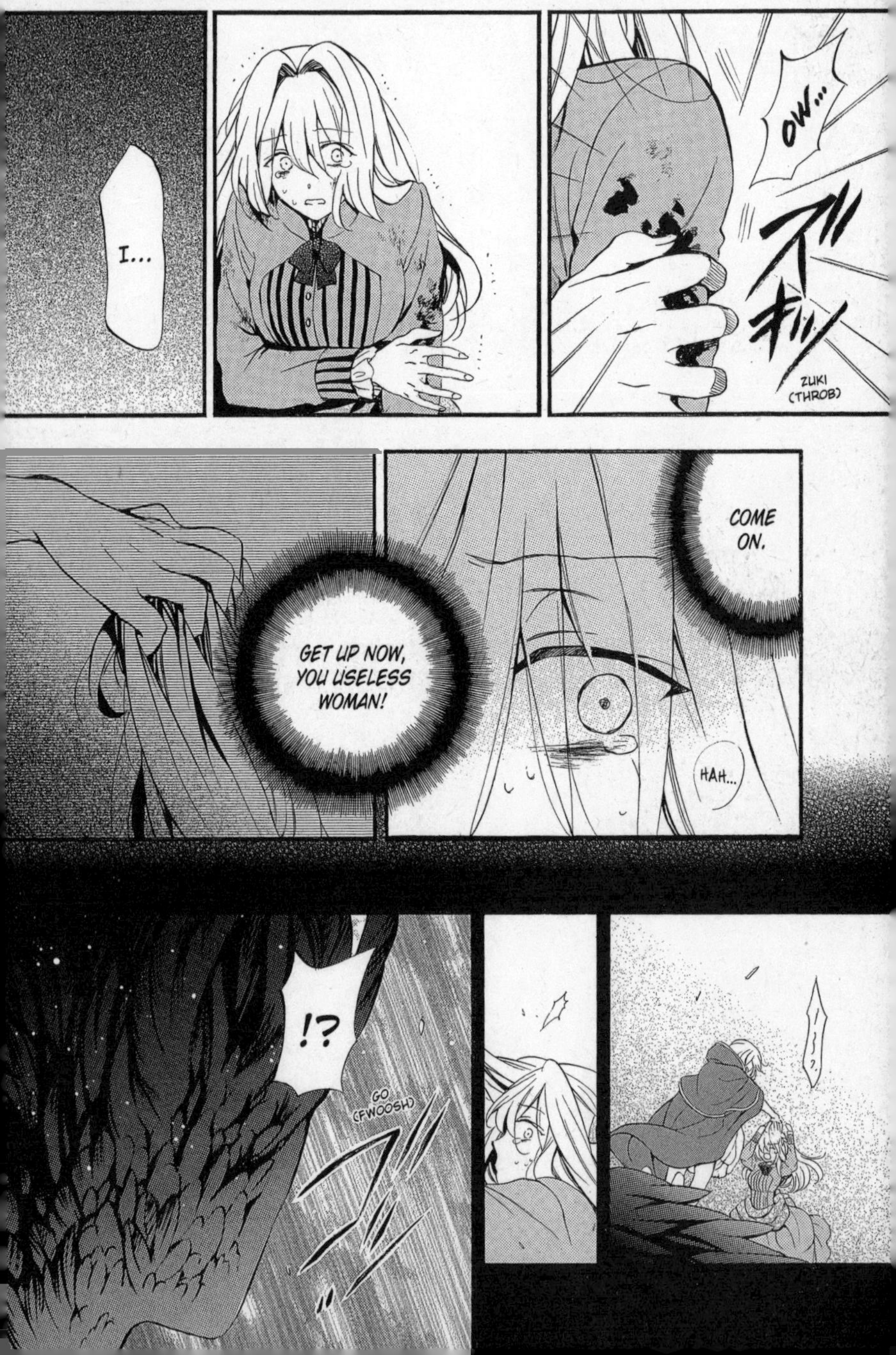

OW...
ZUKI (THROB)
I...
COME ON.
HAH...
GET UP NOW, YOU USELESS WOMAN!
!?
GO (FWOOSH)

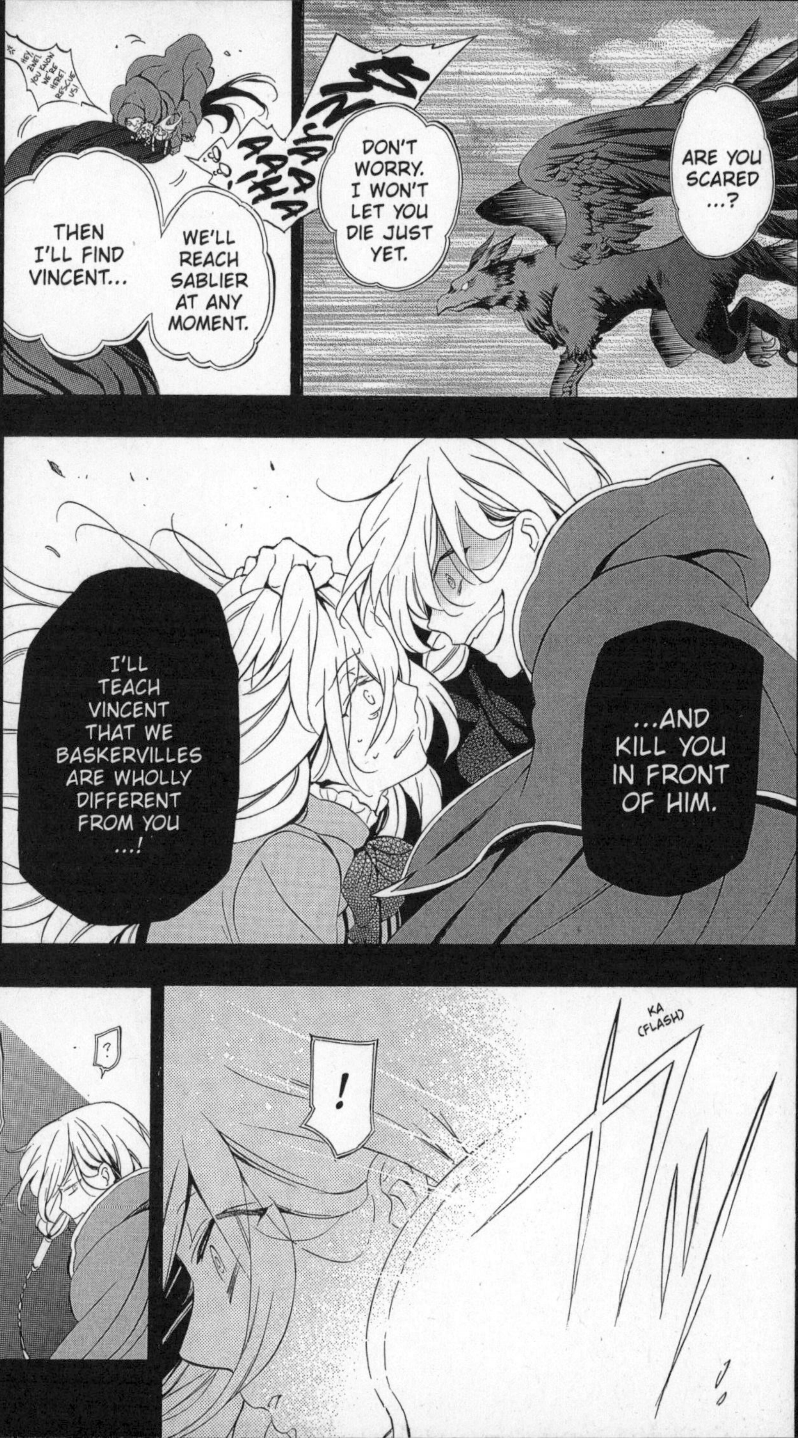
ARE YOU SCARED ...?
DON'T WORRY. I WON'T LET YOU DIE JUST YET.
GNYAAAA AAAHA!
HEY, ZWEI! YOU KNOW WE'RE HERE! RESCUE US!
WE'LL REACH SABLIER AT ANY MOMENT.
THEN I'LL FIND VINCENT...
...AND KILL YOU IN FRONT OF HIM.
I'LL TEACH VINCENT THAT WE BASKERVILLES ARE WHOLLY DIFFERENT FROM YOU ...!
KA (FLASH)
!
?
WHA—!?

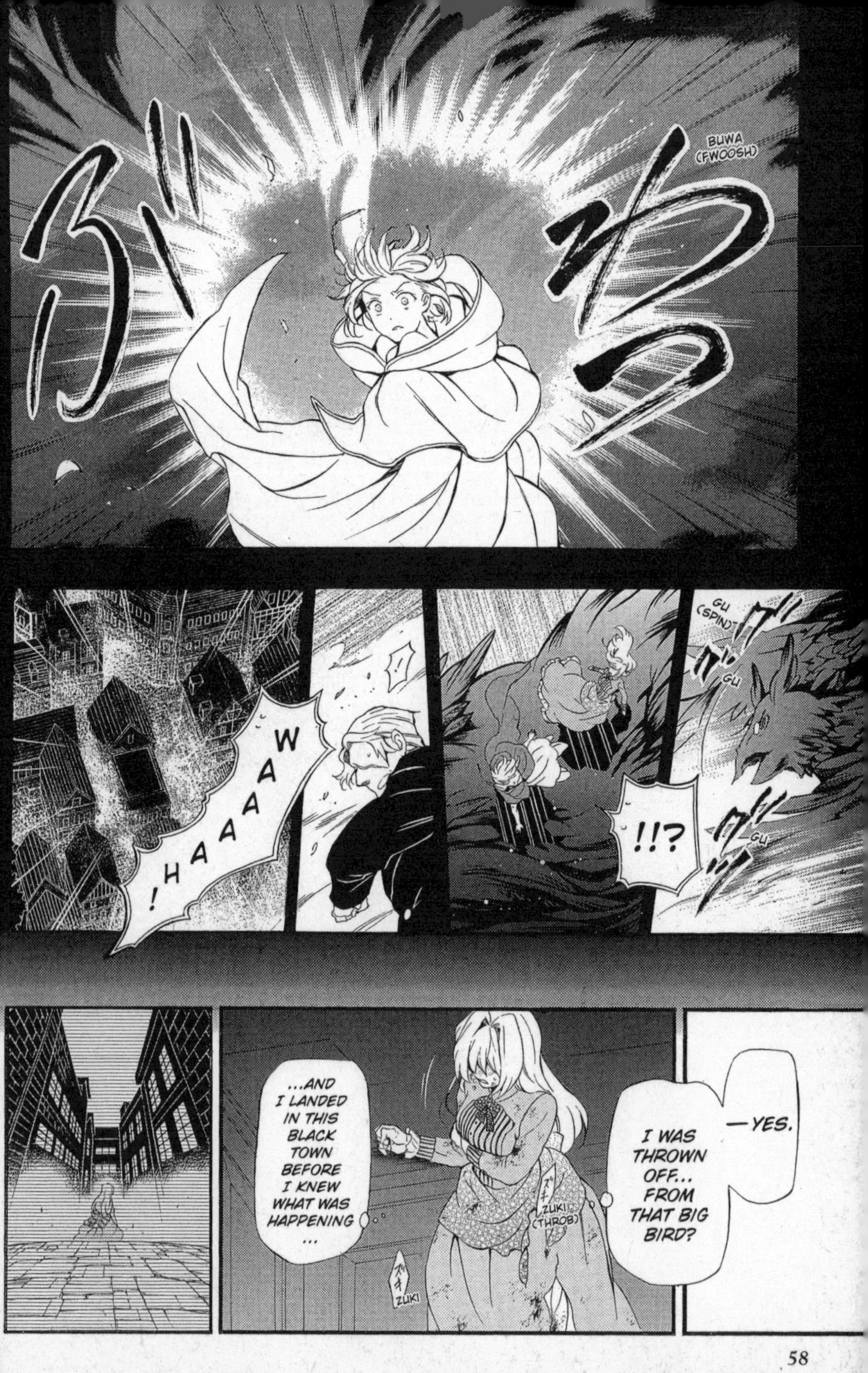
BUWA (FWOOSH)
GU (SPIN)
GU
GU
!!?
!
WAAAH!
—YES.
I WAS THROWN OFF... FROM THAT BIG BIRD?
...AND I LANDED IN THIS BLACK TOWN BEFORE I KNEW WHAT WAS HAPPENING ...
ZUKI (THROB)
ZUKI

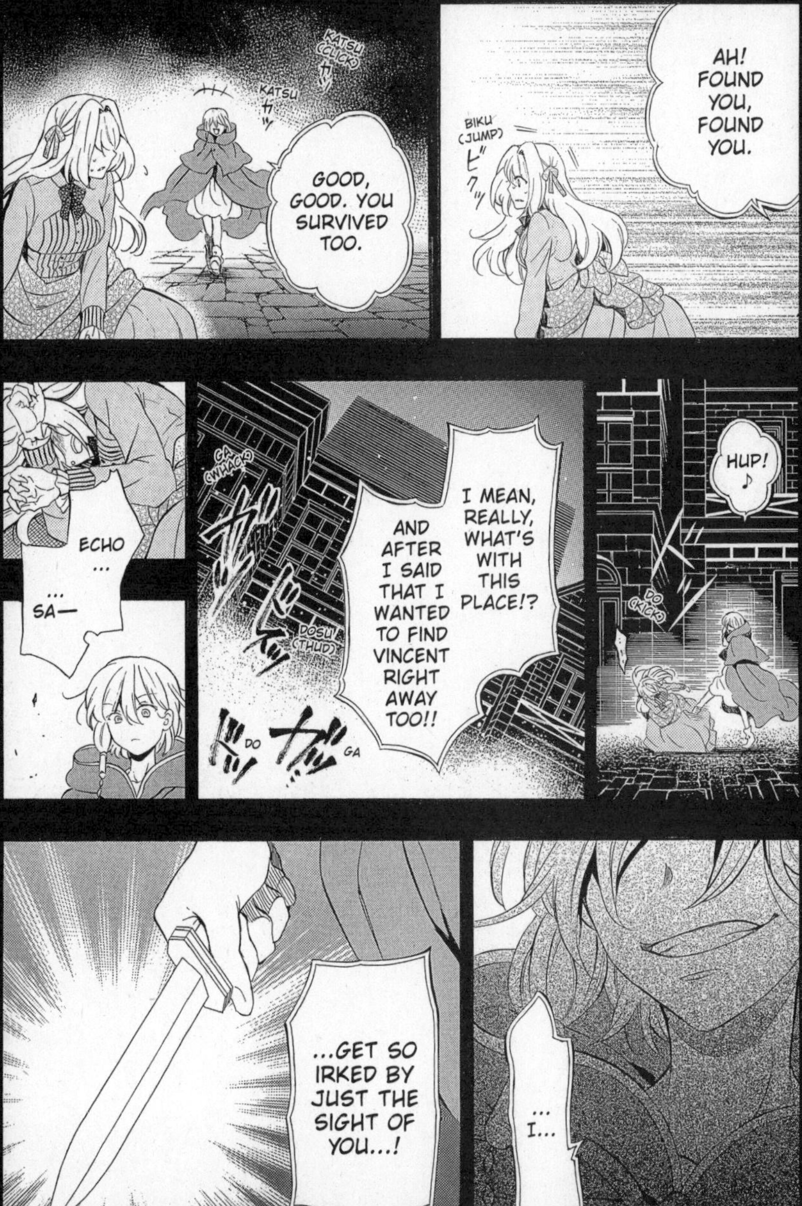
AH! FOUND YOU, FOUND YOU.
BIKU (JUMP)
KATSU (CLICK)
KATSU
GOOD, GOOD. YOU SURVIVED TOO.
HUP! ♪
DO (KICK)
I MEAN, REALLY, WHAT'S WITH THIS PLACE!?
AND AFTER I SAID THAT I WANTED TO FIND VINCENT RIGHT AWAY TOO!!
GA (WHACK)
DOSU (THUD)
DO
GA
ECHO...
...SA—
... I...
...GET SO IRKED BY JUST THE SIGHT OF YOU...!

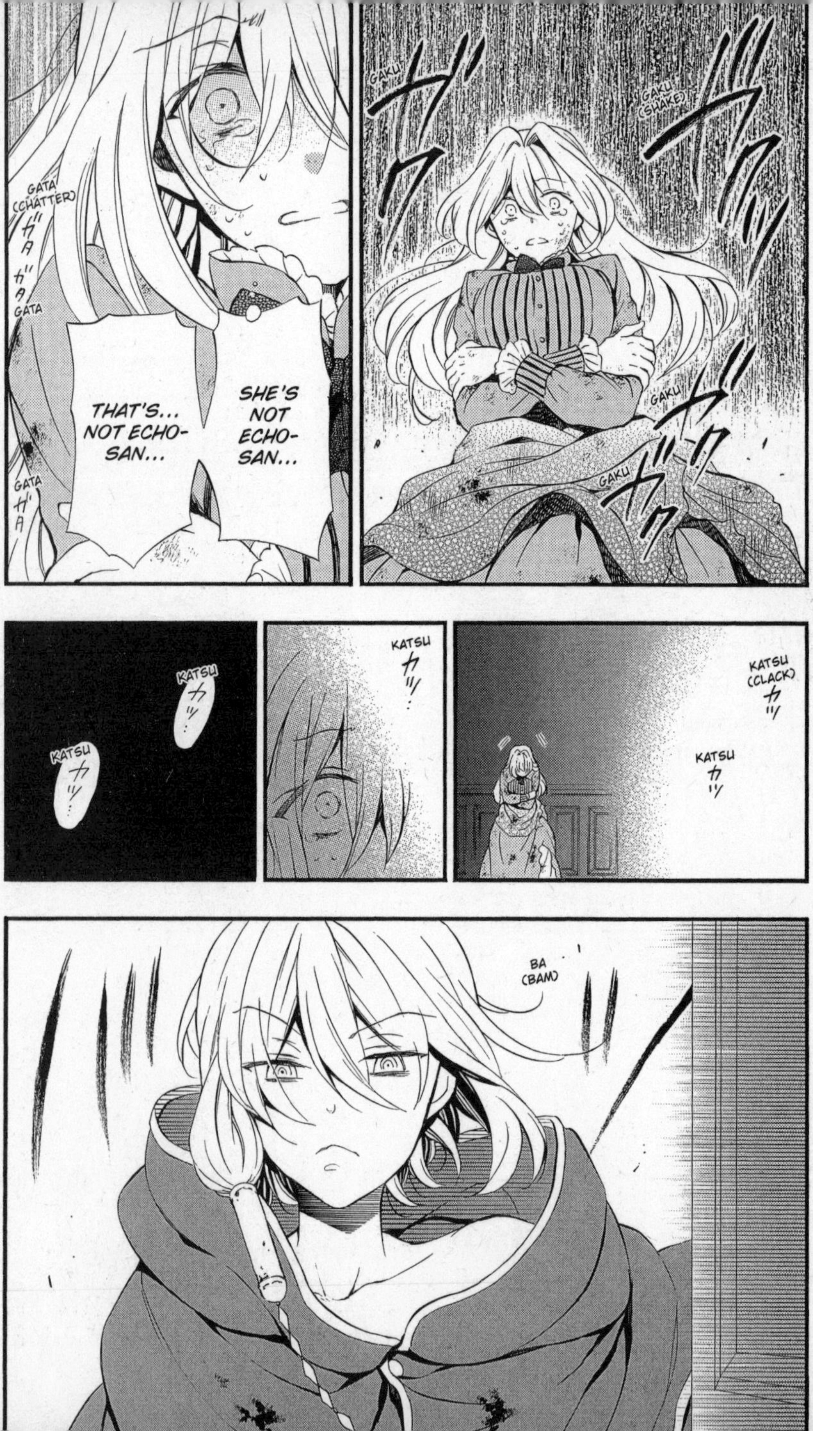

GAKU
GAKU (SHAKE)
GAKU
GAKU
GATA (CHATTER)
ガタ
ガタ
GATA
SHE'S NOT ECHO-SAN...
THAT'S... NOT ECHO-SAN...
GATA
ガタ
KATSU (CLACK)
カッ
KATSU
カッ
KATSU
カッ...
KATSU
カッ...
KATSU
カッ...
BA (BAM)

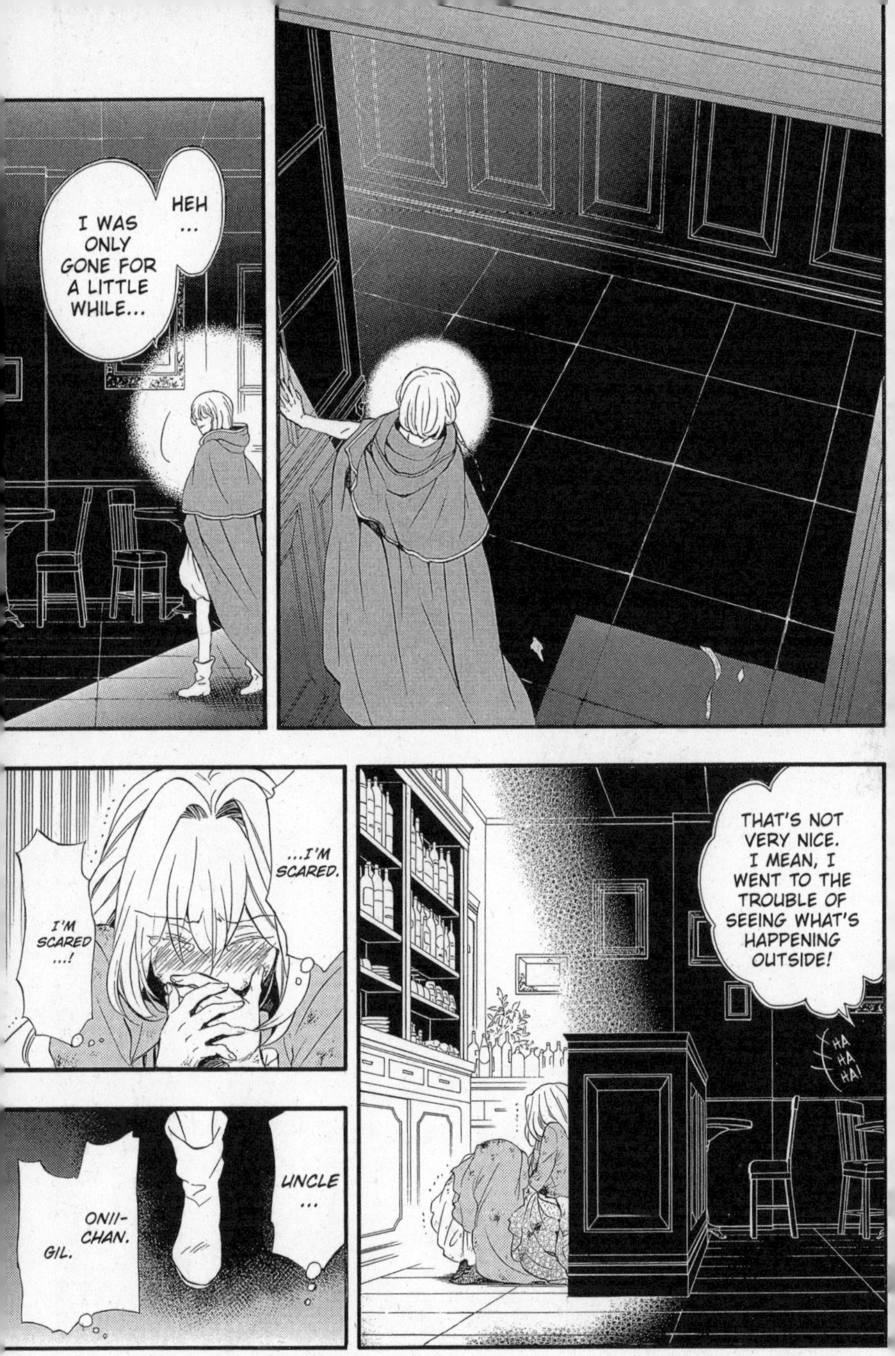
HEH ...
I WAS ONLY GONE FOR A LITTLE WHILE...
THAT'S NOT VERY NICE. I MEAN, I WENT TO THE TROUBLE OF SEEING WHAT'S HAPPENING OUTSIDE!
HA HA HA!
...I'M SCARED.
I'M SCARED ...!
UNCLE ...
ONII-CHAN.
GIL.

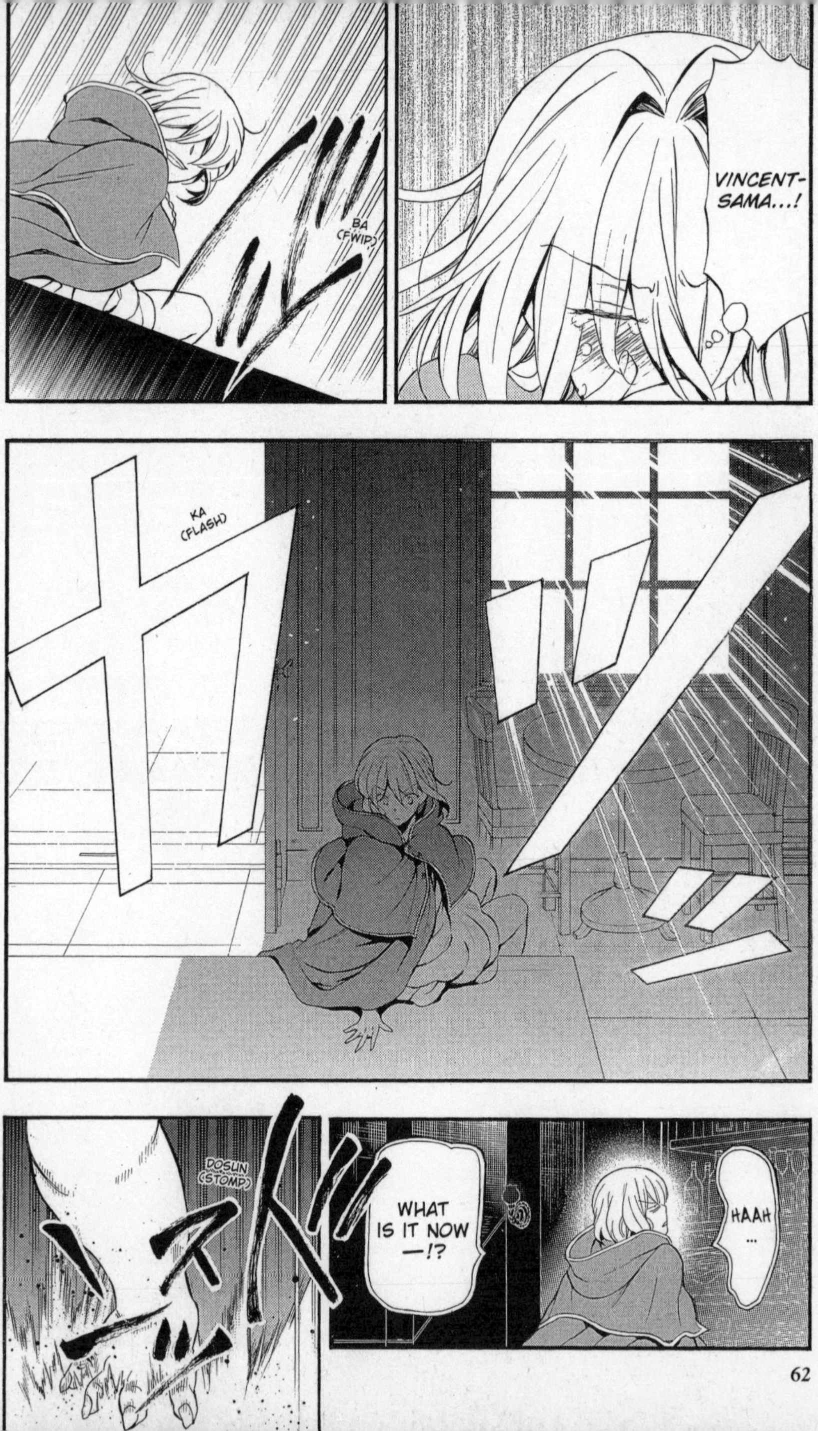
VINCENT-SAMA...!
BA (FWIP)
KA (FLASH)
HAAH ...
WHAT IS IT NOW —!?
DOSUN (STOMP)

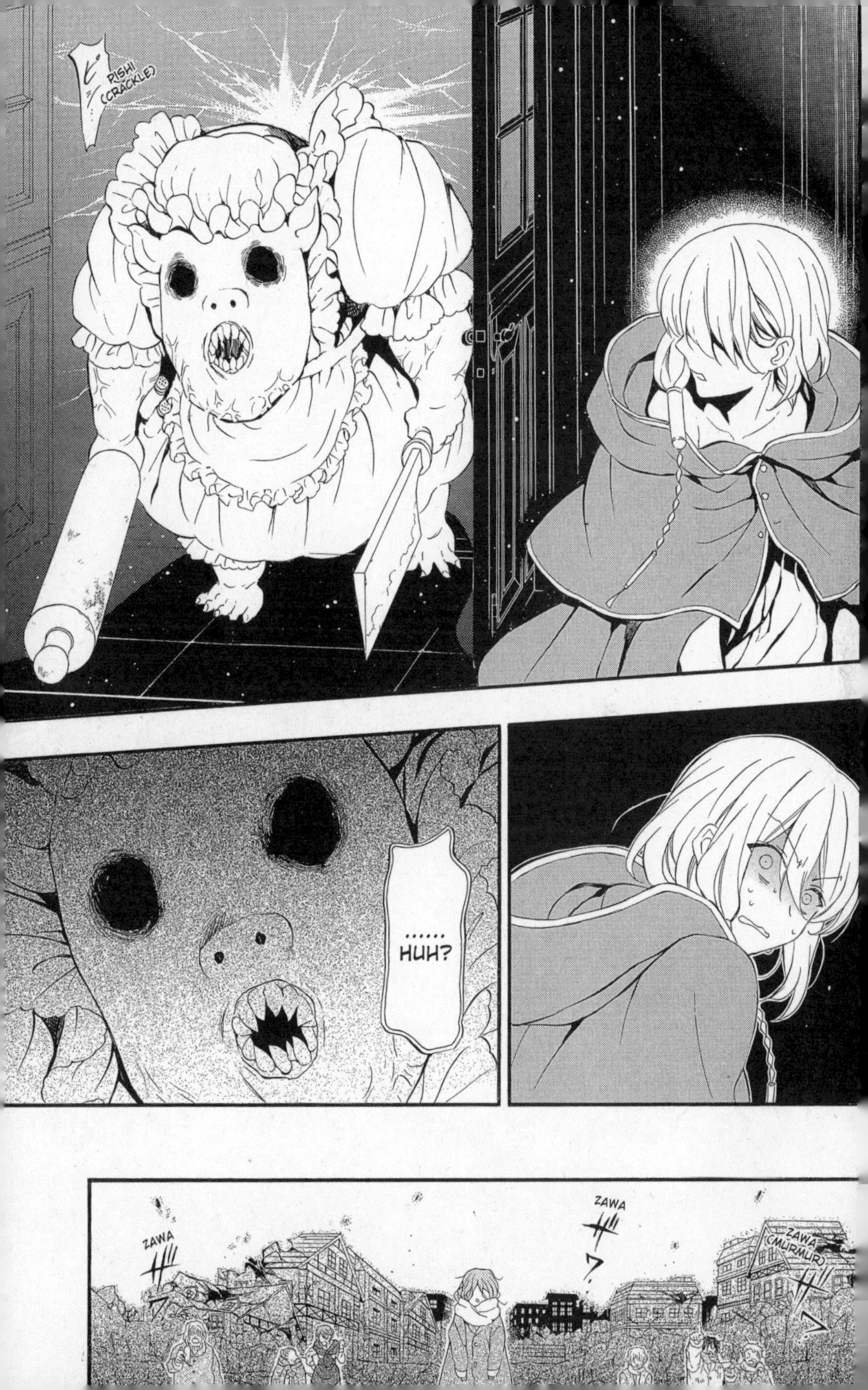
PISHI (CRACKLE)
...... HUH?
ZAWA (MURMUR)
ZAWA
ZAWA

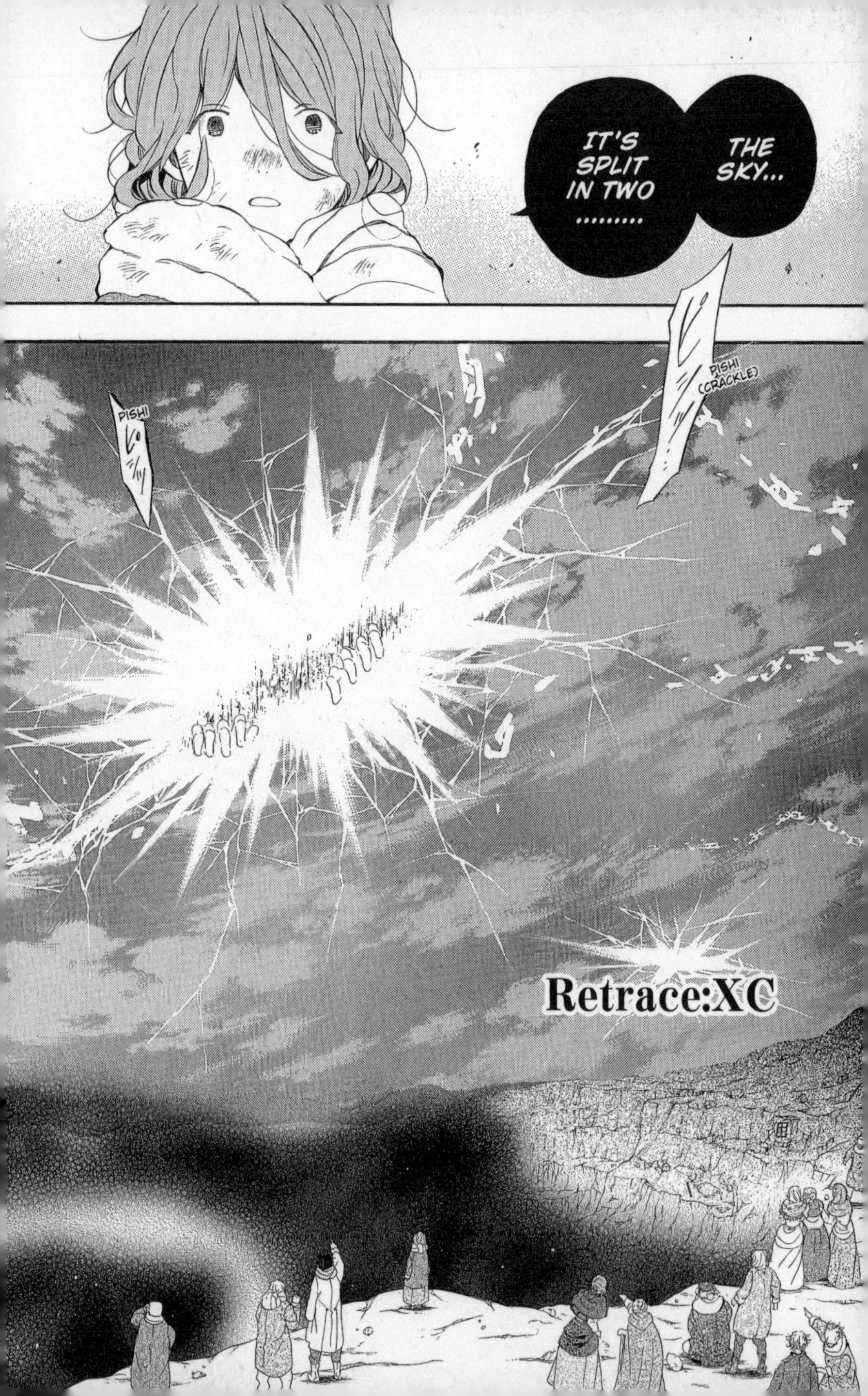
THE SKY...
IT'S SPLIT IN TWO ....
PISHI (CRACKLE)
PISHI
Retrace:XC

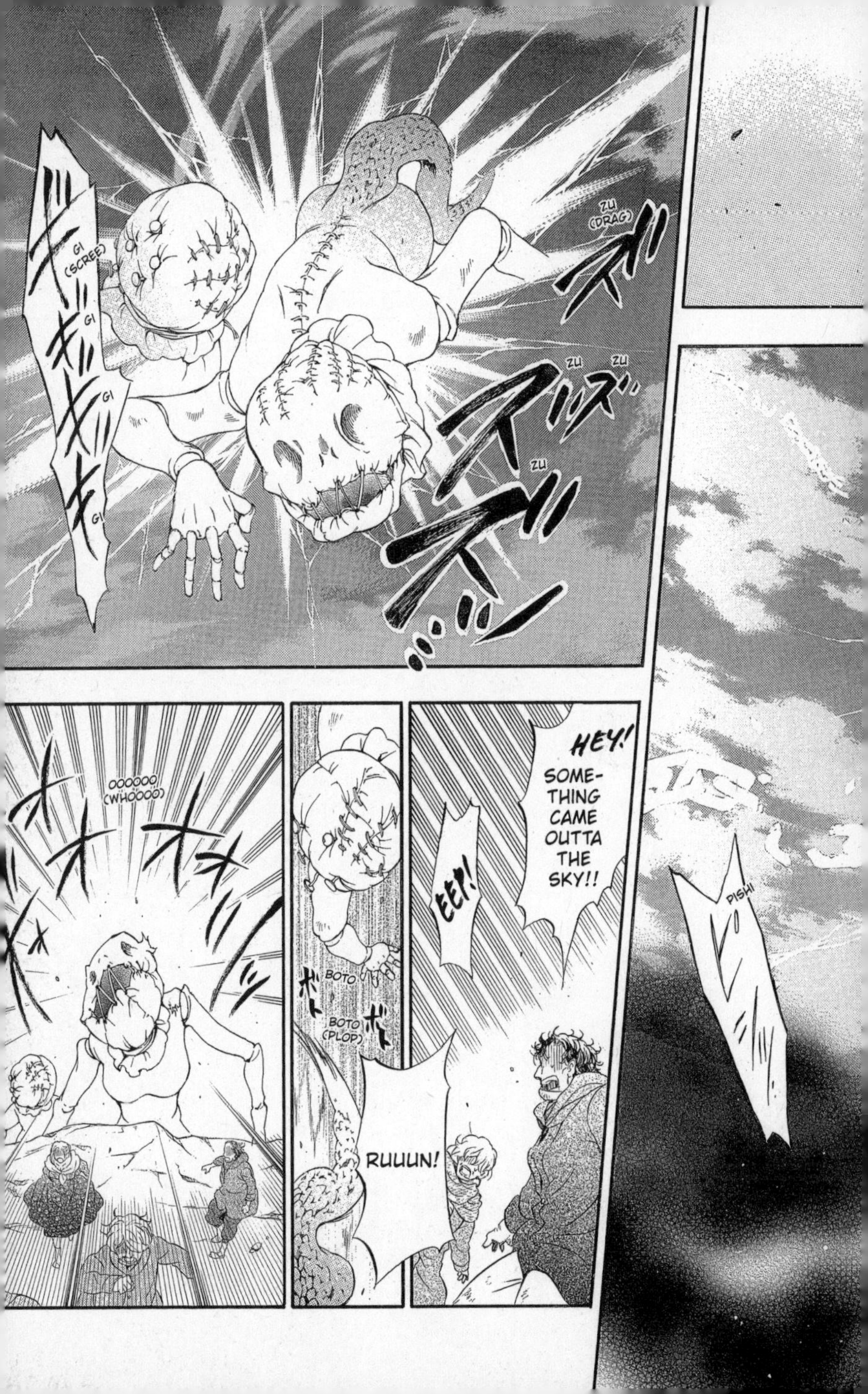
PISHI
GI (SCREE)
GI
GI
GI
ZU (DRAG)
ZU
ZU
ZU
HEY!
SOMETHING CAME OUTTA THE SKY!!
RUUUN!
EEP!
BOTO
BOTO (PLOP)
OOOOOO (WHOOOO)

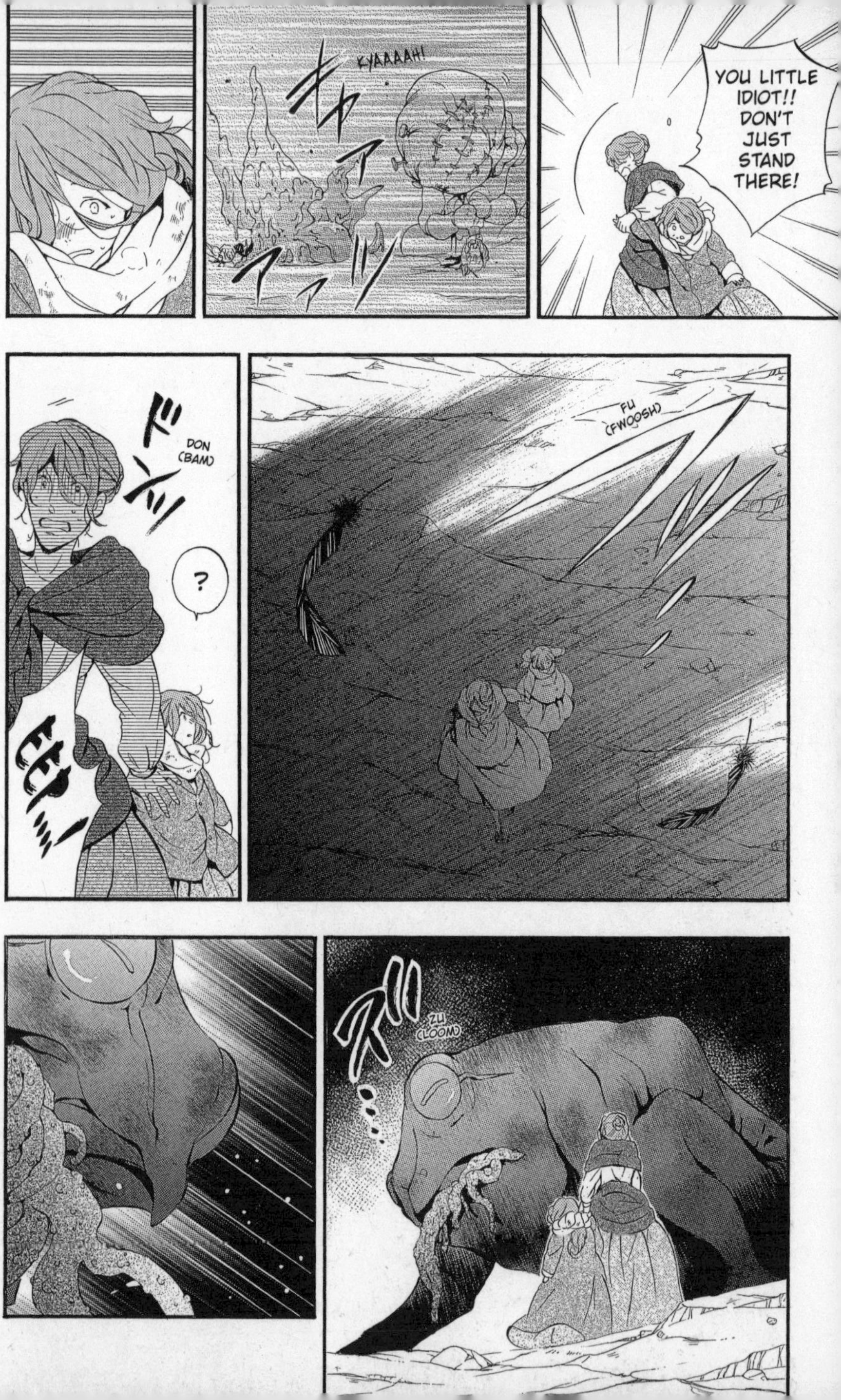
YOU LITTLE IDIOT!! DON'T JUST STAND THERE!
KYAAAAH!
FU (FWOOSH)
DON (BAM)
?
EEP...!
ZU (LOOM)

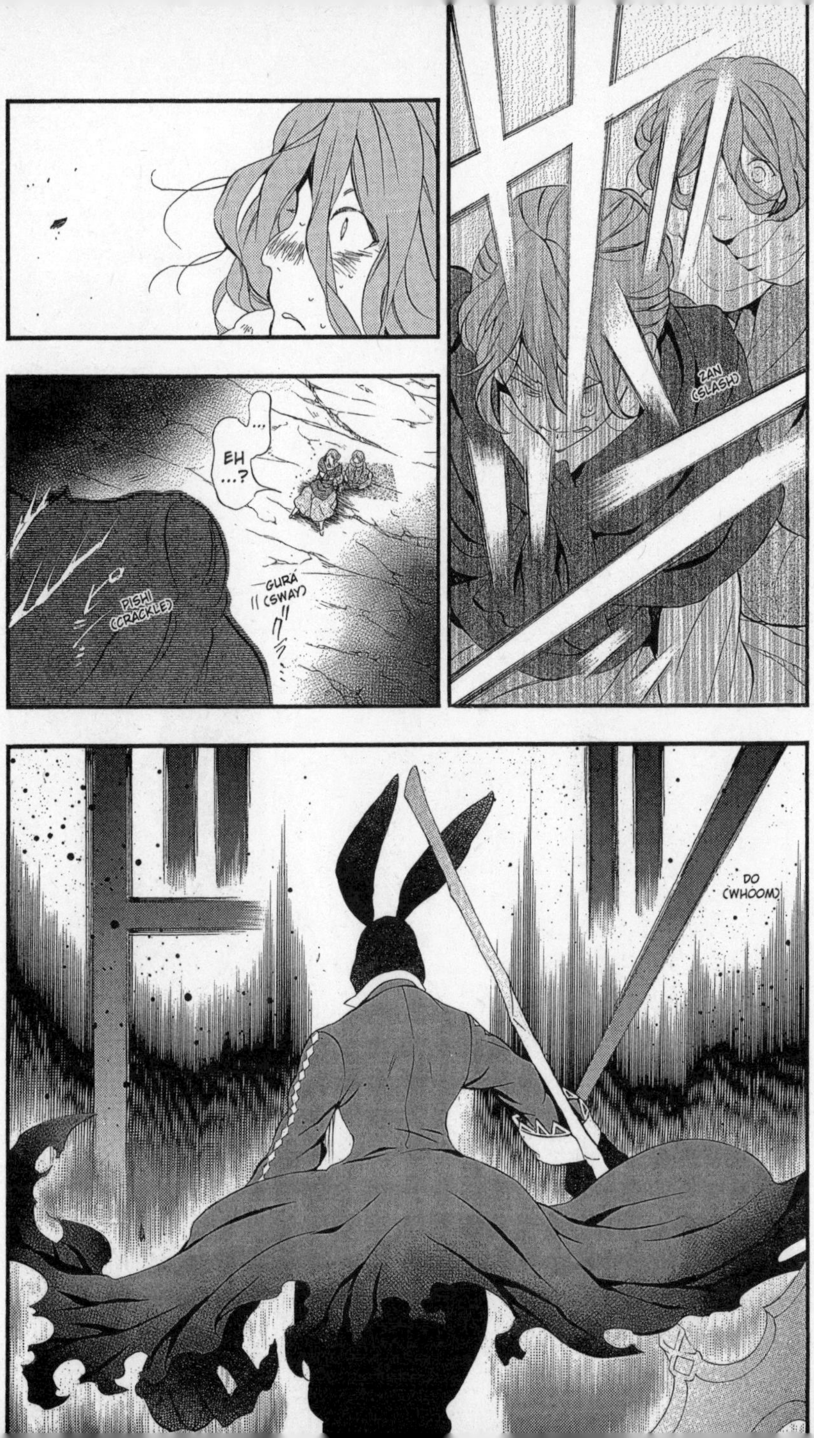
ZAN (SLASH)
... EH ...?
GURA (SWAY)
PISHI (CRACKLE)
DO (WHOOM)

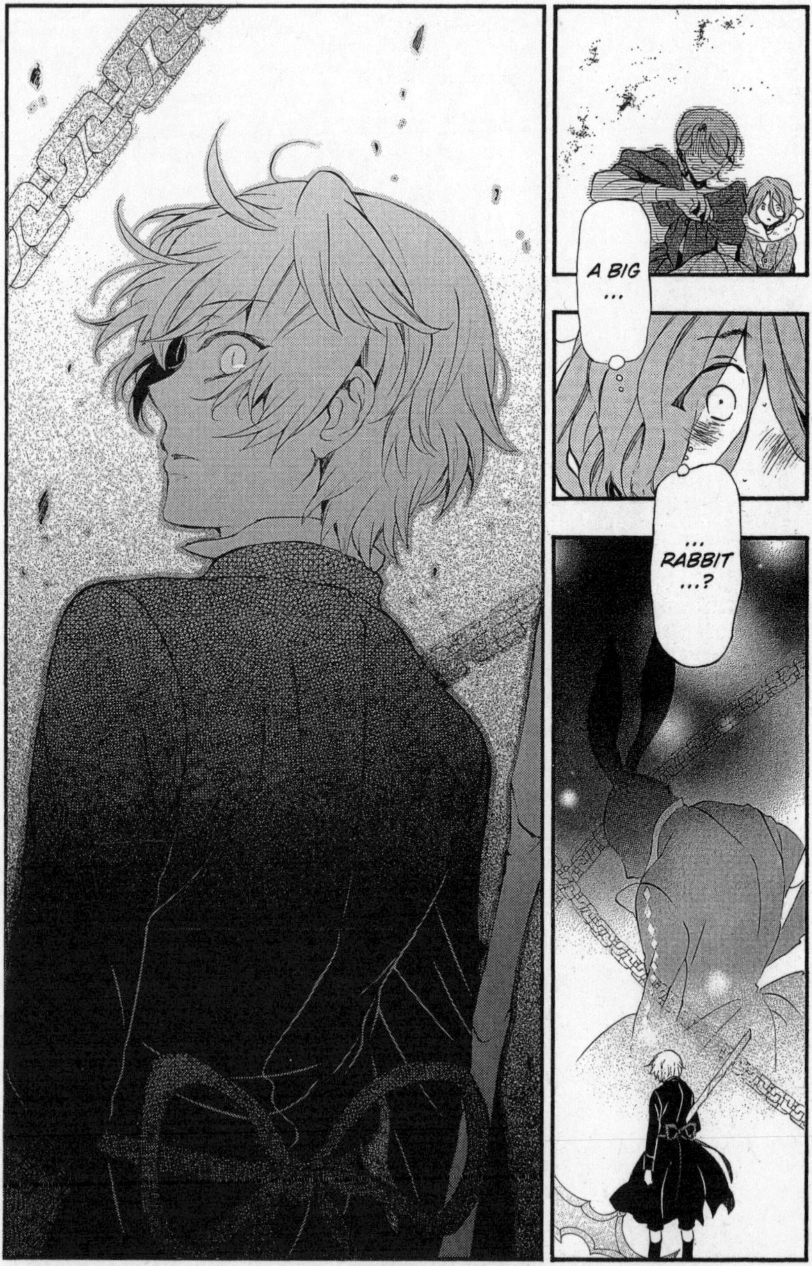
A BIG ...
... RABBIT ...?

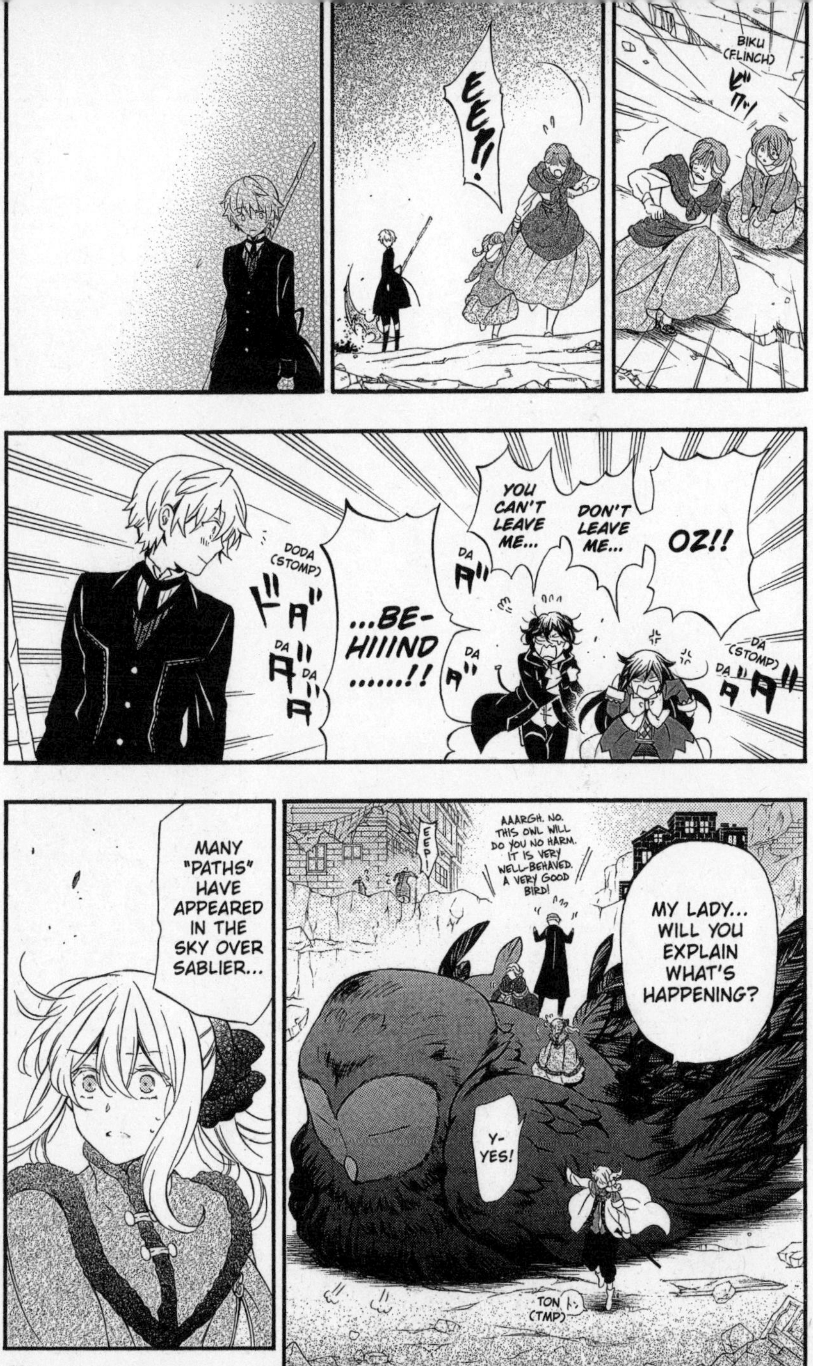
BIKU (FLINCH)
ビクッ
OZ!!
DON'T LEAVE ME...
YOU CAN'T LEAVE ME...
DA (STOMP) DA
DA
...BE-HIIIND ......!!
DODA (STOMP)
DA
DA
MY LADY... WILL YOU EXPLAIN WHAT'S HAPPENING?
AAARGH. NO. THIS OWL WILL DO YOU NO HARM. IT IS VERY WELL-BEHAVED. A VERY GOOD BIRD!
EEP!
Y-YES!
TON (TMP)
MANY "PATHS" HAVE APPEARED IN THE SKY OVER SABLIER...

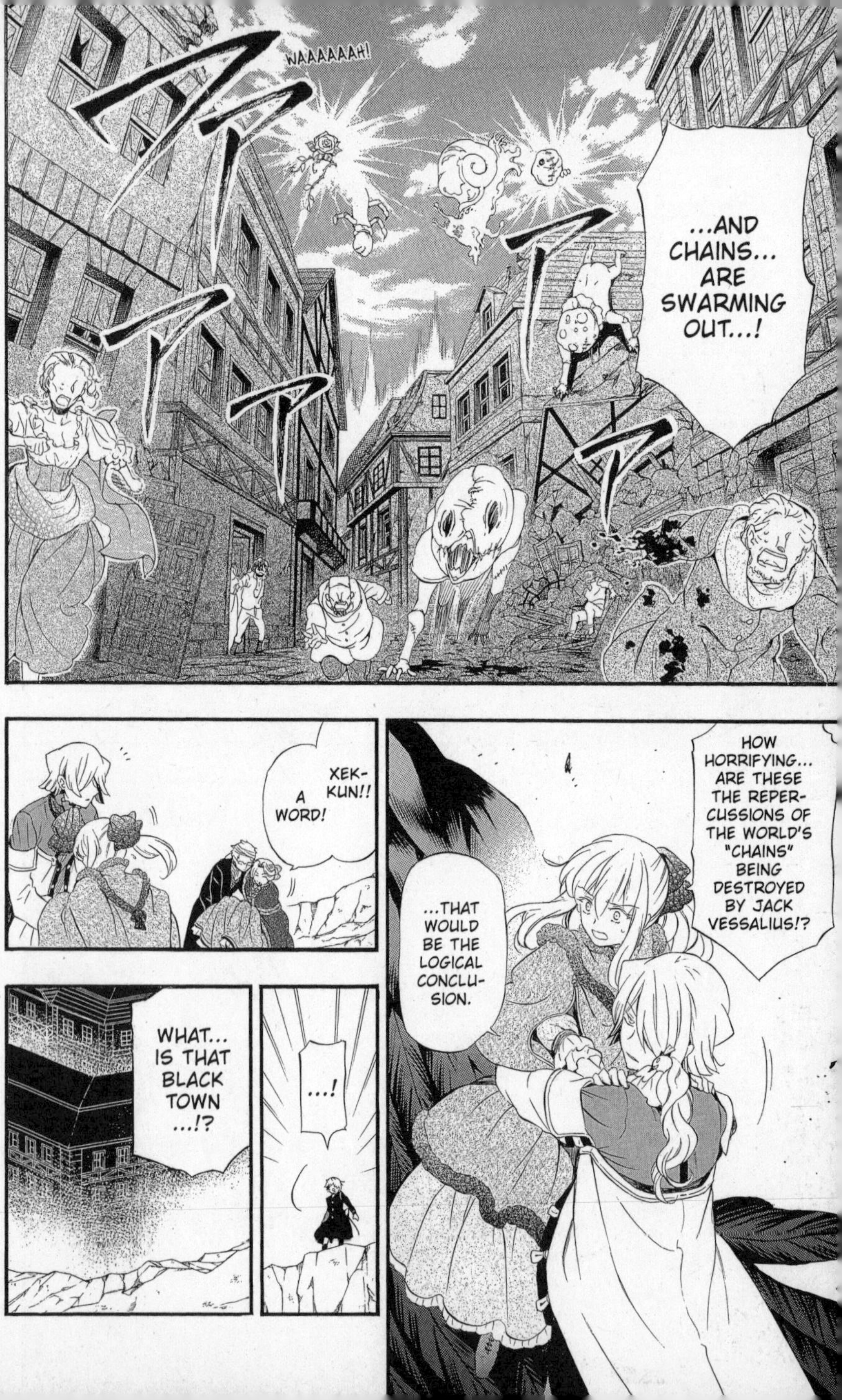
WAAAAAAH!
...AND CHAINS... ARE SWARMING OUT...!
HOW HORRIFYING... ARE THESE THE REPERCUSSIONS OF THE WORLD'S "CHAINS" BEING DESTROYED BY JACK VESSALIUS!?
...THAT WOULD BE THE LOGICAL CONCLUSION.
XEK-KUN!! A WORD!
...!
WHAT... IS THAT BLACK TOWN ...!?

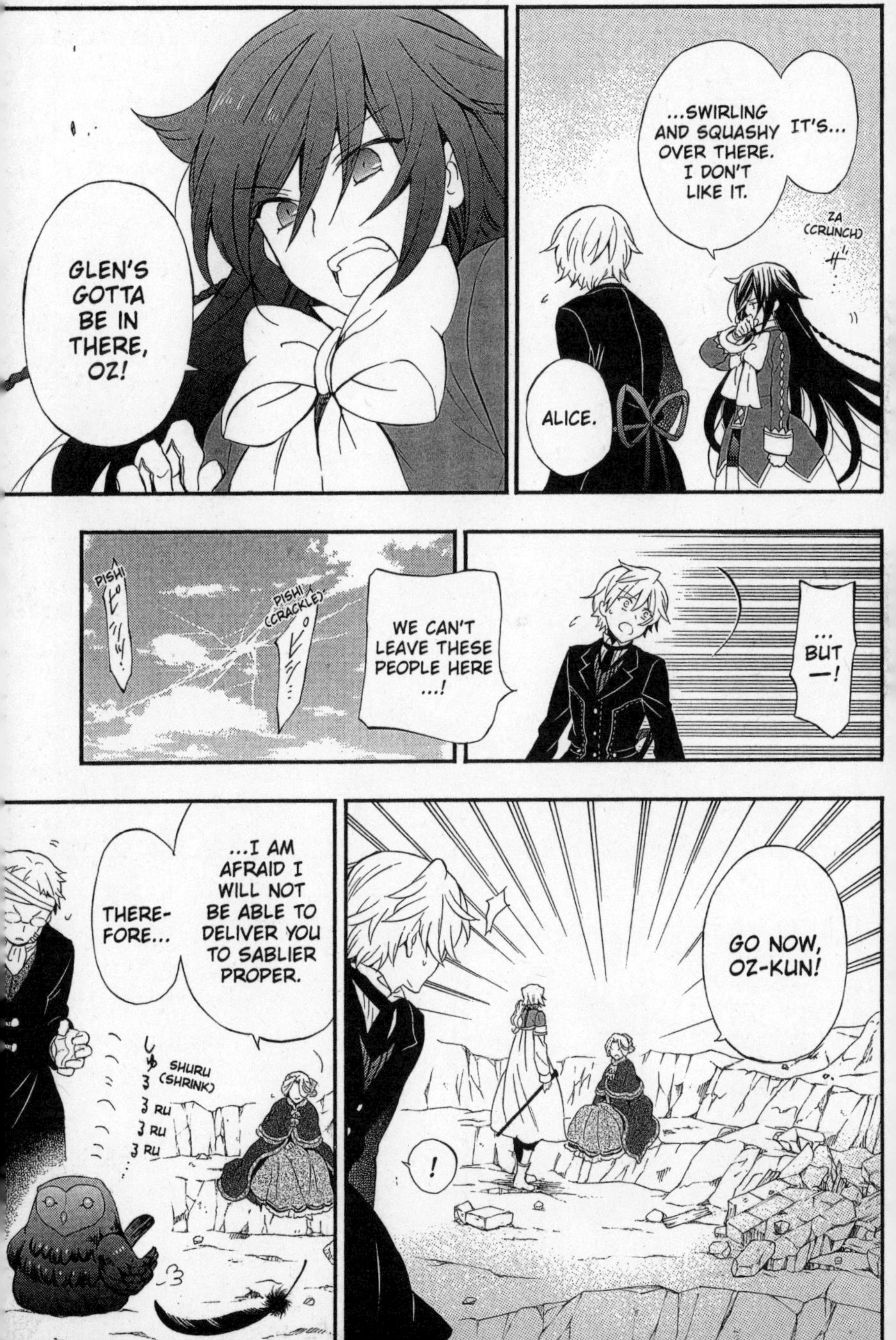
IT'S...
...SWIRLING AND SQUASHY OVER THERE. I DON'T LIKE IT.
ZA (CRUNCH)
ALICE.
GLEN'S GOTTA BE IN THERE, OZ!
...BUT—!
WE CAN'T LEAVE THESE PEOPLE HERE ...!
PISHI (CRACKLE)
PISHI
GO NOW, OZ-KUN!
!
...I AM AFRAID I WILL NOT BE ABLE TO DELIVER YOU TO SABLIER PROPER.
THERE-FORE...
SHURU (SHRINK)
RU
RU
RU

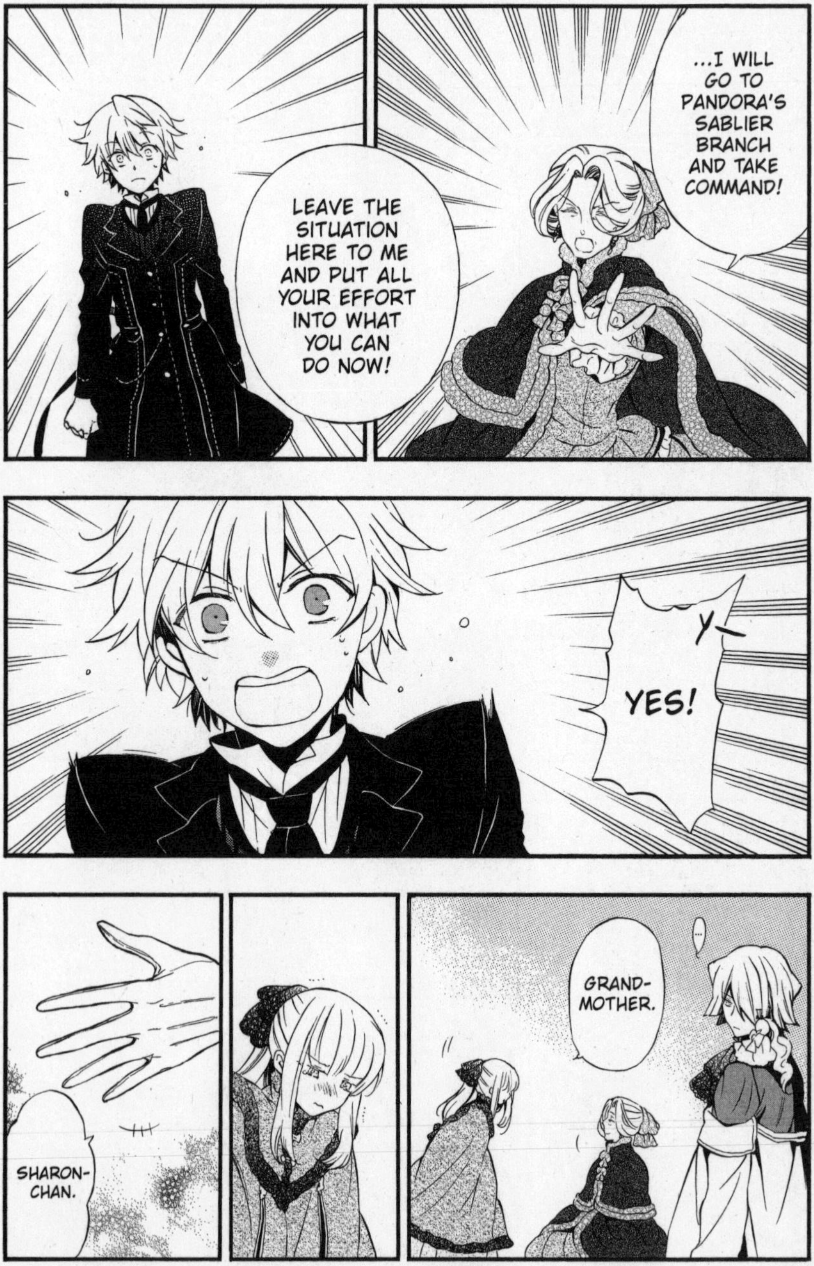
...I WILL GO TO PANDORA'S SABLIER BRANCH AND TAKE COMMAND!
LEAVE THE SITUATION HERE TO ME AND PUT ALL YOUR EFFORT INTO WHAT YOU CAN DO NOW!
Y— YES!
...
GRAND-MOTHER.
...
SHARON-CHAN.

XERXES.

IF I AM BEING HONEST...

...I WANT YOU TO STAY WITH ME.

VERY WELL. BUT PROMISE ME YOU WILL RETURN.

YES... I AM SORRY, GRANDMOTHER.

I WILL...!

....

TAKE CARE OF SHERYL-SAMA.

I WILL.

I—

I! HAVE YET! TO SAY ANYTHING!!

!!

BUT I GUESSED RIGHT!

YOU'LL JUST BE A LIABILITY IF YOU COME WIIIIITH!

KYAH HA!

POSU (PAT)

THE REST IS UP TO YOU.

GOOD.

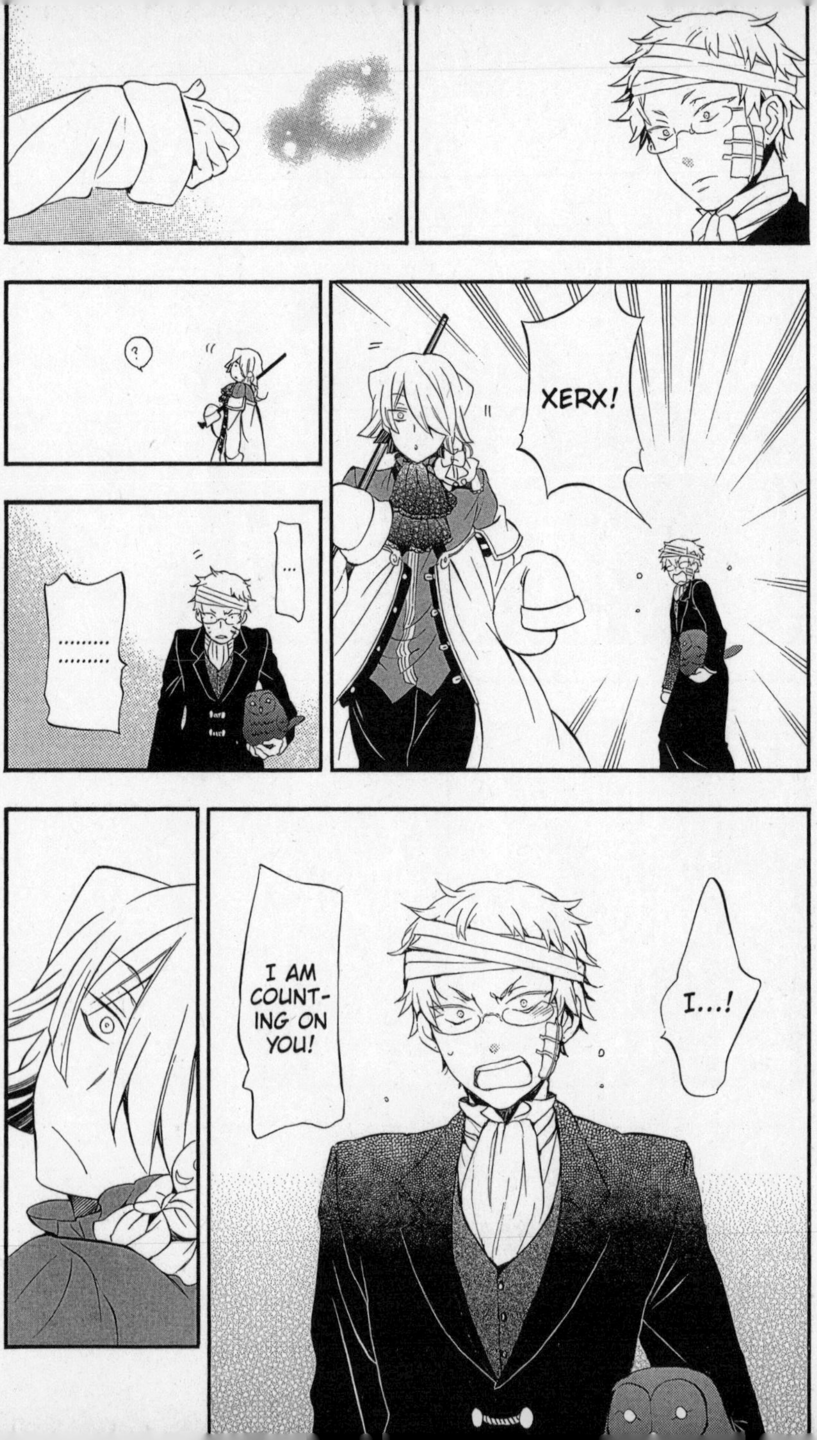
XERX!
?
...
....
....
I...!
I AM COUNTING ON YOU!

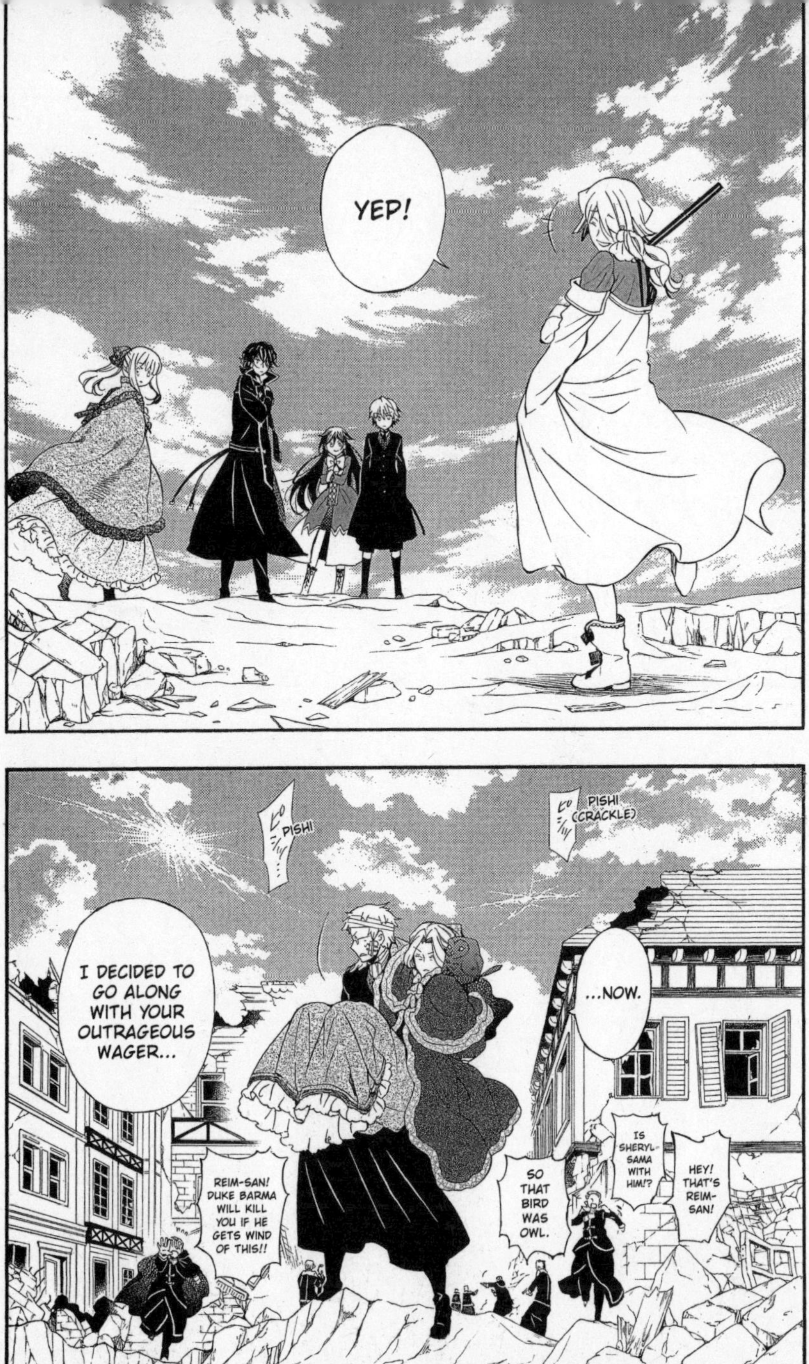
YEP!
PISHI (CRACKLE)
PISHI
I DECIDED TO GO ALONG WITH YOUR OUTRAGEOUS WAGER...
...NOW.
HEY! THAT'S REIM-SAN!
IS SHERYL-SAMA WITH HIM!?
SO THAT BIRD WAS OWL.
REIM-SAN! DUKE BARMA WILL KILL YOU IF HE GETS WIND OF THIS!!

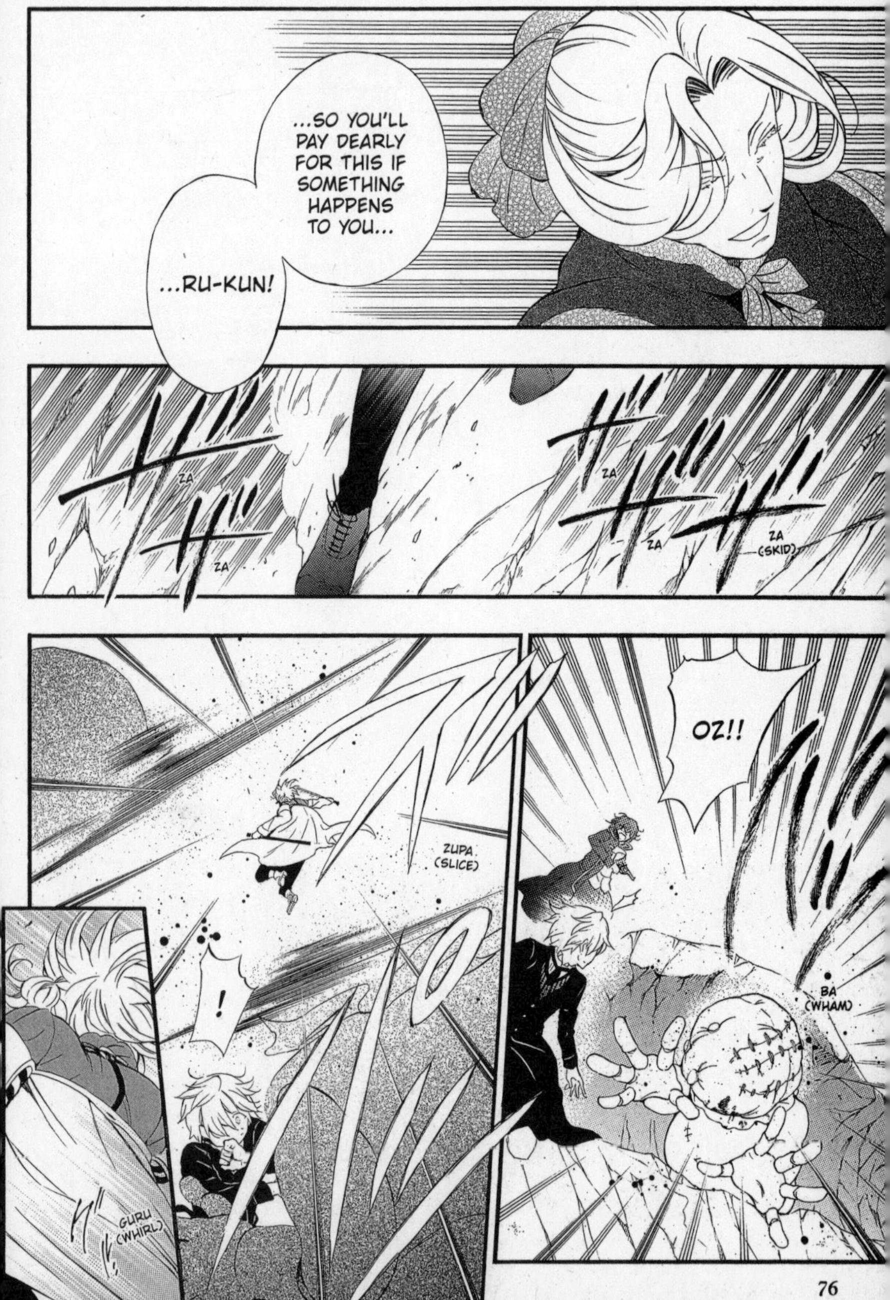
...SO YOU'LL PAY DEARLY FOR THIS IF SOMETHING HAPPENS TO YOU...
...RU-KUN!
ZA (SKID)
ZA
ZA
ZA
ZA
OZ!!
BA (WHAM)
ZUPA (SLICE)
!
GURU (WHIRL)

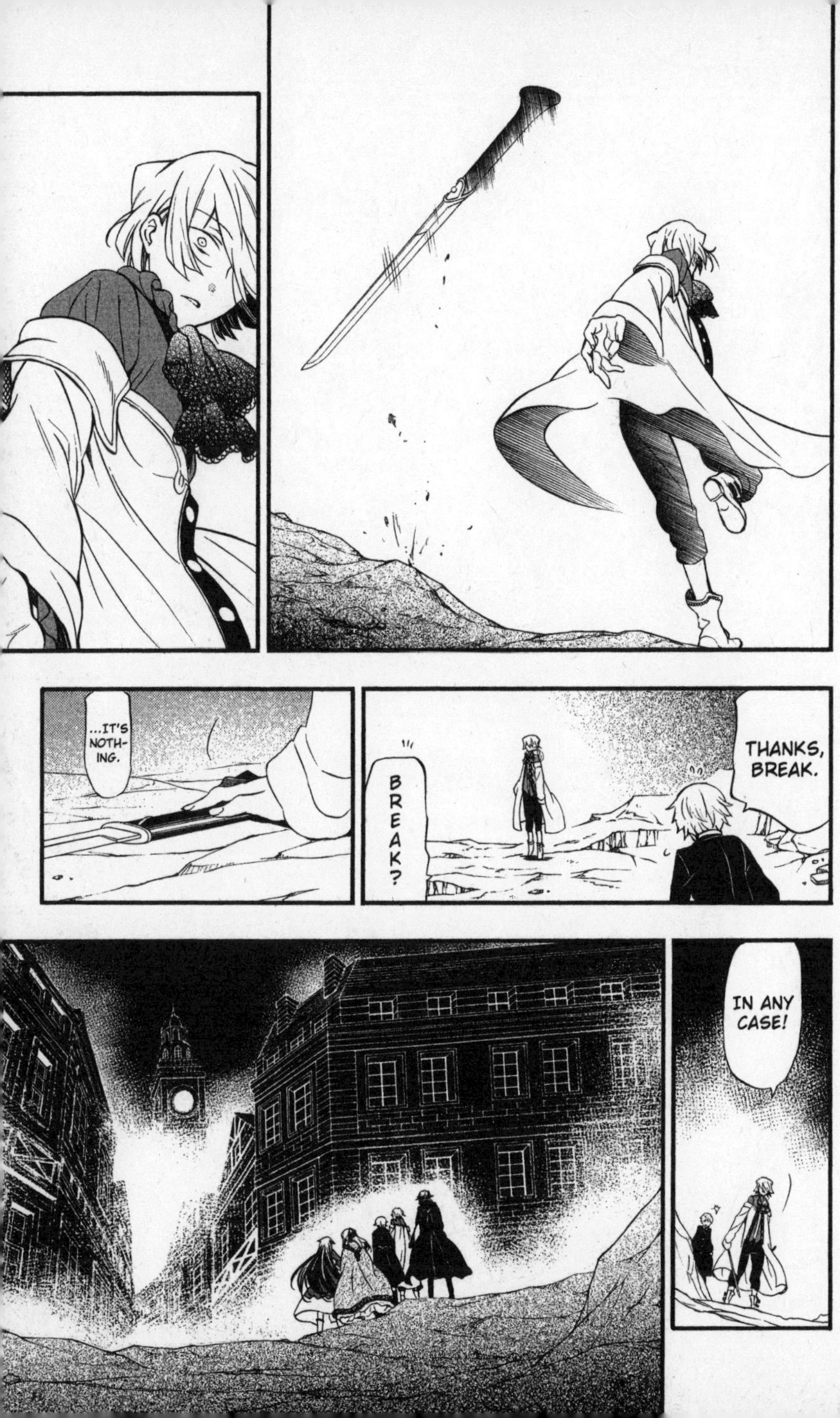
THANKS, BREAK.
BREAK?
...IT'S NOTHING.
IN ANY CASE!

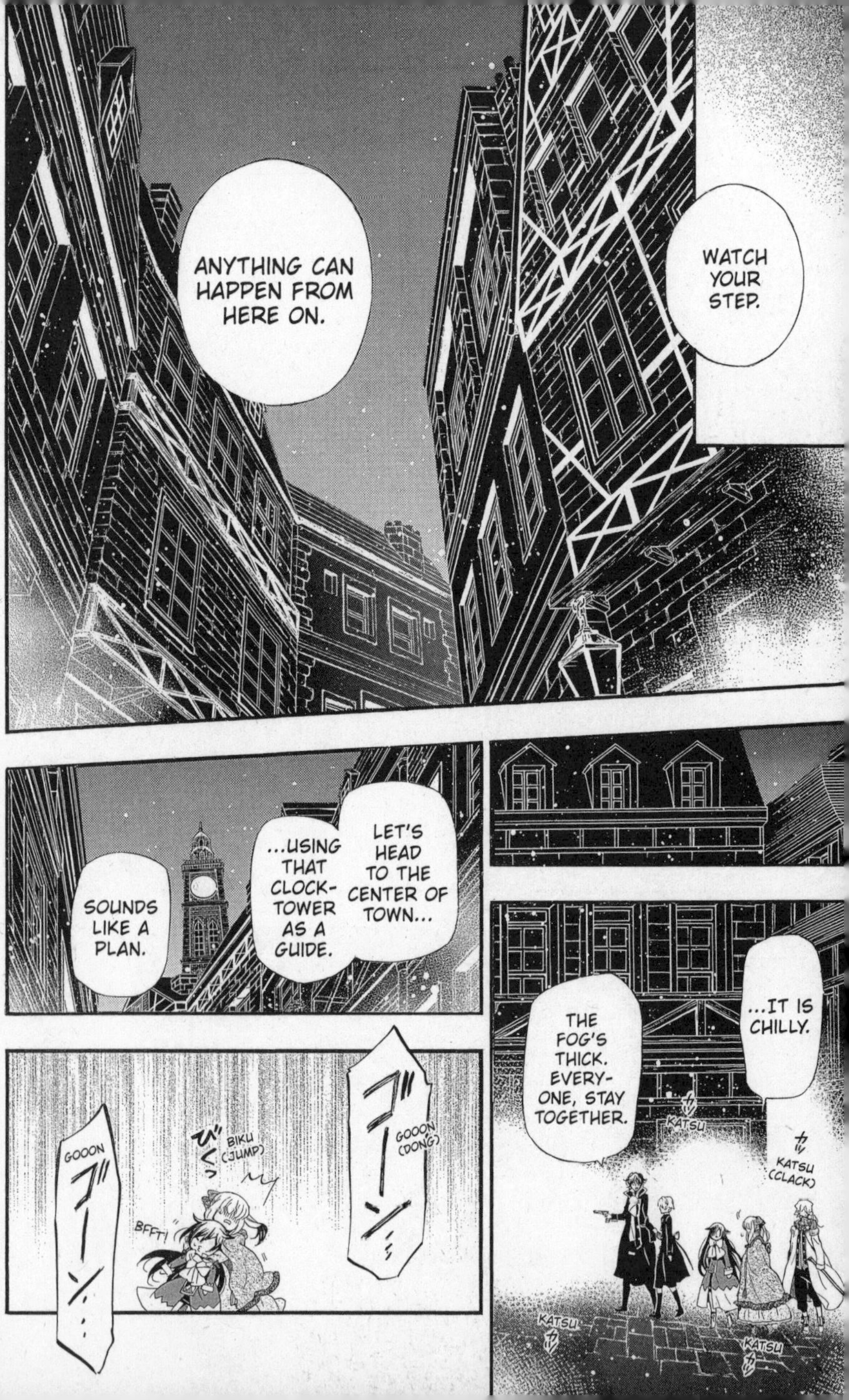

WATCH YOUR STEP.
ANYTHING CAN HAPPEN FROM HERE ON.
...IT IS CHILLY.
THE FOG'S THICK. EVERY-ONE, STAY TOGETHER.
KATSU
KATSU (CLACK)
KATSU
KATSU
LET'S HEAD TO THE CENTER OF TOWN...
...USING THAT CLOCK-TOWER AS A GUIDE.
SOUNDS LIKE A PLAN.
GOOON (DONG)
BIKU (JUMP)
GOOON
BFFT!

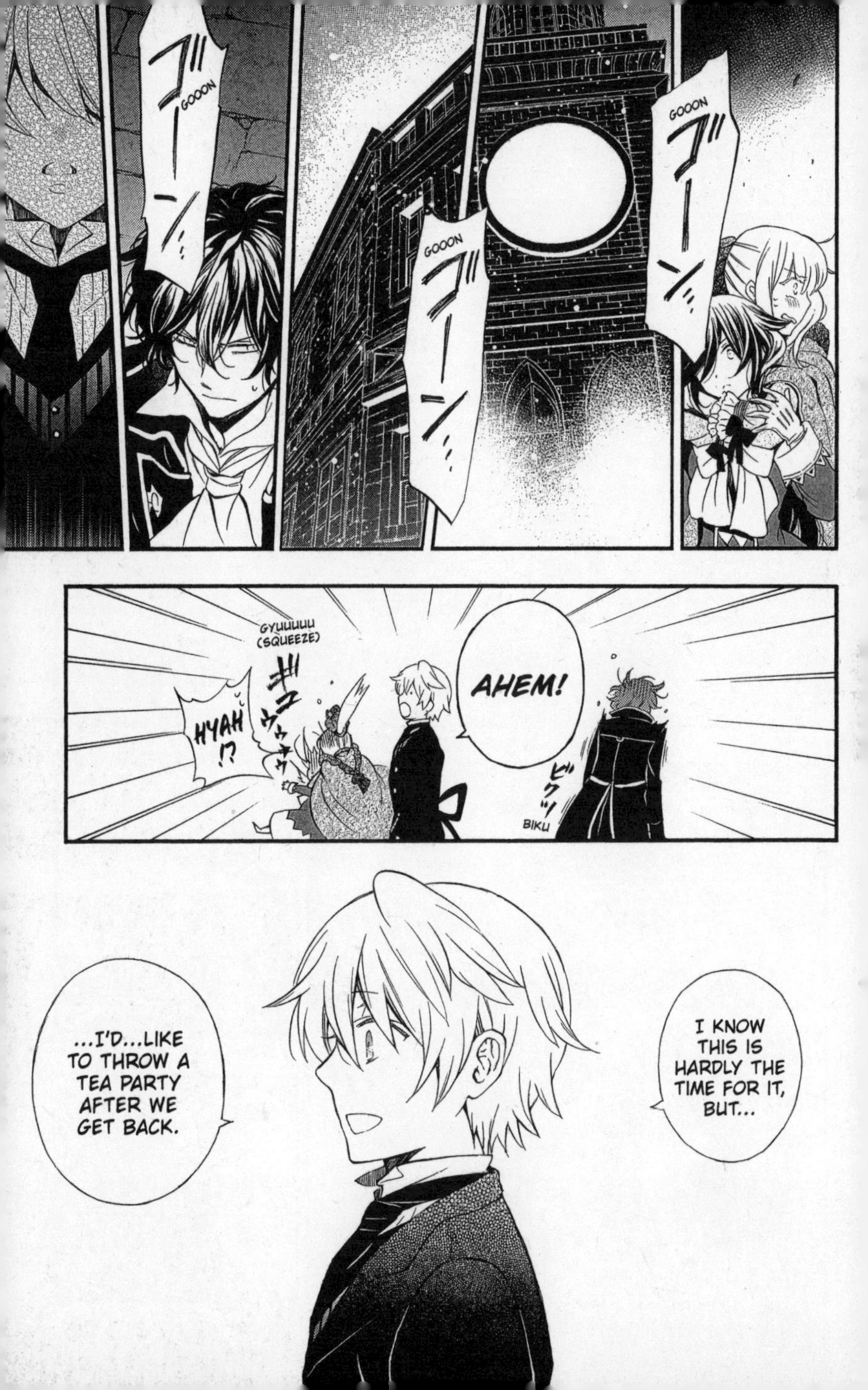
GOOON
GOOON
GOOON
AHEM!
BIKU
GYUUUUU (SQUEEZE)
HYAH!?
I KNOW THIS IS HARDLY THE TIME FOR IT, BUT...
...I'D...LIKE TO THROW A TEA PARTY AFTER WE GET BACK.

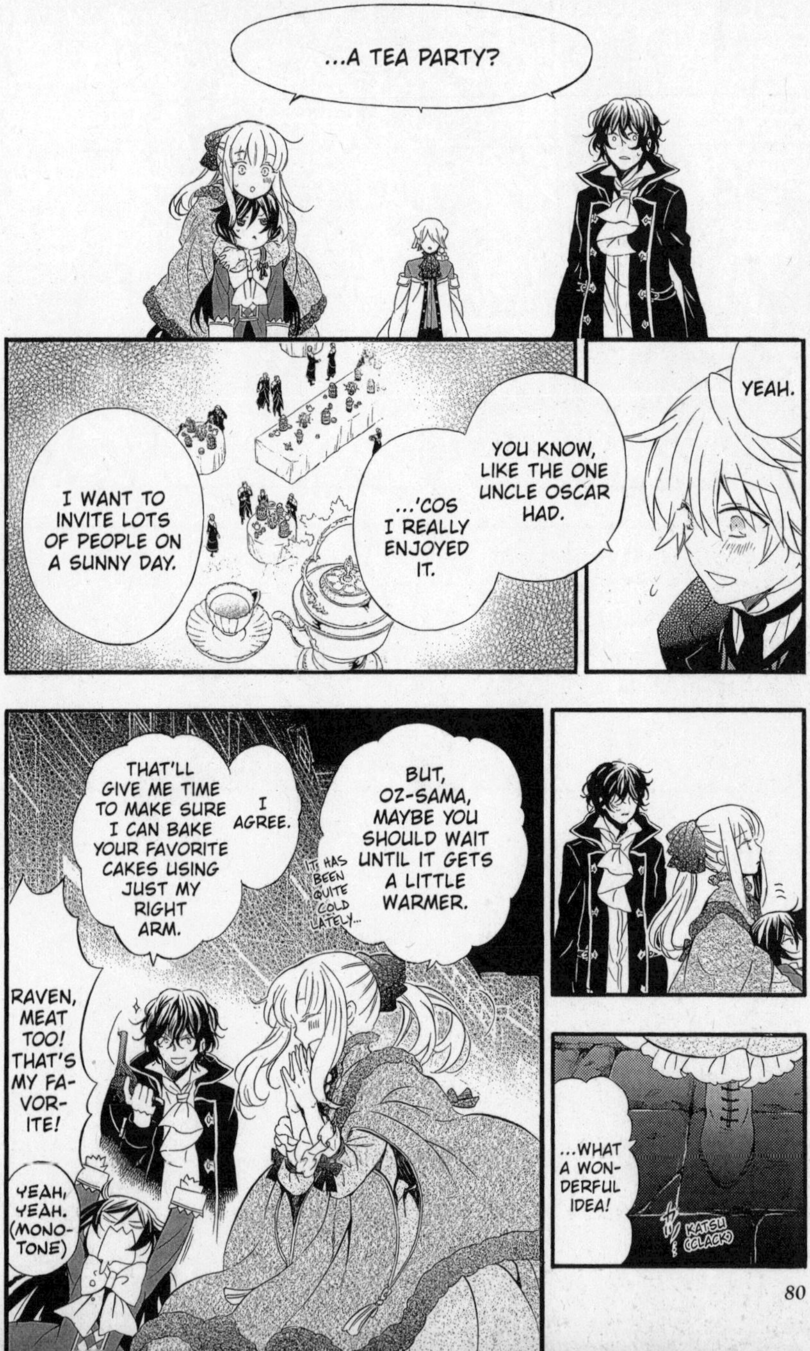
...A TEA PARTY?
YEAH.
YOU KNOW, LIKE THE ONE UNCLE OSCAR HAD.
...'COS I REALLY ENJOYED IT.
I WANT TO INVITE LOTS OF PEOPLE ON A SUNNY DAY.
...WHAT A WONDERFUL IDEA!
KATSU (CLACK)
BUT, OZ-SAMA, MAYBE YOU SHOULD WAIT UNTIL IT GETS A LITTLE WARMER.
IT HAS BEEN QUITE COLD LATELY...
I AGREE.
THAT'LL GIVE ME TIME TO MAKE SURE I CAN BAKE YOUR FAVORITE CAKES USING JUST MY RIGHT ARM.
RAVEN, MEAT TOO! THAT'S MY FAVORITE!
YEAH, YEAH. (MONOTONE)

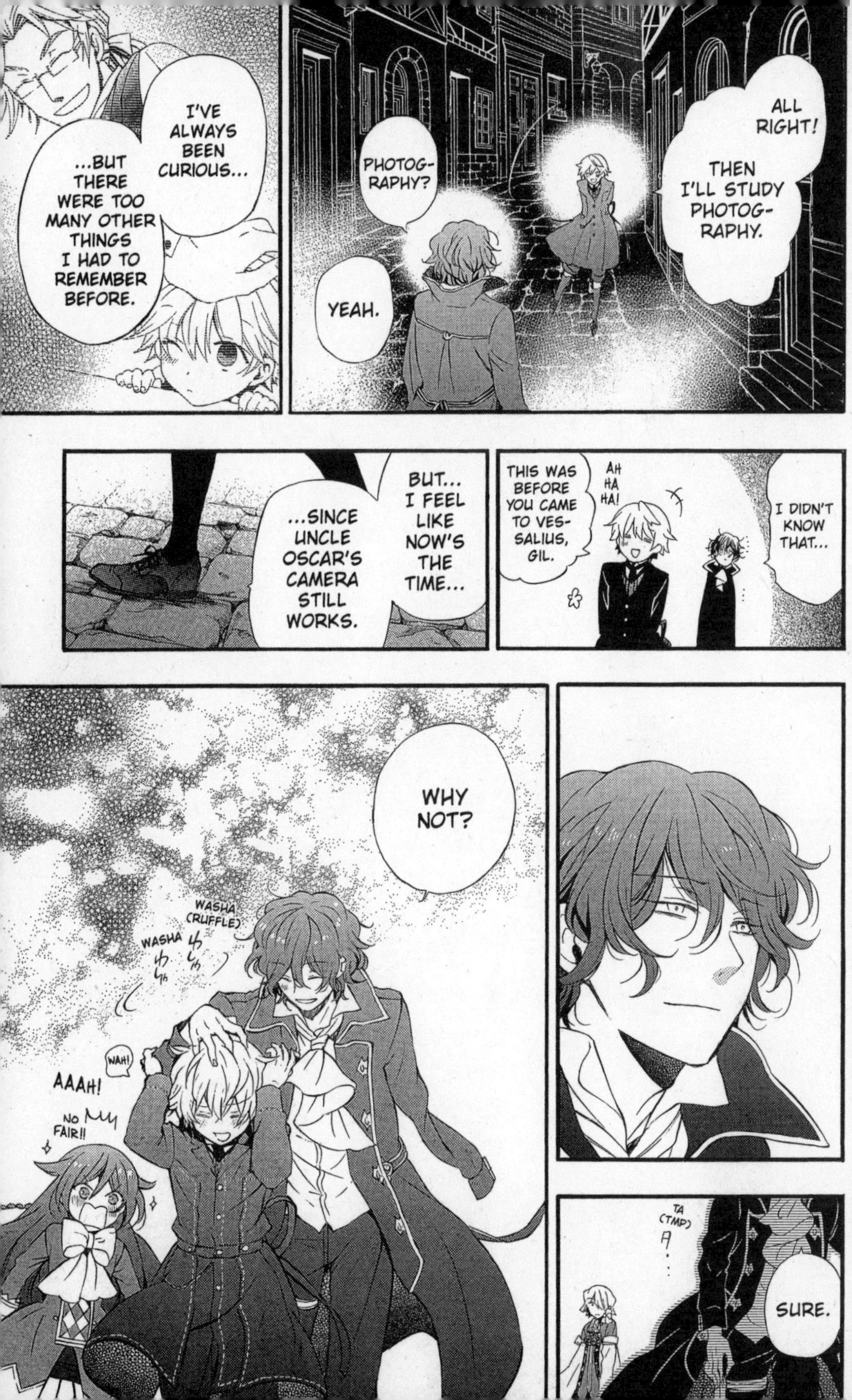
ALL RIGHT!
THEN I'LL STUDY PHOTOG-RAPHY.
PHOTOG-RAPHY?
YEAH.
I'VE ALWAYS BEEN CURIOUS...
...BUT THERE WERE TOO MANY OTHER THINGS I HAD TO REMEMBER BEFORE.
I DIDN'T KNOW THAT...
AH HA HA!
THIS WAS BEFORE YOU CAME TO VES-SALIUS, GIL.
BUT... I FEEL LIKE NOW'S THE TIME...
...SINCE UNCLE OSCAR'S CAMERA STILL WORKS.
TA (TMP)
SURE.
WHY NOT?
WASHA (RUFFLE)
WASHA
WAH!
AAAH!
NO FAIR!!

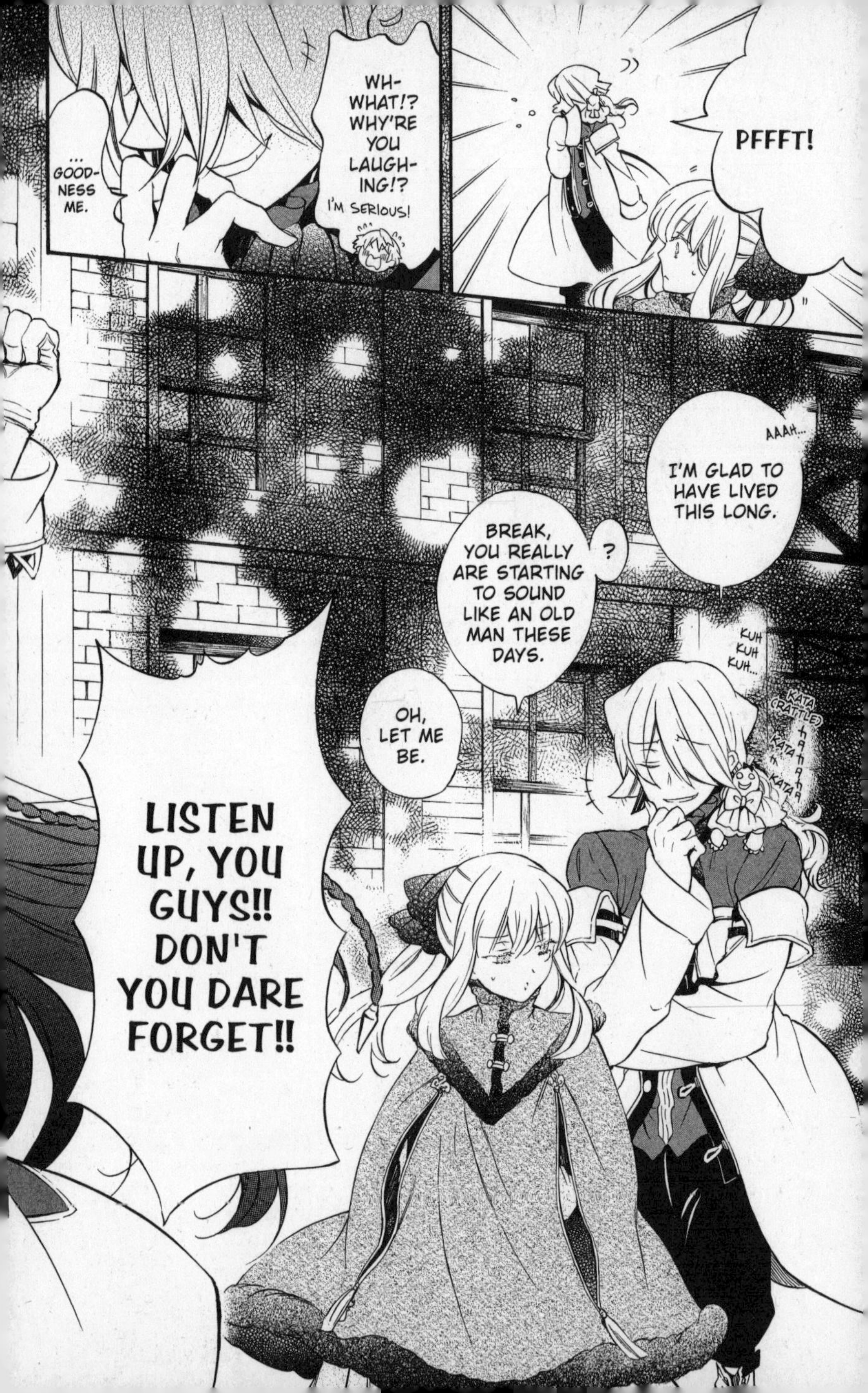
PFFFT!
WH-WHAT!? WHY'RE YOU LAUGHING!?
I'M SERIOUS!
...GOODNESS ME.
AAAH...
I'M GLAD TO HAVE LIVED THIS LONG.
?
BREAK, YOU REALLY ARE STARTING TO SOUND LIKE AN OLD MAN THESE DAYS.
KUH KUH KUH...
KATA (RATTLE)
KATA
KATA
OH, LET ME BE.
LISTEN UP, YOU GUYS!! DON'T YOU DARE FORGET!!

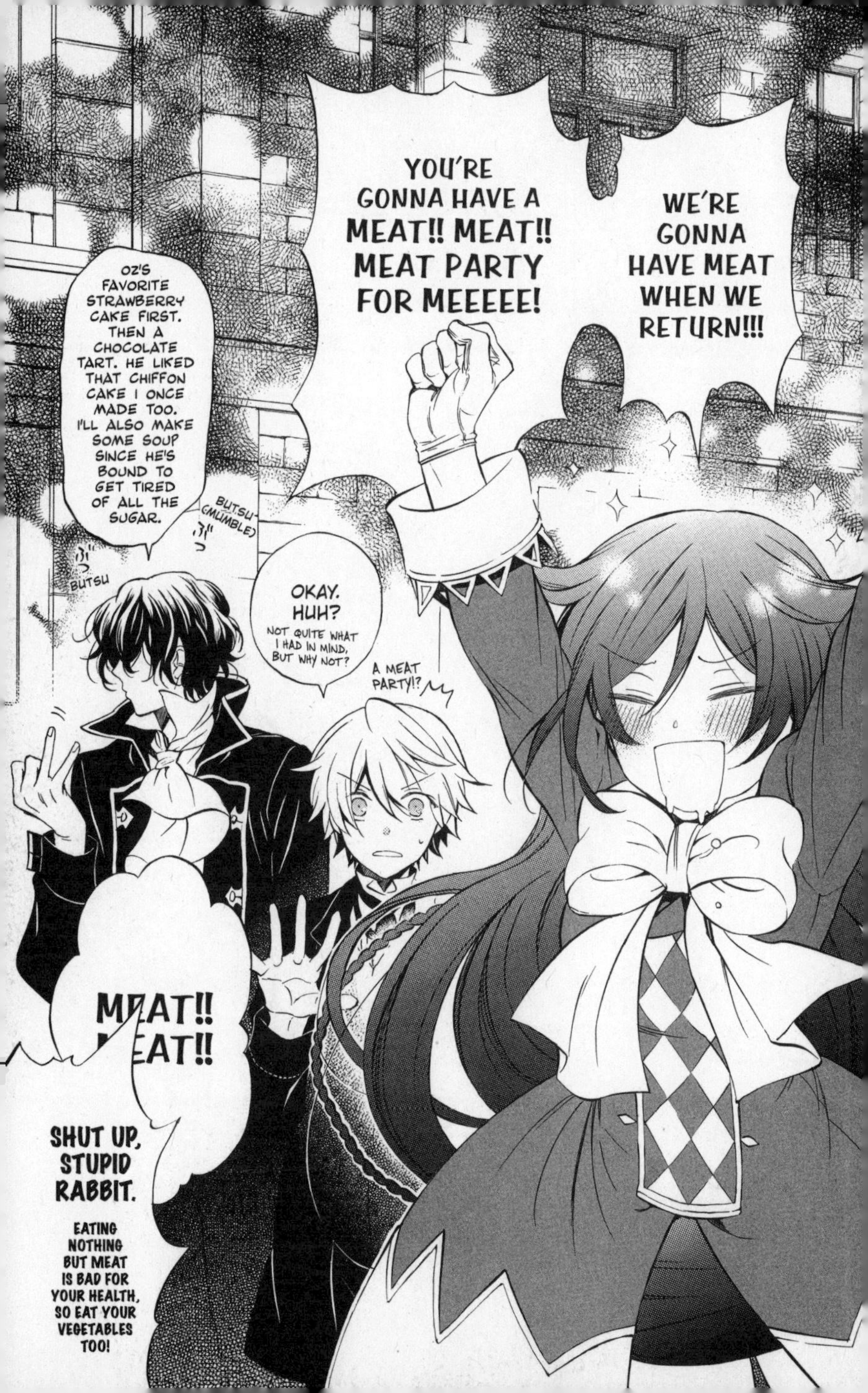
WE'RE GONNA HAVE MEAT WHEN WE RETURN!!!
YOU'RE GONNA HAVE A MEAT!! MEAT!! MEAT PARTY FOR MEEEEE!
OZ'S FAVORITE STRAWBERRY CAKE FIRST. THEN A CHOCOLATE TART. HE LIKED THAT CHIFFON CAKE I ONCE MADE TOO. I'LL ALSO MAKE SOME SOUP SINCE HE'S BOUND TO GET TIRED OF ALL THE SUGAR.
BUTSU (MUMBLE)
BUTSU
OKAY. HUH?
NOT QUITE WHAT I HAD IN MIND, BUT WHY NOT?
A MEAT PARTY!?
MEAT!! MEAT!!
SHUT UP, STUPID RABBIT.
EATING NOTHING BUT MEAT IS BAD FOR YOUR HEALTH, SO EAT YOUR VEGETABLES TOO!

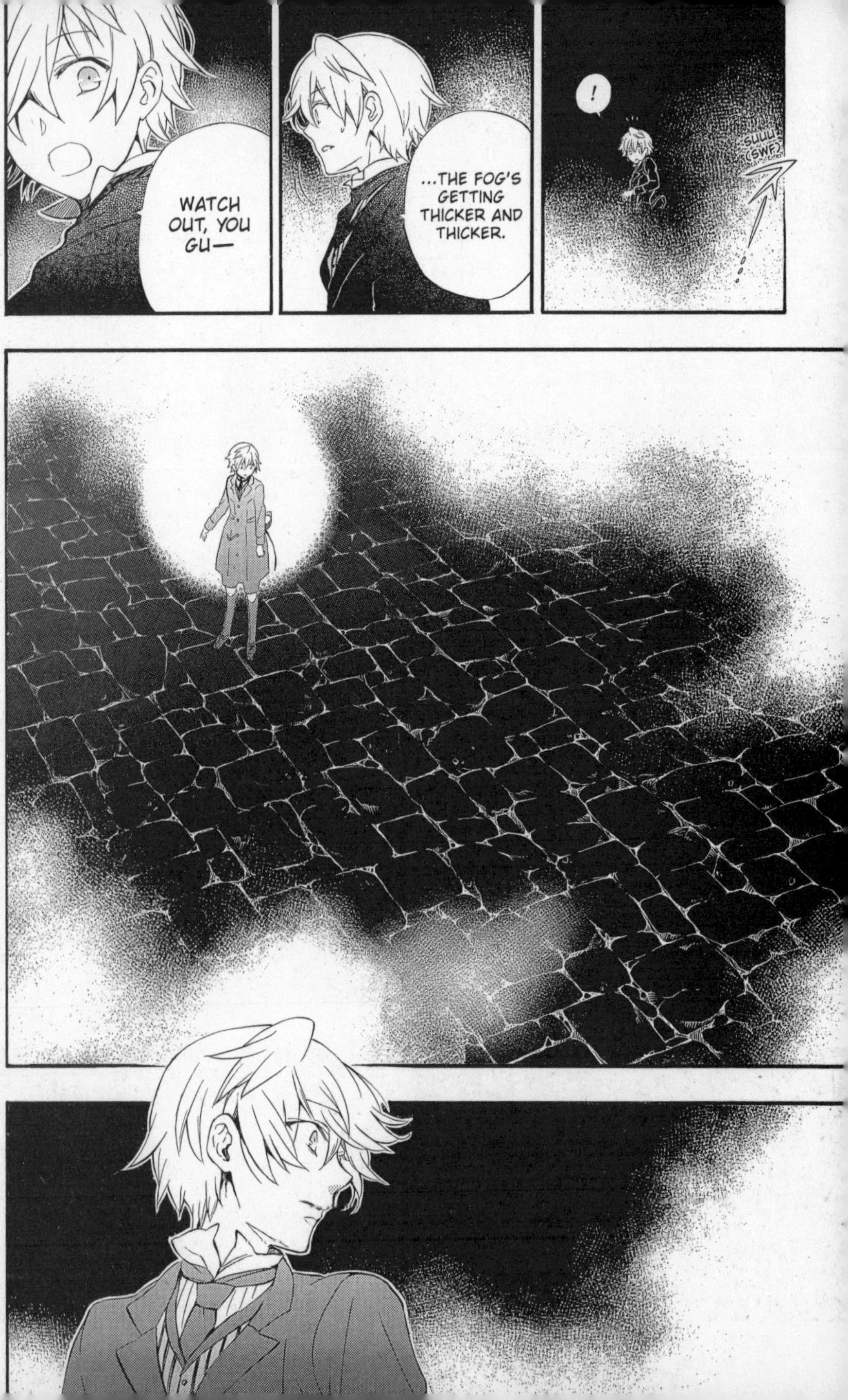
!
SUUU (SWF)
...THE FOG'S GETTING THICKER AND THICKER.
WATCH OUT, YOU GU—

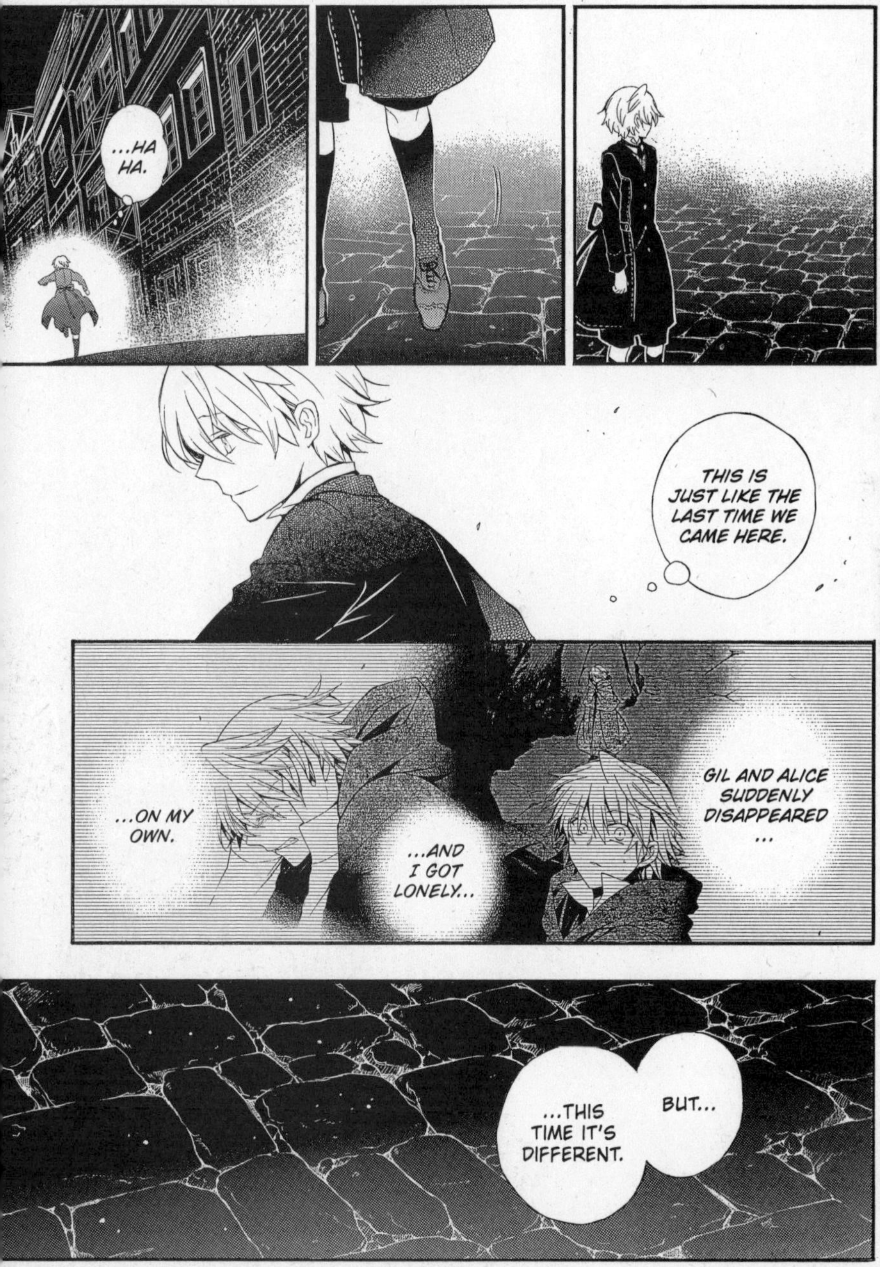
...HA HA.
THIS IS JUST LIKE THE LAST TIME WE CAME HERE.
GIL AND ALICE SUDDENLY DISAPPEARED ...
...AND I GOT LONELY...
...ON MY OWN.
BUT...
...THIS TIME IT'S DIFFERENT.

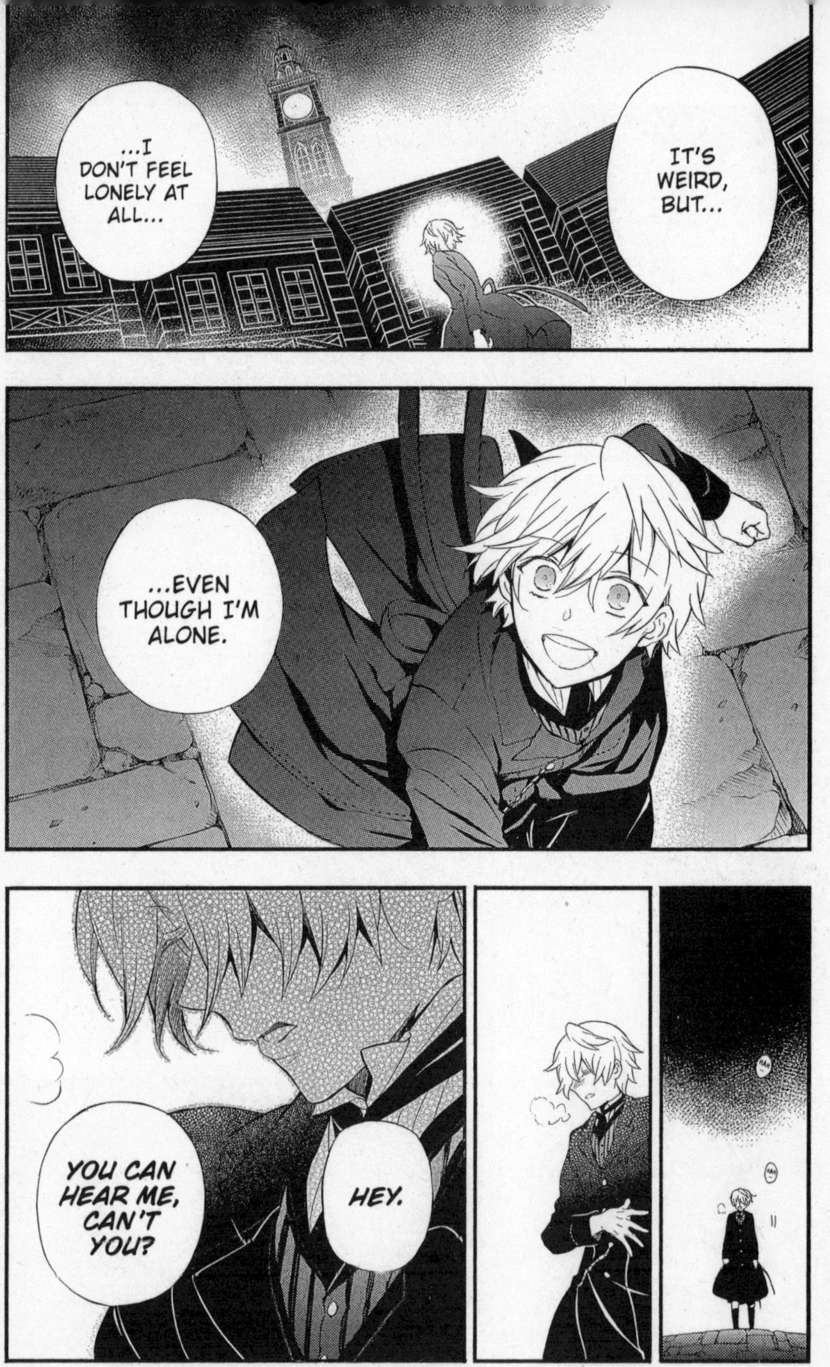
IT'S WEIRD, BUT...
...I DON'T FEEL LONELY AT ALL...
...EVEN THOUGH I'M ALONE.
HEY.
YOU CAN HEAR ME, CAN'T YOU?

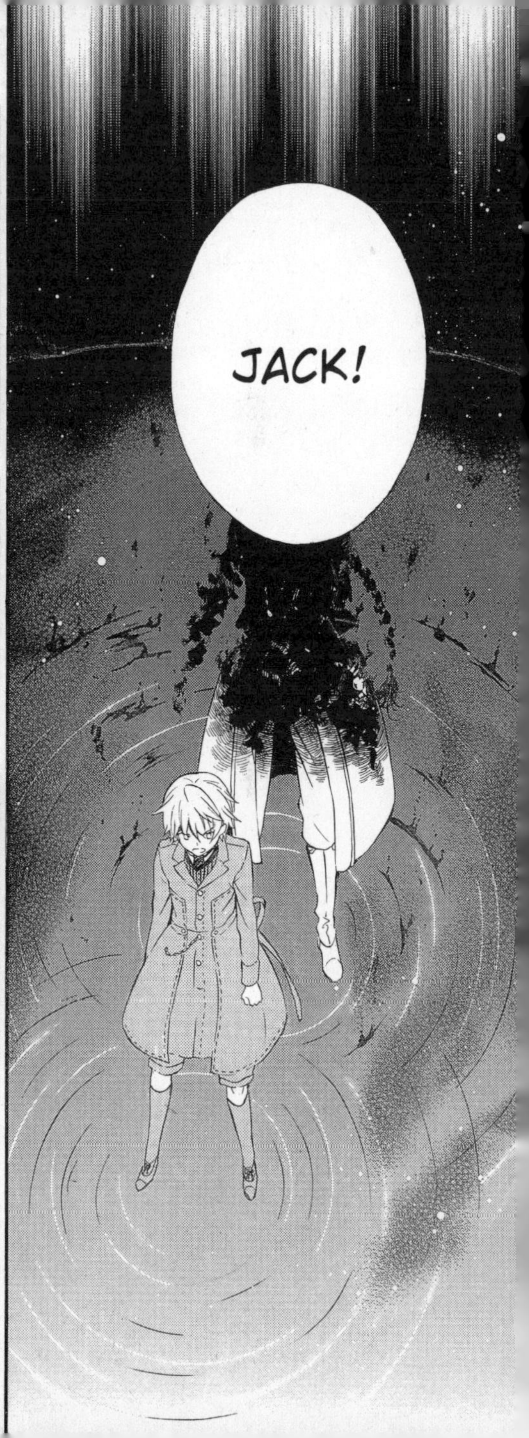
JACK!

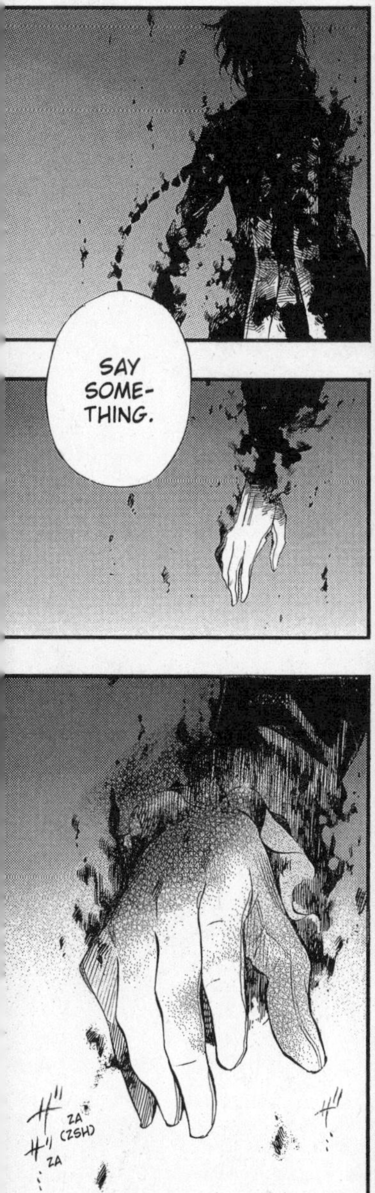
SAY SOME-THING.
ZA (ZSH) ZA

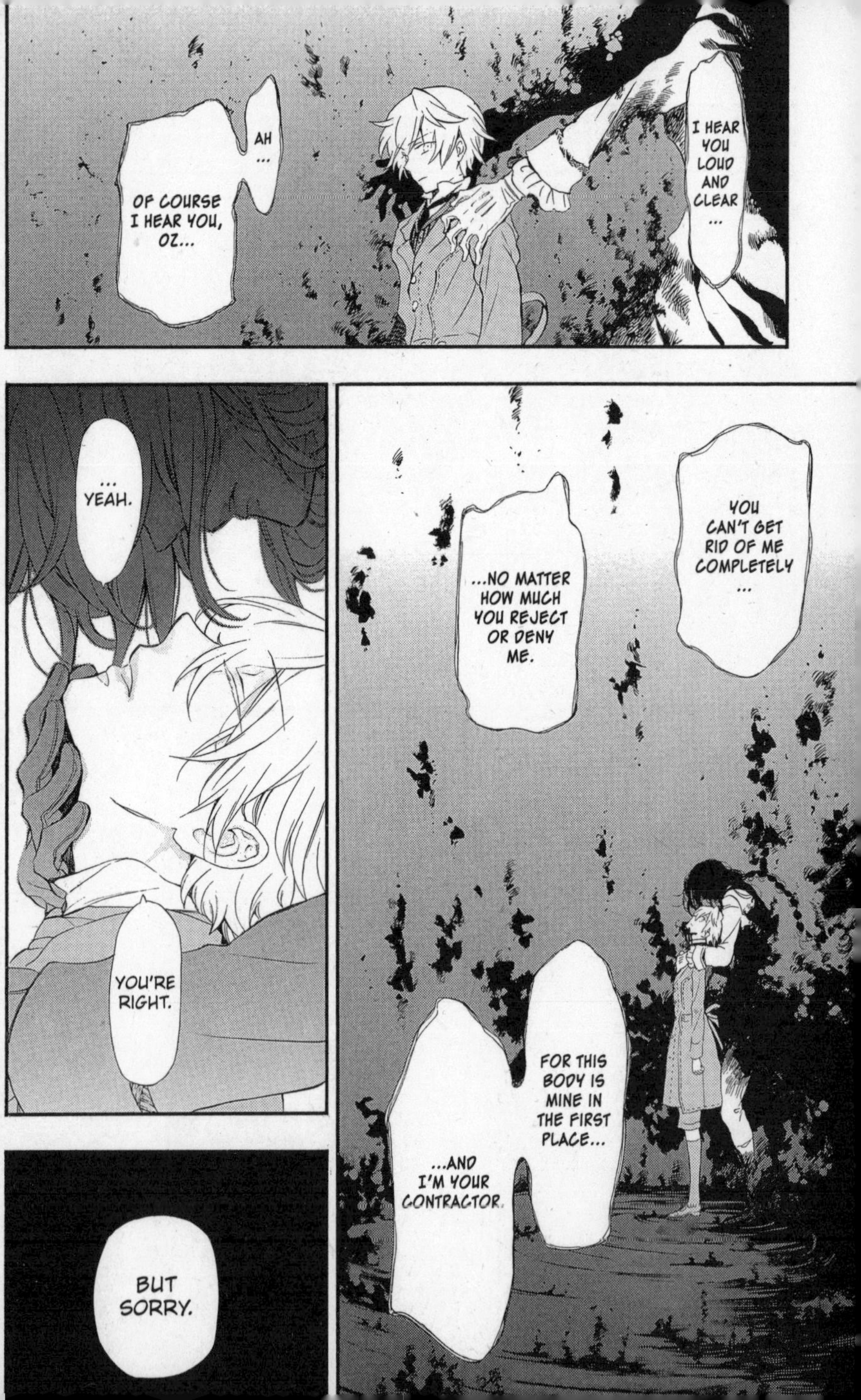
I HEAR YOU LOUD AND CLEAR...
AH...
OF COURSE I HEAR YOU, OZ...
YOU CAN'T GET RID OF ME COMPLETELY...
...NO MATTER HOW MUCH YOU REJECT OR DENY ME.
FOR THIS BODY IS MINE IN THE FIRST PLACE...
...AND I'M YOUR CONTRACTOR.
...YEAH.
YOU'RE RIGHT.
BUT SORRY.

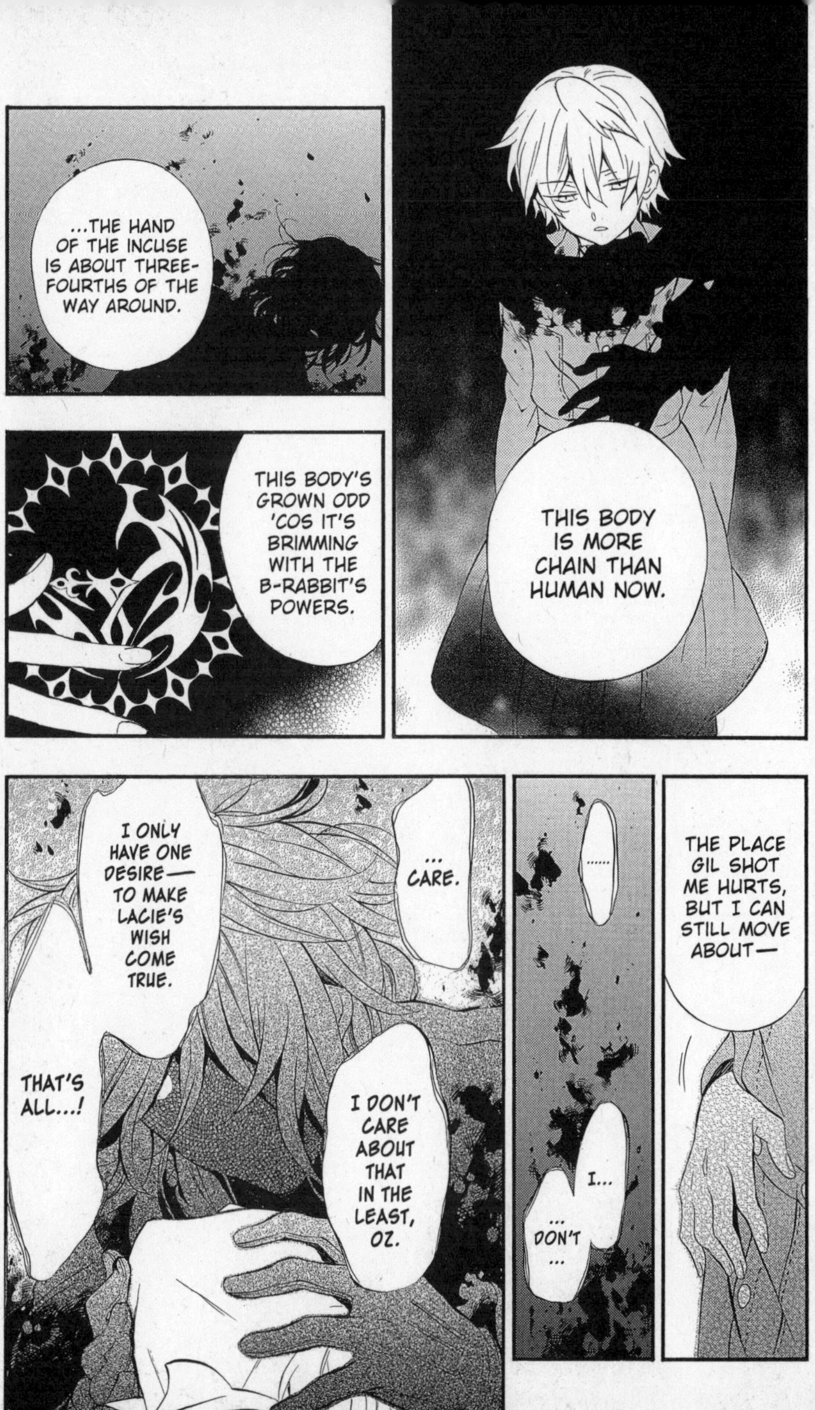
THIS BODY IS MORE CHAIN THAN HUMAN NOW.
...THE HAND OF THE INCUSE IS ABOUT THREE-FOURTHS OF THE WAY AROUND.
THIS BODY'S GROWN ODD 'COS IT'S BRIMMING WITH THE B-RABBIT'S POWERS.
THE PLACE GIL SHOT ME HURTS, BUT I CAN STILL MOVE ABOUT—
......
I...
...DON'T...
...CARE.
I ONLY HAVE ONE DESIRE—TO MAKE LACIE'S WISH COME TRUE.
I DON'T CARE ABOUT THAT IN THE LEAST, OZ.
THAT'S ALL...!

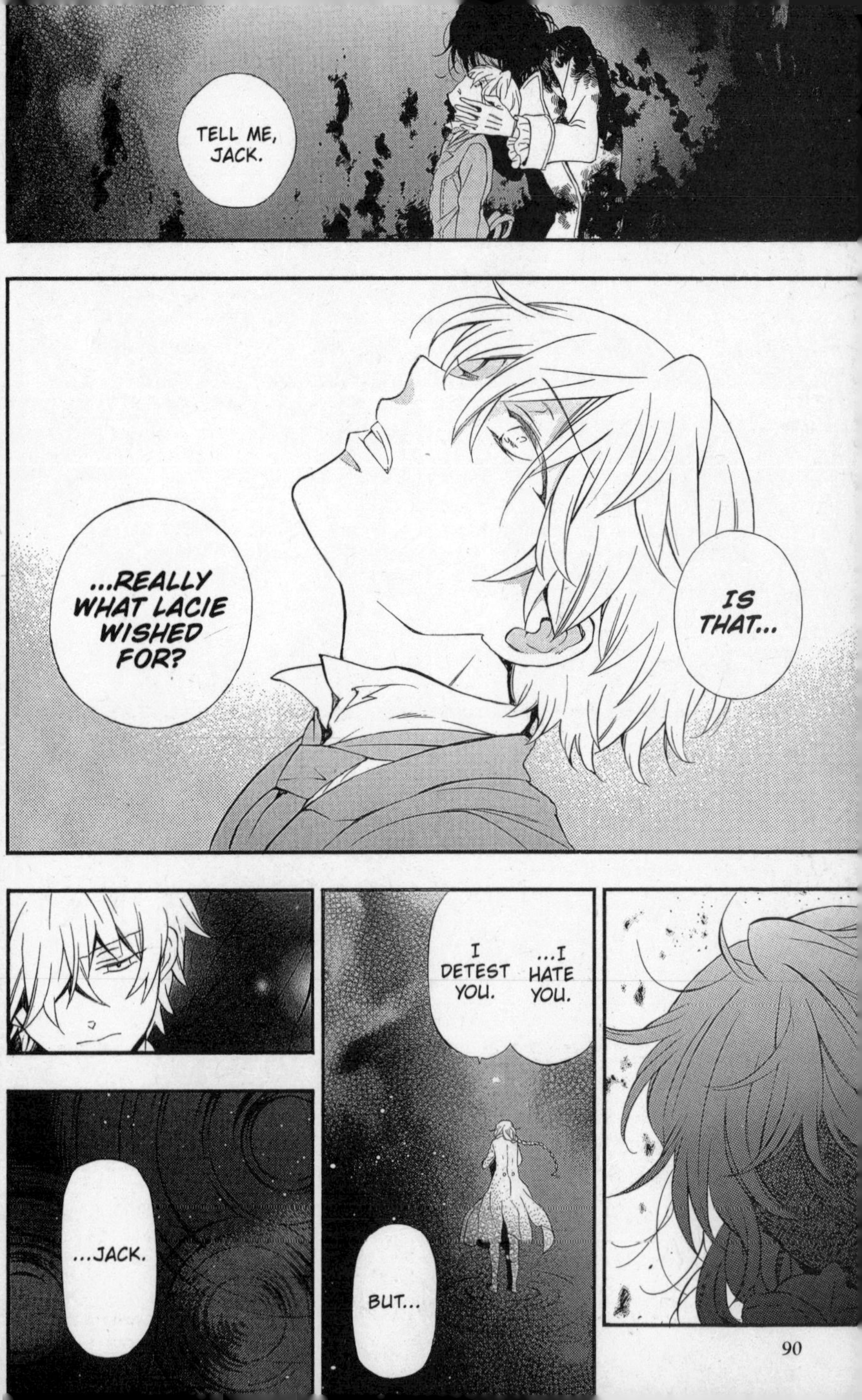
TELL ME, JACK.
IS THAT...
...REALLY WHAT LACIE WISHED FOR?
...I HATE YOU.
I DETEST YOU.
BUT...
...JACK.

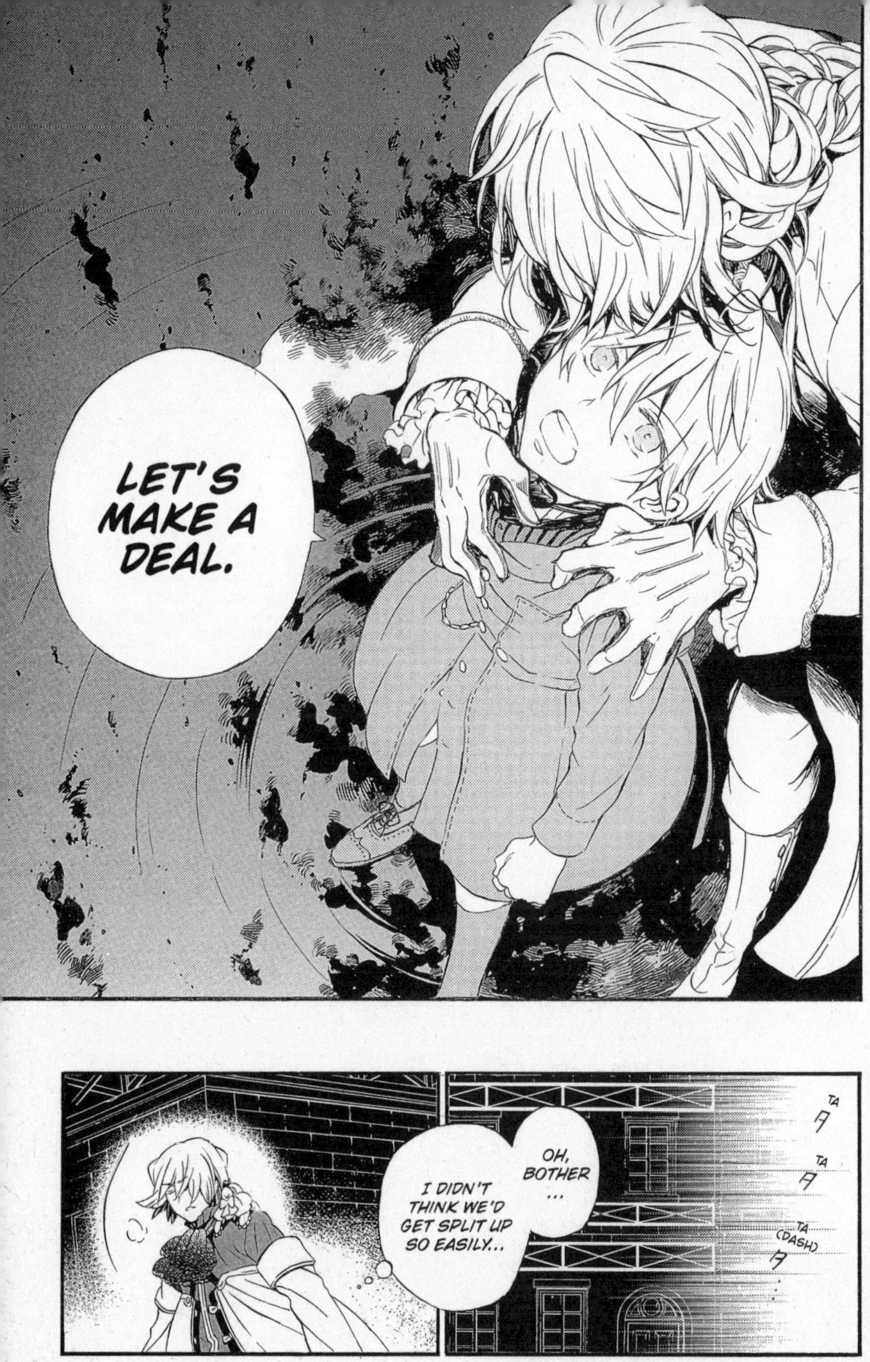
LET'S MAKE A DEAL.
TA TA TA (DASH)
OH, BOTHER...
I DIDN'T THINK WE'D GET SPLIT UP SO EASILY...

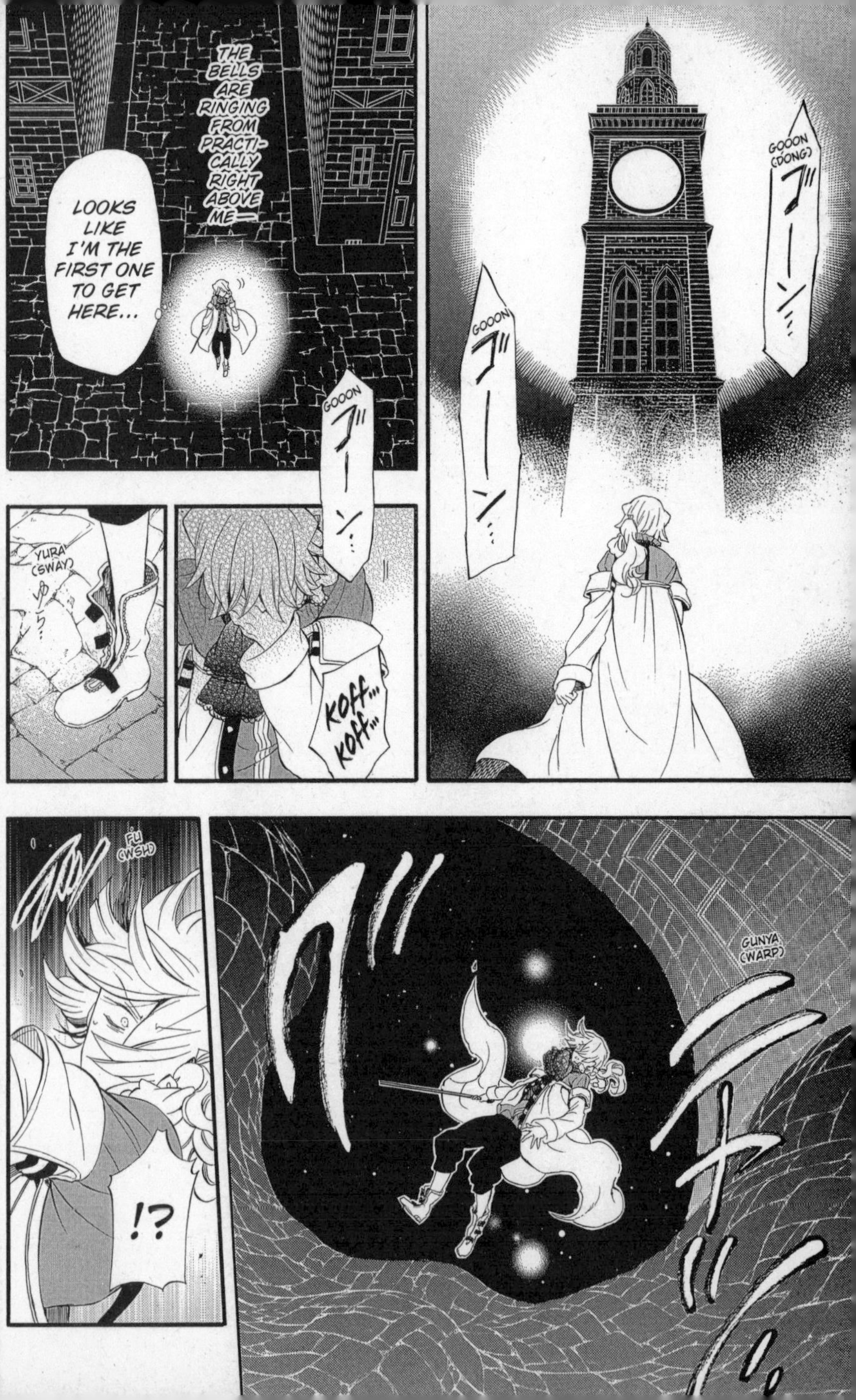

GOOON (DONG)
ゴーン…
GOOON
ゴーン…
THE BELLS ARE RINGING FROM PRACTICALLY RIGHT ABOVE ME—
LOOKS LIKE I'M THE FIRST ONE TO GET HERE...
GOOON
ゴーン…
KOFF... KOFF...
YURA (SWAY)
ゆら…
GUNYA (WARP)
FU (WSH)
!?

DO (THUD)
KUH ...!
DO
DO
DO
GURA (WHORL)
GURA
GURA
I CAN'T HEAR THE BELLS ANYMORE...
I'VE...
...BEEN HURLED OFF TO YET ANOTHER LOCATION.
KATSU (CLACK)
KATSU
HAH...

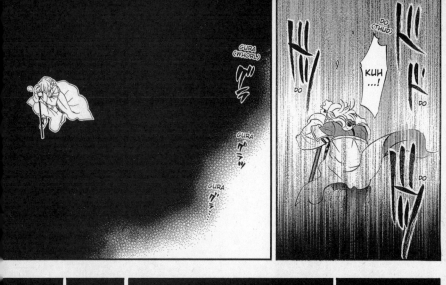

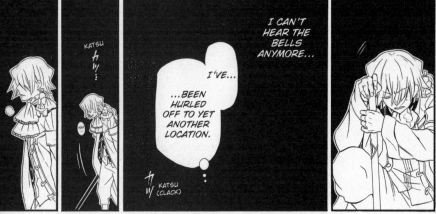

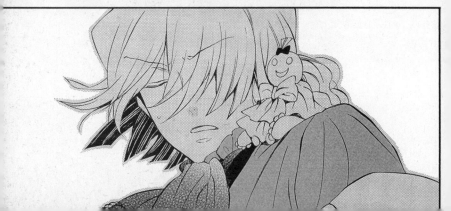

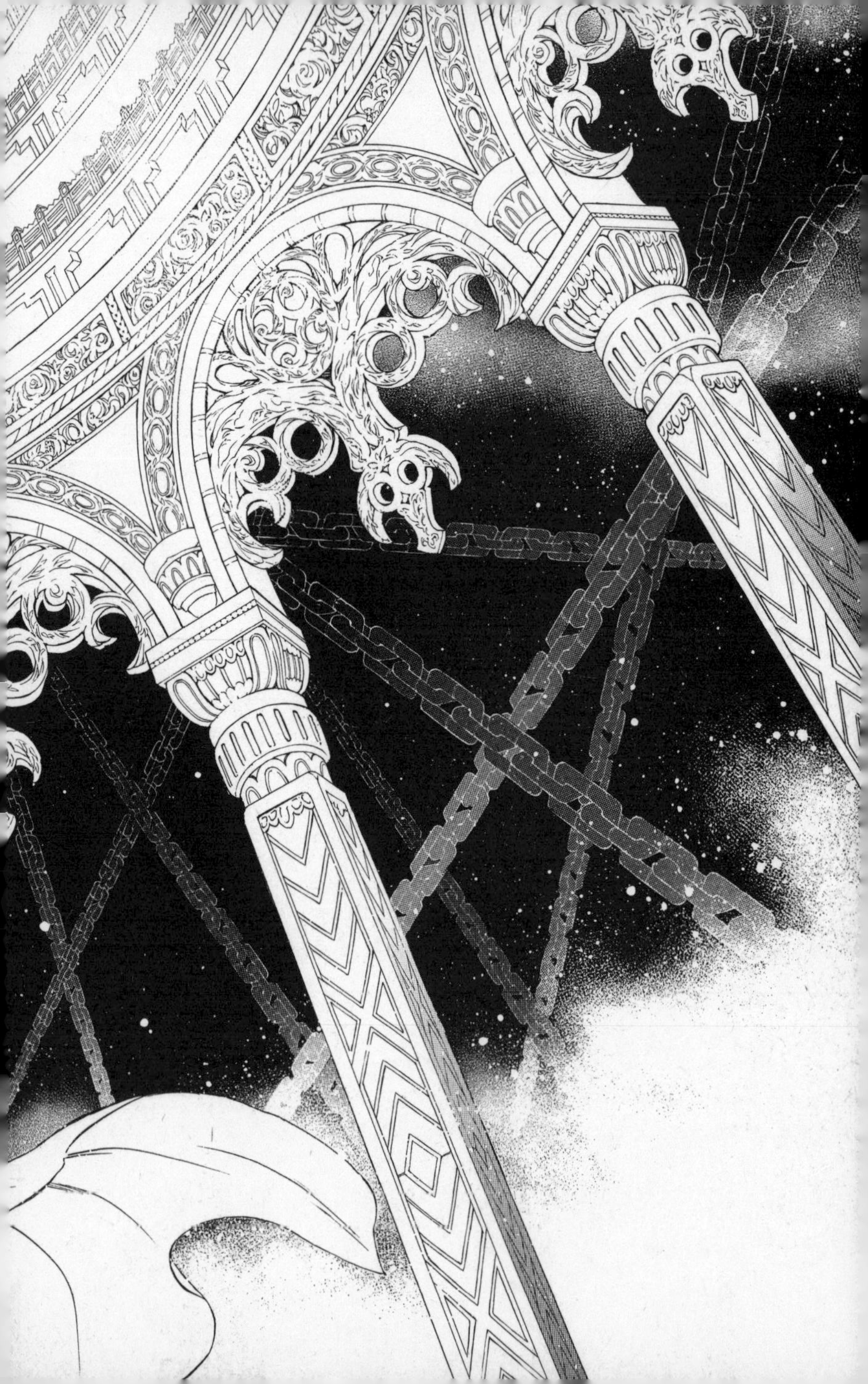

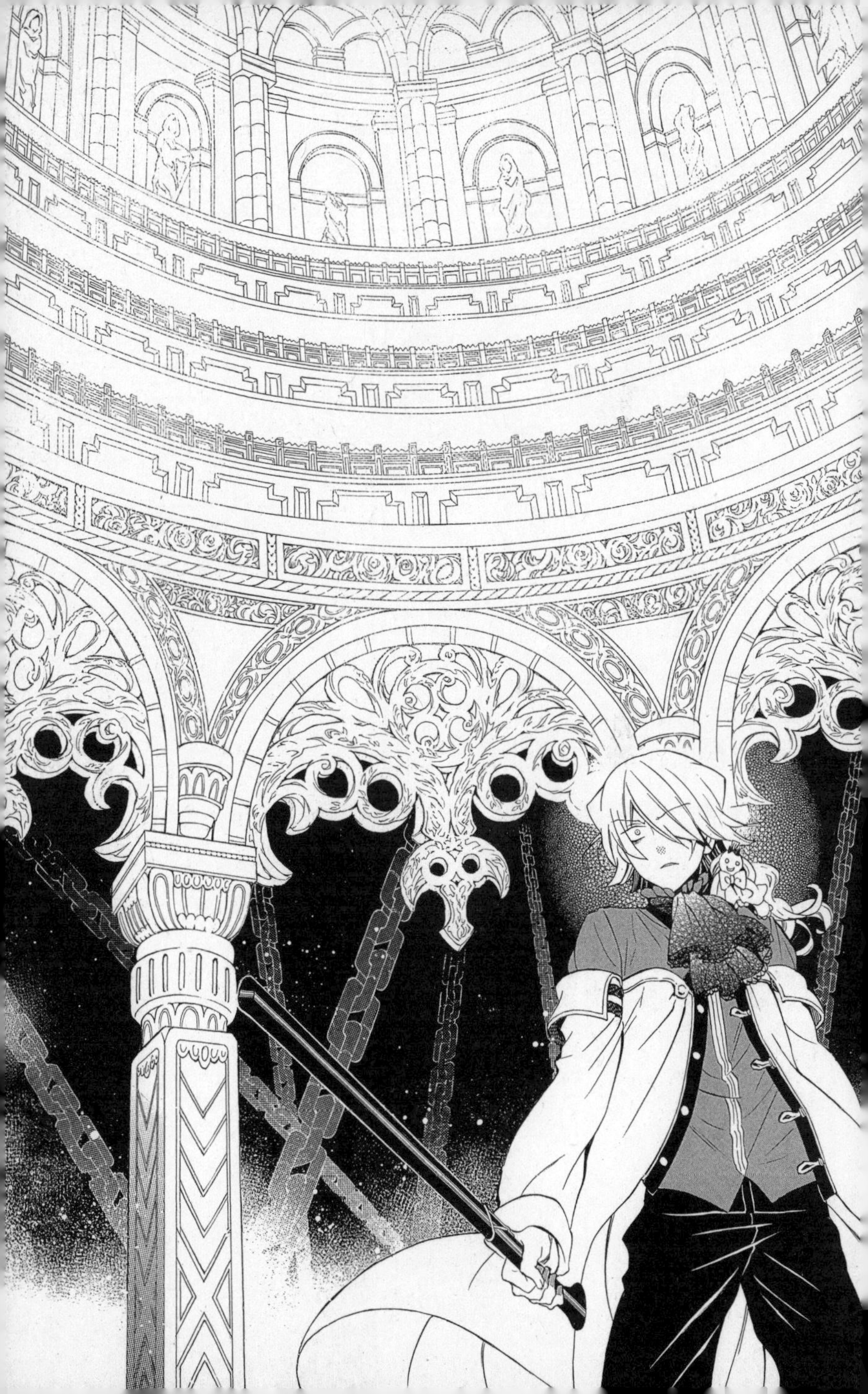

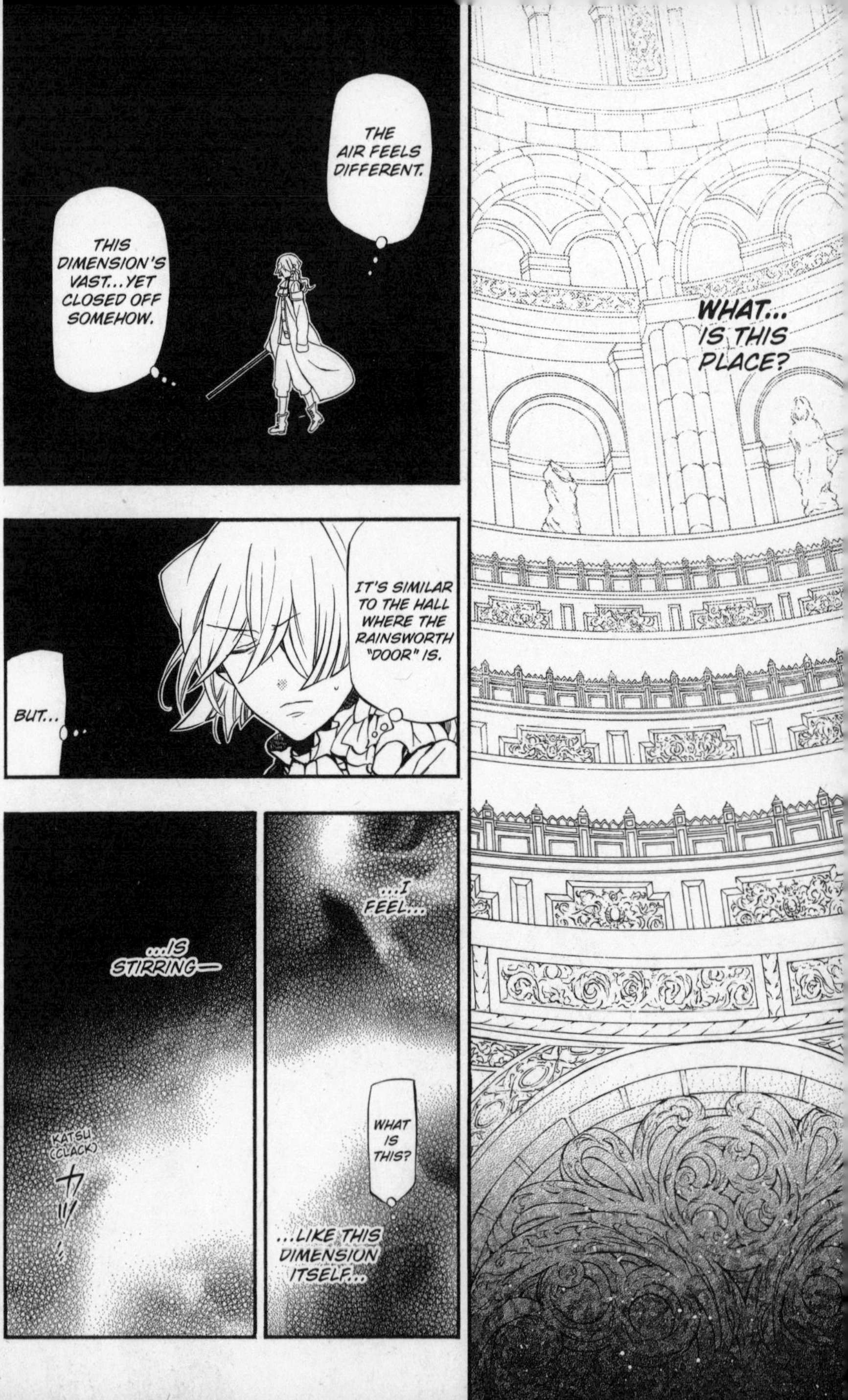
WHAT... IS THIS PLACE?
THE AIR FEELS DIFFERENT.
THIS DIMENSION'S VAST...YET CLOSED OFF SOMEHOW.
IT'S SIMILAR TO THE HALL WHERE THE RAINSWORTH "DOOR" IS.
BUT...
...I FEEL...
WHAT IS THIS?
...LIKE THIS DIMENSION ITSELF...
...IS STIRRING—
KATSU (CLACK)

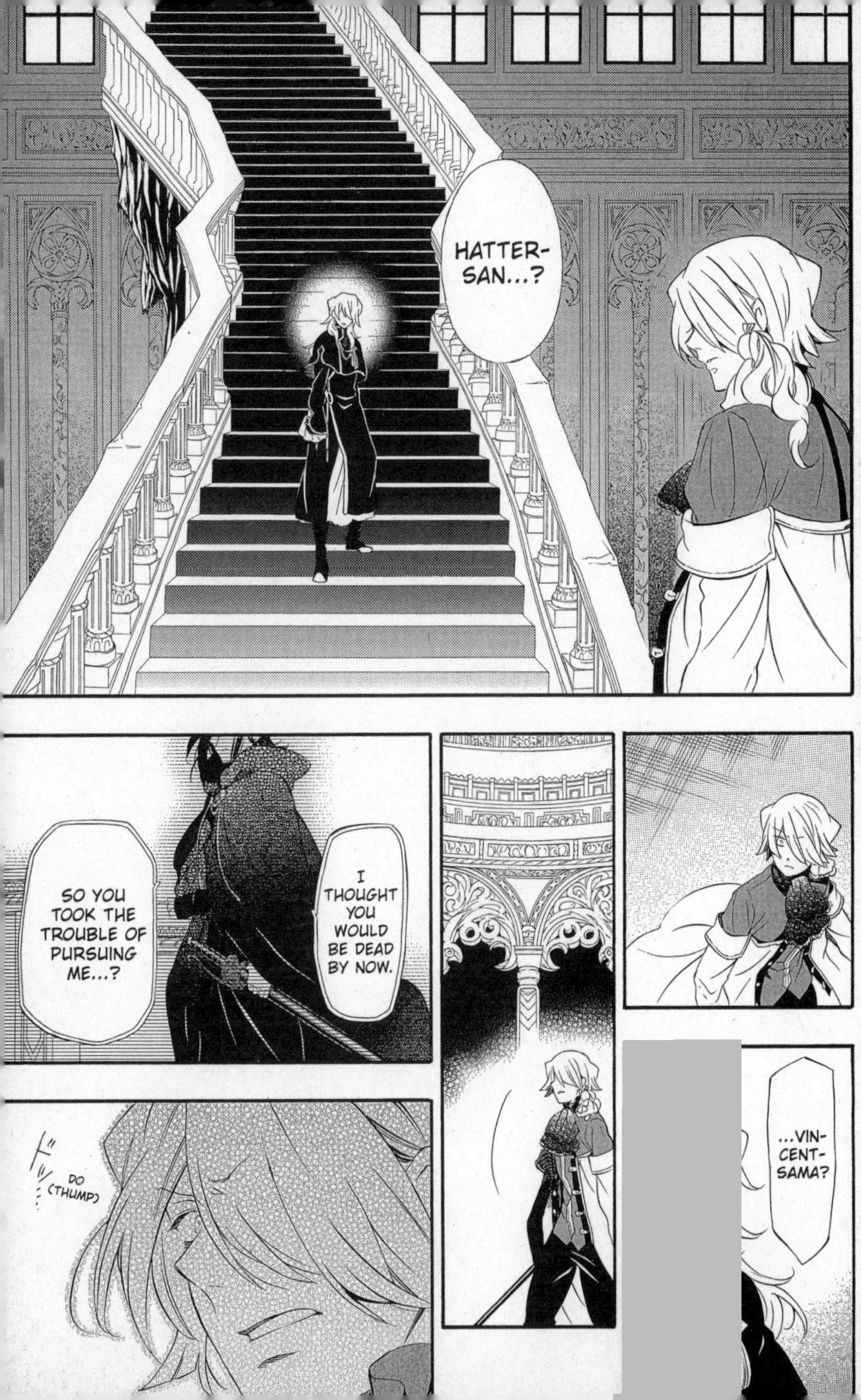
HATTER-SAN...?
...VIN-CENT-SAMA?
I THOUGHT YOU WOULD BE DEAD BY NOW.
SO YOU TOOK THE TROUBLE OF PURSUING ME...?
DO (THUMP)

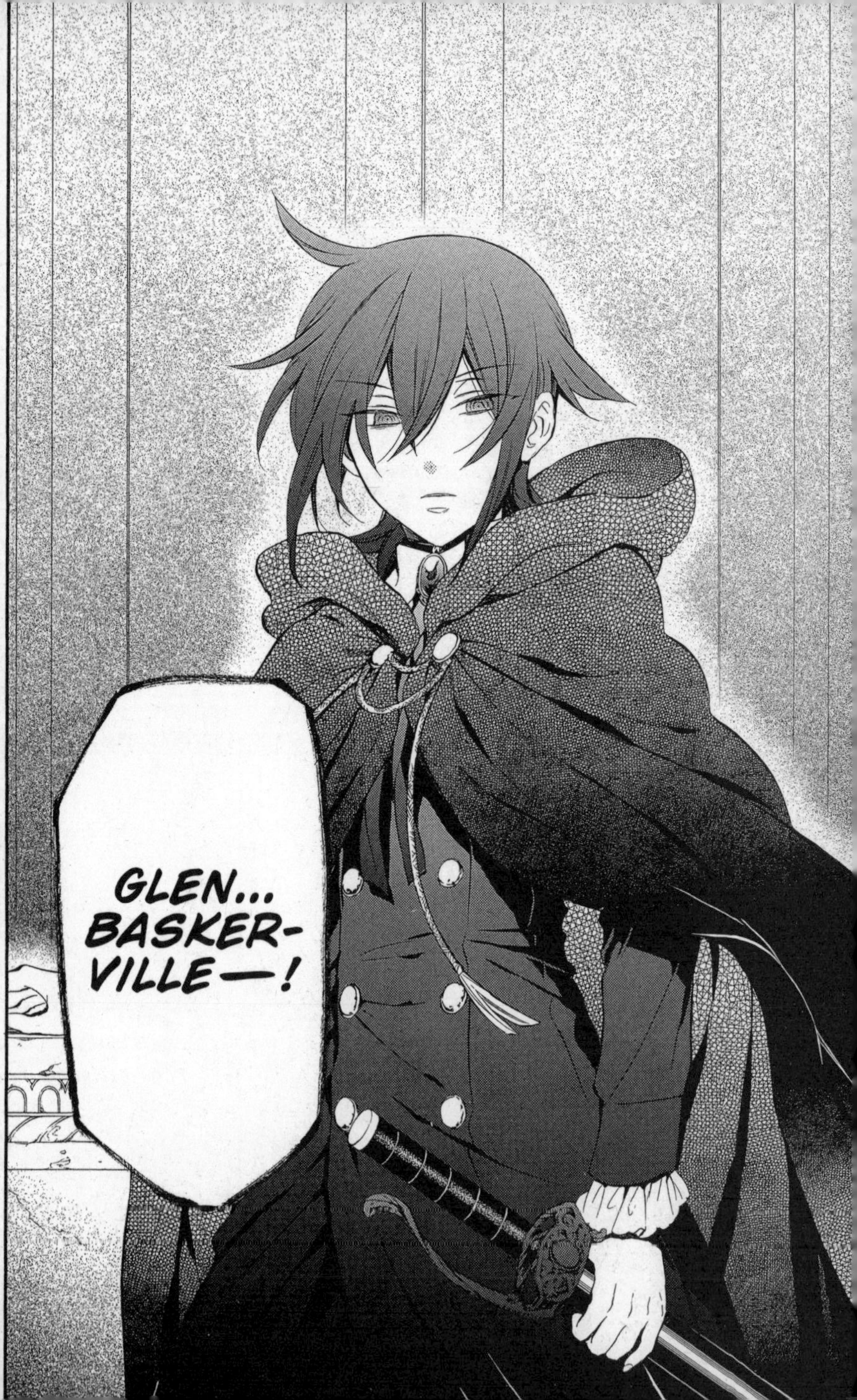
GLEN... BASKER-VILLE—!

Retrace:XC Clocktower

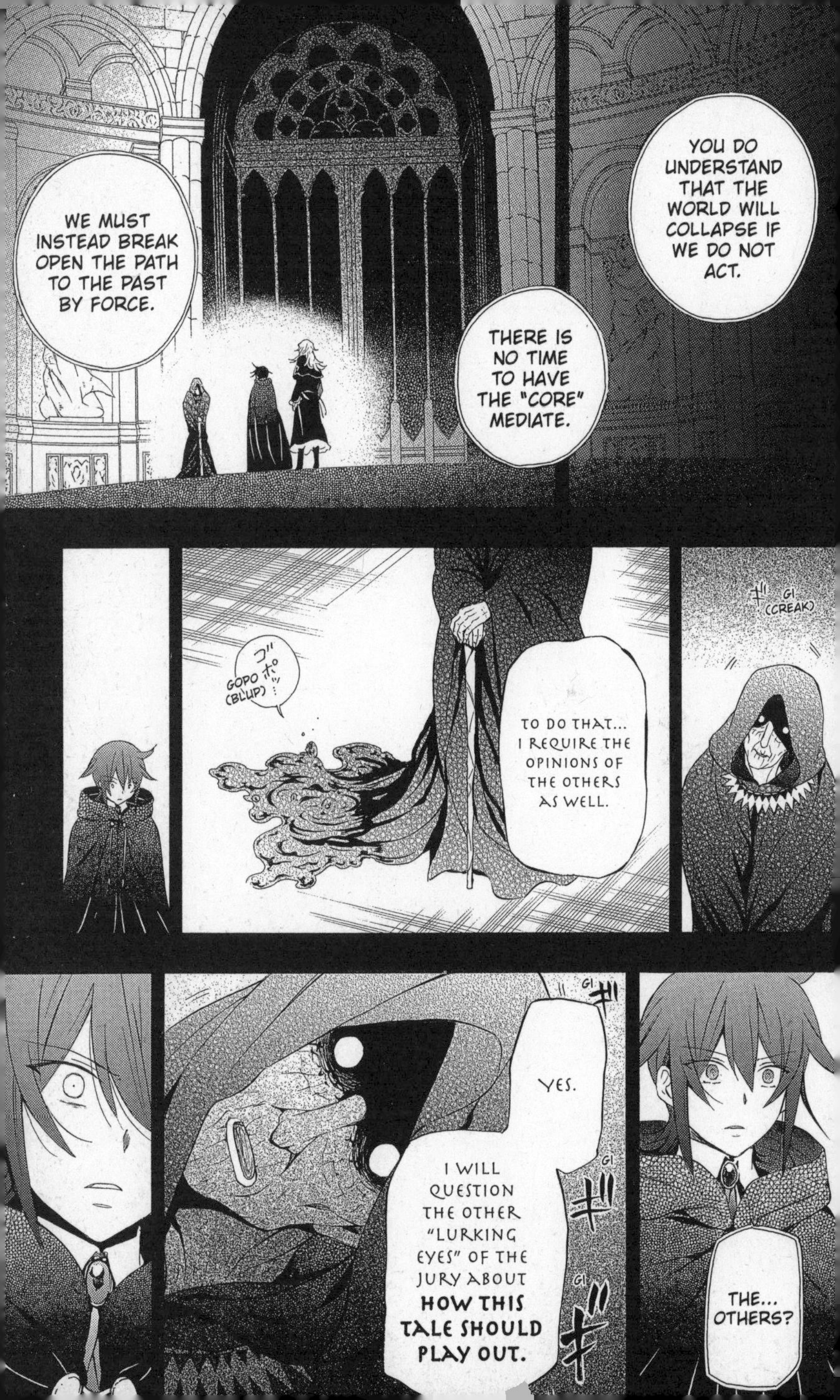

YOU DO UNDERSTAND THAT THE WORLD WILL COLLAPSE IF WE DO NOT ACT.
THERE IS NO TIME TO HAVE THE "CORE" MEDIATE.
WE MUST INSTEAD BREAK OPEN THE PATH TO THE PAST BY FORCE.
ギ
GI (CREAK)
TO DO THAT... I REQUIRE THE OPINIONS OF THE OTHERS AS WELL.
ゴポッ…
GOPO (BLUP)
THE... OTHERS?
ギ
GI
YES.
I WILL QUESTION THE OTHER "LURKING EYES" OF THE JURY ABOUT **HOW THIS TALE SHOULD PLAY OUT.**
ギ
GI
ギ
GI

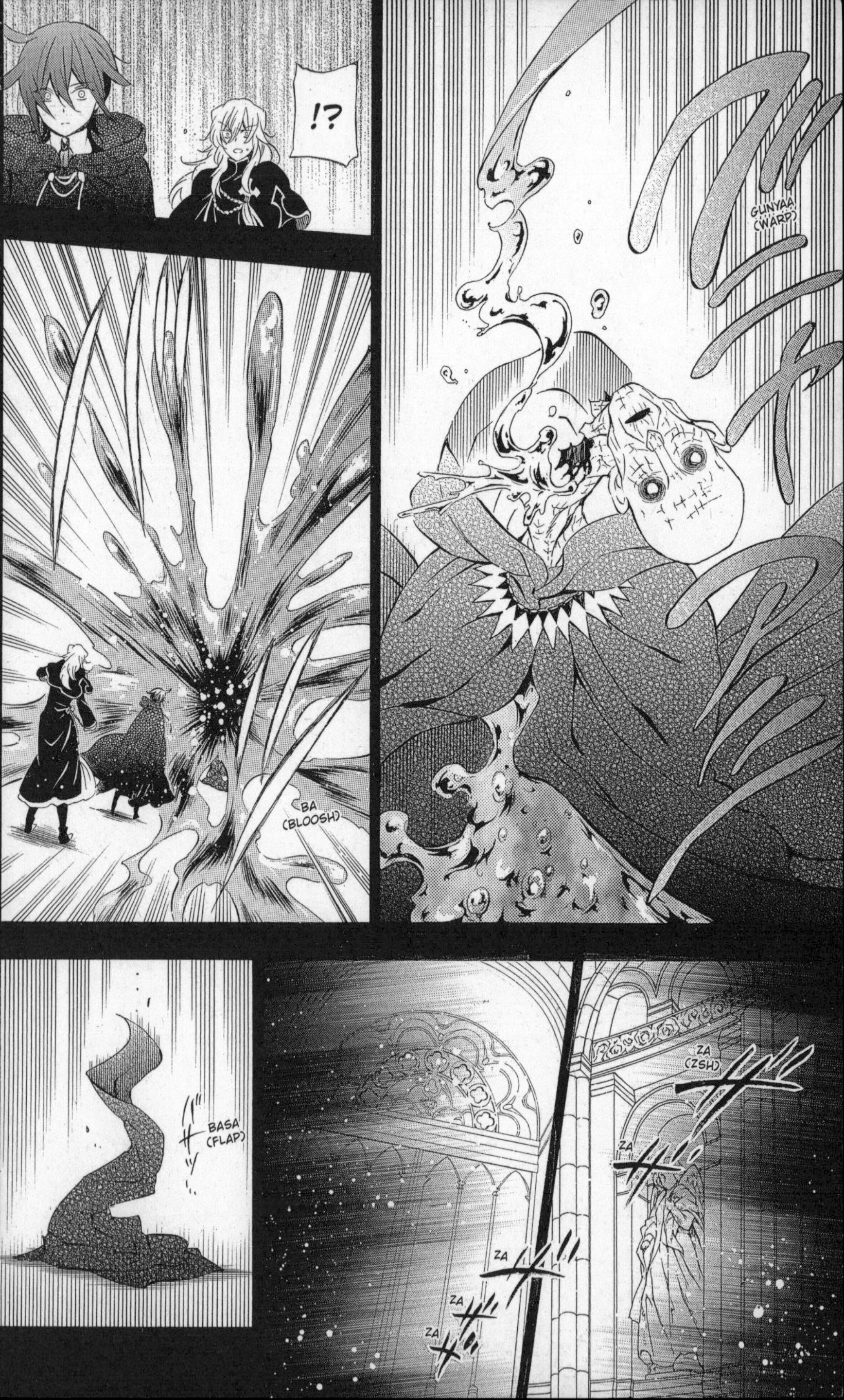
GUNYAA (WARP)
!?
BA (BLOOSH)
ZA (ZSH)
ZA
ZA
ZA
ZA
BASA (FLAP)

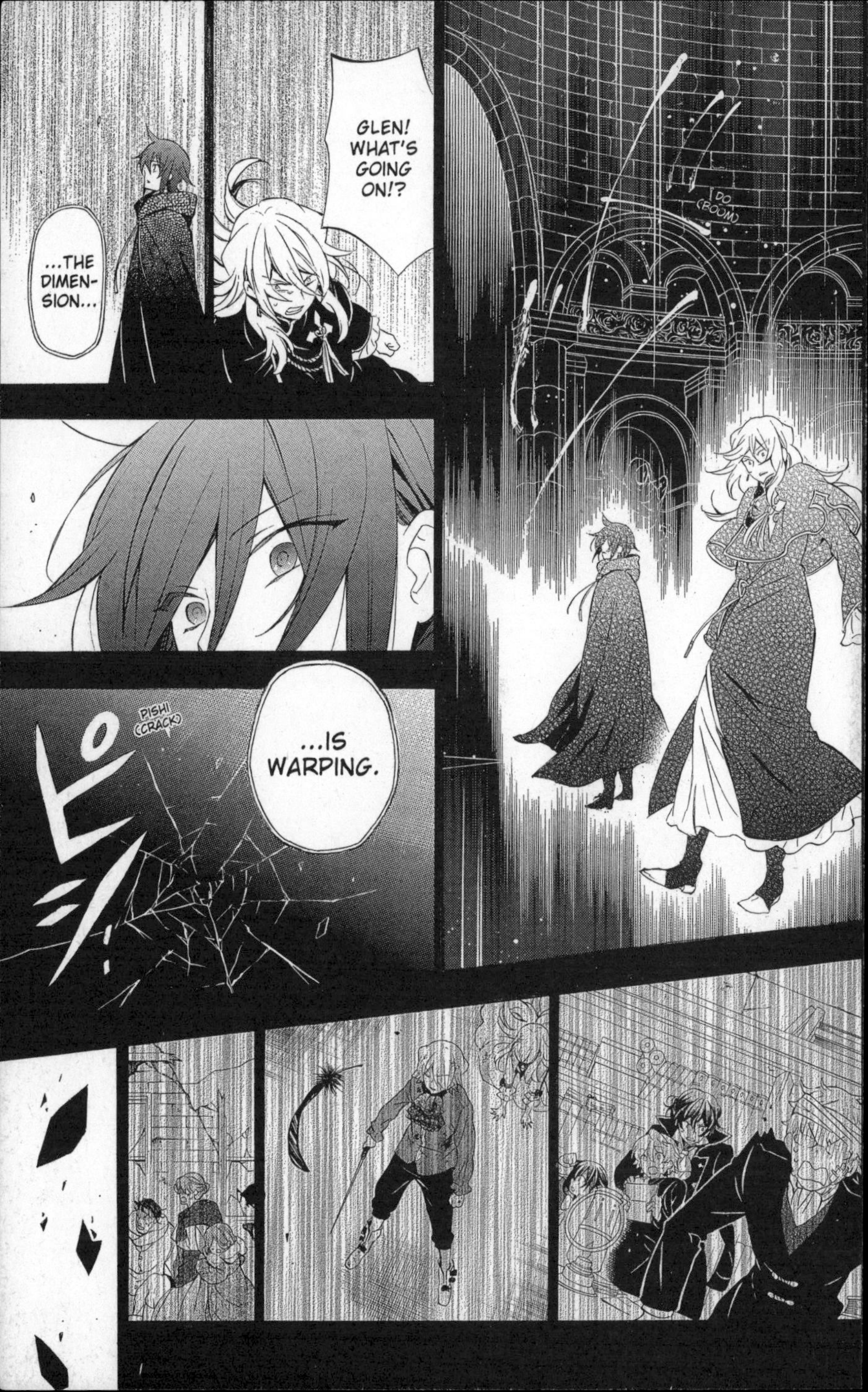
DO (BOOM)
GLEN! WHAT'S GOING ON!?
...THE DIMENSION...
...IS WARPING.
PISHI (CRACK)

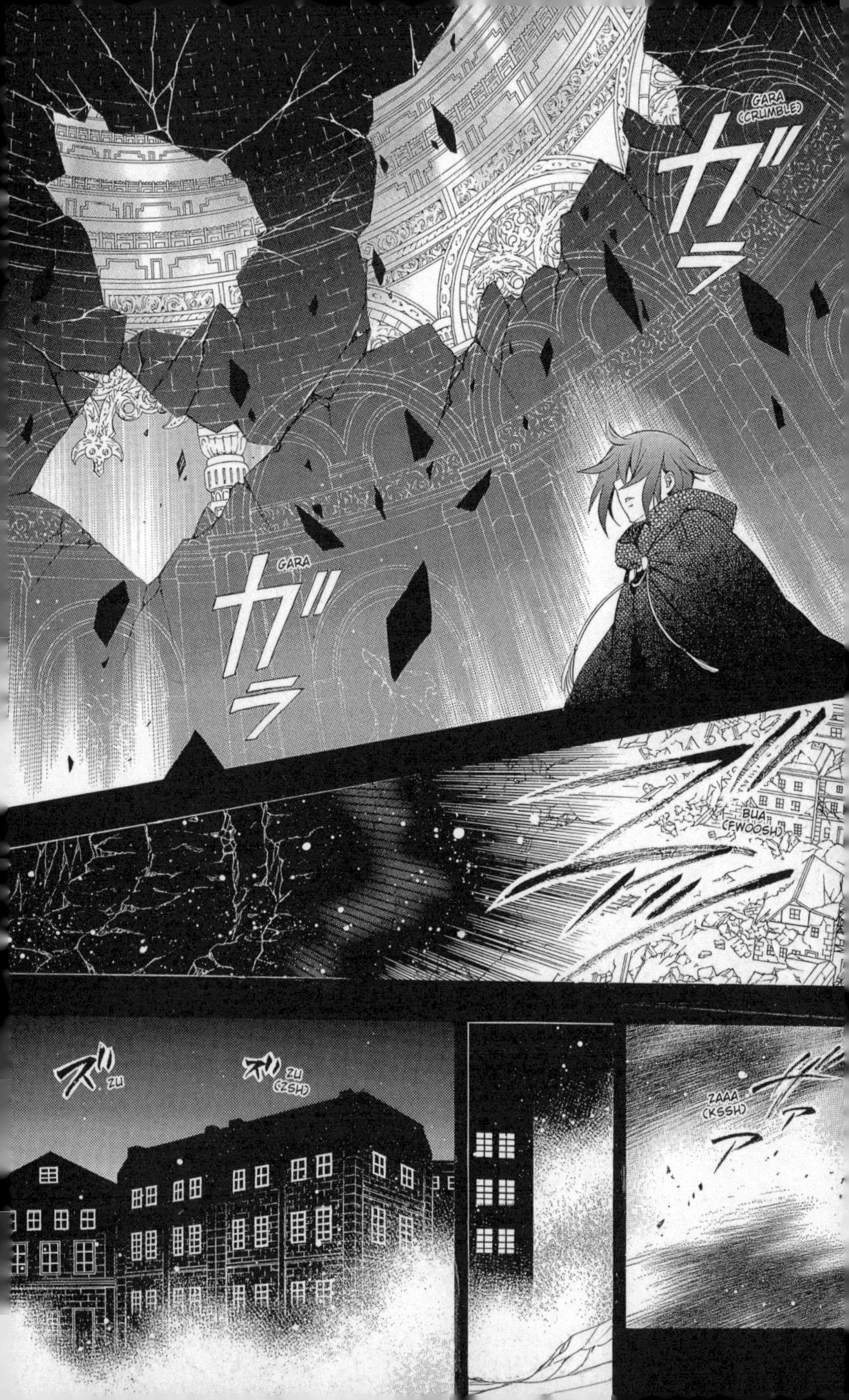

ガラ
GARA (CRUMBLE)
ガラ
GARA
BUA (FWOOSH)
ZAAA (KSSH)
ZU (ZSH)
ZU

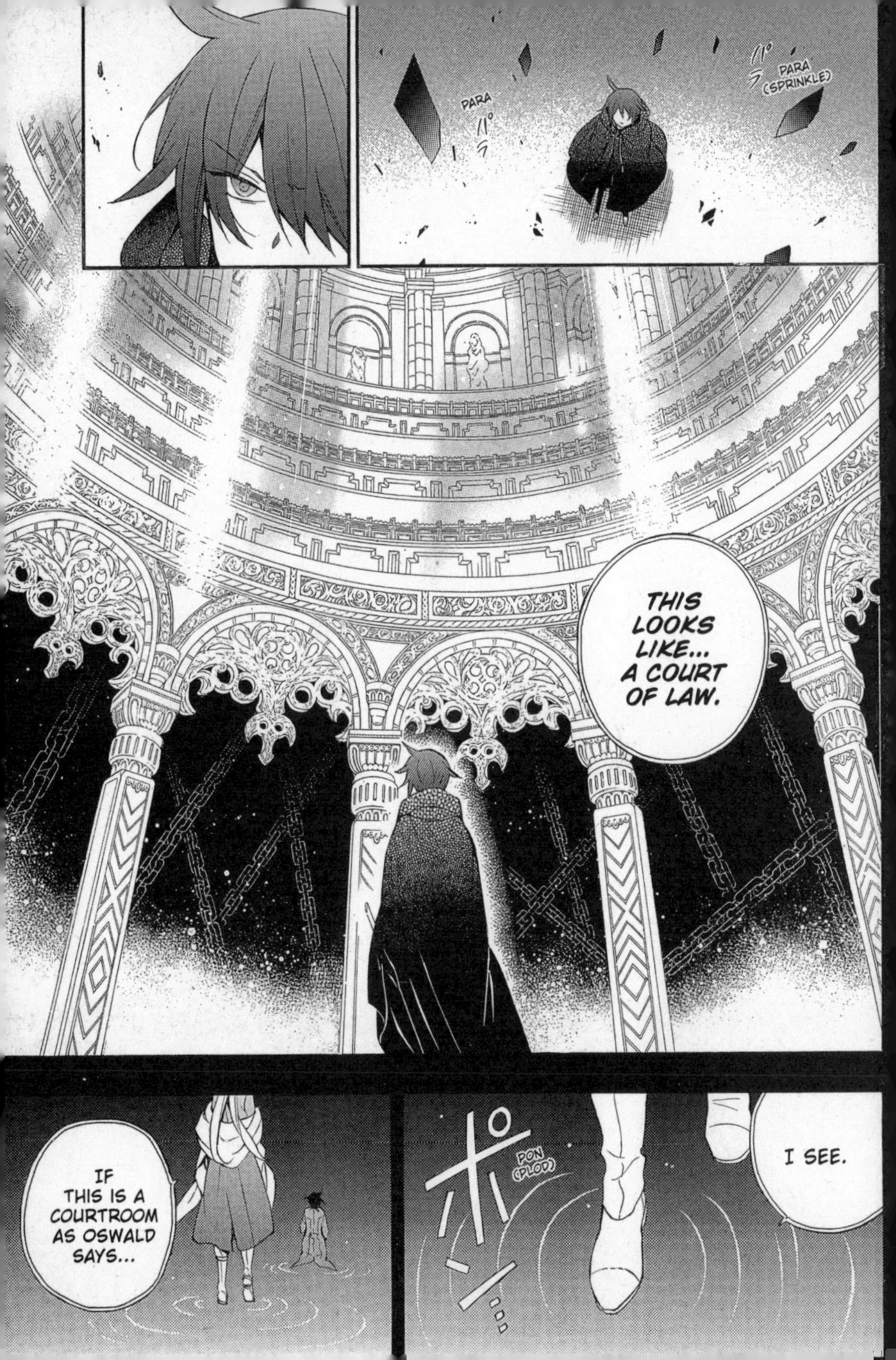
PARA (SPRINKLE)
PARA
THIS LOOKS LIKE... A COURT OF LAW.
I SEE.
PON (PLOD)
IF THIS IS A COURTROOM AS OSWALD SAYS...

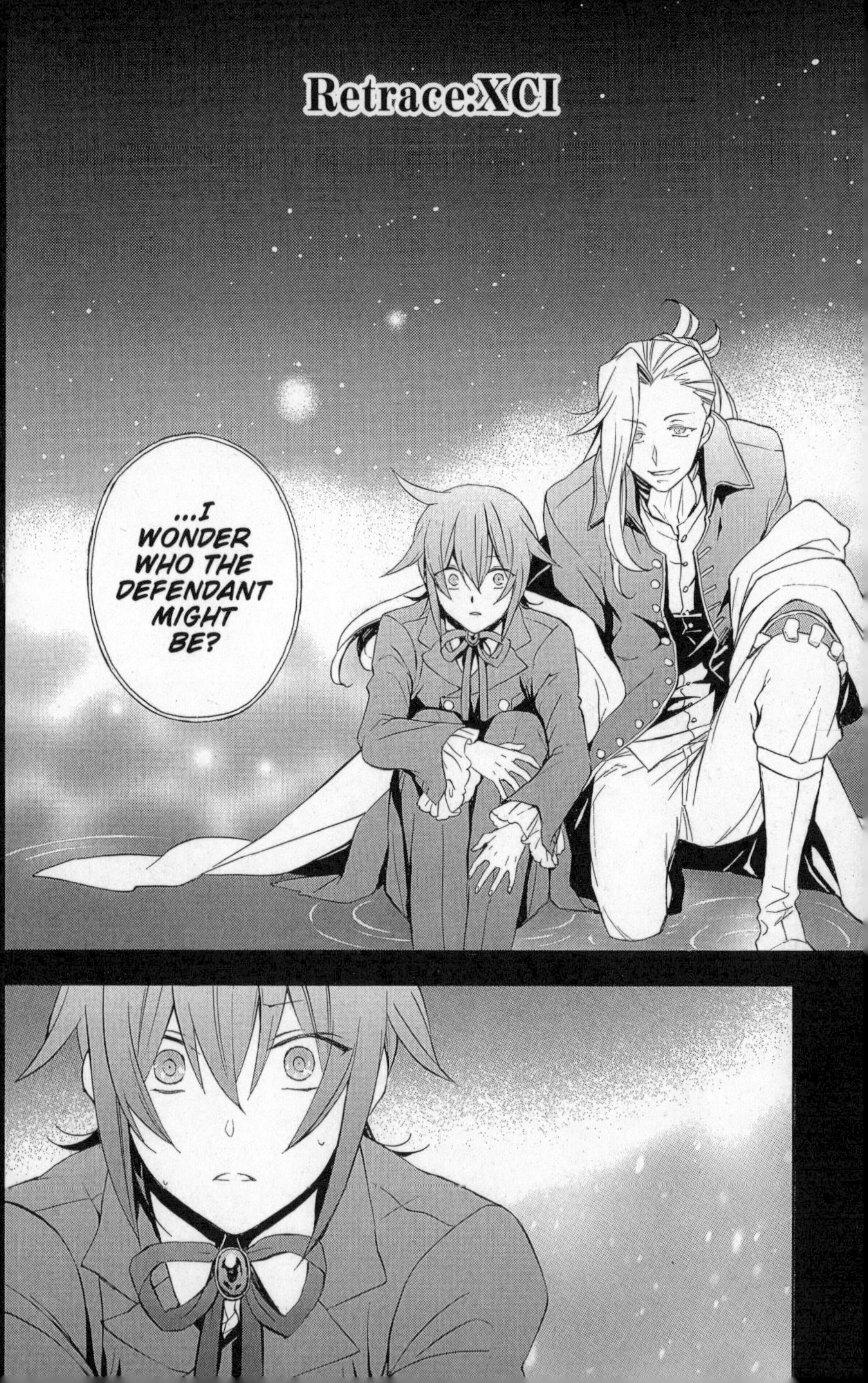
Retrace:XCI
...I WONDER WHO THE DEFENDANT MIGHT BE?

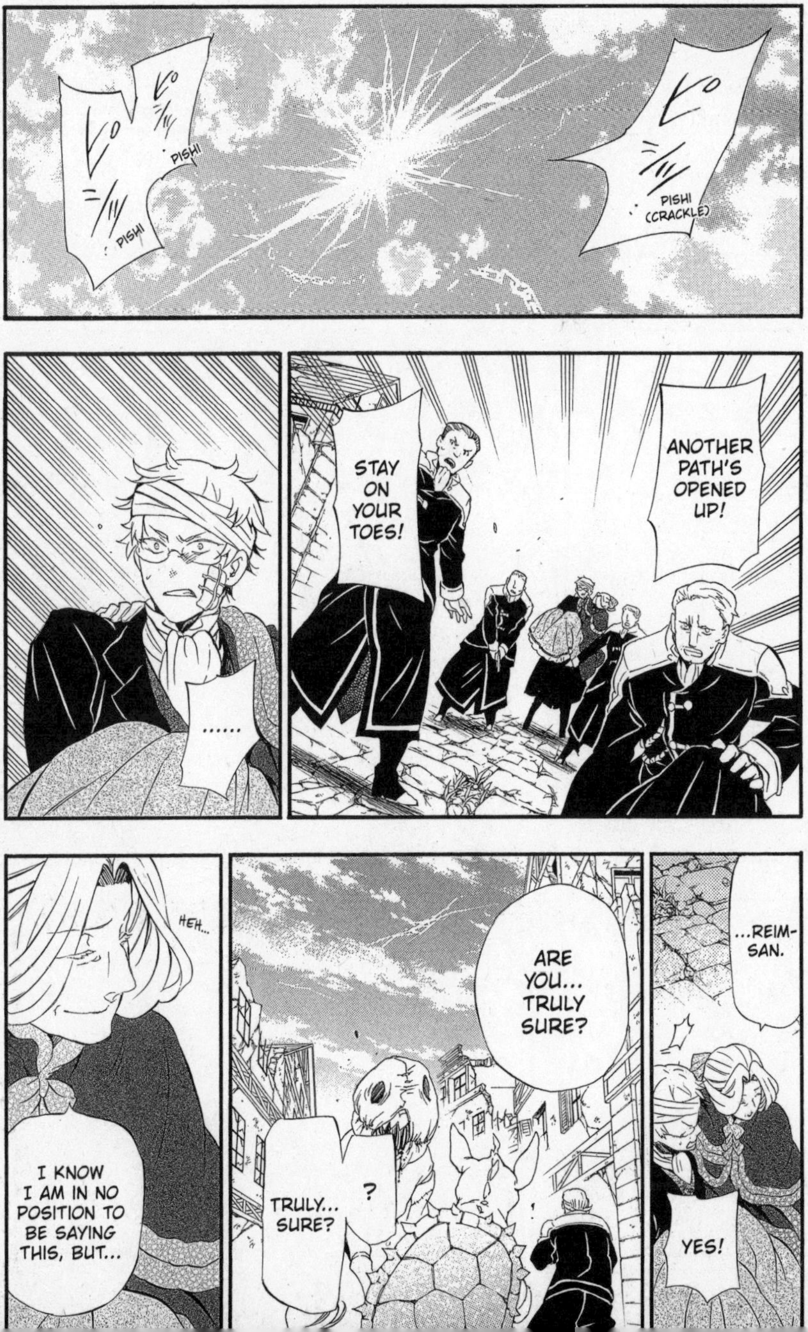
PISHI (CRACKLE)
PISHI
PISHI
ANOTHER PATH'S OPENED UP!
STAY ON YOUR TOES!
......
...REIM-SAN.
YES!
ARE YOU... TRULY SURE?
?
TRULY... SURE?
HEH...
I KNOW I AM IN NO POSITION TO BE SAYING THIS, BUT...

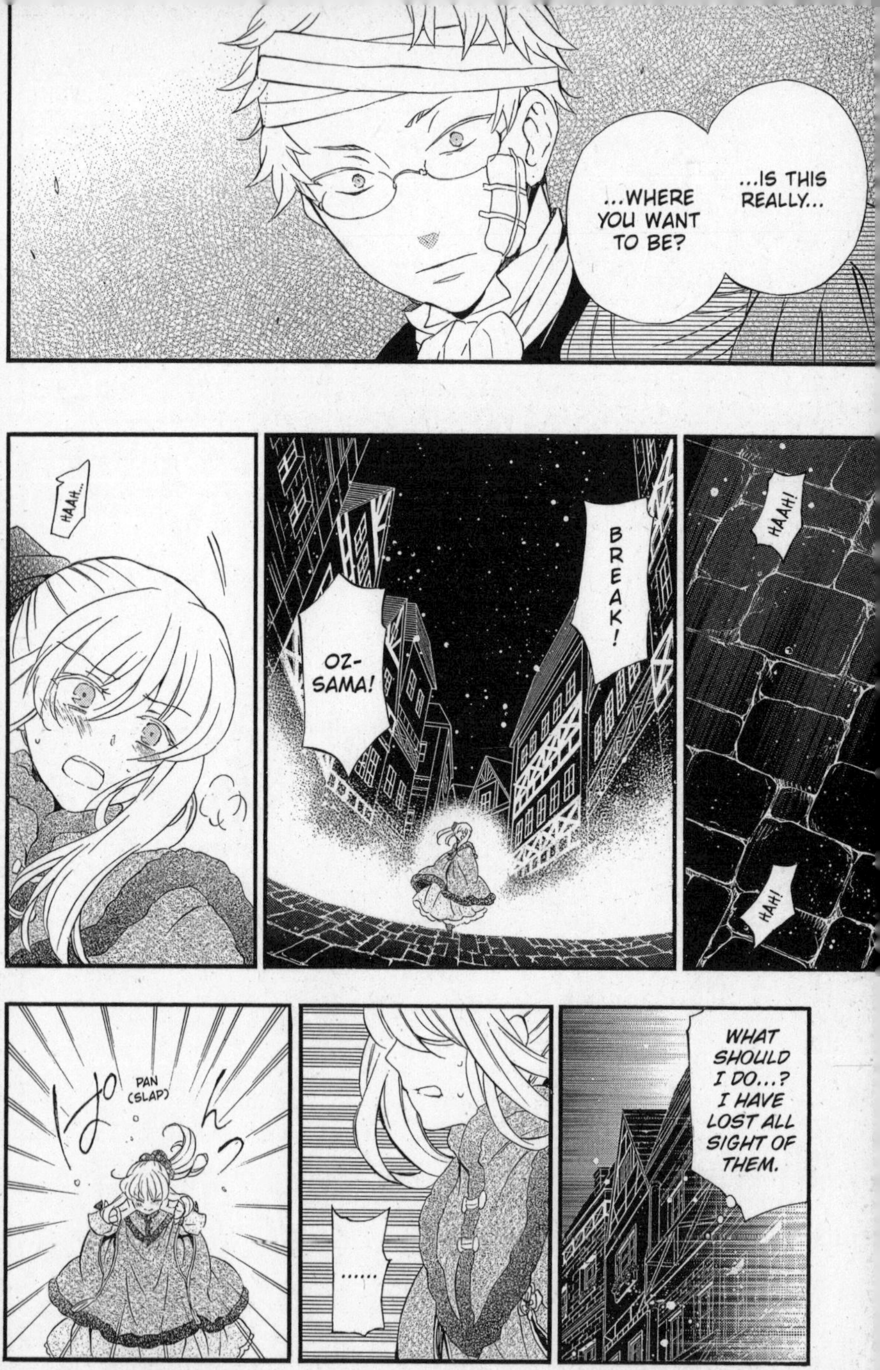
...IS THIS REALLY...
...WHERE YOU WANT TO BE?
HAAH!
HAH!
BREAK!
OZ-SAMA!
HAAH...
WHAT SHOULD I DO...? I HAVE LOST ALL SIGHT OF THEM.
......
PAN (SLAP)

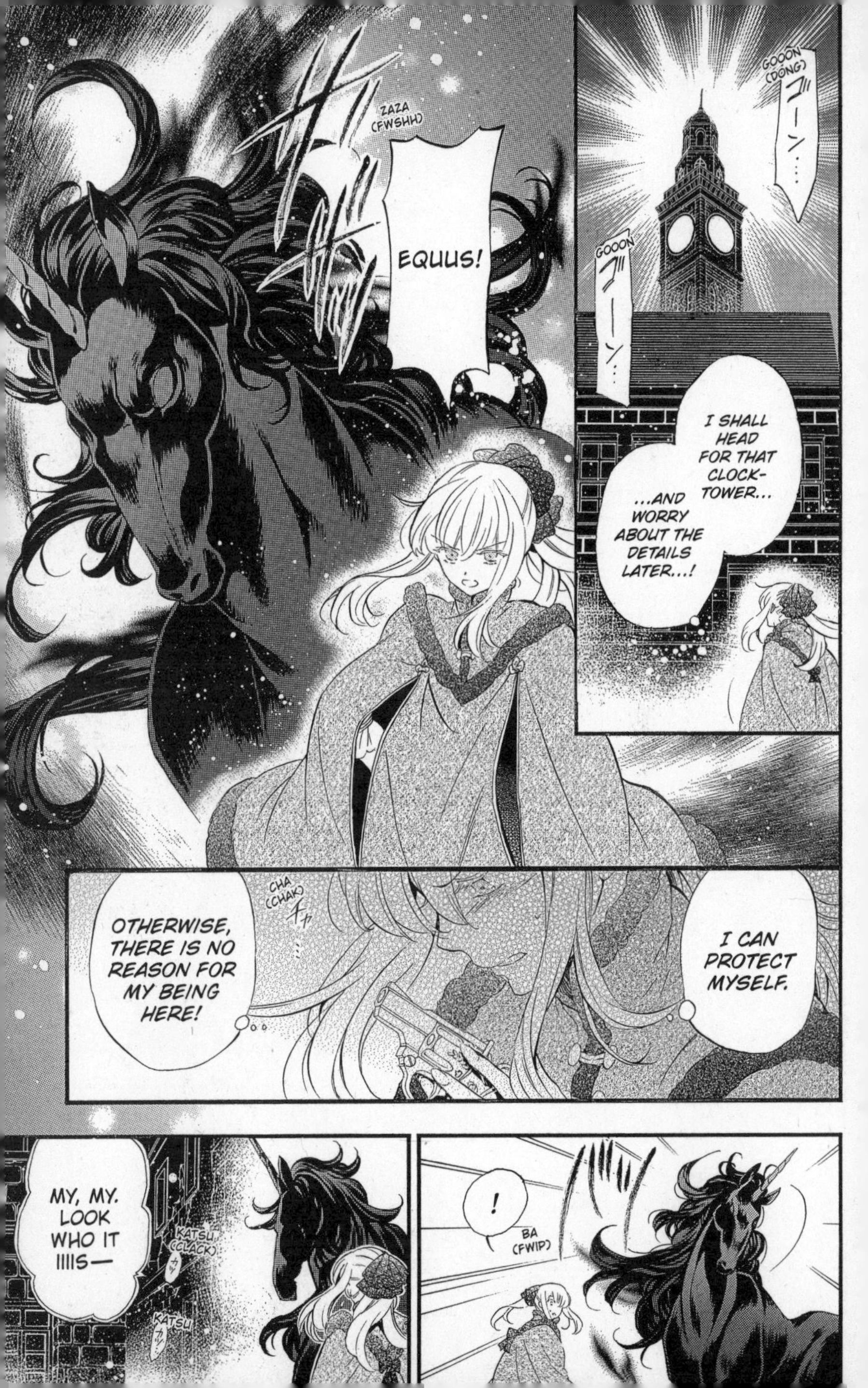

GOOON (DONG)
ゴーン…
GOOON
ゴーン…
I SHALL HEAD FOR THAT CLOCK-TOWER...
...AND WORRY ABOUT THE DETAILS LATER...!
ZAZA (FWSHH)
EQUUS!
I CAN PROTECT MYSELF.
CHA (CHAK)
OTHERWISE, THERE IS NO REASON FOR MY BEING HERE!
!
BA (FWIP)
MY, MY. LOOK WHO IT IIIIS—
KATSU (CLACK)
KATSU

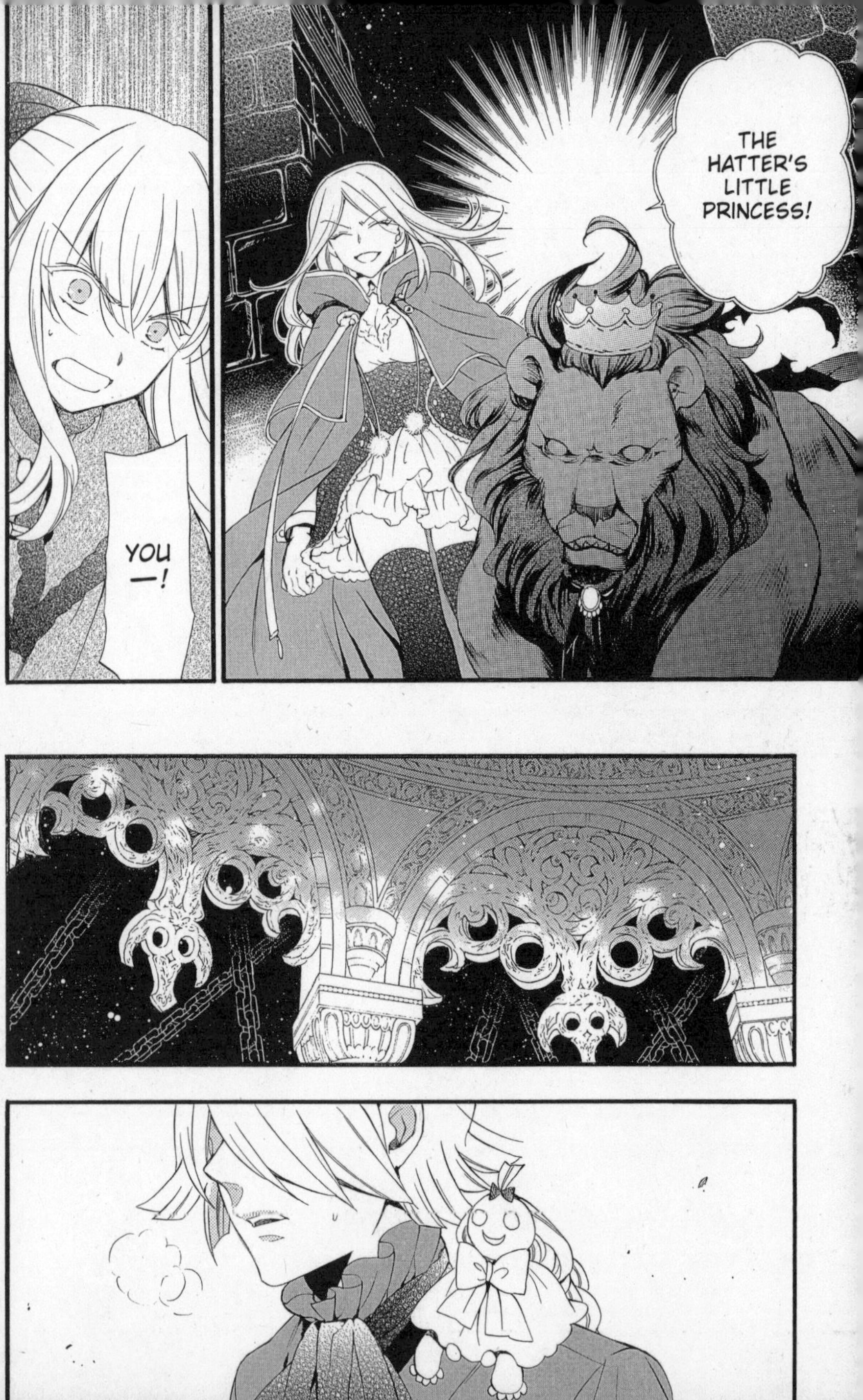
THE HATTER'S LITTLE PRINCESS!
YOU—!

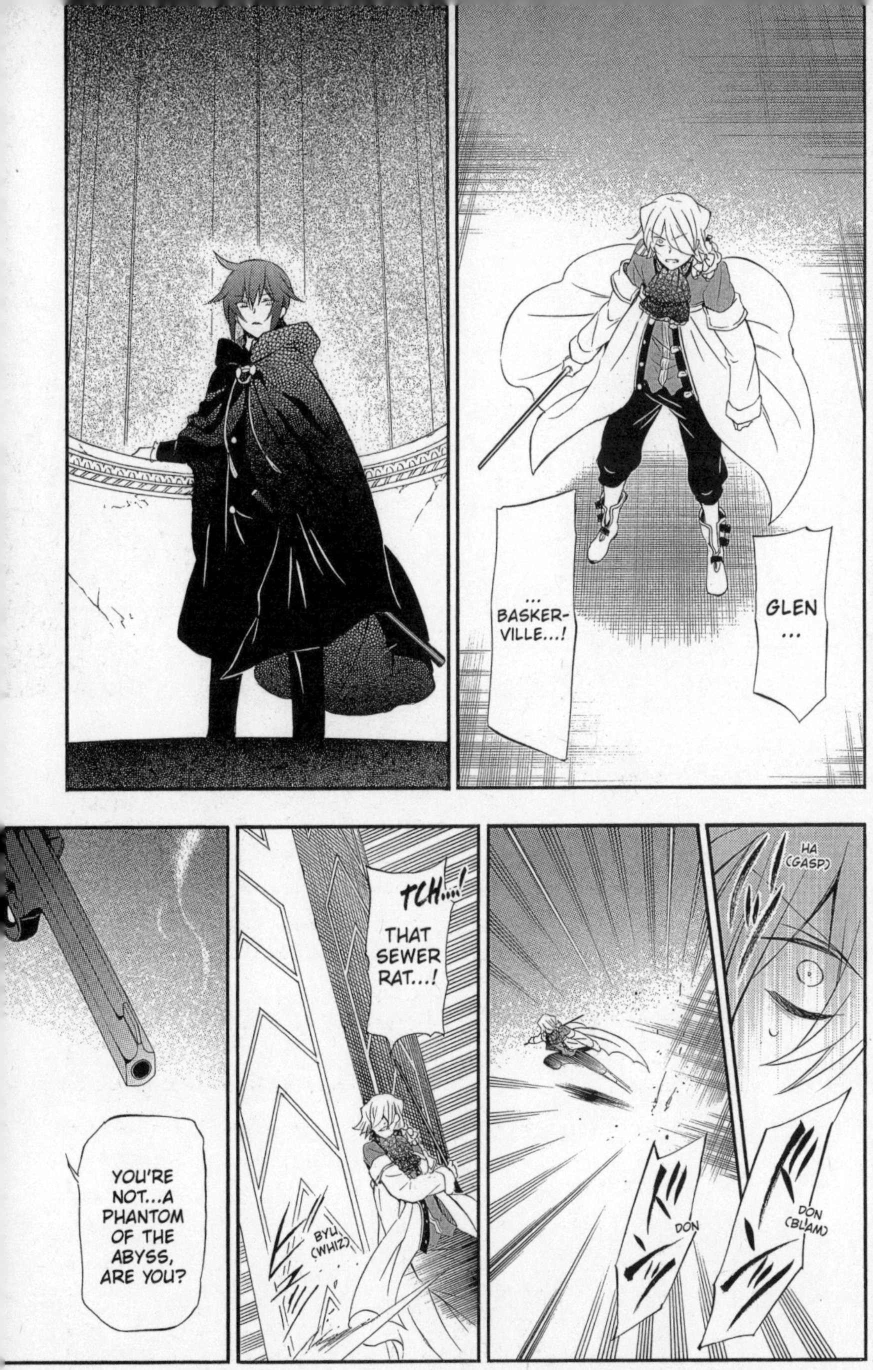
GLEN...
...BASKERVILLE...!
HA (GASP)
DON (BLAM)
DON
TCH...!
THAT SEWER RAT...!
BYU (WHIZ)
YOU'RE NOT...A PHANTOM OF THE ABYSS, ARE YOU?

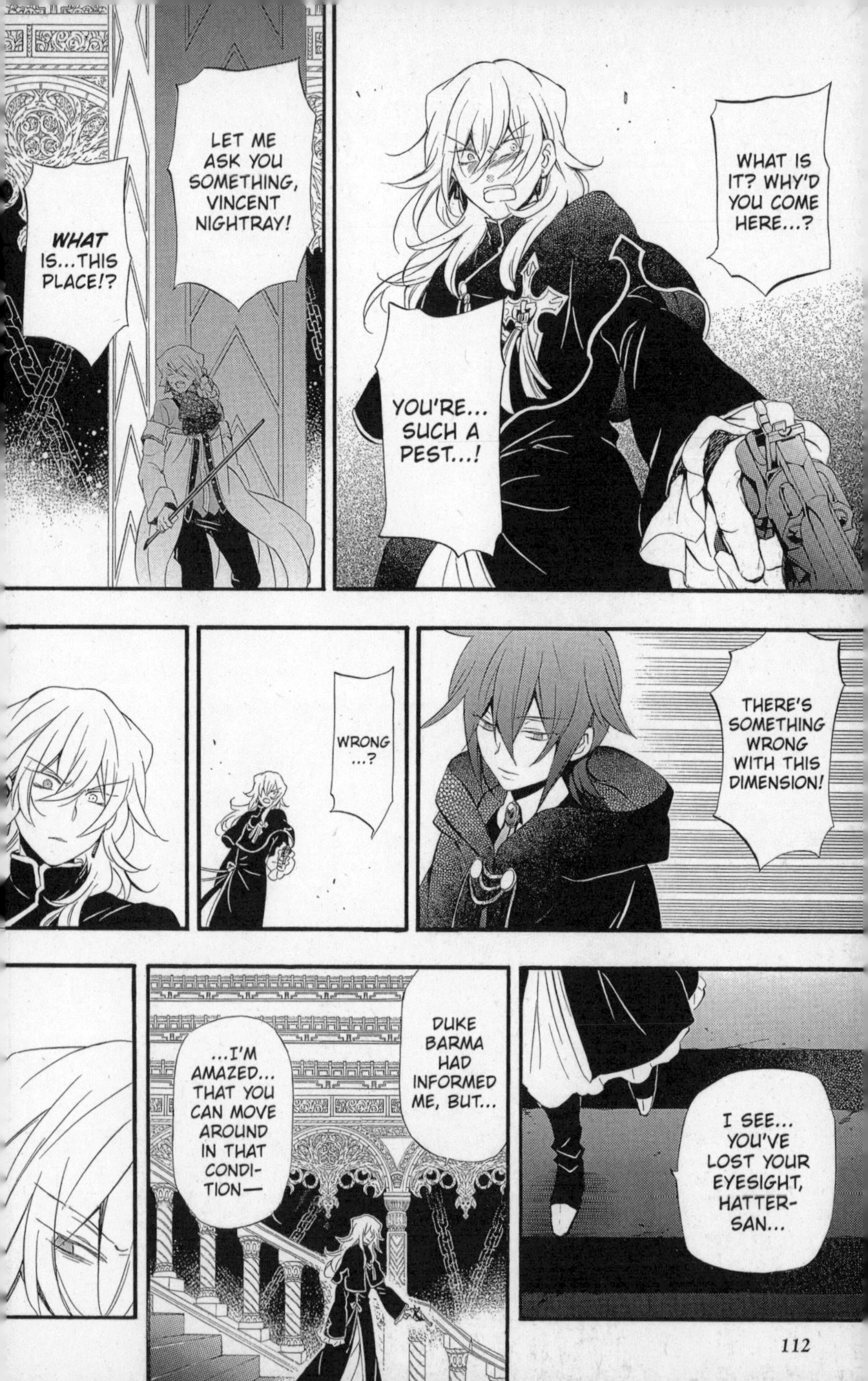
WHAT IS IT? WHY'D YOU COME HERE...?
YOU'RE... SUCH A PEST...!
LET ME ASK YOU SOMETHING, VINCENT NIGHTRAY!
WHAT IS...THIS PLACE!?
THERE'S SOMETHING WRONG WITH THIS DIMENSION!
WRONG...?
I SEE... YOU'VE LOST YOUR EYESIGHT, HATTER-SAN...
DUKE BARMA HAD INFORMED ME, BUT...
...I'M AMAZED... THAT YOU CAN MOVE AROUND IN THAT CONDI-TION—

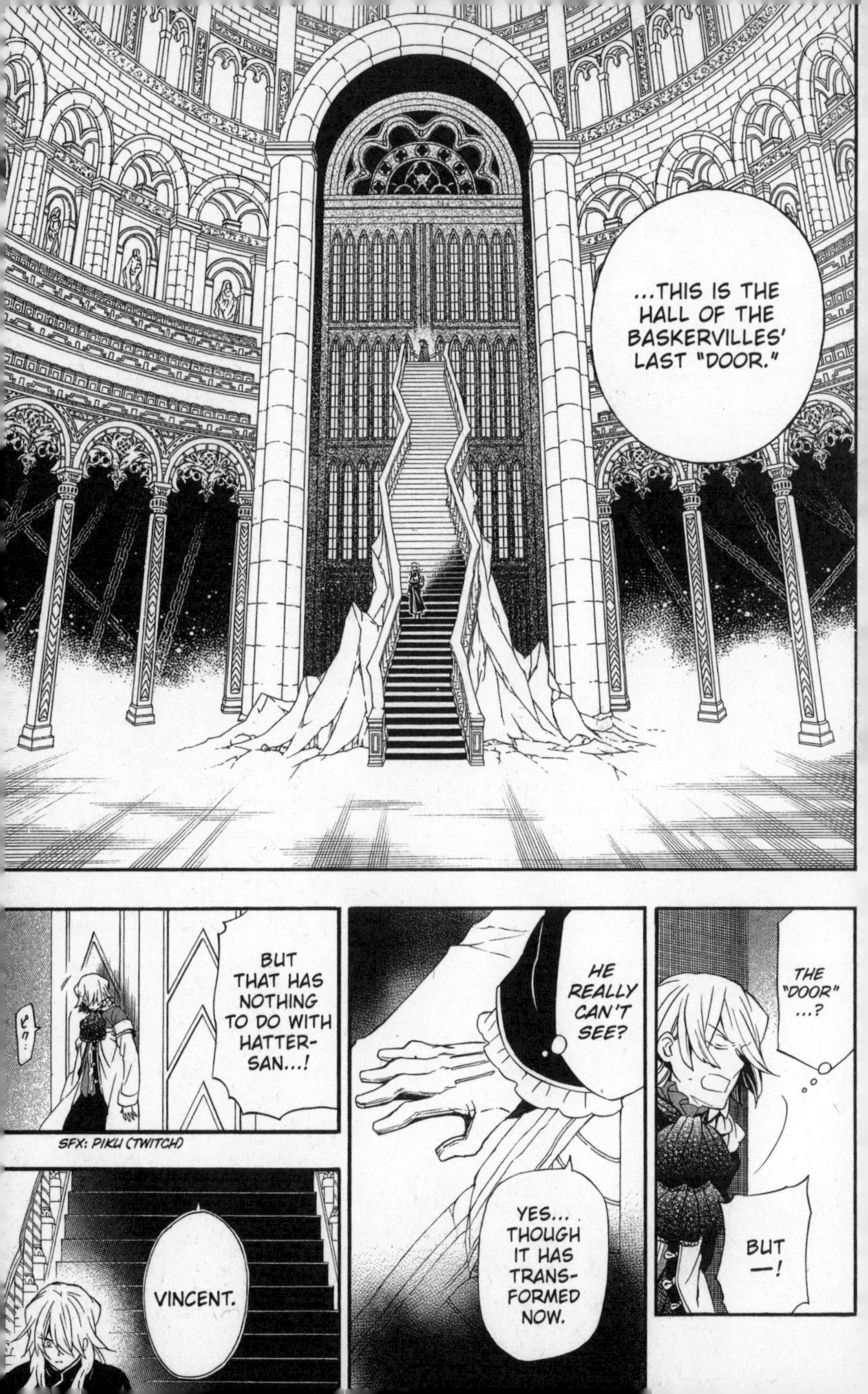
...THIS IS THE HALL OF THE BASKERVILLES' LAST "DOOR."
THE "DOOR" ...?
BUT—!
HE REALLY CAN'T SEE?
YES... THOUGH IT HAS TRANS-FORMED NOW.
BUT THAT HAS NOTHING TO DO WITH HATTER-SAN...!
SFX: PIKU (TWITCH)
VINCENT.

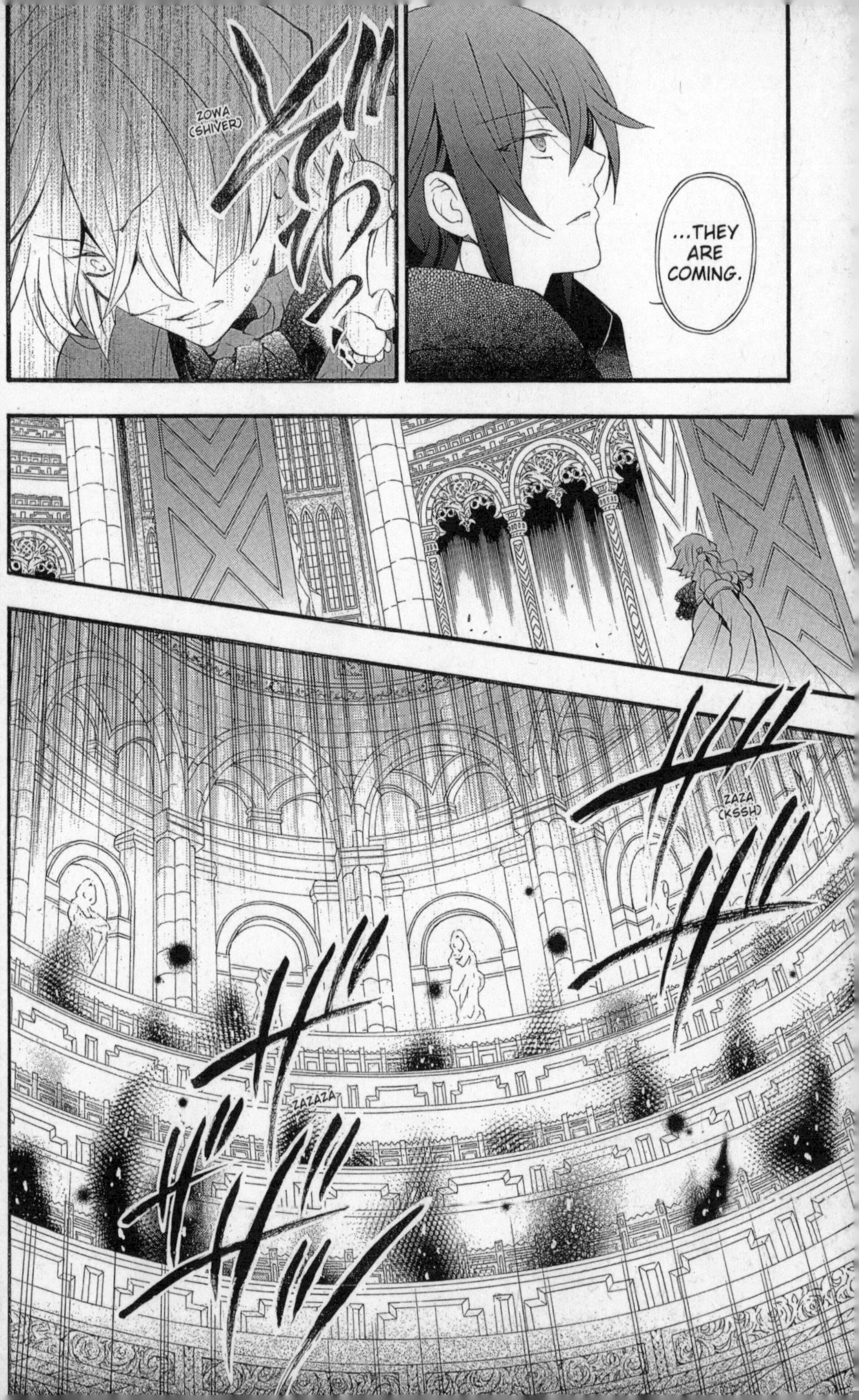
...THEY ARE COMING.
ZOWA (SHIVER)
ZAZA (KSSH)
ZAZAZA

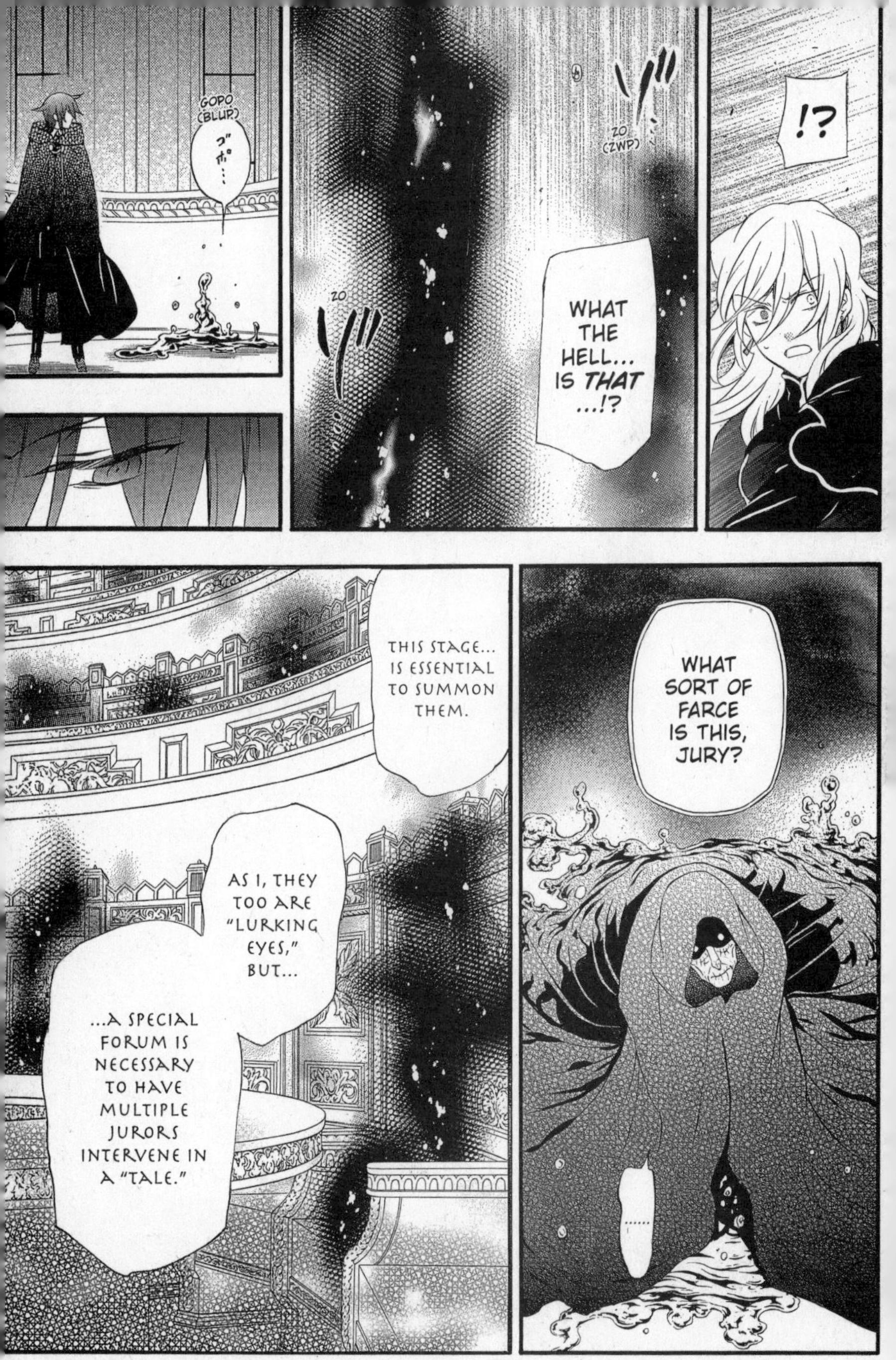
!?
WHAT THE HELL... IS *THAT* ...!?
ZO (ZWP)
ZO
GOPO (BLUP)
ゴポ…
WHAT SORT OF FARCE IS THIS, JURY?
......
THIS STAGE... IS ESSENTIAL TO SUMMON THEM.
AS I, THEY TOO ARE "LURKING EYES," BUT...
...A SPECIAL FORUM IS NECESSARY TO HAVE MULTIPLE JURORS INTERVENE IN A "TALE."

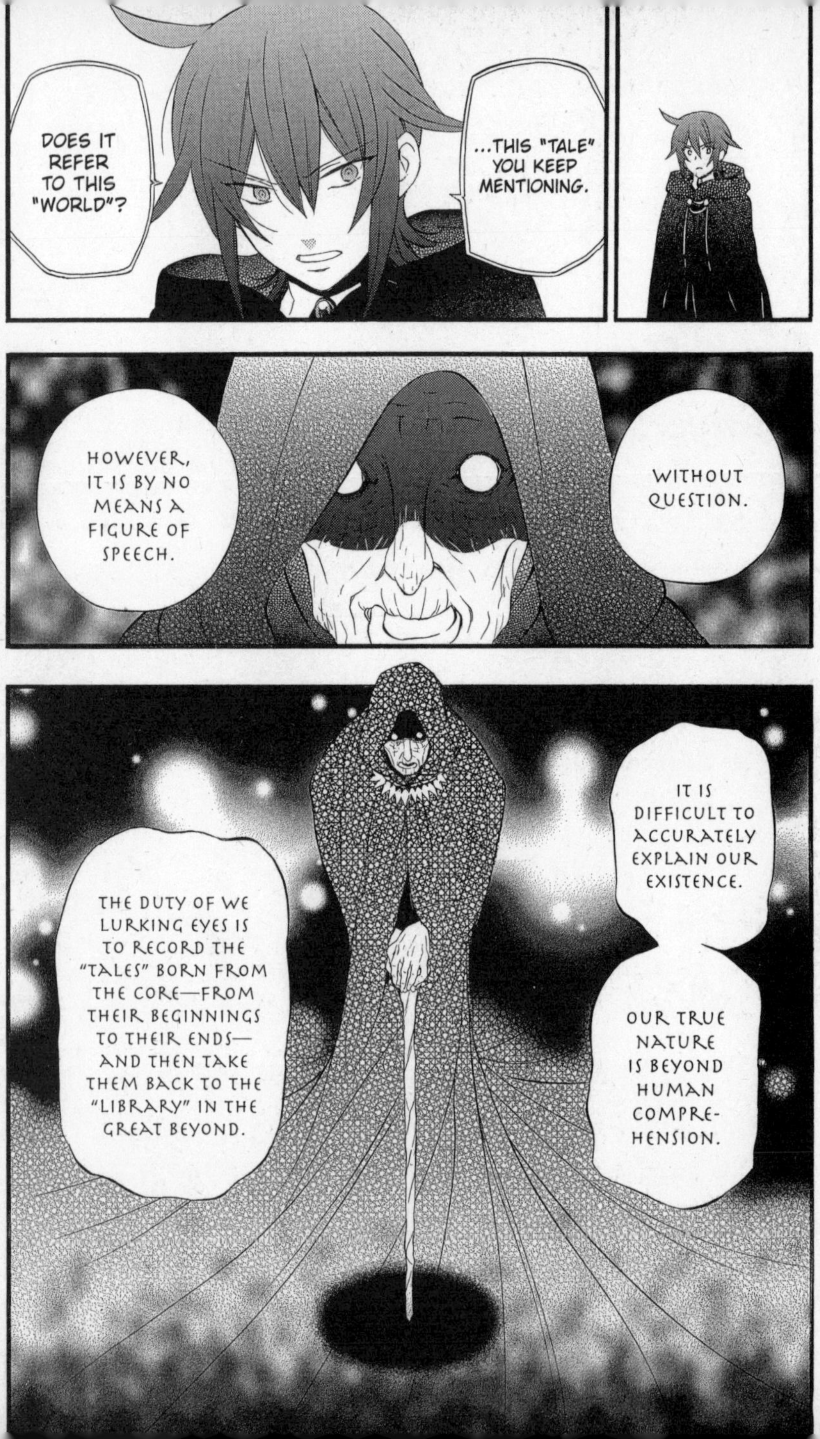
...THIS "TALE" YOU KEEP MENTIONING.
DOES IT REFER TO THIS "WORLD"?
WITHOUT QUESTION.
HOWEVER, IT IS BY NO MEANS A FIGURE OF SPEECH.
IT IS DIFFICULT TO ACCURATELY EXPLAIN OUR EXISTENCE.
OUR TRUE NATURE IS BEYOND HUMAN COMPRE-HENSION.
THE DUTY OF WE LURKING EYES IS TO RECORD THE "TALES" BORN FROM THE CORE—FROM THEIR BEGINNINGS TO THEIR ENDS—AND THEN TAKE THEM BACK TO THE "LIBRARY" IN THE GREAT BEYOND.

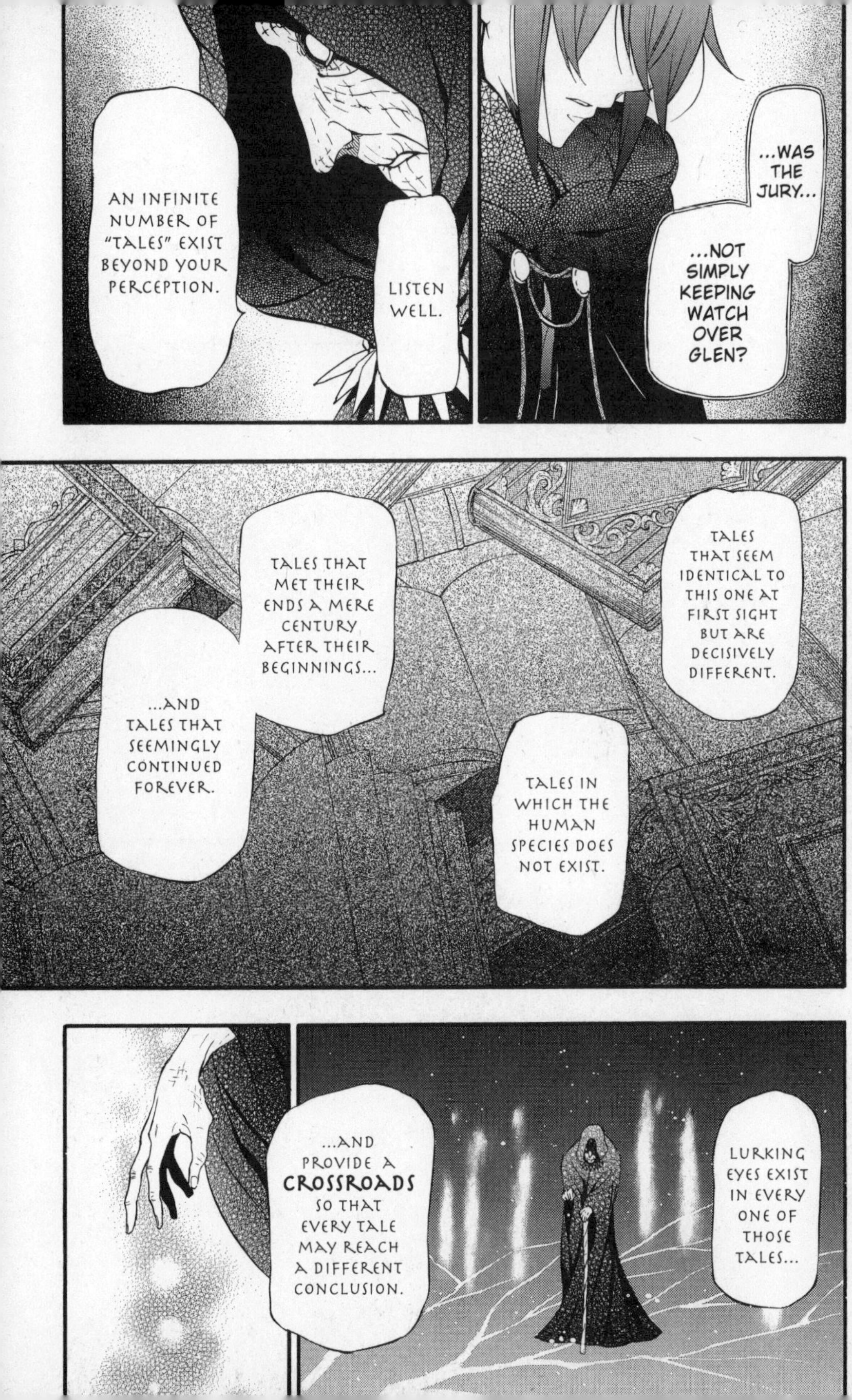
...WAS THE JURY...
...NOT SIMPLY KEEPING WATCH OVER GLEN?
LISTEN WELL.
AN INFINITE NUMBER OF "TALES" EXIST BEYOND YOUR PERCEPTION.
TALES THAT SEEM IDENTICAL TO THIS ONE AT FIRST SIGHT BUT ARE DECISIVELY DIFFERENT.
TALES IN WHICH THE HUMAN SPECIES DOES NOT EXIST.
TALES THAT MET THEIR ENDS A MERE CENTURY AFTER THEIR BEGINNINGS...
...AND TALES THAT SEEMINGLY CONTINUED FOREVER.
LURKING EYES EXIST IN EVERY ONE OF THOSE TALES...
...AND PROVIDE A CROSSROADS SO THAT EVERY TALE MAY REACH A DIFFERENT CONCLUSION.

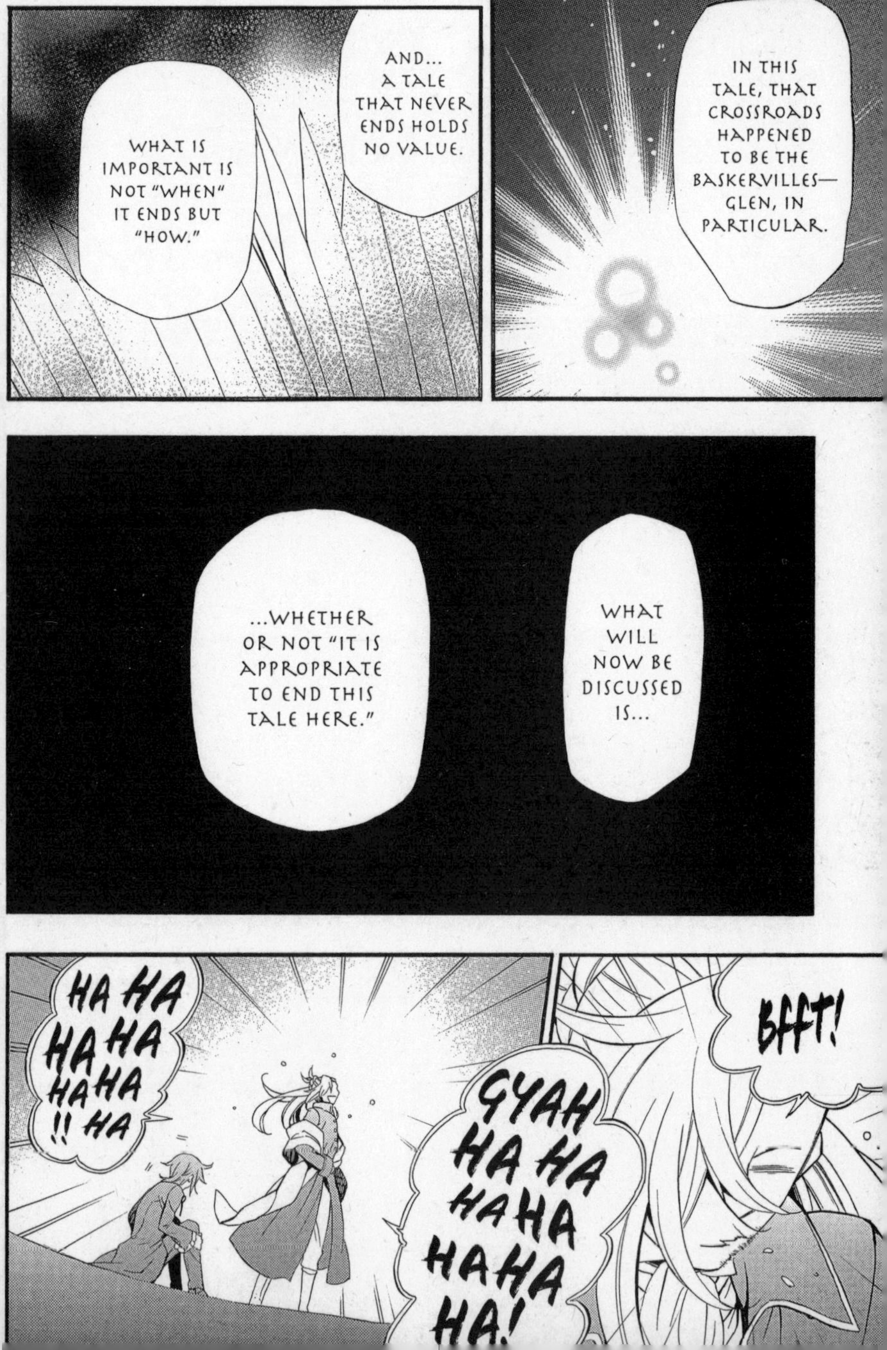
IN THIS TALE, THAT CROSSROADS HAPPENED TO BE THE BASKERVILLES—GLEN, IN PARTICULAR.
AND... A TALE THAT NEVER ENDS HOLDS NO VALUE.
WHAT IS IMPORTANT IS NOT "WHEN" IT ENDS BUT "HOW."
WHAT WILL NOW BE DISCUSSED IS...
...WHETHER OR NOT "IT IS APPROPRIATE TO END THIS TALE HERE."
BFFT!
GYAH HA HA HA HA HA HA HA HA HA!
HA HA HA HA HA HA HA HA!!

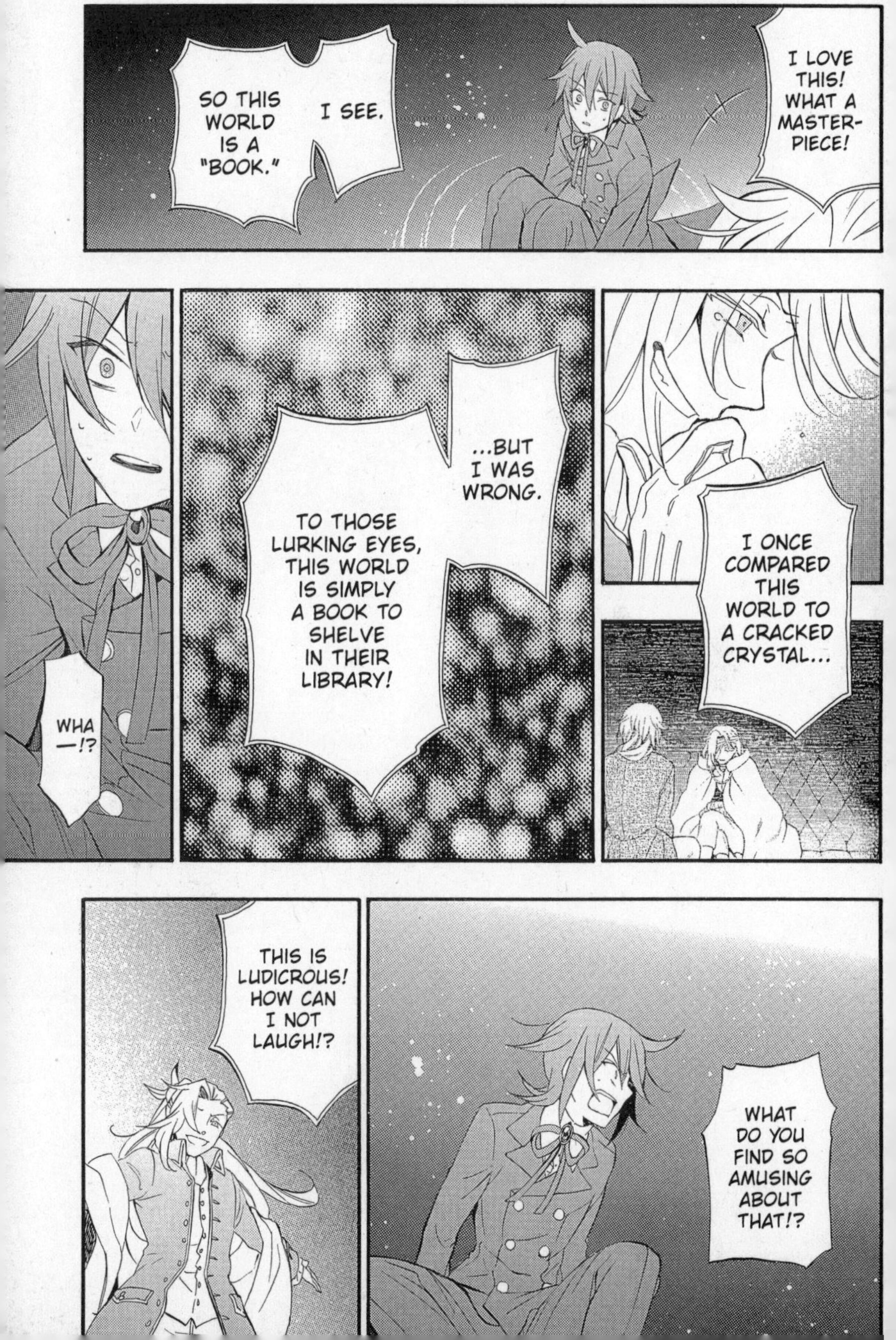
I LOVE THIS! WHAT A MASTERPIECE!
I SEE.
SO THIS WORLD IS A "BOOK."
I ONCE COMPARED THIS WORLD TO A CRACKED CRYSTAL...
...BUT I WAS WRONG.
TO THOSE LURKING EYES, THIS WORLD IS SIMPLY A BOOK TO SHELVE IN THEIR LIBRARY!
WHA—!?
WHAT DO YOU FIND SO AMUSING ABOUT THAT!?
THIS IS LUDICROUS! HOW CAN I NOT LAUGH!?

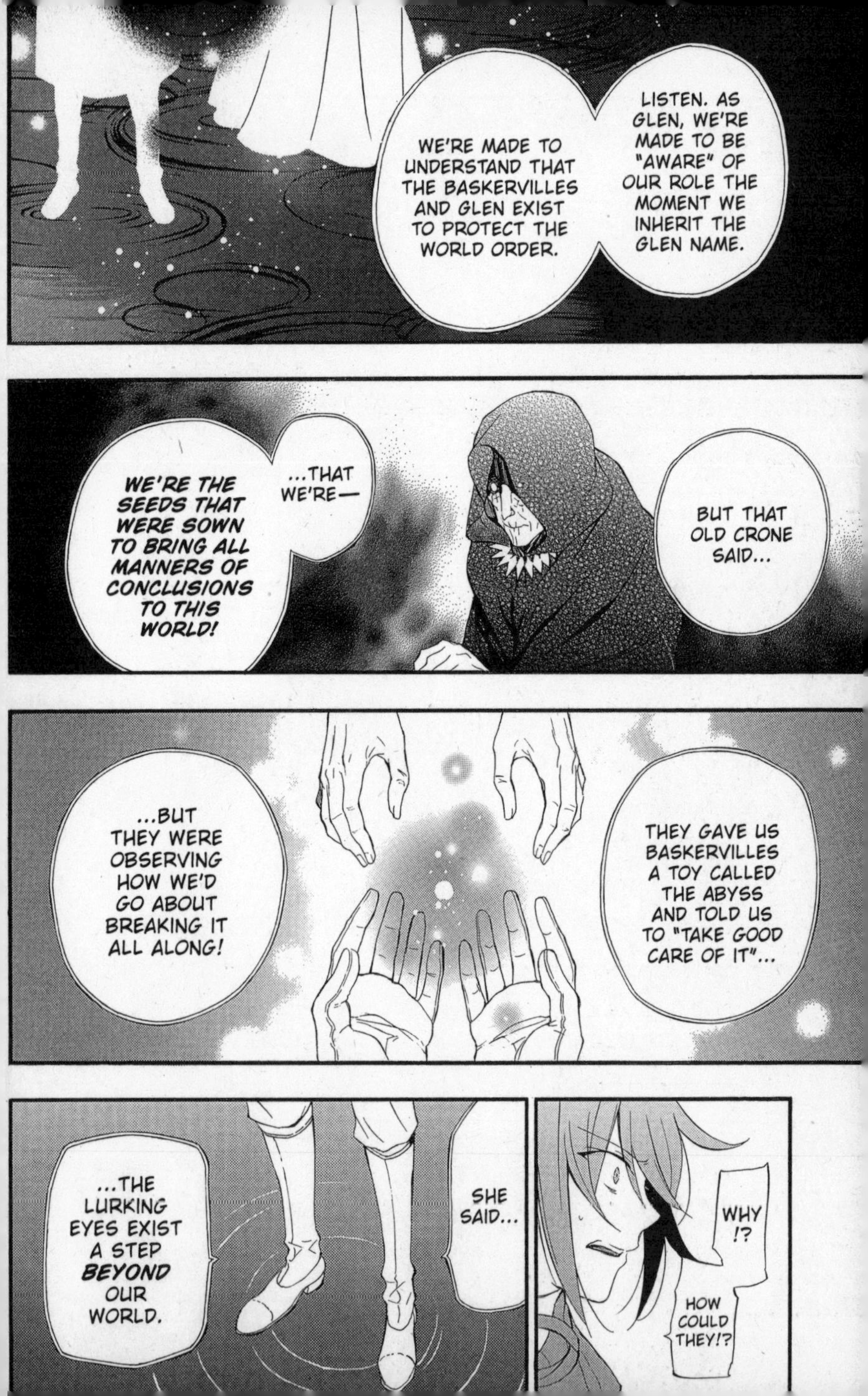
LISTEN. AS GLEN, WE'RE MADE TO BE "AWARE" OF OUR ROLE THE MOMENT WE INHERIT THE GLEN NAME.
WE'RE MADE TO UNDERSTAND THAT THE BASKERVILLES AND GLEN EXIST TO PROTECT THE WORLD ORDER.
BUT THAT OLD CRONE SAID...
...THAT WE'RE—
WE'RE THE SEEDS THAT WERE SOWN TO BRING ALL MANNERS OF CONCLUSIONS TO THIS WORLD!
THEY GAVE US BASKERVILLES A TOY CALLED THE ABYSS AND TOLD US TO "TAKE GOOD CARE OF IT"...
...BUT THEY WERE OBSERVING HOW WE'D GO ABOUT BREAKING IT ALL ALONG!
WHY!?
HOW COULD THEY!?
SHE SAID...
...THE LURKING EYES EXIST A STEP BEYOND OUR WORLD.

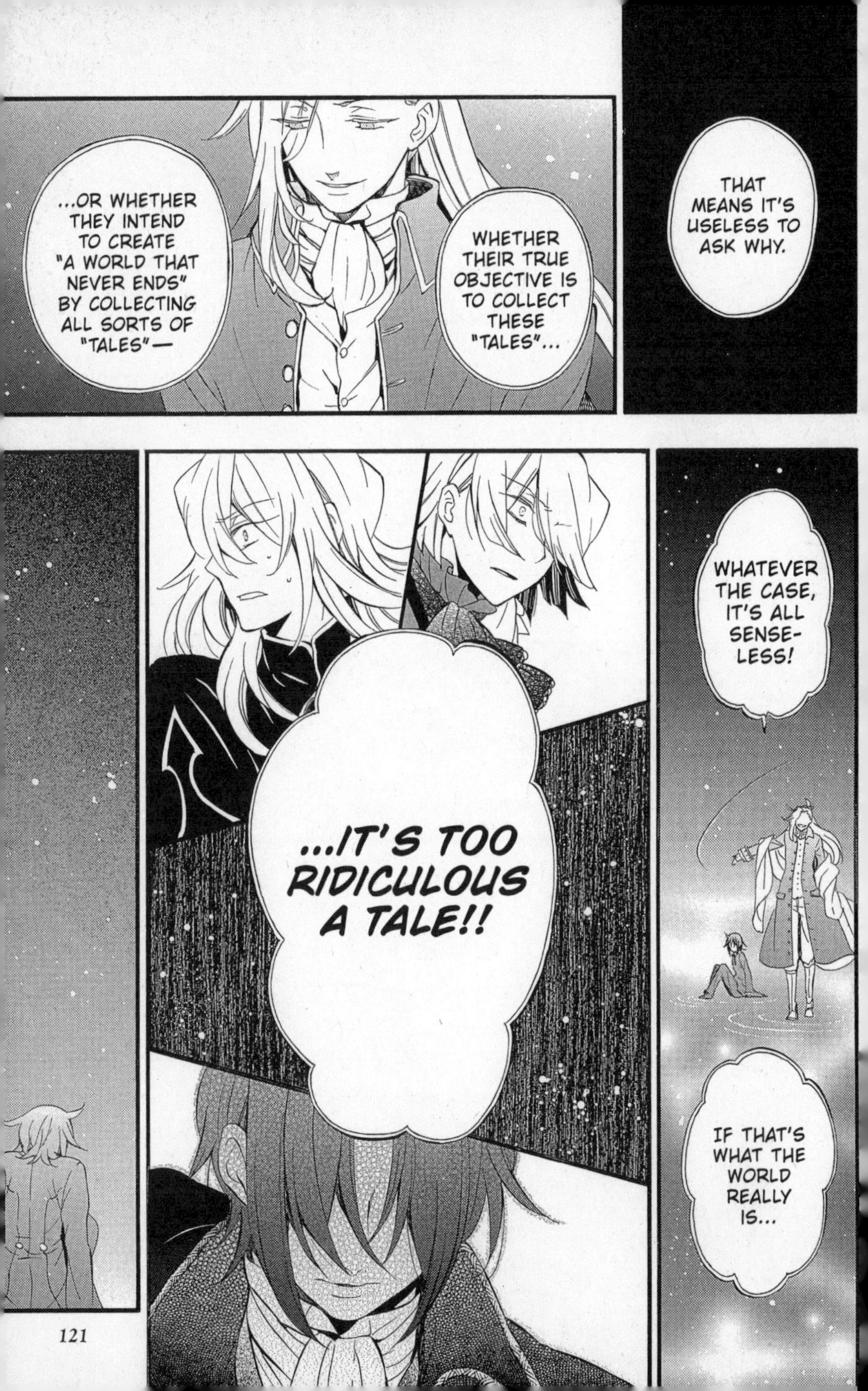
THAT MEANS IT'S USELESS TO ASK WHY.
WHETHER THEIR TRUE OBJECTIVE IS TO COLLECT THESE "TALES"...
...OR WHETHER THEY INTEND TO CREATE "A WORLD THAT NEVER ENDS" BY COLLECTING ALL SORTS OF "TALES"—
WHATEVER THE CASE, IT'S ALL SENSE-LESS!
IF THAT'S WHAT THE WORLD REALLY IS...
...IT'S TOO RIDICULOUS A TALE!!

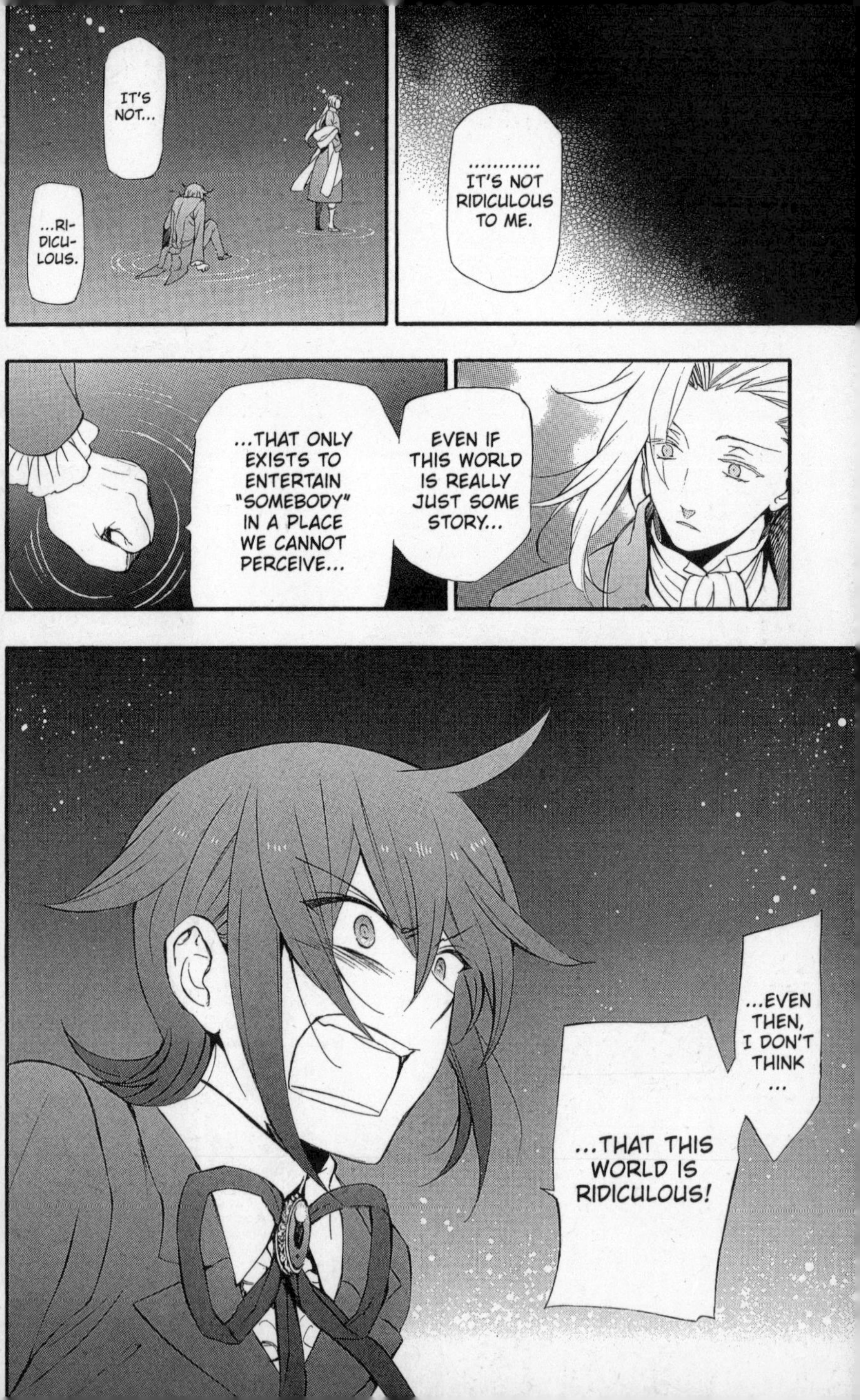
.... IT'S NOT RIDICULOUS TO ME.
IT'S NOT...
...RI-DICU-LOUS.
EVEN IF THIS WORLD IS REALLY JUST SOME STORY...
...THAT ONLY EXISTS TO ENTERTAIN "SOMEBODY" IN A PLACE WE CANNOT PERCEIVE...
...EVEN THEN, I DON'T THINK ...
...THAT THIS WORLD IS RIDICULOUS!

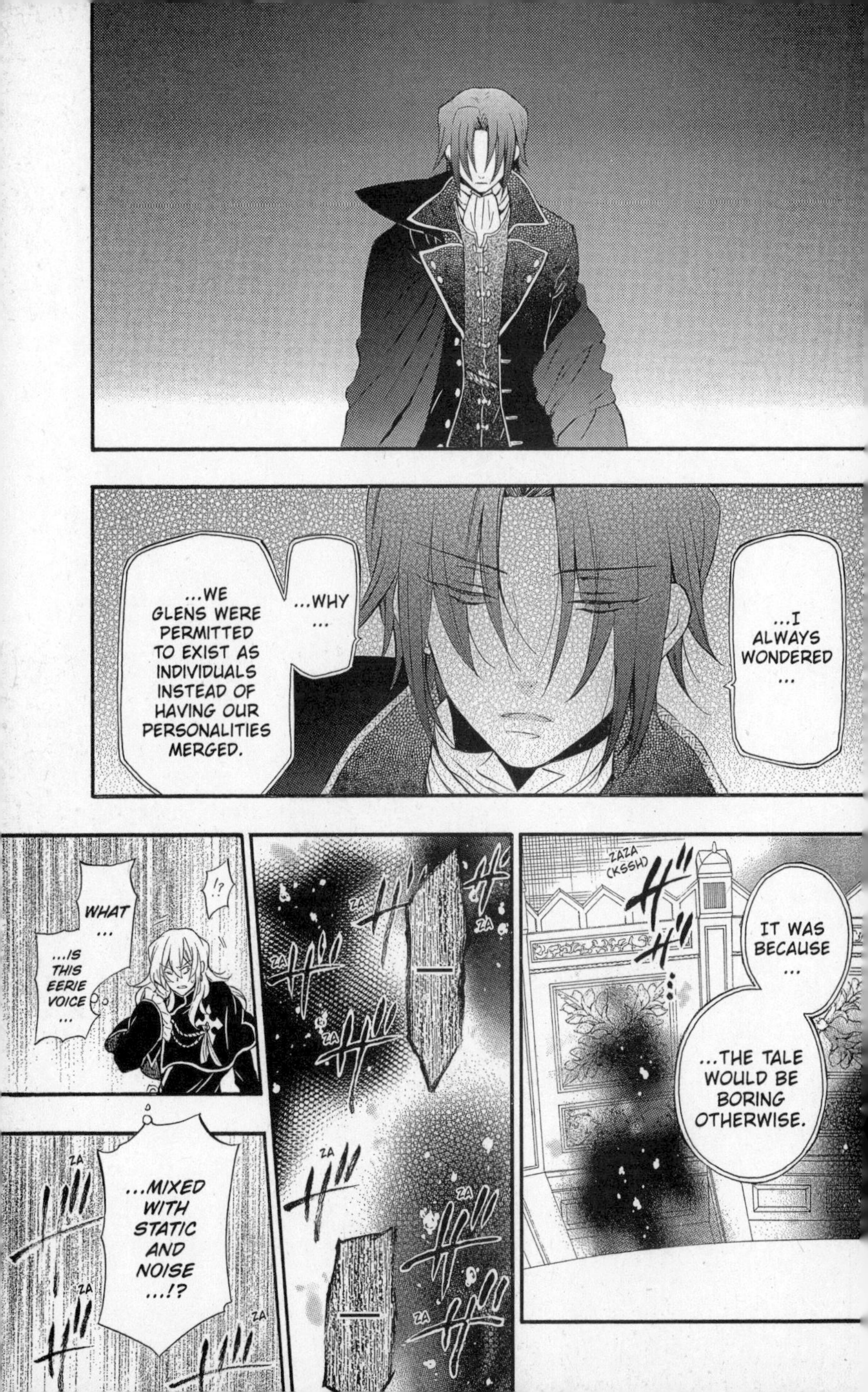
...I ALWAYS WONDERED ...
...WHY ...
...WE GLENS WERE PERMITTED TO EXIST AS INDIVIDUALS INSTEAD OF HAVING OUR PERSONALITIES MERGED.
ZAZA (KSSH)
IT WAS BECAUSE ...
...THE TALE WOULD BE BORING OTHERWISE.
ZA
ZA
ZA
ZA
ZA
ZA
ZA
!?
WHAT ...
...IS THIS EERIE VOICE ...
ZA
...MIXED WITH STATIC AND NOISE ...!?
ZA
ZA

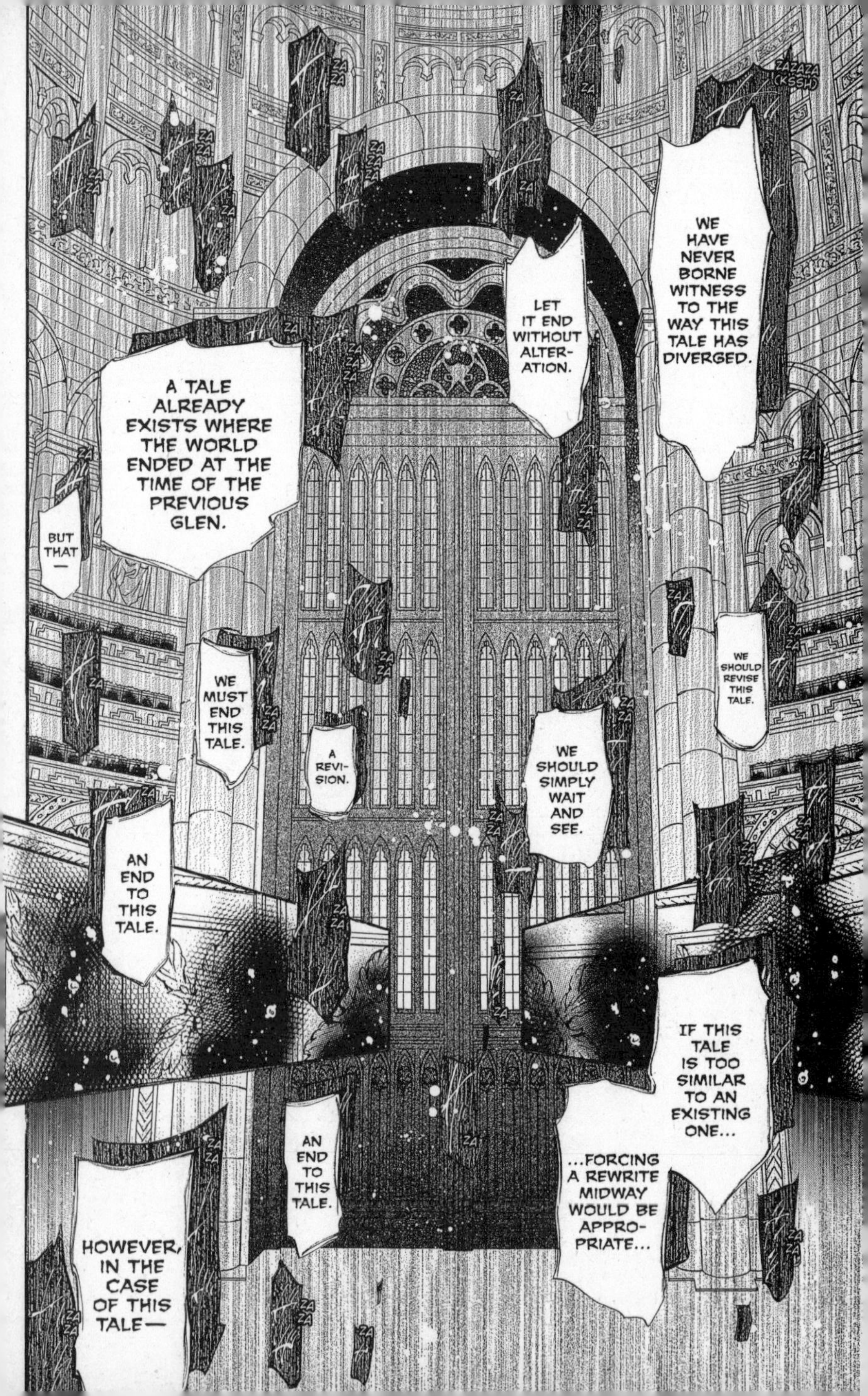
ZAZA (KSSH)
WE HAVE NEVER BORNE WITNESS TO THE WAY THIS TALE HAS DIVERGED.
LET IT END WITHOUT ALTER-ATION.
A TALE ALREADY EXISTS WHERE THE WORLD ENDED AT THE TIME OF THE PREVIOUS GLEN.
BUT THAT—
WE SHOULD REVISE THIS TALE.
WE SHOULD SIMPLY WAIT AND SEE.
A REVI-SION.
WE MUST END THIS TALE.
AN END TO THIS TALE.
IF THIS TALE IS TOO SIMILAR TO AN EXISTING ONE...
...FORCING A REWRITE MIDWAY WOULD BE APPRO-PRIATE...
AN END TO THIS TALE.
HOWEVER, IN THE CASE OF THIS TALE—

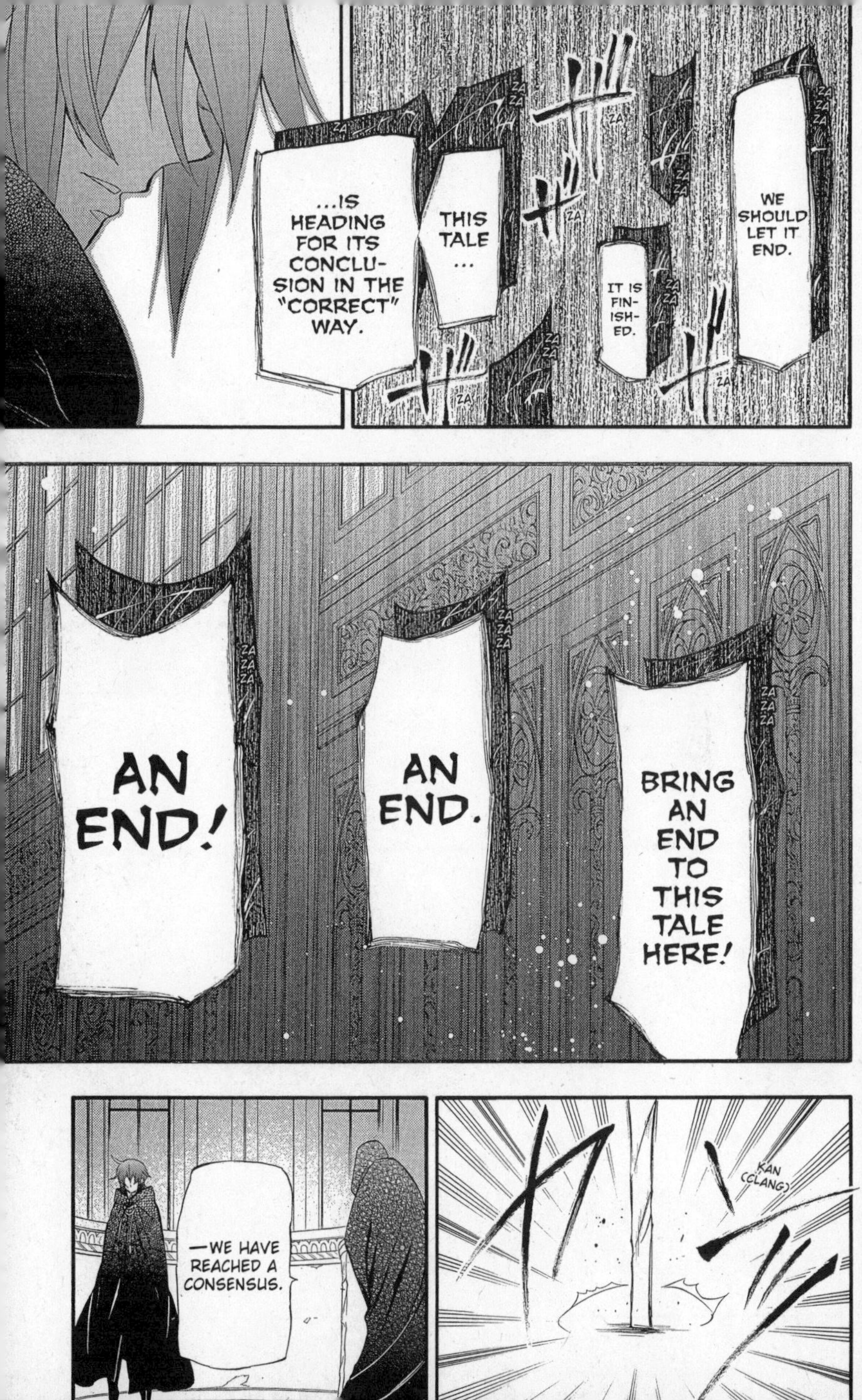
ZA ZA ZA
WE SHOULD LET IT END.
ZA
IT IS FIN-ISH-ED.
ZA ZA
ZA ZA ZA
THIS TALE ...
...IS HEADING FOR ITS CONCLU-SION IN THE "CORRECT" WAY.
ZA
ZA ZA
ZA
ZA ZA ZA
BRING AN END TO THIS TALE HERE!
ZA ZA ZA
AN END.
ZA ZA ZA
AN END!
KAN (CLANG)
—WE HAVE REACHED A CONSENSUS.

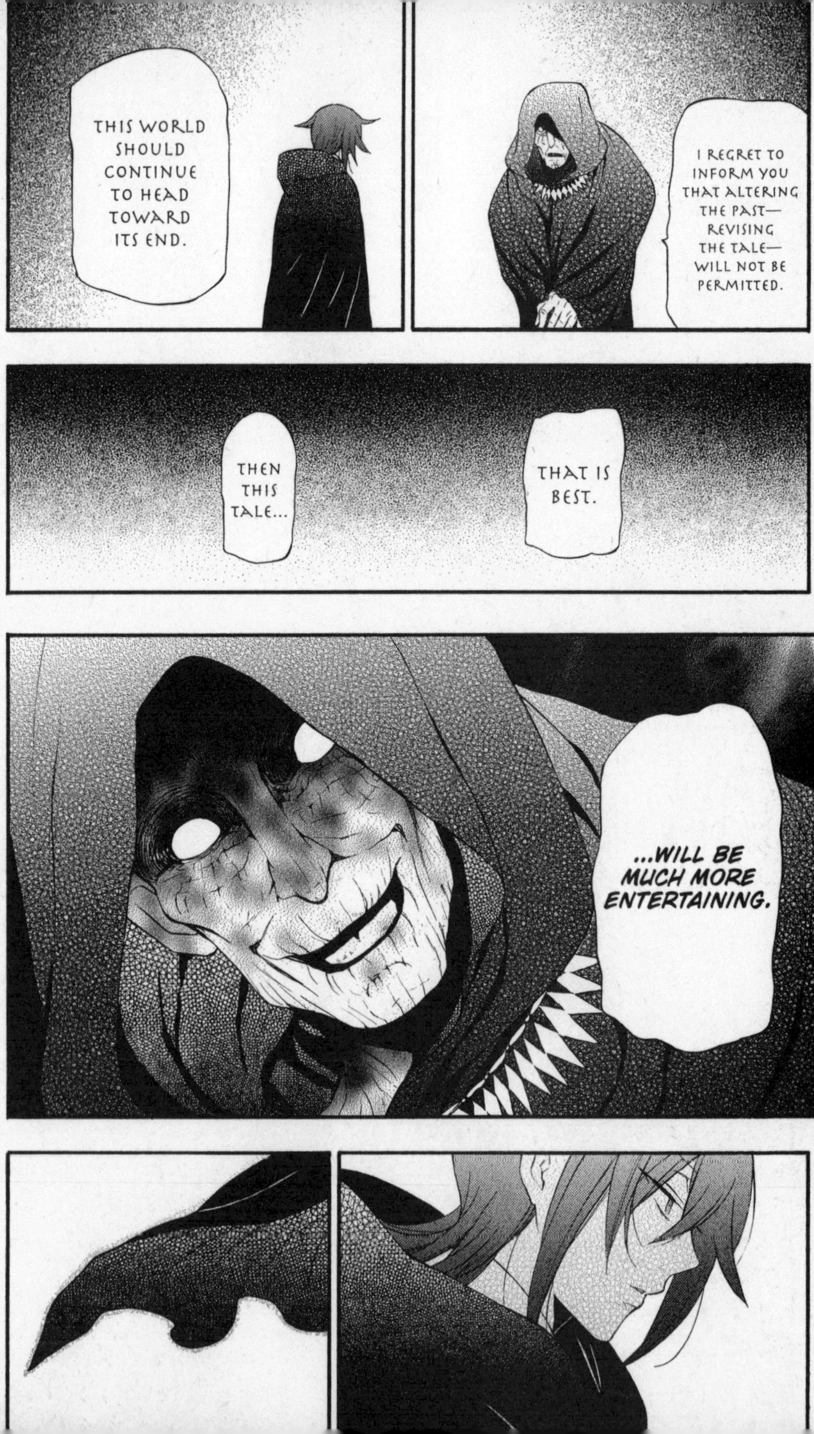
I REGRET TO INFORM YOU THAT ALTERING THE PAST—REVISING THE TALE—WILL NOT BE PERMITTED.
THIS WORLD SHOULD CONTINUE TO HEAD TOWARD ITS END.
THAT IS BEST.
THEN THIS TALE...
...WILL BE MUCH MORE ENTERTAINING.

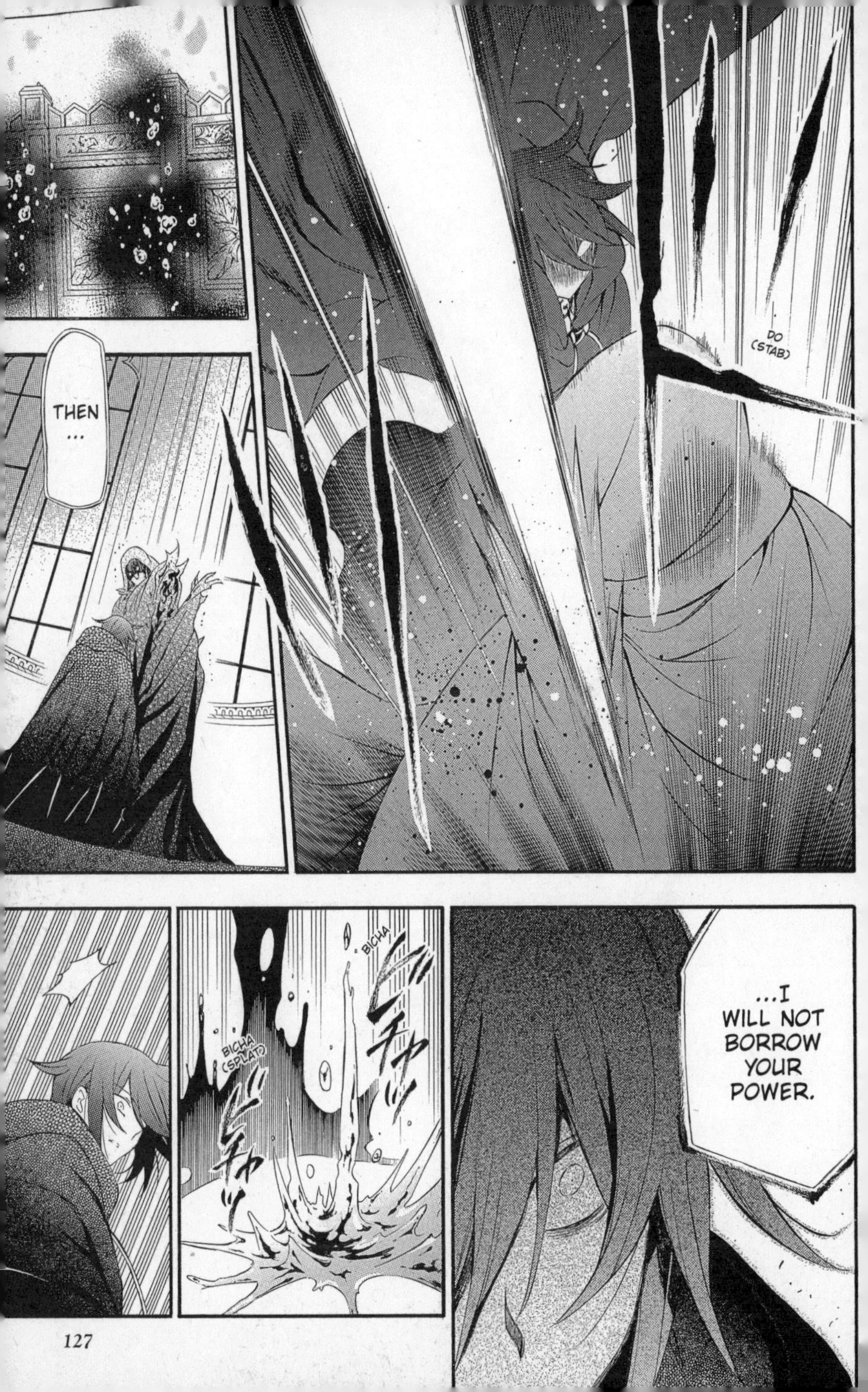
DO (STAB)
THEN ...
...I WILL NOT BORROW YOUR POWER.
BICHA
BICHA (SPLAT)

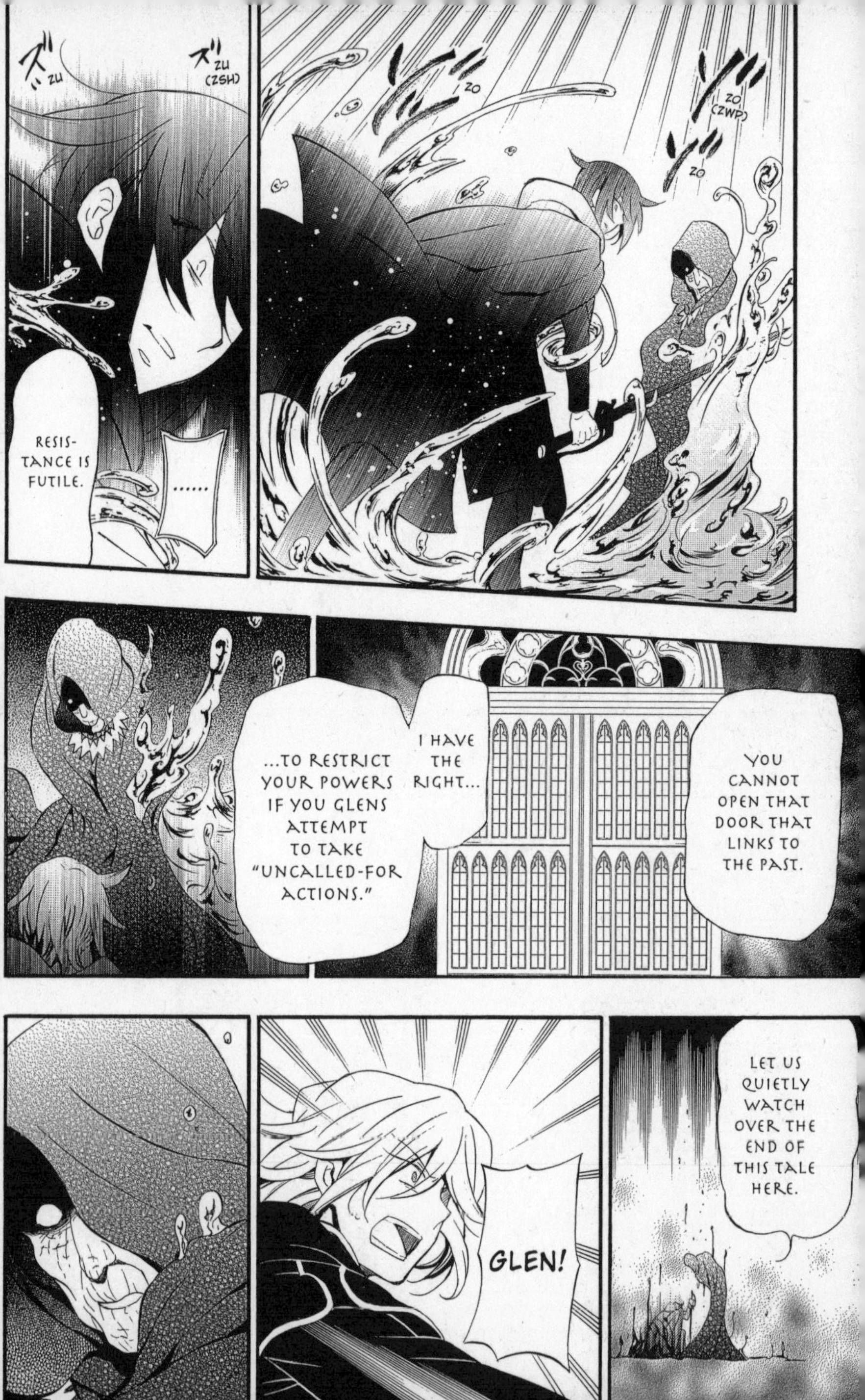
ゾ ZO (ZWP)
ゾ ZO
ゾ ZO
ズ ZU (ZSH)
ズ ZU
......
RESIS-TANCE IS FUTILE.
YOU CANNOT OPEN THAT DOOR THAT LINKS TO THE PAST.
I HAVE THE RIGHT...
...TO RESTRICT YOUR POWERS IF YOU GLENS ATTEMPT TO TAKE "UNCALLED-FOR ACTIONS."
LET US QUIETLY WATCH OVER THE END OF THIS TALE HERE.
GLEN!

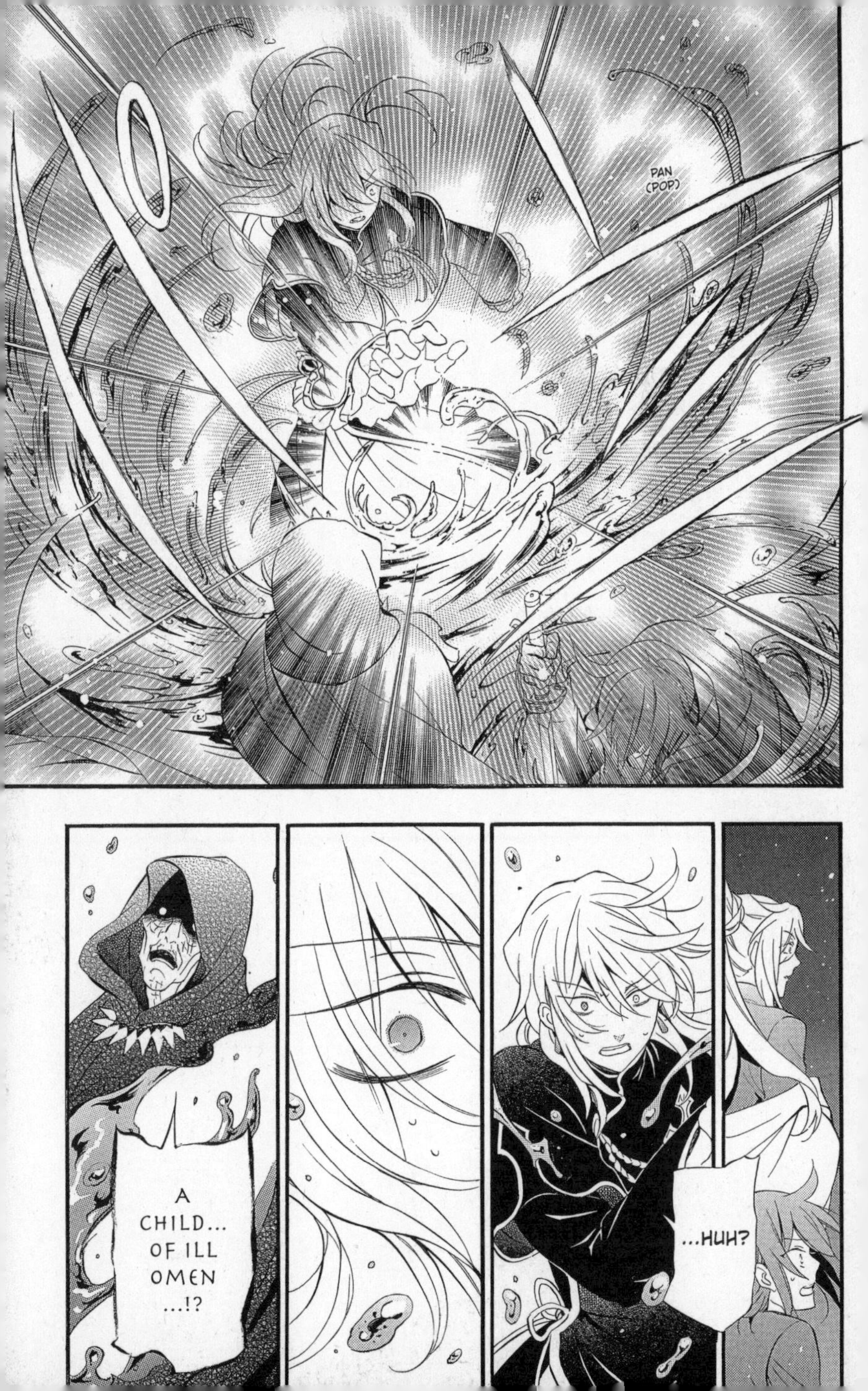
PAN (POP)
...HUH?
A CHILD... OF ILL OMEN ...!?

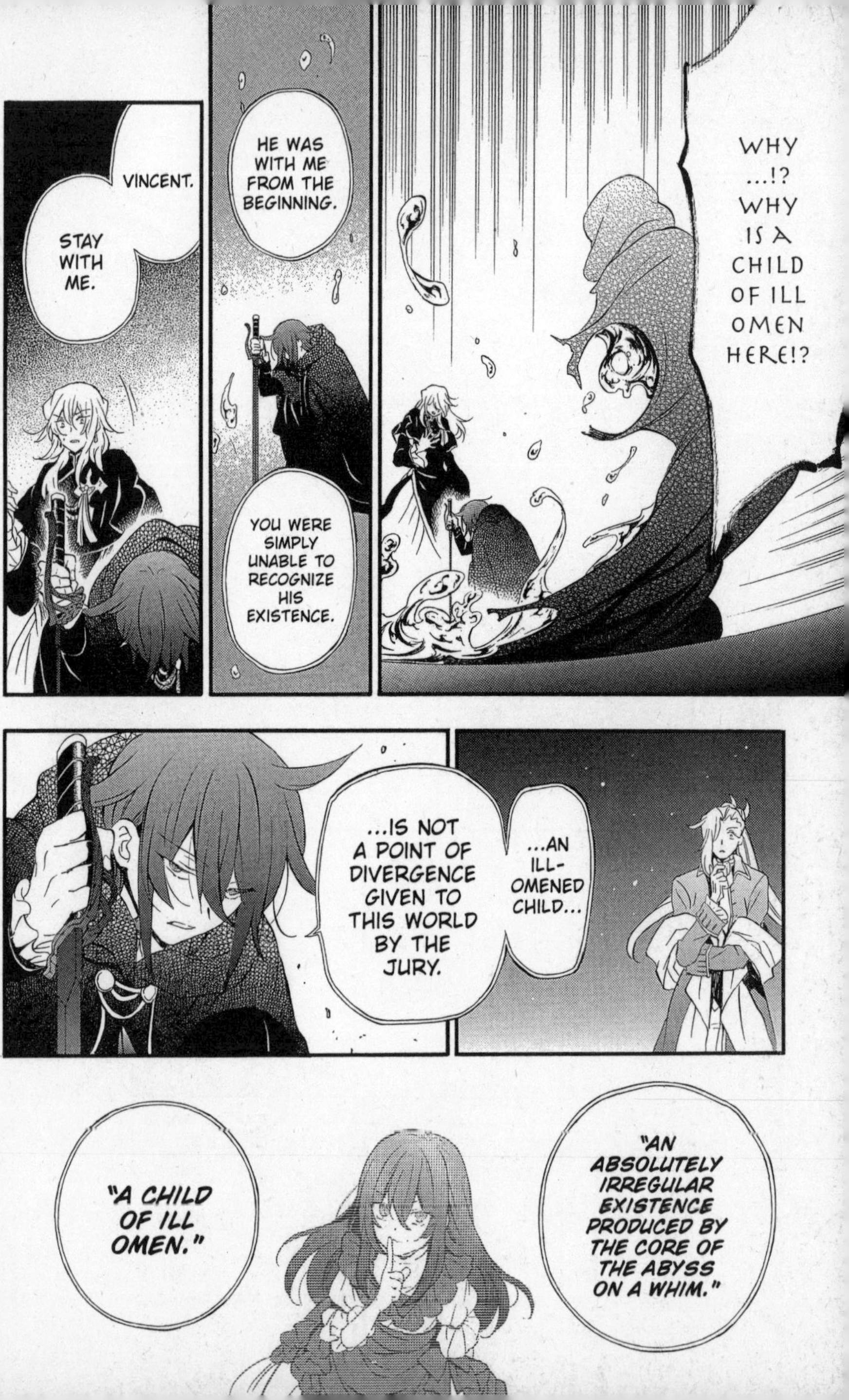
WHY ...!? WHY IS A CHILD OF ILL OMEN HERE!?
HE WAS WITH ME FROM THE BEGINNING.
YOU WERE SIMPLY UNABLE TO RECOGNIZE HIS EXISTENCE.
VINCENT.
STAY WITH ME.
...AN ILL-OMENED CHILD...
...IS NOT A POINT OF DIVERGENCE GIVEN TO THIS WORLD BY THE JURY.
"AN ABSOLUTELY IRREGULAR EXISTENCE PRODUCED BY THE CORE OF THE ABYSS ON A WHIM."
"A CHILD OF ILL OMEN."

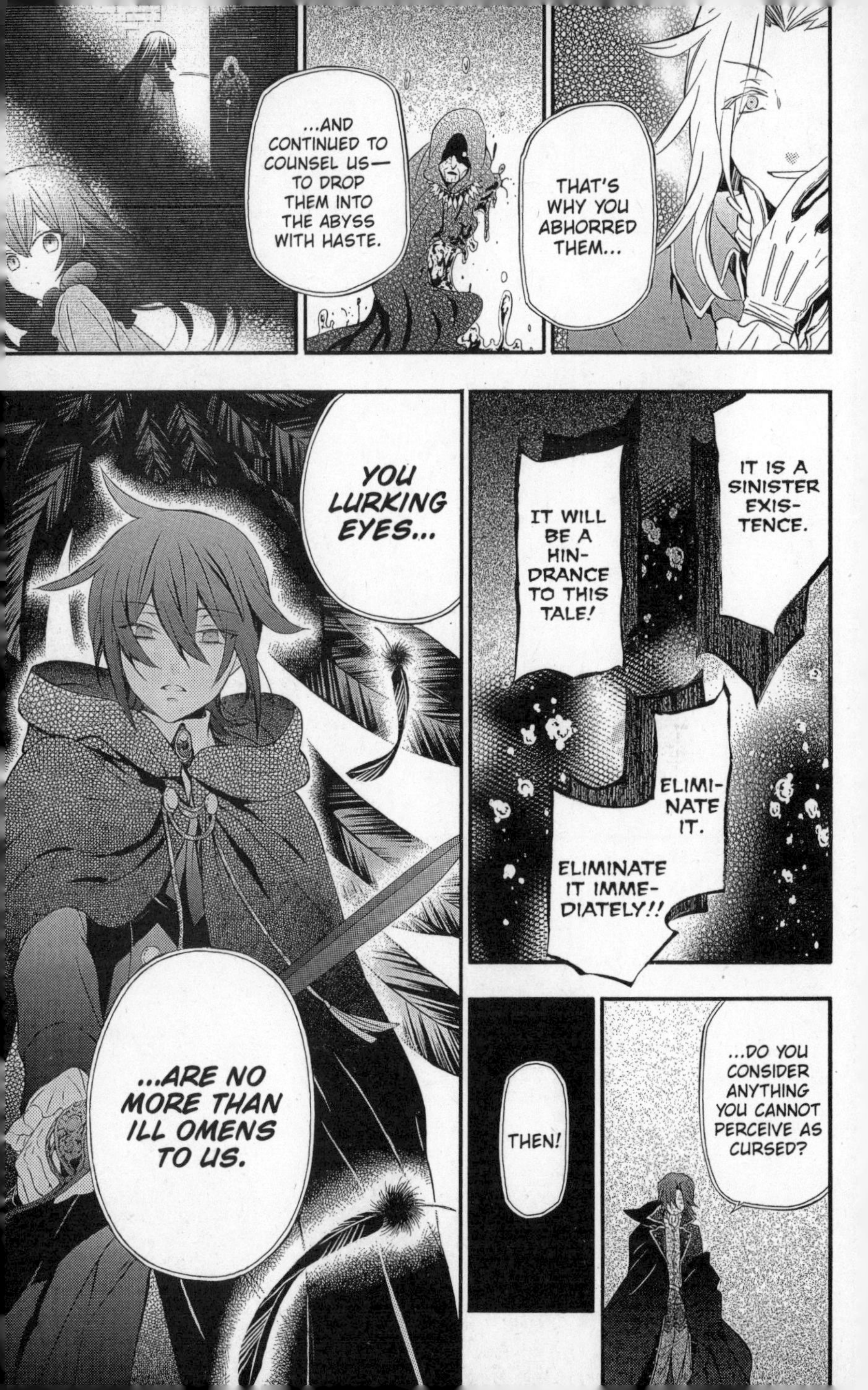
THAT'S WHY YOU ABHORRED THEM...
...AND CONTINUED TO COUNSEL US— TO DROP THEM INTO THE ABYSS WITH HASTE.
IT IS A SINISTER EXIS- TENCE.
IT WILL BE A HIN- DRANCE TO THIS TALE!
ELIMI- NATE IT.
ELIMINATE IT IMME- DIATELY!!
...DO YOU CONSIDER ANYTHING YOU CANNOT PERCEIVE AS CURSED?
THEN!
YOU LURKING EYES...
...ARE NO MORE THAN ILL OMENS TO US.

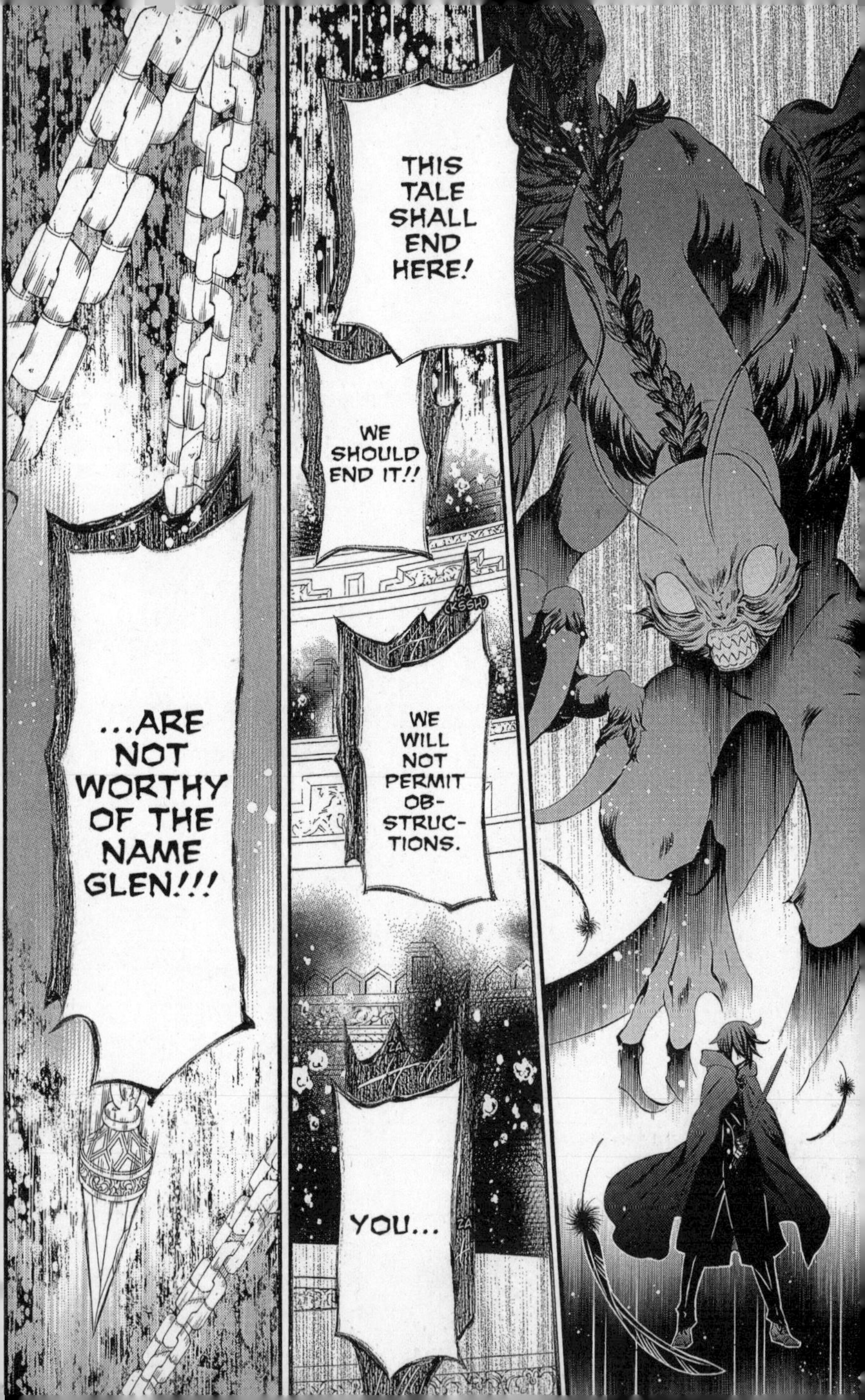
THIS TALE SHALL END HERE!
WE SHOULD END IT!!
ZA (KSSH)
WE WILL NOT PERMIT OB-STRUC-TIONS.
ZA
YOU...
ZA
...ARE NOT WORTHY OF THE NAME GLEN!!!

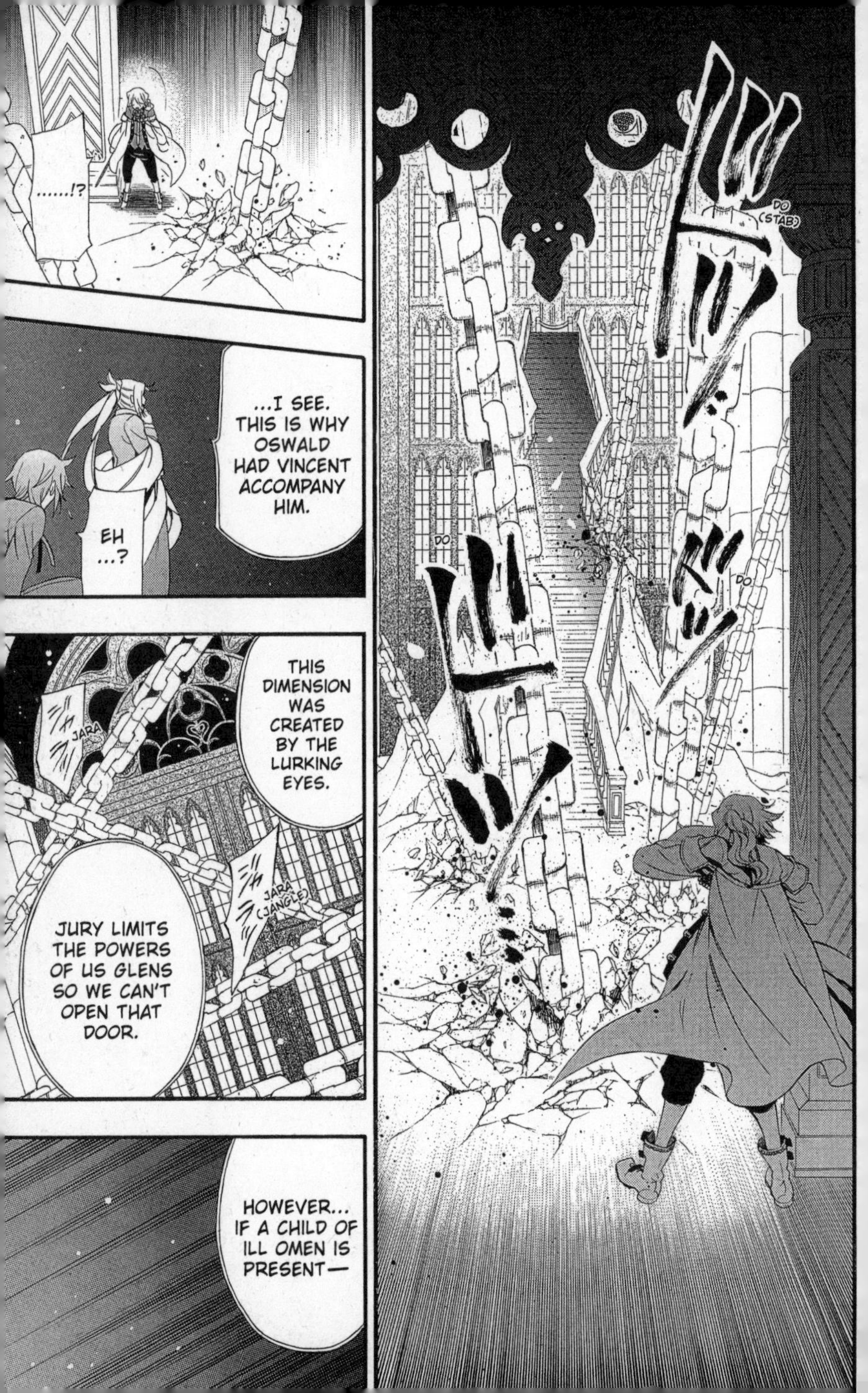
DO (STAB)
DO
DO
......!?
...I SEE. THIS IS WHY OSWALD HAD VINCENT ACCOMPANY HIM.
EH ...?
THIS DIMENSION WAS CREATED BY THE LURKING EYES.
JARA
JARA (JANGLE)
JURY LIMITS THE POWERS OF US GLENS SO WE CAN'T OPEN THAT DOOR.
HOWEVER... IF A CHILD OF ILL OMEN IS PRESENT—

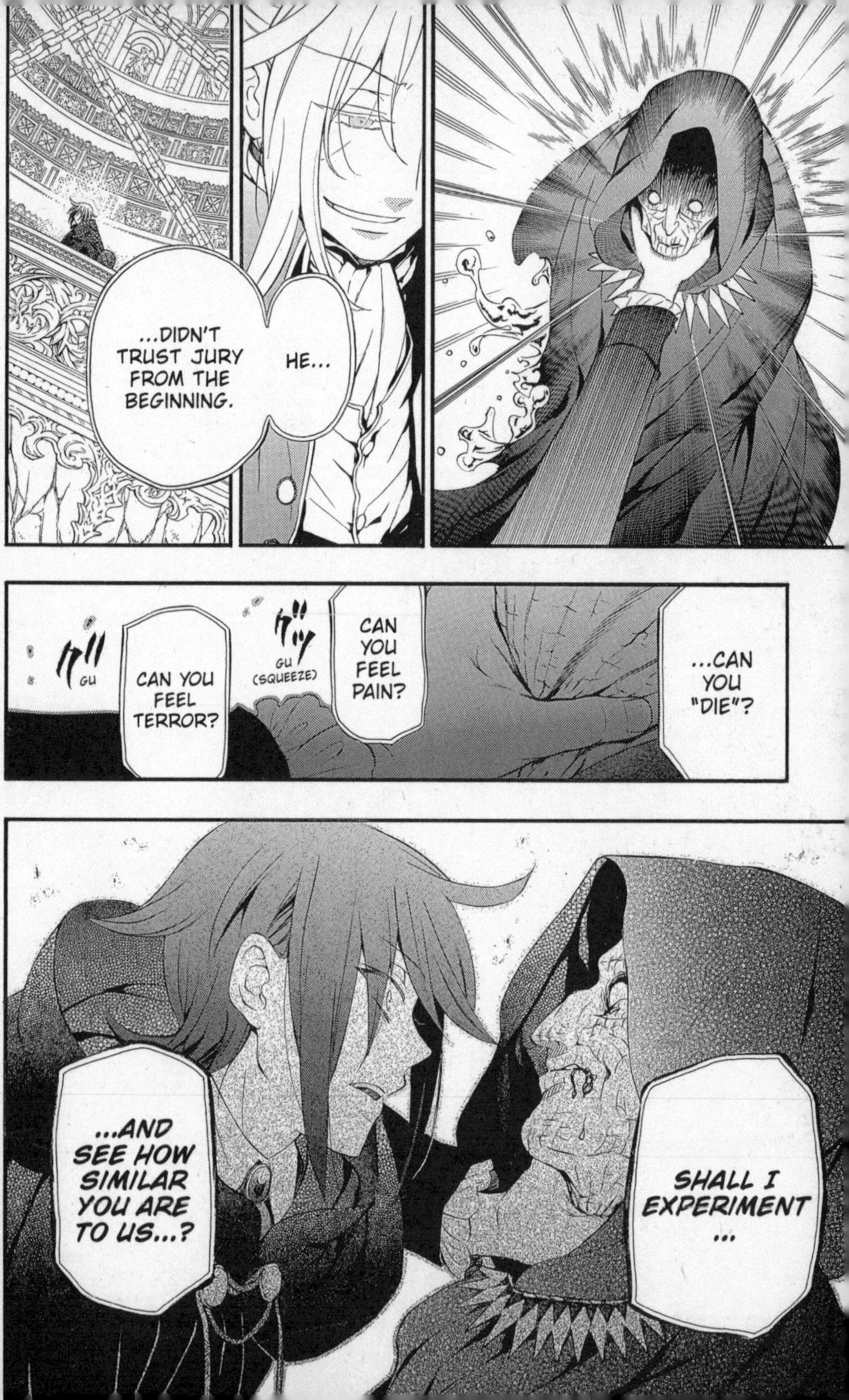
HE...
...DIDN'T TRUST JURY FROM THE BEGINNING.
...CAN YOU "DIE"?
CAN YOU FEEL PAIN?
GU (SQUEEZE)
CAN YOU FEEL TERROR?
GU
SHALL I EXPERIMENT ...
...AND SEE HOW SIMILAR YOU ARE TO US...?

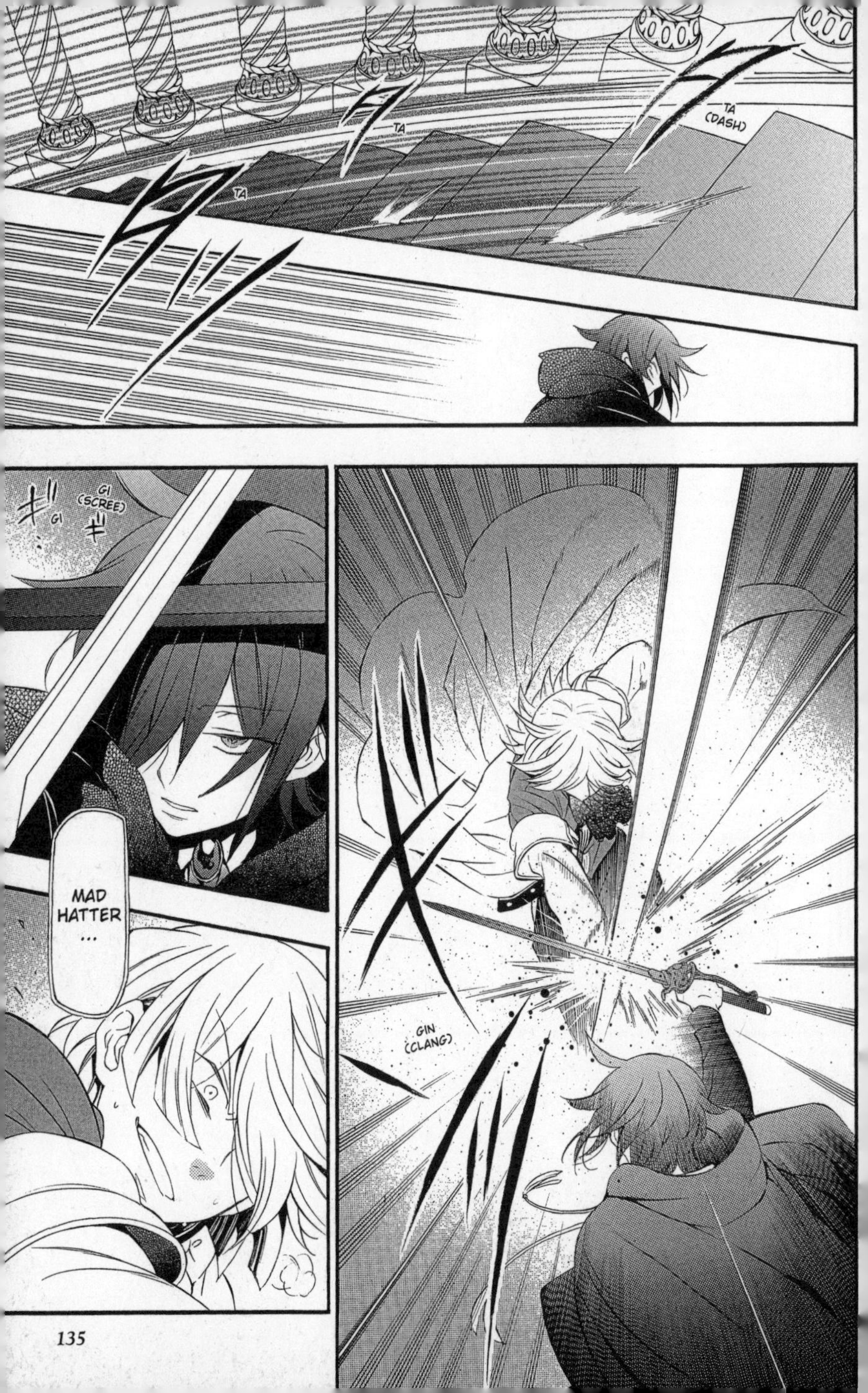
TA (DASH)
TA
TA
GIN (CLANG)
GI (SCREE)
GI
MAD HATTER ...

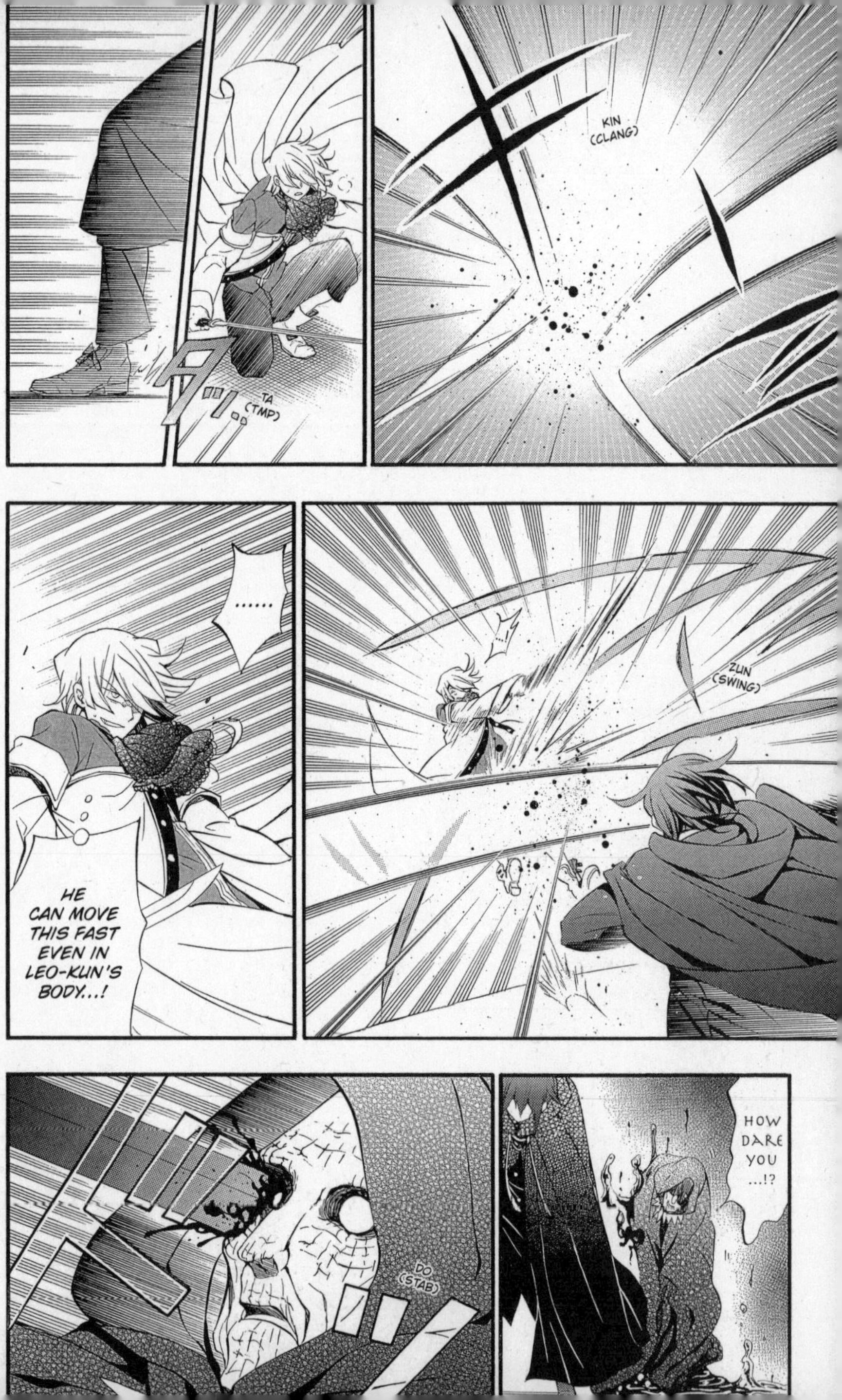
KIN (CLANG)
TA (TMP)
ZUN (SWING)
......
HE CAN MOVE THIS FAST EVEN IN LEO-KUN'S BODY...!
HOW DARE YOU ...!?
DO (STAB)

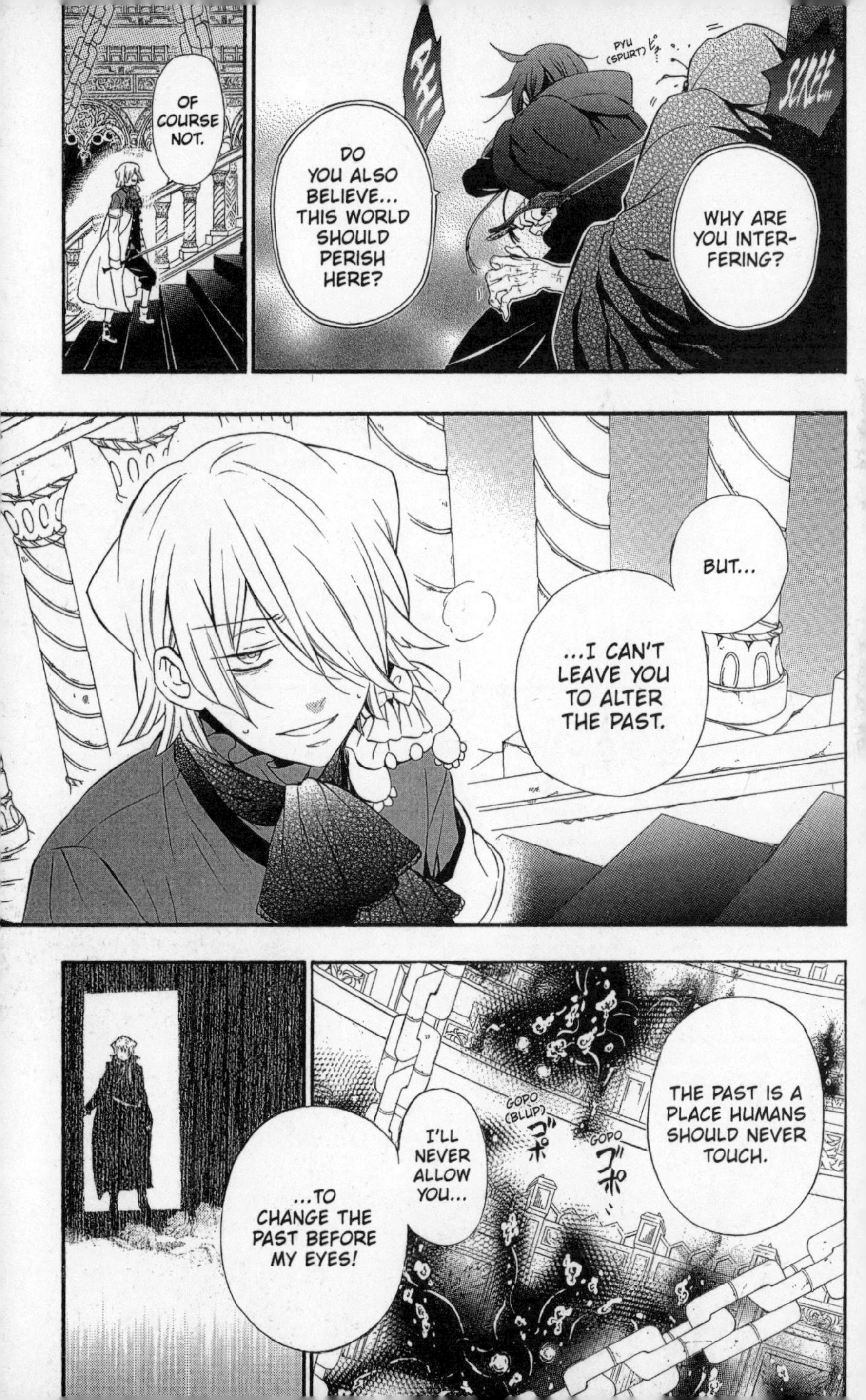
PYU (SPURT)
WHY ARE YOU INTER-FERING?
AH!
DO YOU ALSO BELIEVE... THIS WORLD SHOULD PERISH HERE?
OF COURSE NOT.
BUT...
...I CAN'T LEAVE YOU TO ALTER THE PAST.
THE PAST IS A PLACE HUMANS SHOULD NEVER TOUCH.
GOPO
GOPO (BLUP)
I'LL NEVER ALLOW YOU...
...TO CHANGE THE PAST BEFORE MY EYES!

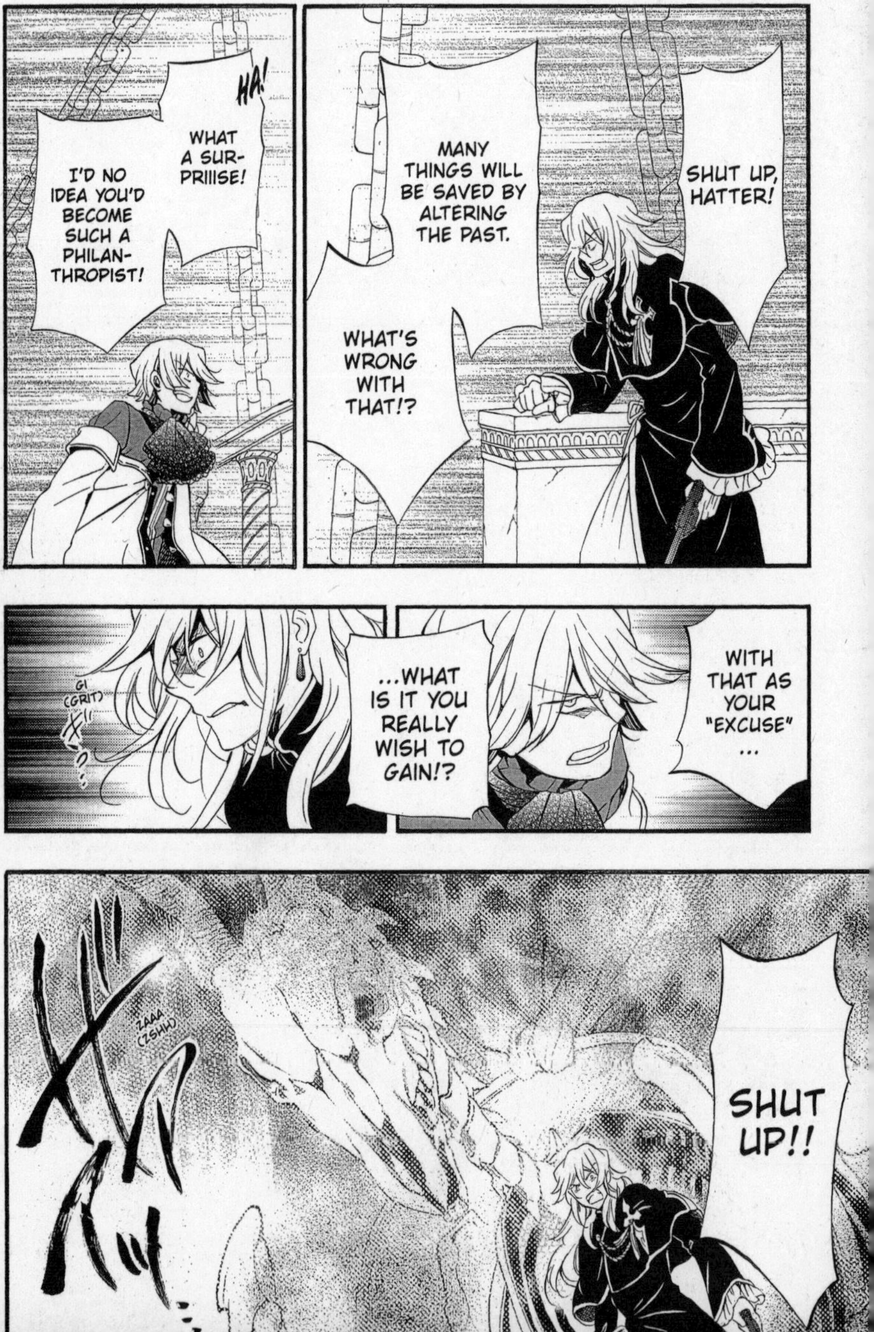
SHUT UP, HATTER!
MANY THINGS WILL BE SAVED BY ALTERING THE PAST.
WHAT'S WRONG WITH THAT!?
HA!
WHAT A SUR-PRIIISE!
I'D NO IDEA YOU'D BECOME SUCH A PHILAN-THROPIST!
WITH THAT AS YOUR "EXCUSE" ...
...WHAT IS IT YOU REALLY WISH TO GAIN!?
GI (GRIT)
SHUT UP!!
ZAAA (ZSHH)

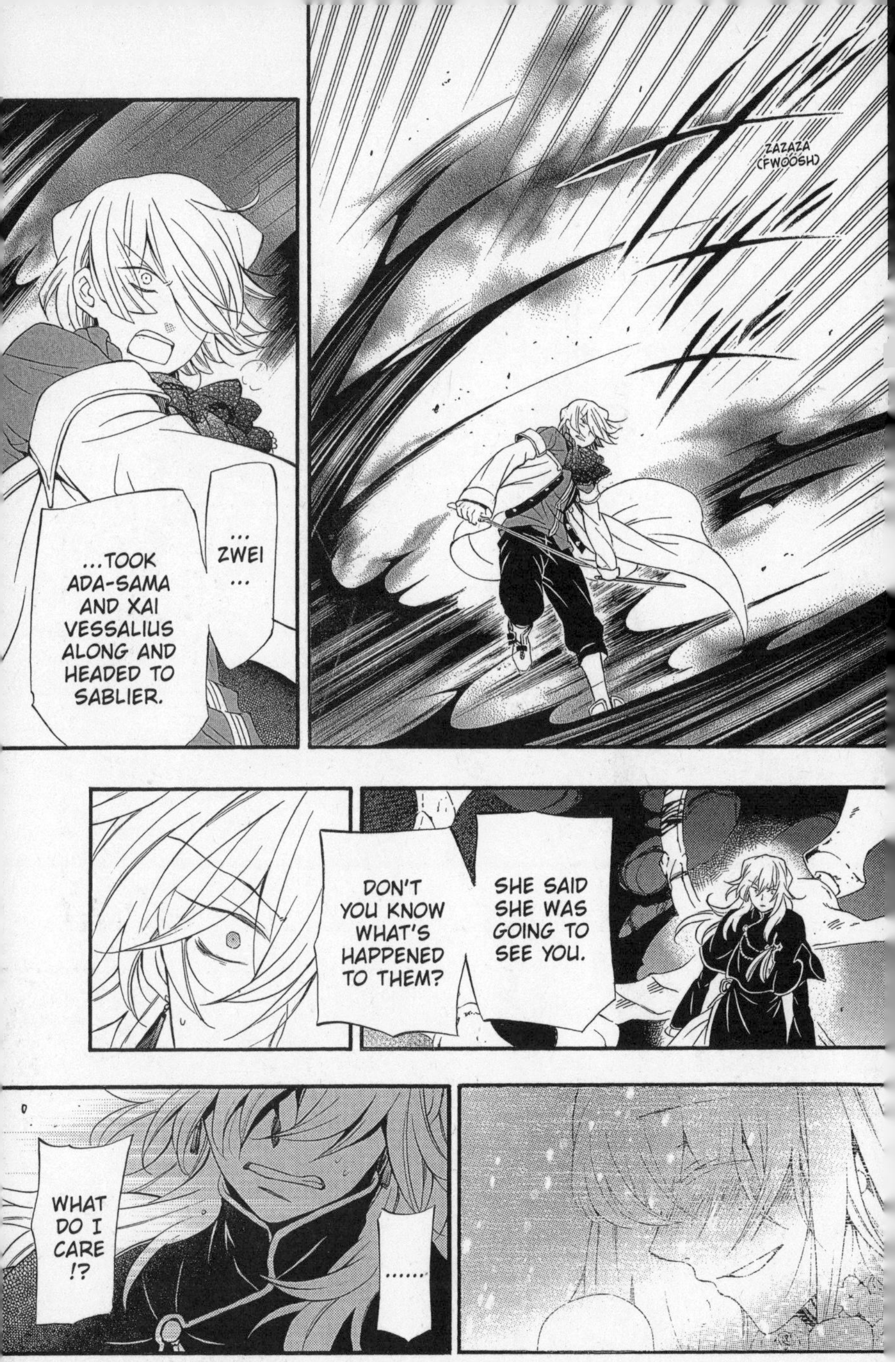
ZAZAZA (FWOOSH)
...ZWEI...
...TOOK ADA-SAMA AND XAI VESSALIUS ALONG AND HEADED TO SABLIER.
SHE SAID SHE WAS GOING TO SEE YOU.
DON'T YOU KNOW WHAT'S HAPPENED TO THEM?
......
WHAT DO I CARE !?

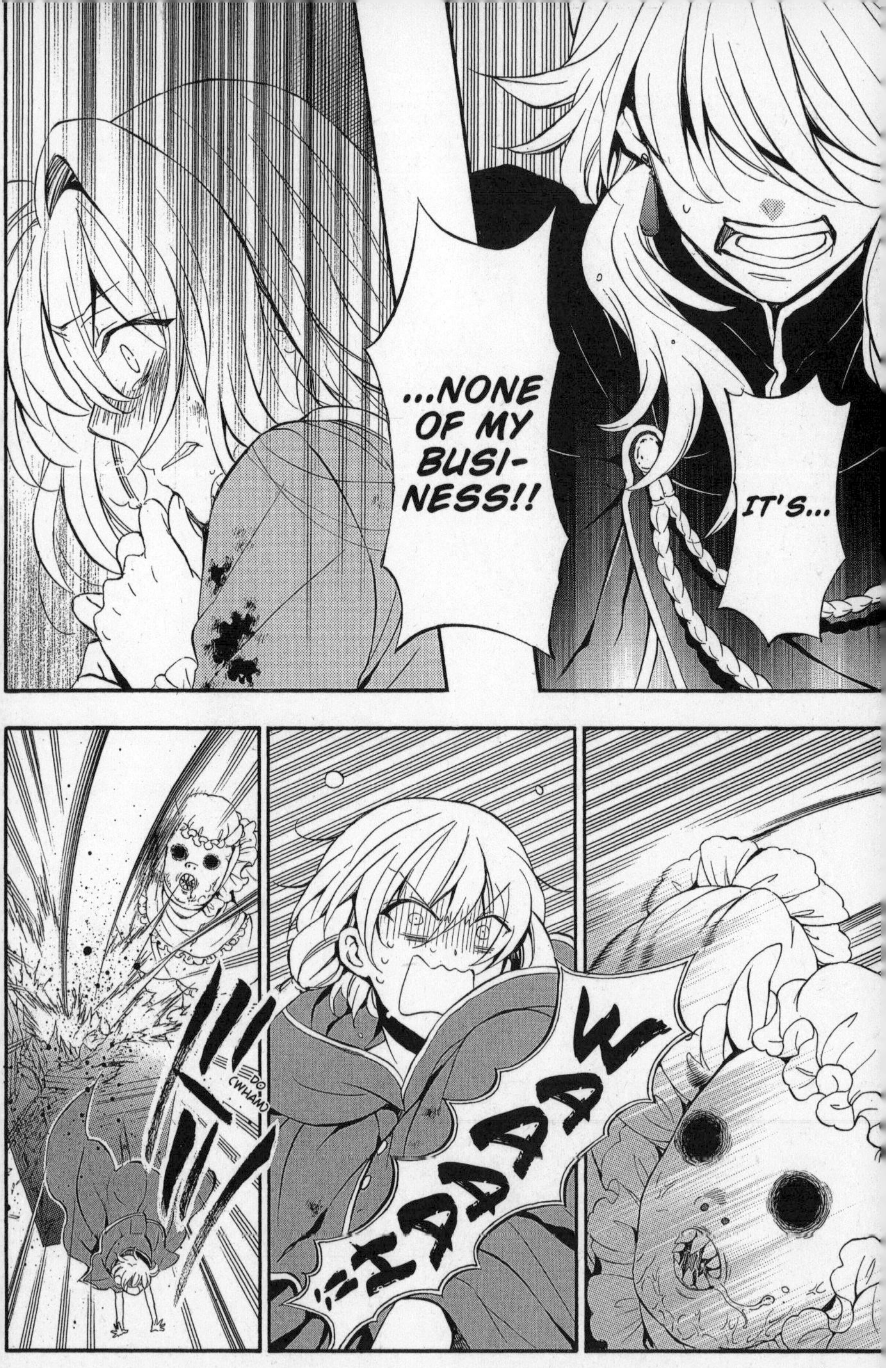
IT'S...
...NONE OF MY BUSI-NESS!!
WAAAAAH!!
DO (WHAM)

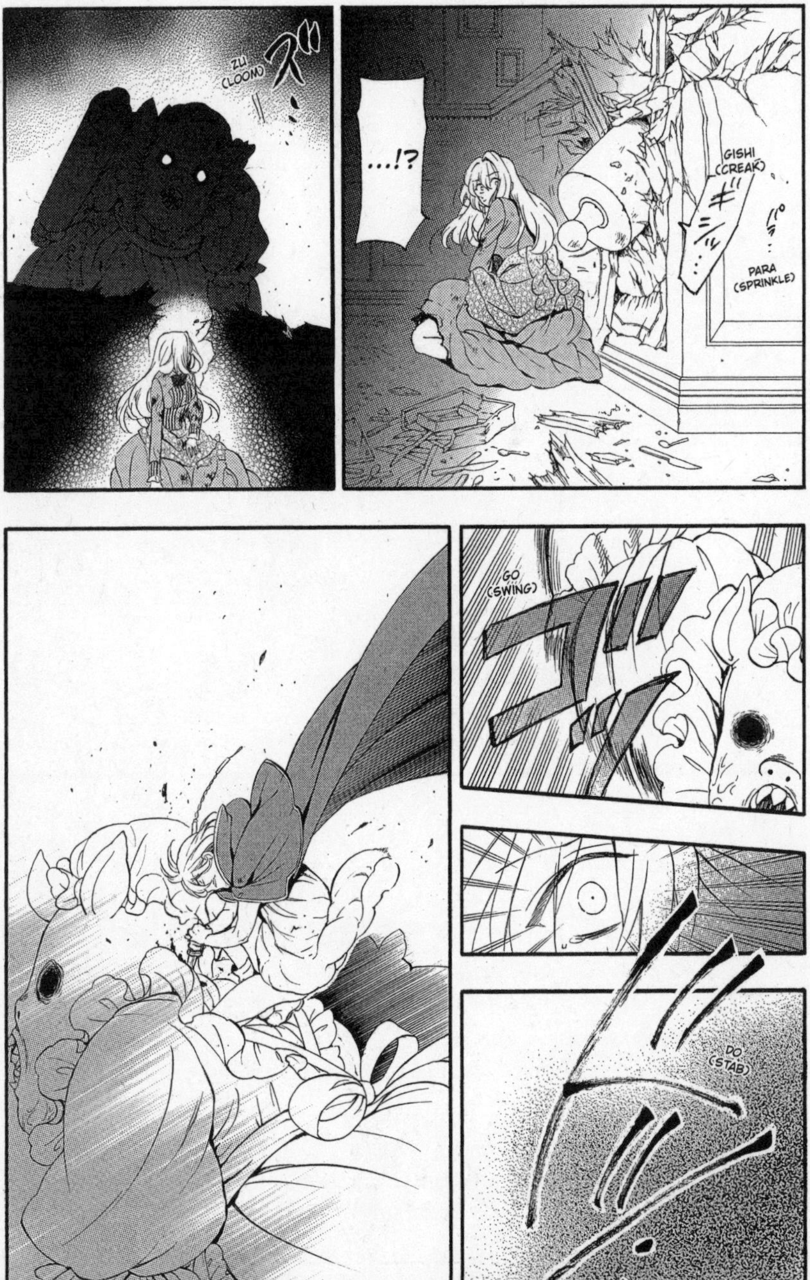
...!?
GISHI (CREAK)
PARA (SPRINKLE)
ZU (LOOM)
GO (SWING)
DO (STAB)

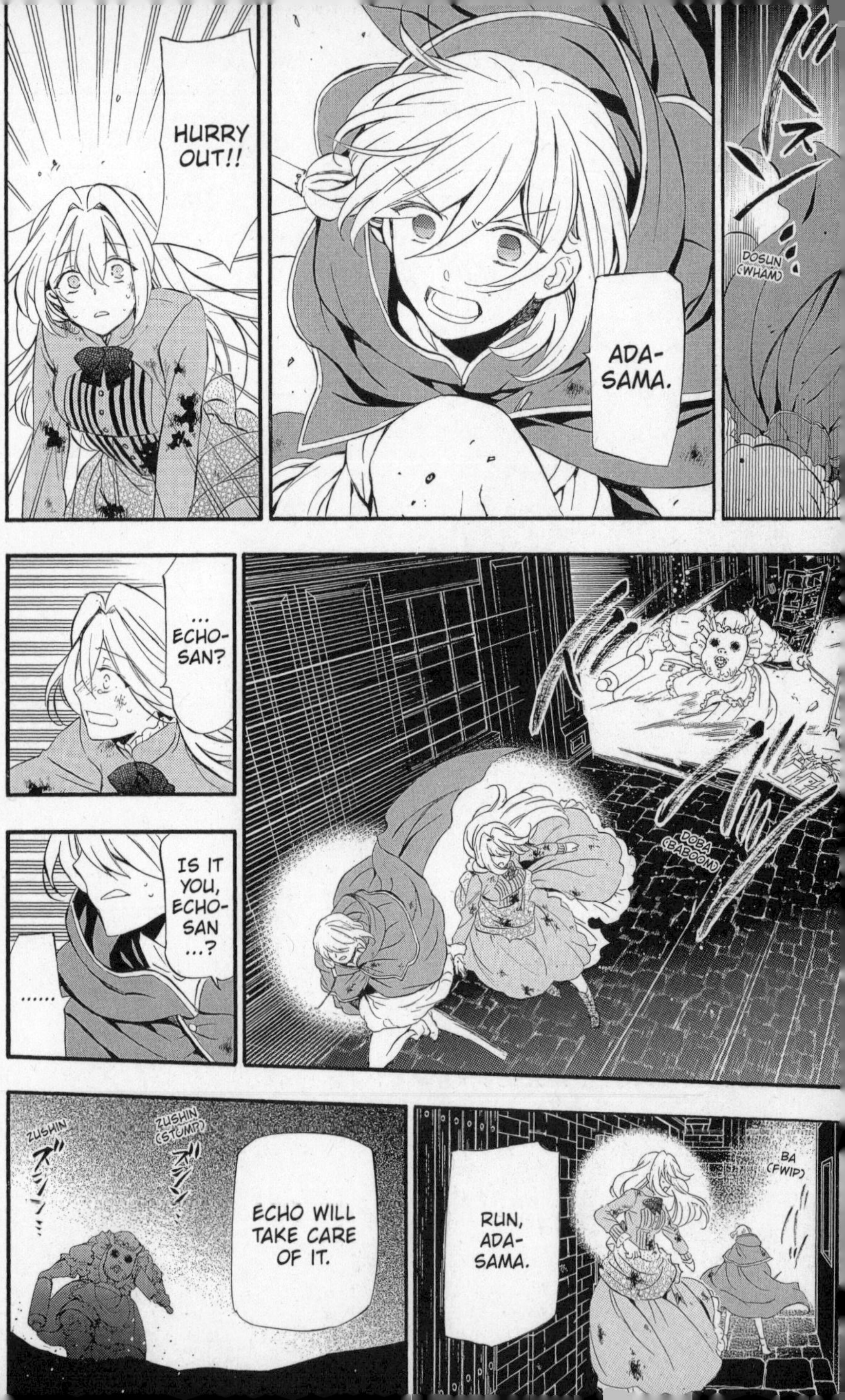
DOSUN (WHAM)
ADA-SAMA.
HURRY OUT!!
DOBA (BABOOM)
... ECHO-SAN?
IS IT YOU, ECHO-SAN ...?
......
BA (FWIP)
RUN, ADA-SAMA.
ZUSHIN (STOMP)
ZUSHIN
ECHO WILL TAKE CARE OF IT.

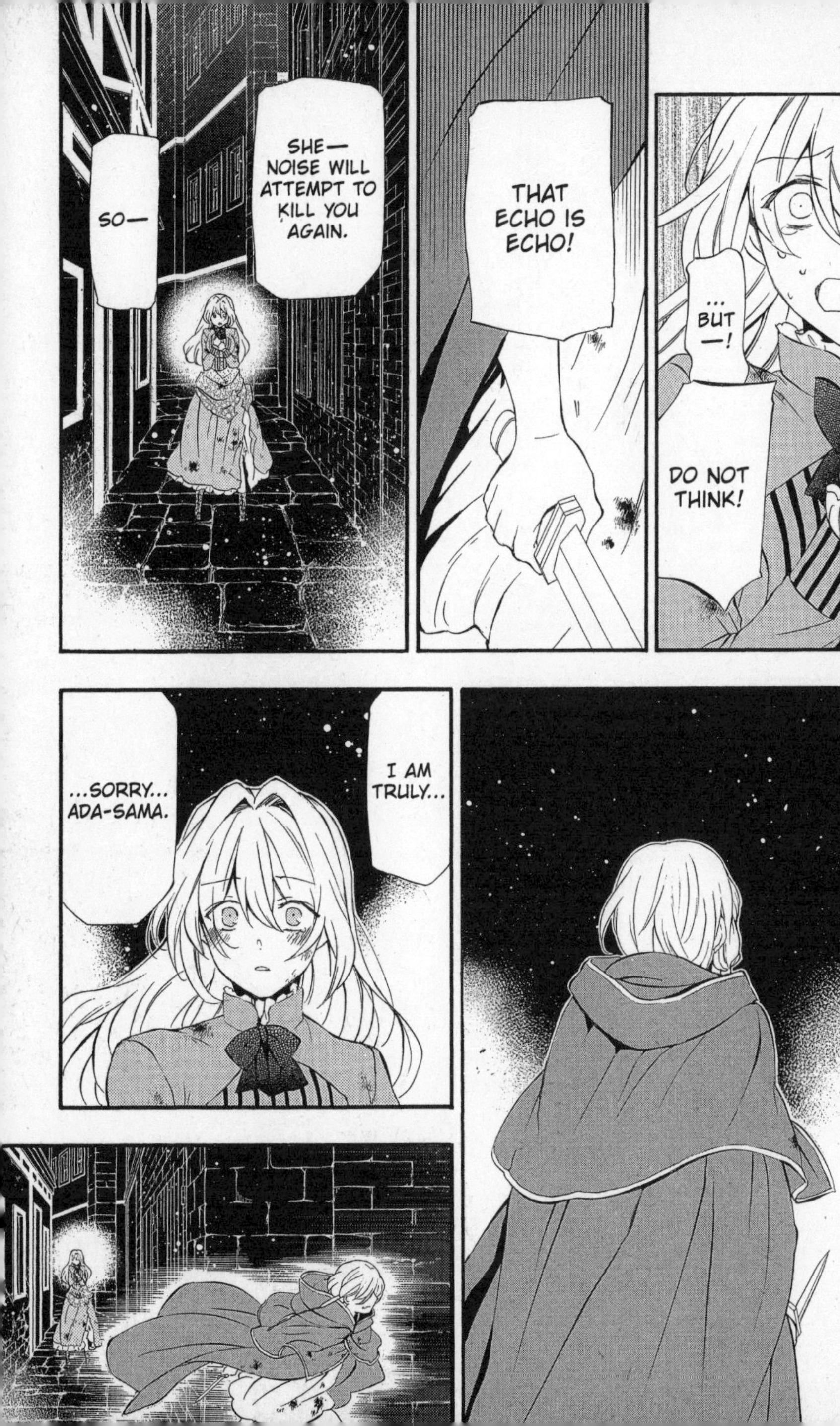
...BUT—!
DO NOT THINK!
THAT ECHO IS ECHO!
SHE—NOISE WILL ATTEMPT TO KILL YOU AGAIN.
SO—
I AM TRULY...
...SORRY... ADA-SAMA.

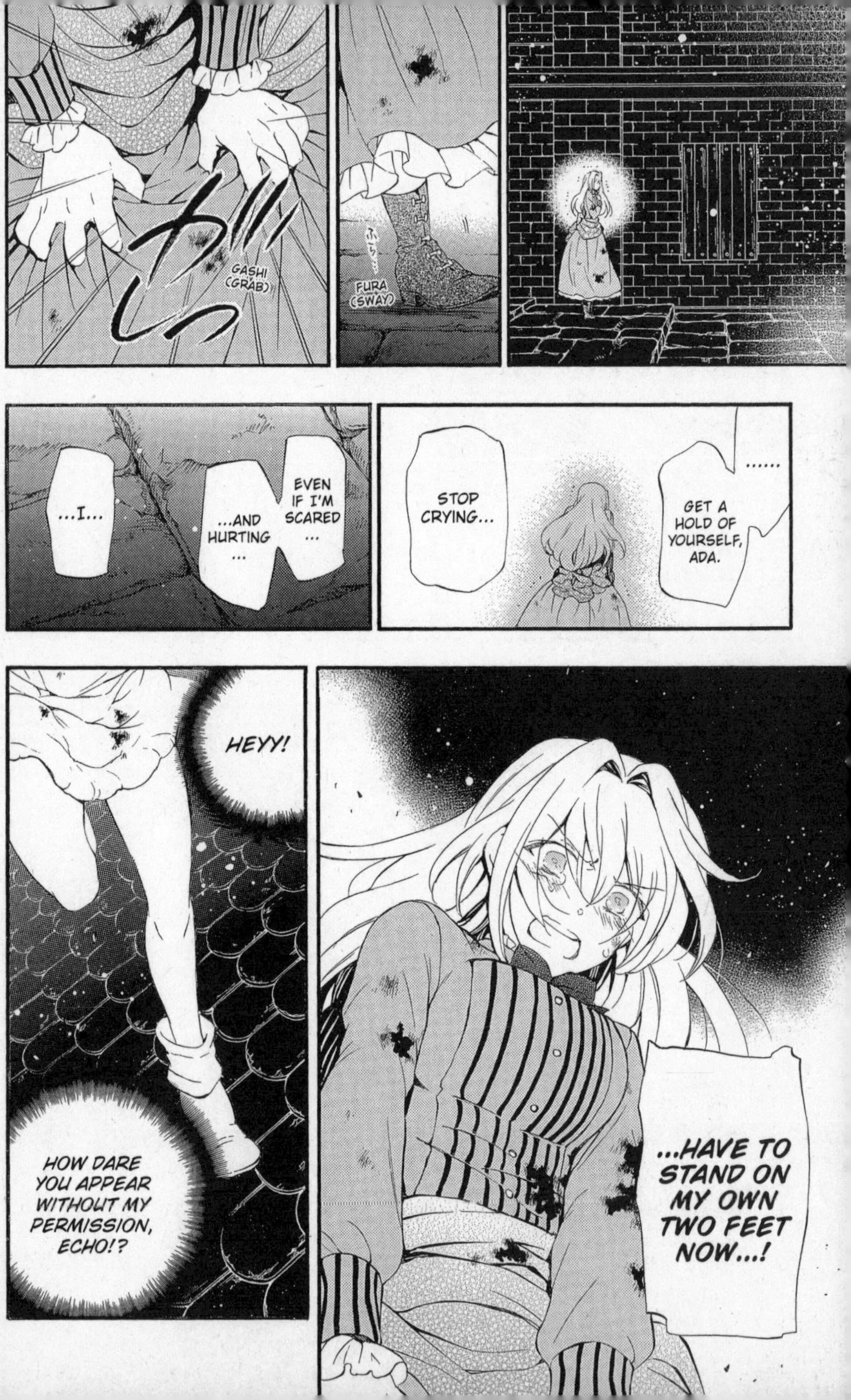
FURA (SWAY)
GASHI (GRAB)
......
GET A HOLD OF YOURSELF, ADA.
STOP CRYING...
EVEN IF I'M SCARED...
...AND HURTING...
...I...
...HAVE TO STAND ON MY OWN TWO FEET NOW...!
HEYY!
HOW DARE YOU APPEAR WITHOUT MY PERMISSION, ECHO!?

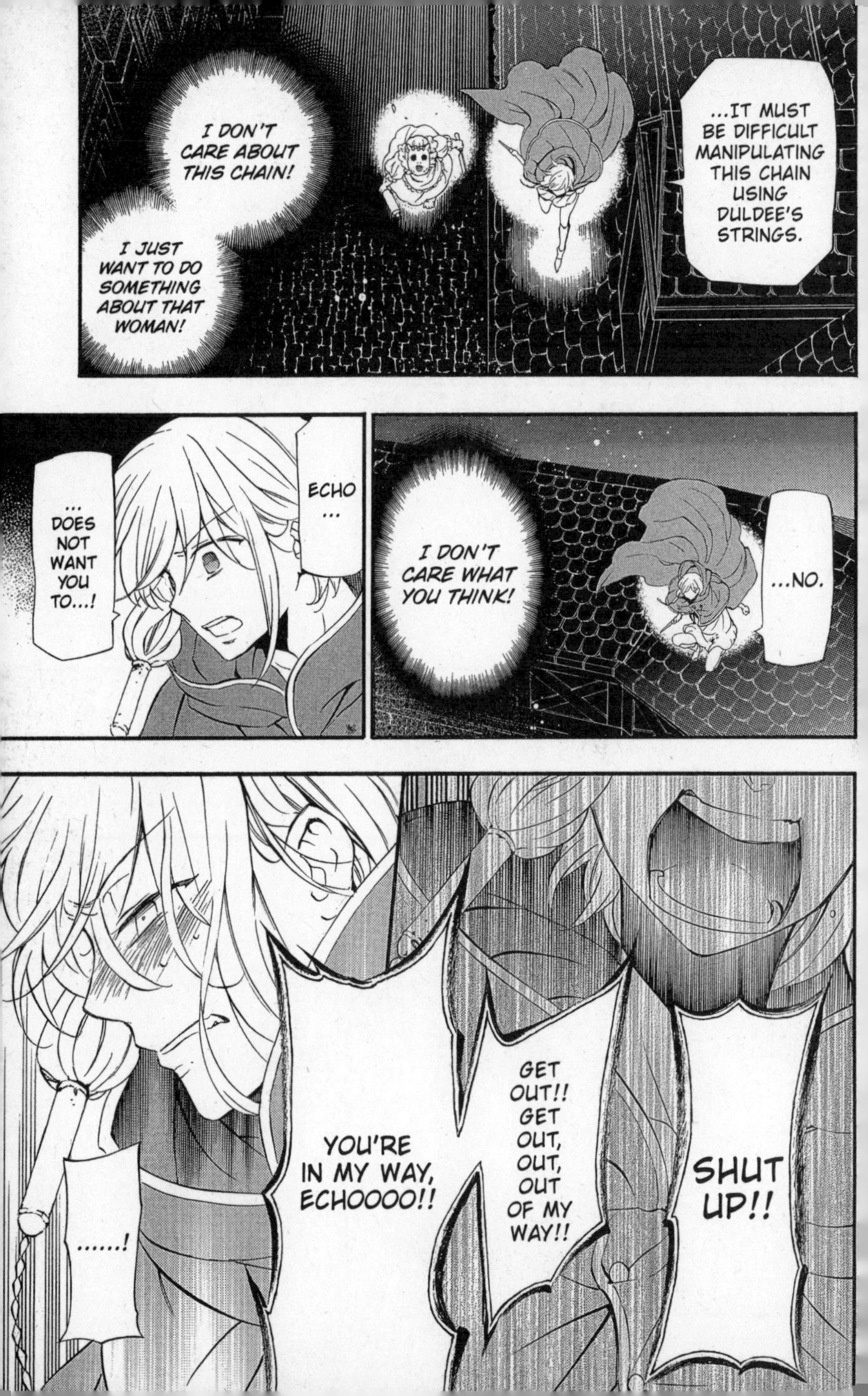
...IT MUST BE DIFFICULT MANIPULATING THIS CHAIN USING DULDEE'S STRINGS.
I DON'T CARE ABOUT THIS CHAIN!
I JUST WANT TO DO SOMETHING ABOUT THAT WOMAN!
...NO.
I DON'T CARE WHAT YOU THINK!
ECHO...
...DOES NOT WANT YOU TO...!
SHUT UP!!
GET OUT!! GET OUT, OUT, OUT OF MY WAY!!
YOU'RE IN MY WAY, ECHOOOO!!
......!

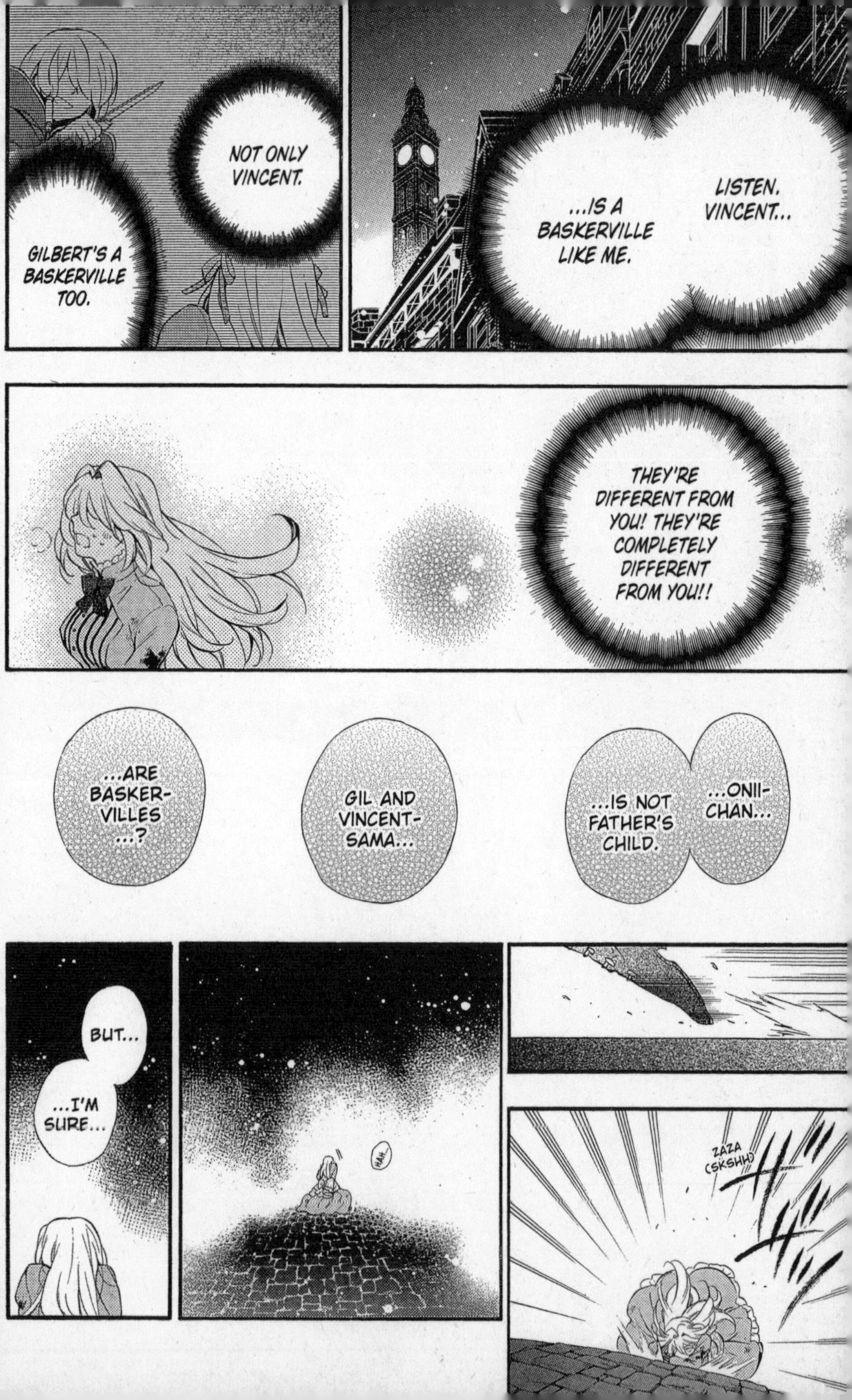
LISTEN. VINCENT...
...IS A BASKERVILLE LIKE ME.
NOT ONLY VINCENT.
GILBERT'S A BASKERVILLE TOO.
THEY'RE DIFFERENT FROM YOU! THEY'RE COMPLETELY DIFFERENT FROM YOU!!
...ONII-CHAN...
...IS NOT FATHER'S CHILD.
GIL AND VINCENT-SAMA...
...ARE BASKERVILLES ...?
ZAZA (SKSHH)
HAH...
BUT...
...I'M SURE...

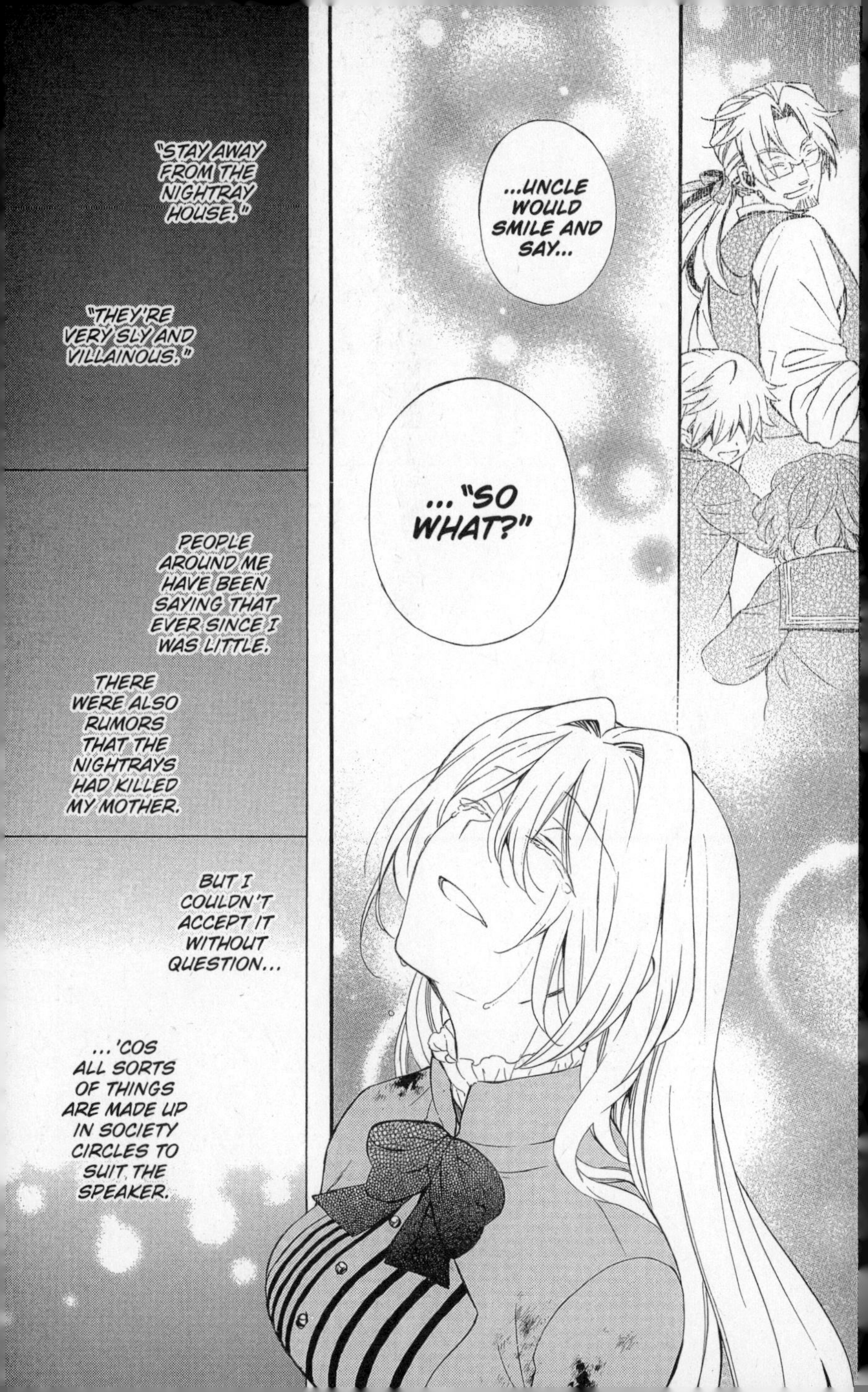
...UNCLE WOULD SMILE AND SAY...
..."SO WHAT?"
"STAY AWAY FROM THE NIGHTRAY HOUSE."
"THEY'RE VERY SLY AND VILLAINOUS."
PEOPLE AROUND ME HAVE BEEN SAYING THAT EVER SINCE I WAS LITTLE.
THERE WERE ALSO RUMORS THAT THE NIGHTRAYS HAD KILLED MY MOTHER.
BUT I COULDN'T ACCEPT IT WITHOUT QUESTION...
...'COS ALL SORTS OF THINGS ARE MADE UP IN SOCIETY CIRCLES TO SUIT THE SPEAKER.

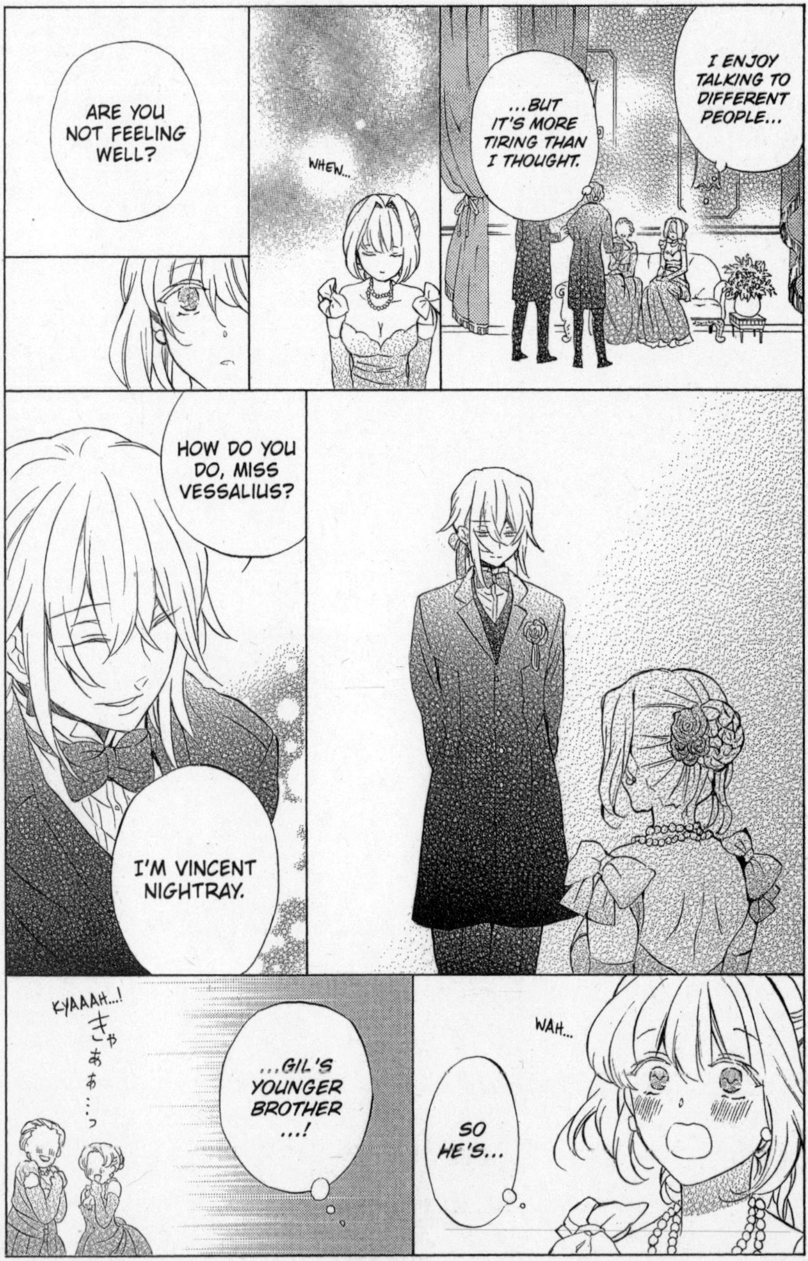
I ENJOY TALKING TO DIFFERENT PEOPLE...
...BUT IT'S MORE TIRING THAN I THOUGHT.
WHEW...
ARE YOU NOT FEELING WELL?
HOW DO YOU DO, MISS VESSALIUS?
I'M VINCENT NIGHTRAY.
WAH...
SO HE'S...
...GIL'S YOUNGER BROTHER ...!
KYAAAH...!
きゃあぁ…っ

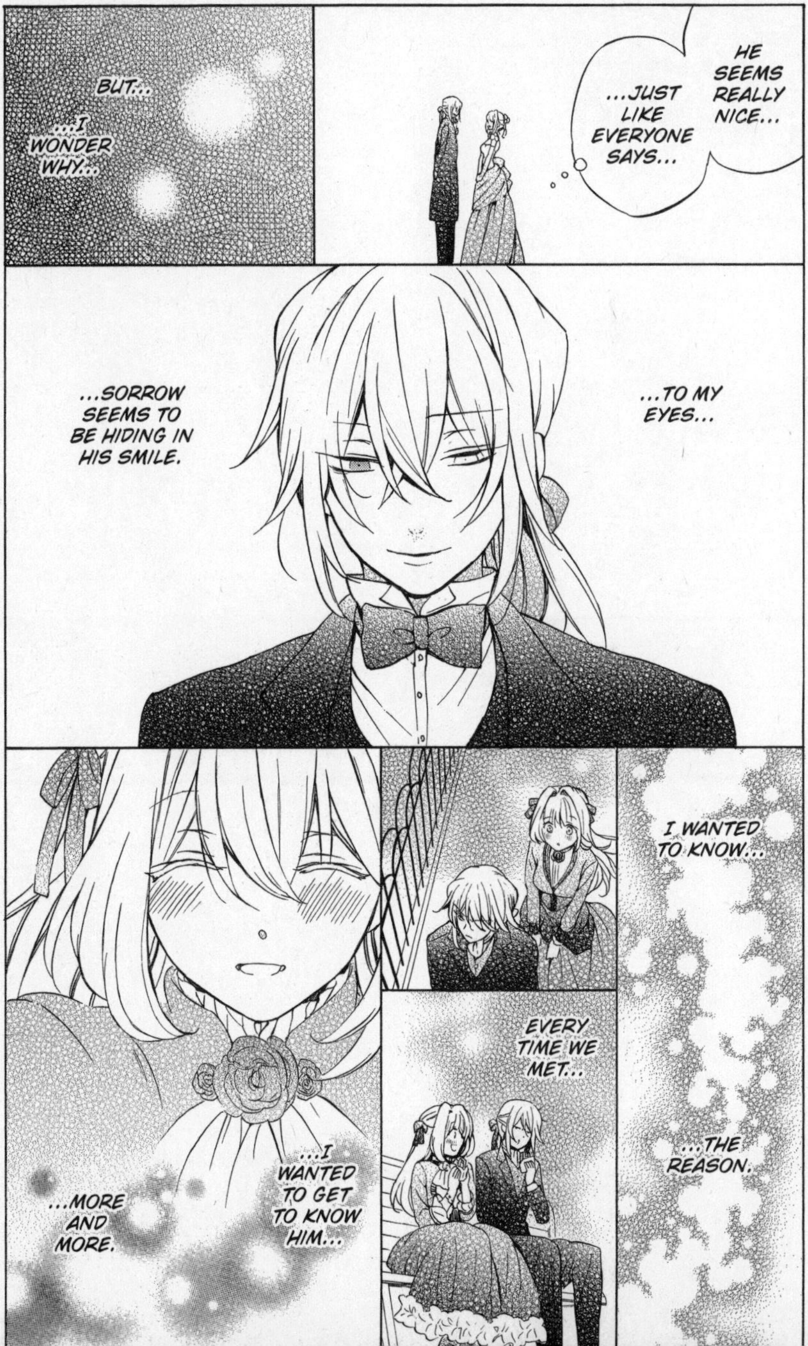
HE SEEMS REALLY NICE...
...JUST LIKE EVERYONE SAYS...
BUT...
...I WONDER WHY...
...TO MY EYES...
...SORROW SEEMS TO BE HIDING IN HIS SMILE.
I WANTED TO KNOW...
...THE REASON.
EVERY TIME WE MET...
...I WANTED TO GET TO KNOW HIM...
...MORE AND MORE.

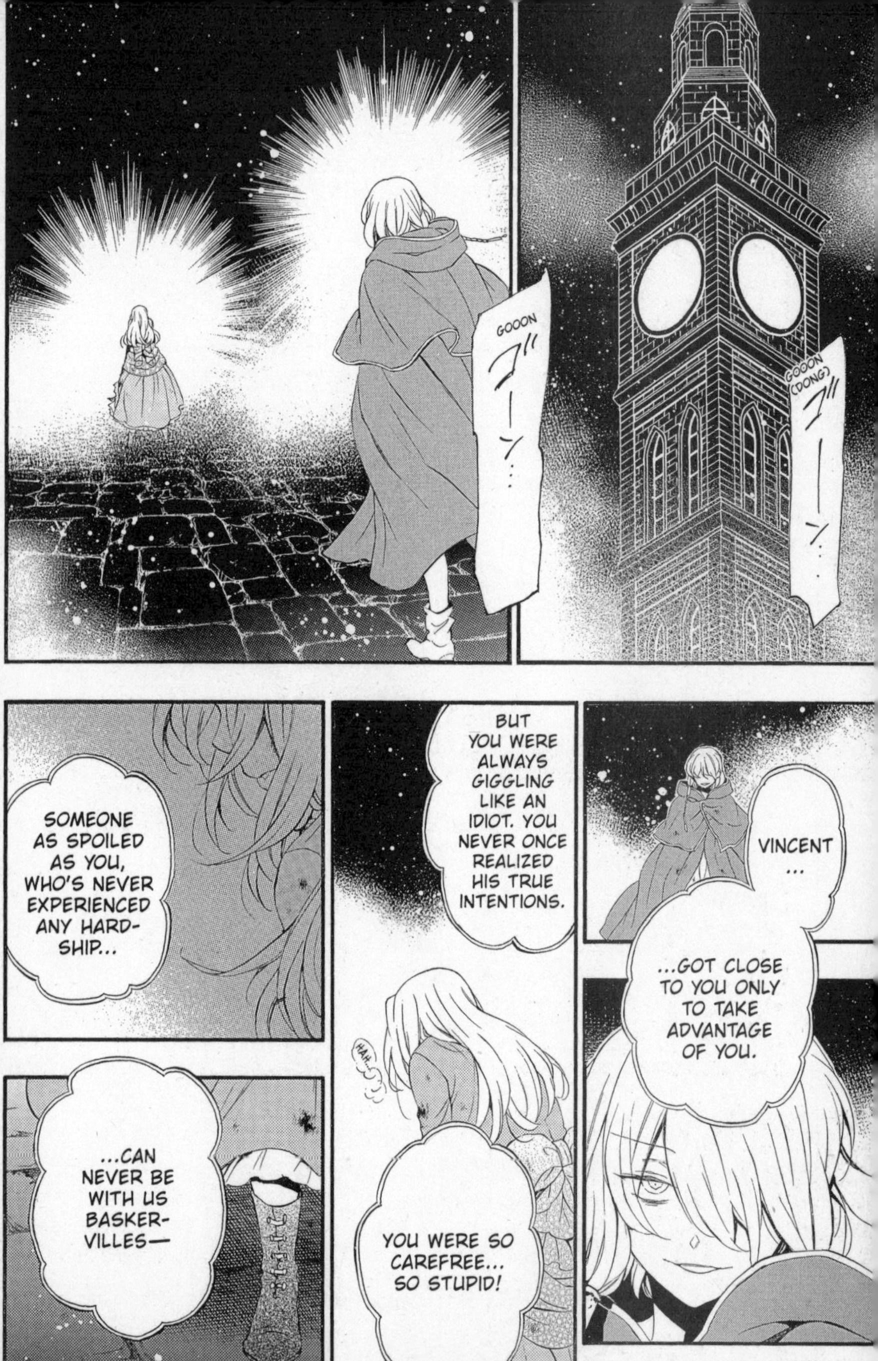
GOOON (DONG)
ゴーン…
GOOON
ゴーン…
VINCENT...
...GOT CLOSE TO YOU ONLY TO TAKE ADVANTAGE OF YOU.
BUT YOU WERE ALWAYS GIGGLING LIKE AN IDIOT. YOU NEVER ONCE REALIZED HIS TRUE INTENTIONS.
HAH...
YOU WERE SO CAREFREE... SO STUPID!
SOMEONE AS SPOILED AS YOU, WHO'S NEVER EXPERIENCED ANY HARDSHIP...
...CAN NEVER BE WITH US BASKERVILLES—

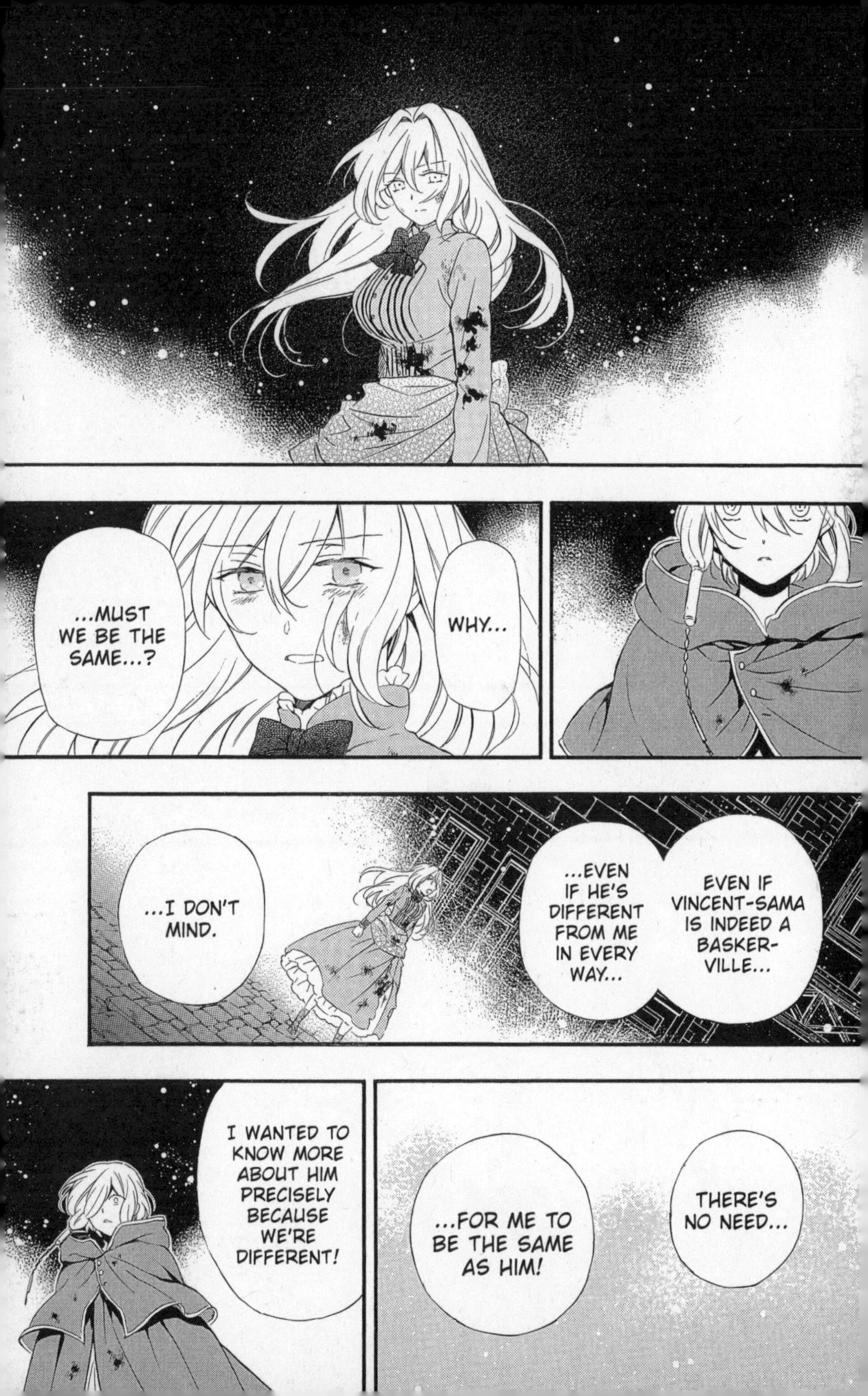
WHY...
...MUST WE BE THE SAME...?
EVEN IF VINCENT-SAMA IS INDEED A BASKER-VILLE...
...EVEN IF HE'S DIFFERENT FROM ME IN EVERY WAY...
...I DON'T MIND.
THERE'S NO NEED...
...FOR ME TO BE THE SAME AS HIM!
I WANTED TO KNOW MORE ABOUT HIM PRECISELY BECAUSE WE'RE DIFFERENT!

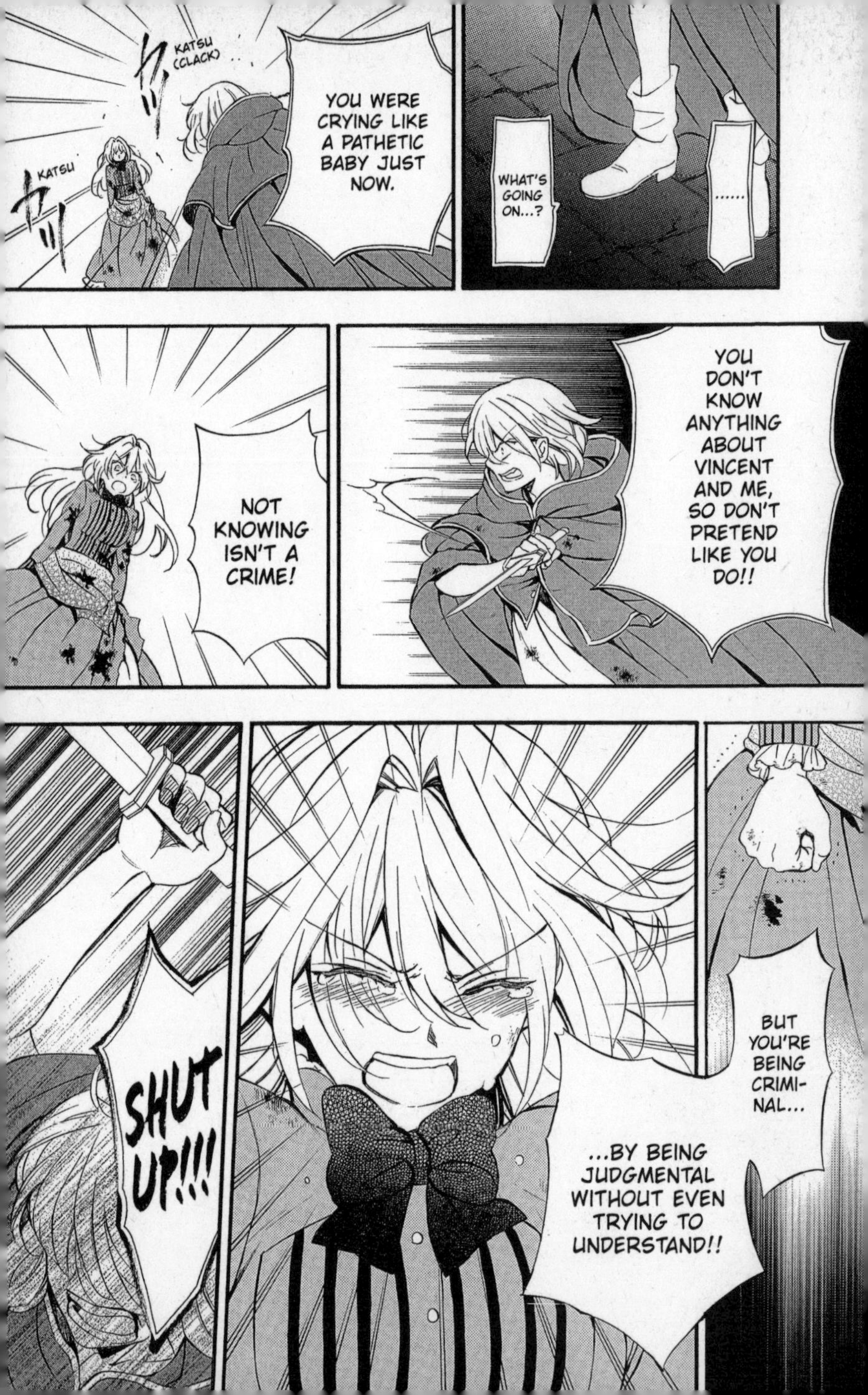

......
WHAT'S GOING ON...?
KATSU (CLACK)
YOU WERE CRYING LIKE A PATHETIC BABY JUST NOW.
KATSU
YOU DON'T KNOW ANYTHING ABOUT VINCENT AND ME, SO DON'T PRETEND LIKE YOU DO!!
NOT KNOWING ISN'T A CRIME!
BUT YOU'RE BEING CRIMI-NAL...
...BY BEING JUDGMENTAL WITHOUT EVEN TRYING TO UNDERSTAND!!
SHUT UP!!!

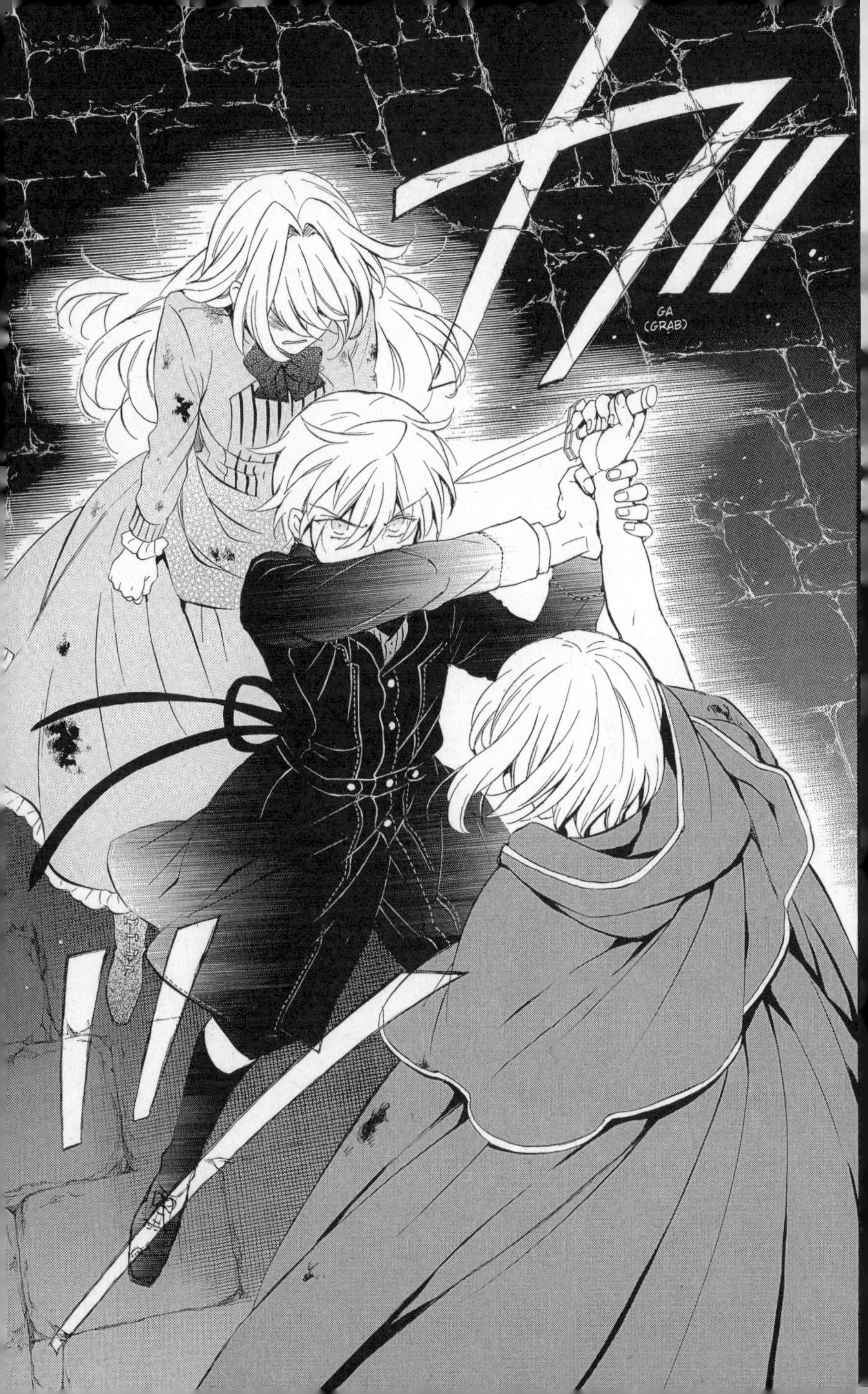
GA
(GRAB)

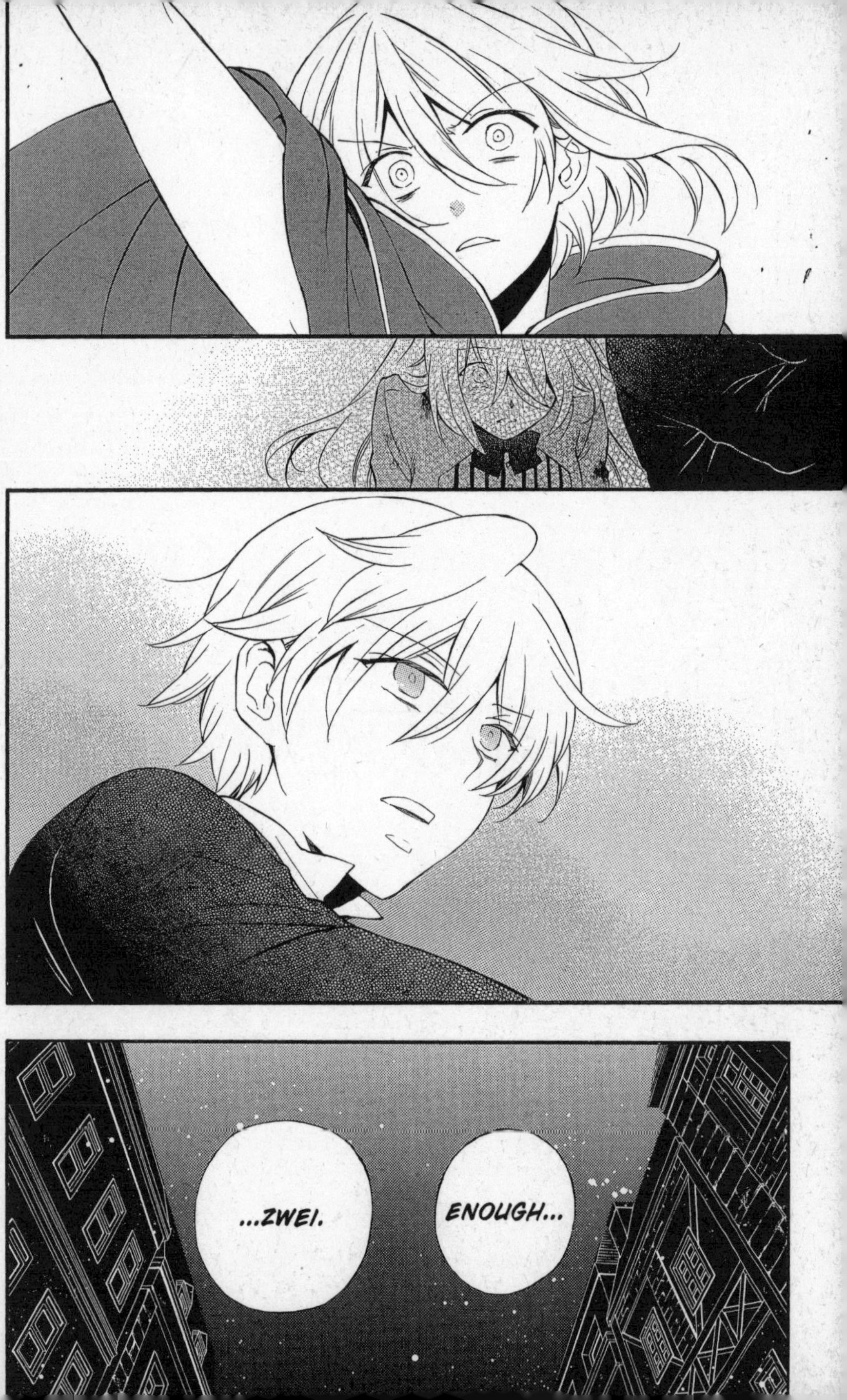
ENOUGH...
...ZWEI.

Retrace:XCI Juror

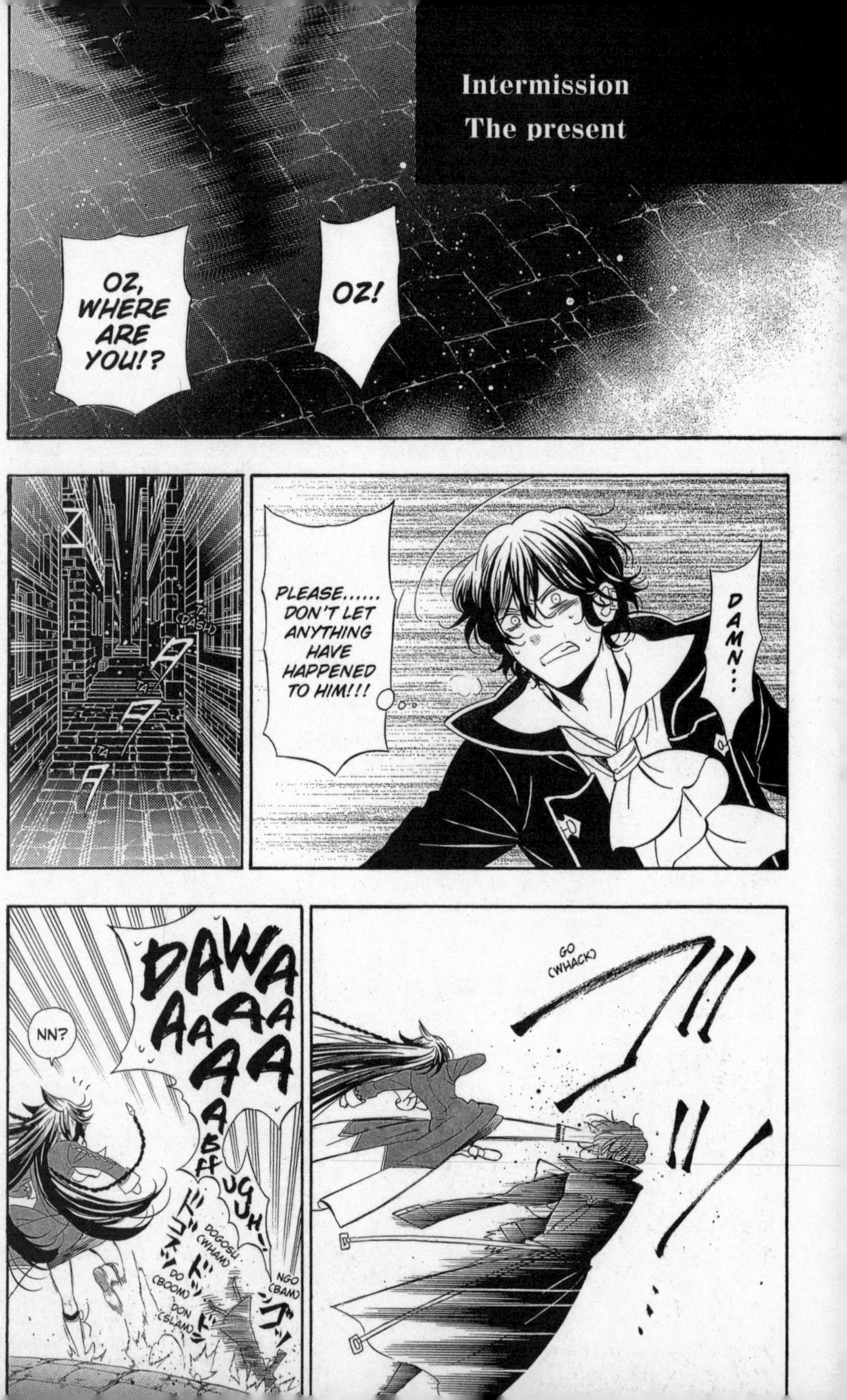
Intermission
The present
OZ!
OZ, WHERE ARE YOU!?
DAMN...
PLEASE...... DON'T LET ANYTHING HAVE HAPPENED TO HIM!!!
TA (DASH)
TA
TA
GO (WHACK)
NN?
DAWAAAAAAAA
UGH!
DOGOSU (WHAM)
DO (BOOM)
DON (SLAM)
NGO (BAM)

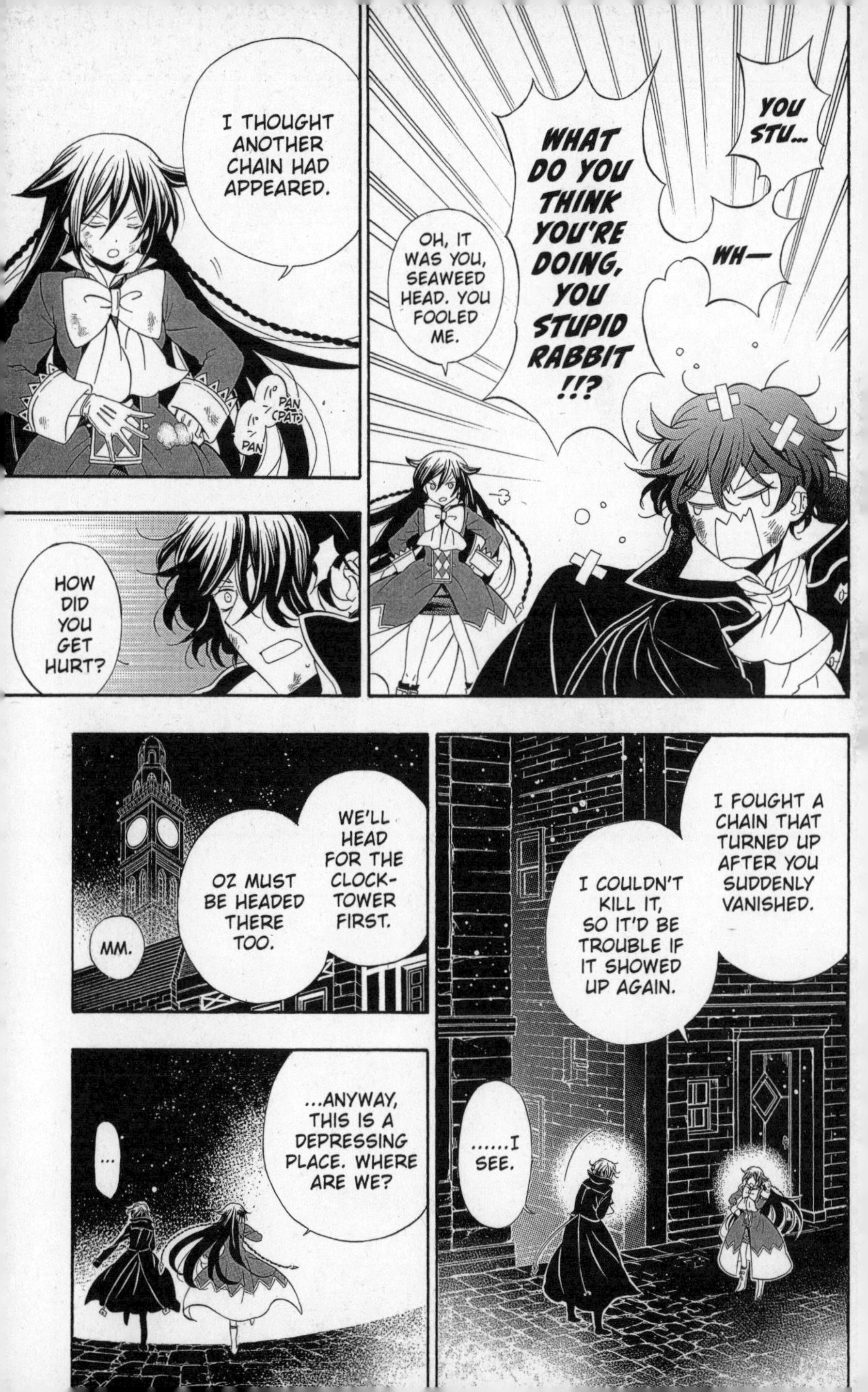
YOU STU...
WH—
WHAT DO YOU THINK YOU'RE DOING, YOU STUPID RABBIT!!?
OH, IT WAS YOU, SEAWEED HEAD. YOU FOOLED ME.
I THOUGHT ANOTHER CHAIN HAD APPEARED.
PAN (PAT) PAN
HOW DID YOU GET HURT?
I FOUGHT A CHAIN THAT TURNED UP AFTER YOU SUDDENLY VANISHED.
I COULDN'T KILL IT, SO IT'D BE TROUBLE IF IT SHOWED UP AGAIN.
......I SEE.
WE'LL HEAD FOR THE CLOCK-TOWER FIRST.
OZ MUST BE HEADED THERE TOO.
MM.
...ANYWAY, THIS IS A DEPRESSING PLACE. WHERE ARE WE?
...

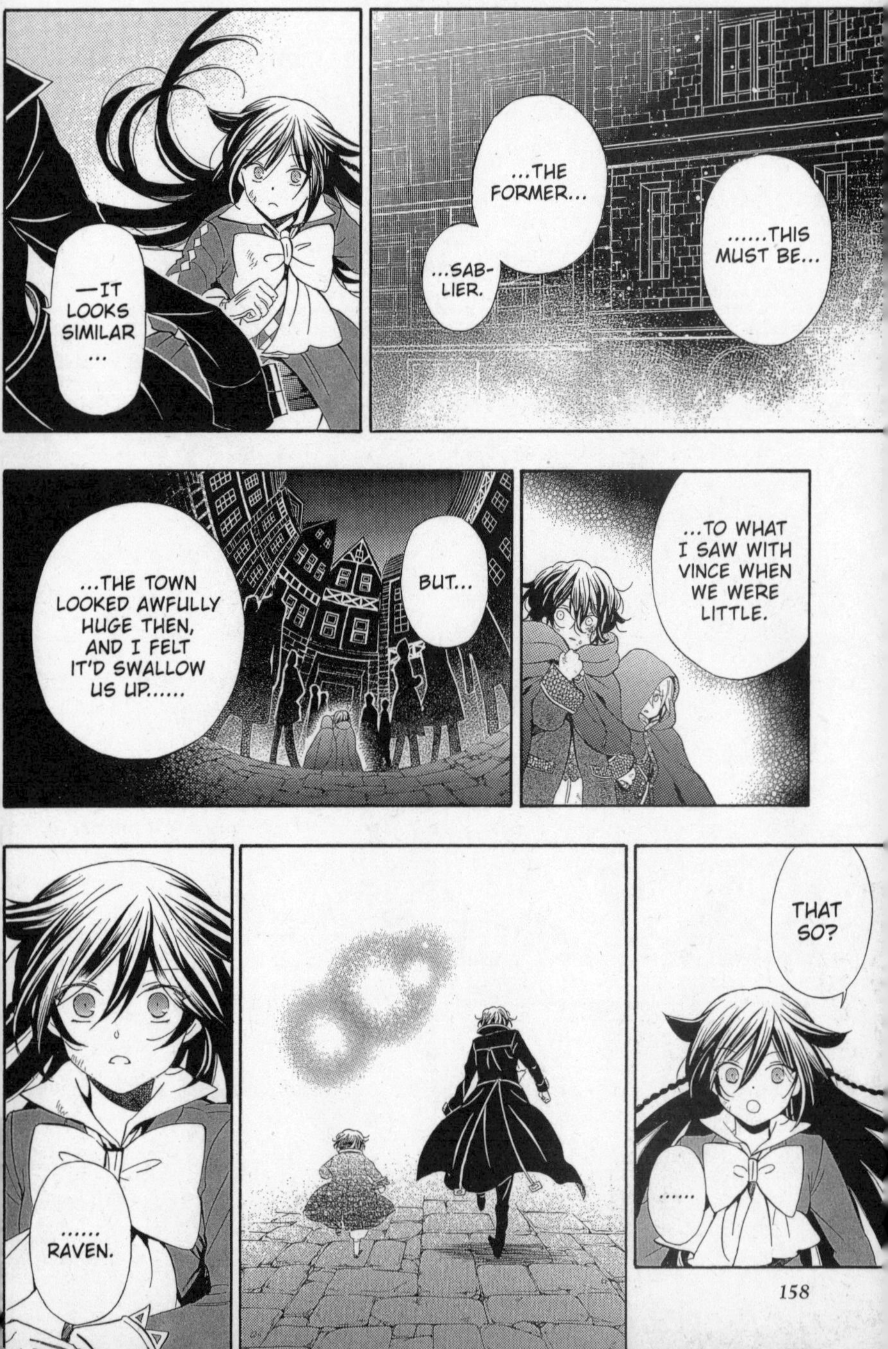

......THIS MUST BE...
...THE FORMER...
...SAB-LIER.
—IT LOOKS SIMILAR ...
...TO WHAT I SAW WITH VINCE WHEN WE WERE LITTLE.
BUT...
...THE TOWN LOOKED AWFULLY HUGE THEN, AND I FELT IT'D SWALLOW US UP......
THAT SO?
......
...... RAVEN.

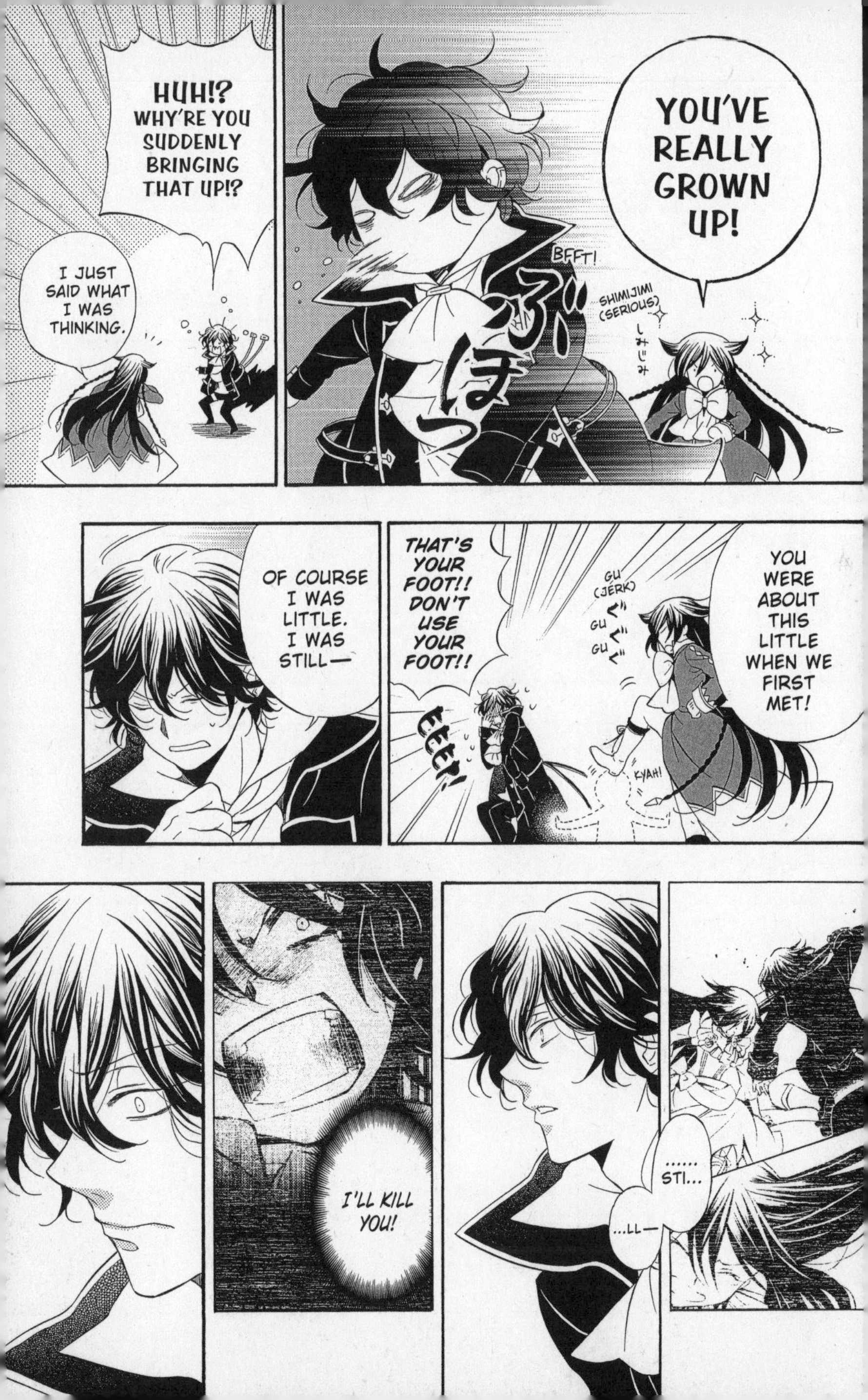
YOU'VE REALLY GROWN UP!
SHIMIJIMI (SERIOUS)
しみじみ
BFFT!
ぶほっ
HUH!? WHY'RE YOU SUDDENLY BRINGING THAT UP!?
I JUST SAID WHAT I WAS THINKING.
YOU WERE ABOUT THIS LITTLE WHEN WE FIRST MET!
GU (JERK)
ぐ GU ぐ GU ぐ
KYAH!
THAT'S YOUR FOOT!! DON'T USE YOUR FOOT!!
EEEK!
OF COURSE I WAS LITTLE. I WAS STILL—
...... STI...
...LL—
I'LL KILL YOU!

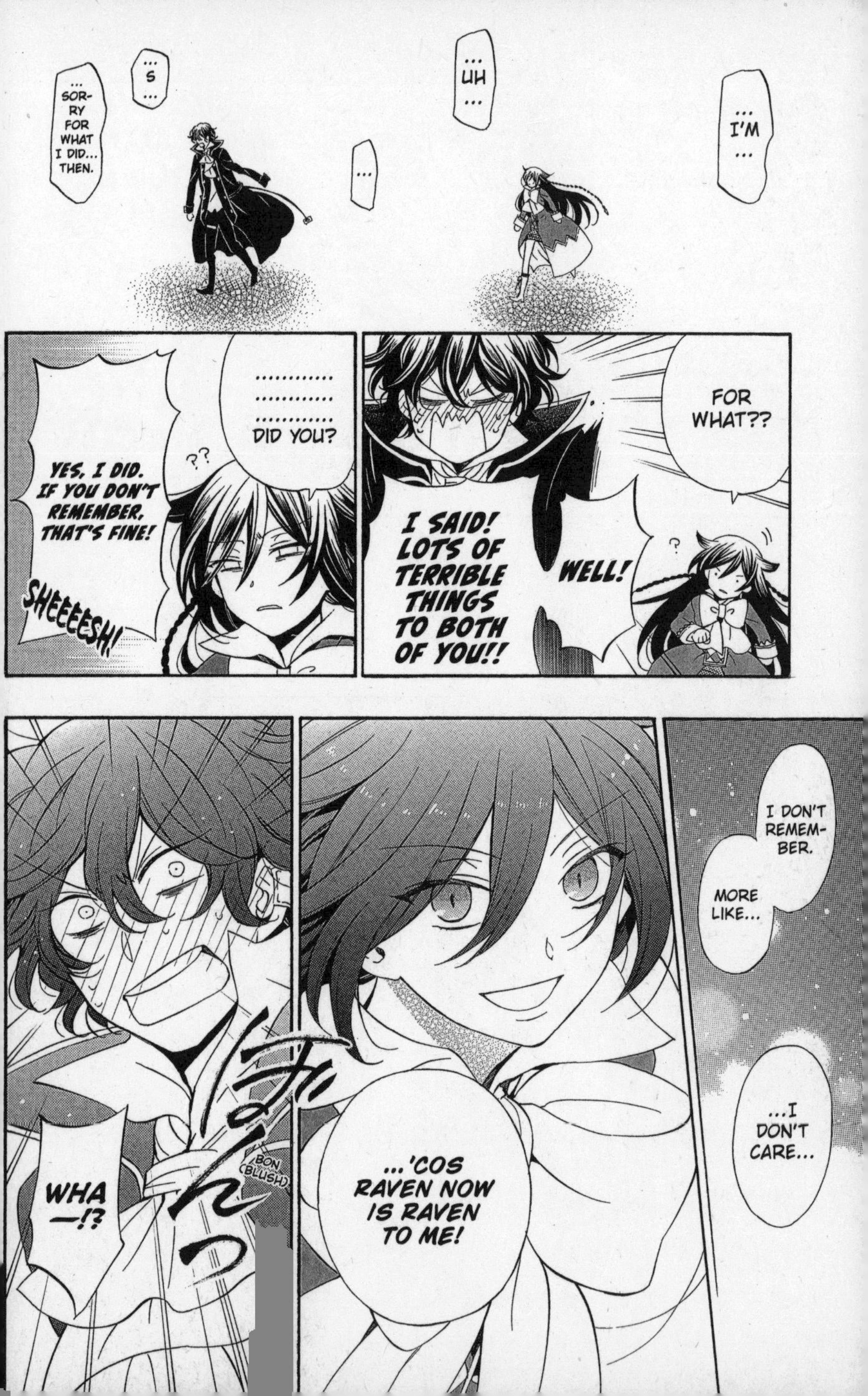
...I'M...
...UH...
...
...S...
...SORRY FOR WHAT I DID... THEN.
FOR WHAT??
WELL!
I SAID! LOTS OF TERRIBLE THINGS TO BOTH OF YOU!!
?
.... DID YOU?
??
YES, I DID. IF YOU DON'T REMEMBER, THAT'S FINE!
SHEEEESH!
I DON'T REMEMBER.
MORE LIKE...
...I DON'T CARE...
...'COS RAVEN NOW IS RAVEN TO ME!
BON (BLUSH)
WHA—!?

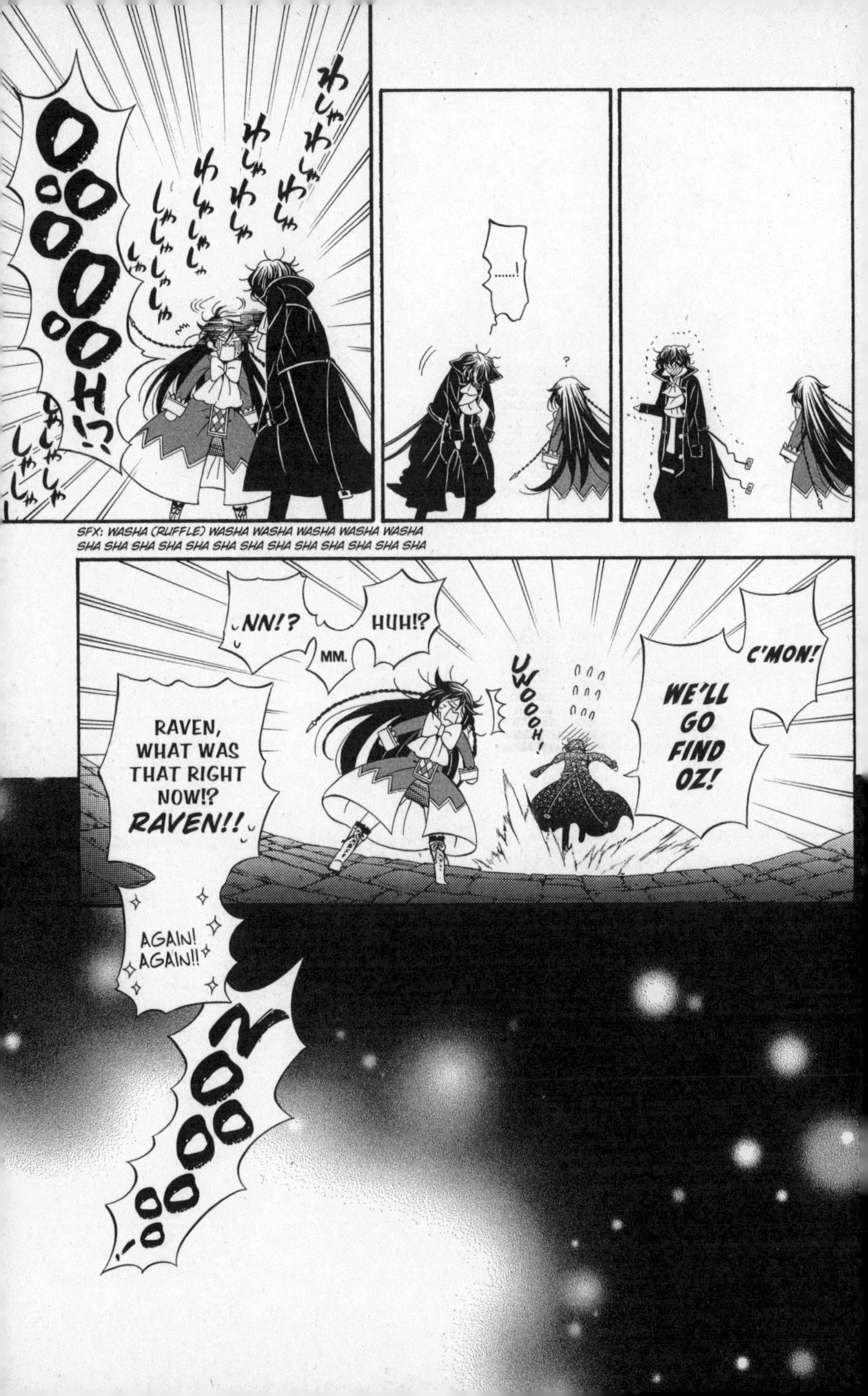
......!
OOOOOOH!?
SFX: WASHA (RUFFLE) WASHA WASHA WASHA WASHA WASHA
SHA SHA SHA SHA SHA SHA SHA SHA SHA SHA SHA SHA SHA
C'MON!
WE'LL GO FIND OZ!
UWOOOH!
HUH!?
MM.
NN!?
RAVEN, WHAT WAS THAT RIGHT NOW!? RAVEN!!
AGAIN! AGAIN!!
OOOOOOO...!

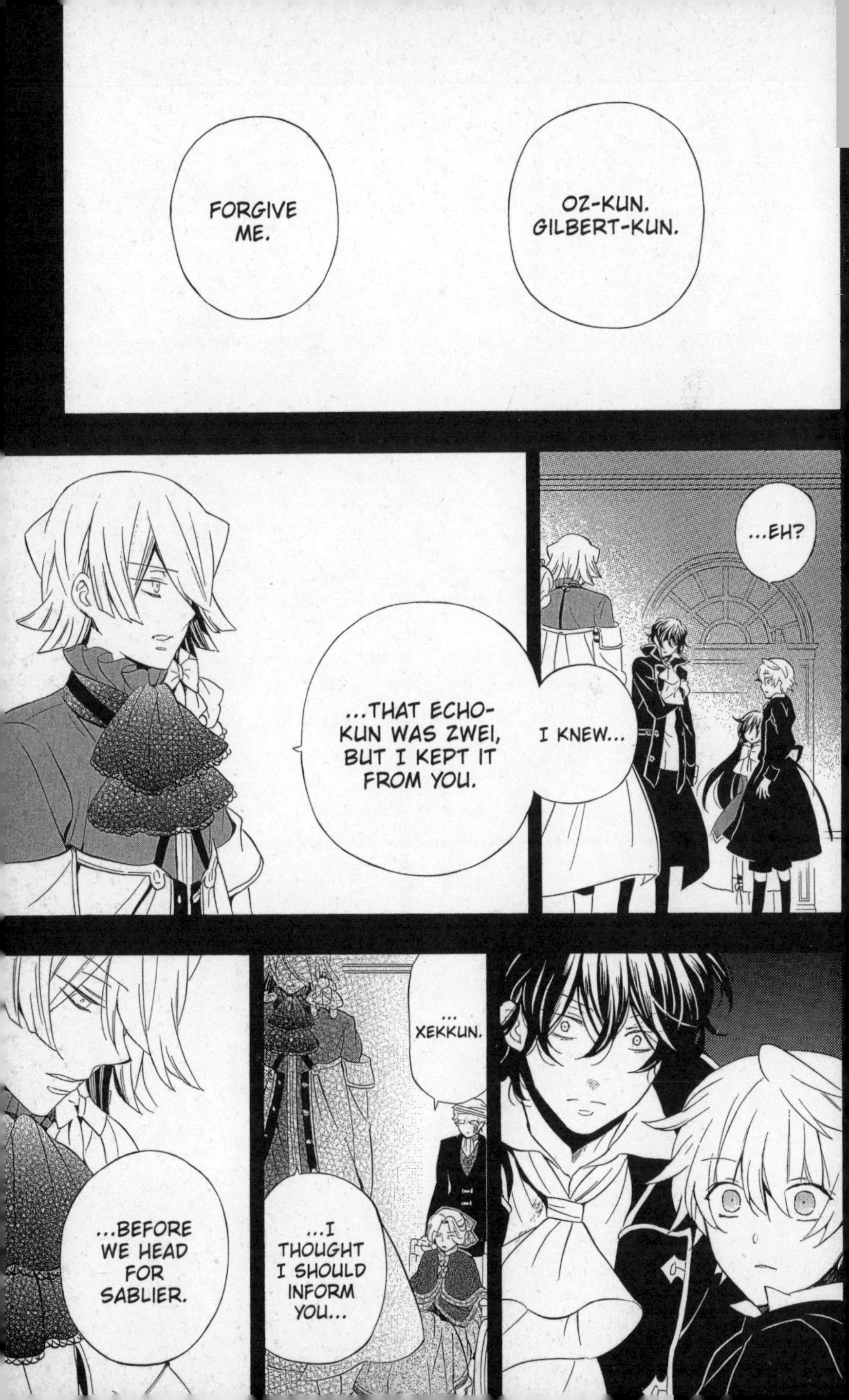
OZ-KUN. GILBERT-KUN.
FORGIVE ME.
...EH?
I KNEW...
...THAT ECHO-KUN WAS ZWEI, BUT I KEPT IT FROM YOU.
... XEKKUN.
...I THOUGHT I SHOULD INFORM YOU...
...BEFORE WE HEAD FOR SABLIER.

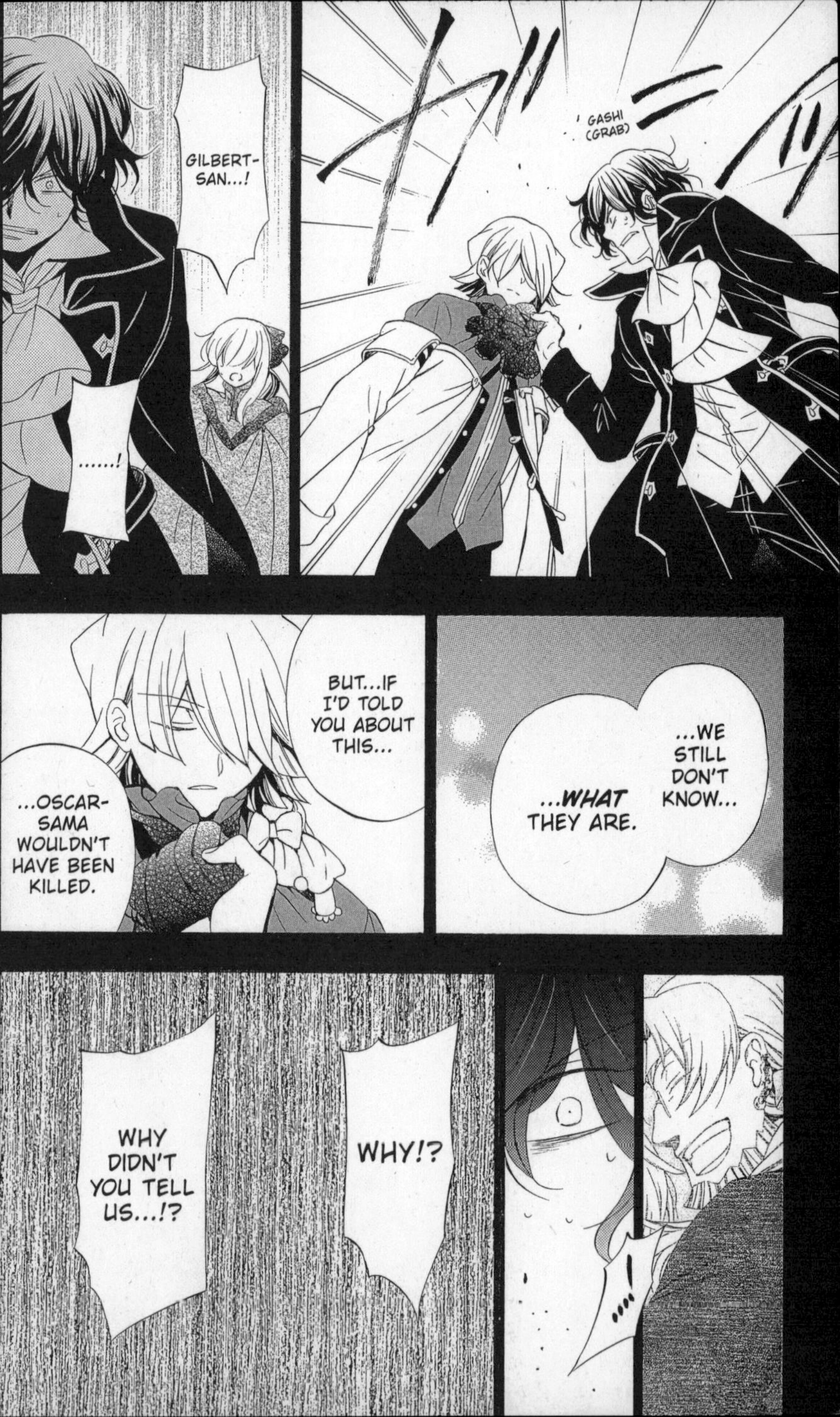
GASHI (GRAB)
GILBERT-SAN...!
......!
...WE STILL DON'T KNOW...
...*WHAT* THEY ARE.
BUT...IF I'D TOLD YOU ABOUT THIS...
...OSCAR-SAMA WOULDN'T HAVE BEEN KILLED.
...!
WHY!?
WHY DIDN'T YOU TELL US...!?

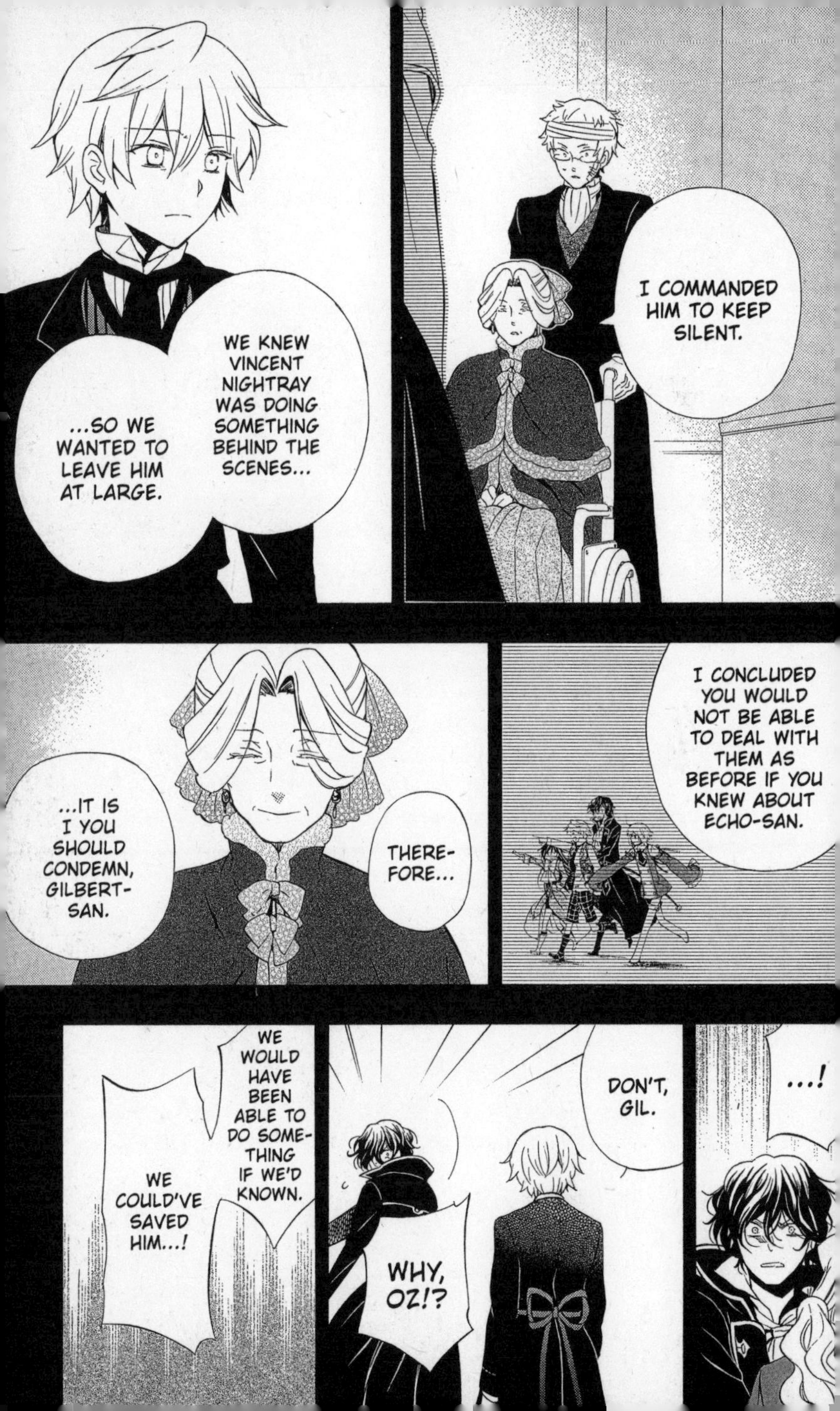
I COMMANDED HIM TO KEEP SILENT.
WE KNEW VINCENT NIGHTRAY WAS DOING SOMETHING BEHIND THE SCENES...
...SO WE WANTED TO LEAVE HIM AT LARGE.
I CONCLUDED YOU WOULD NOT BE ABLE TO DEAL WITH THEM AS BEFORE IF YOU KNEW ABOUT ECHO-SAN.
THERE-FORE...
...IT IS I YOU SHOULD CONDEMN, GILBERT-SAN.
...!
DON'T, GIL.
WHY, OZ!?
WE WOULD HAVE BEEN ABLE TO DO SOME-THING IF WE'D KNOWN.
WE COULD'VE SAVED HIM...!

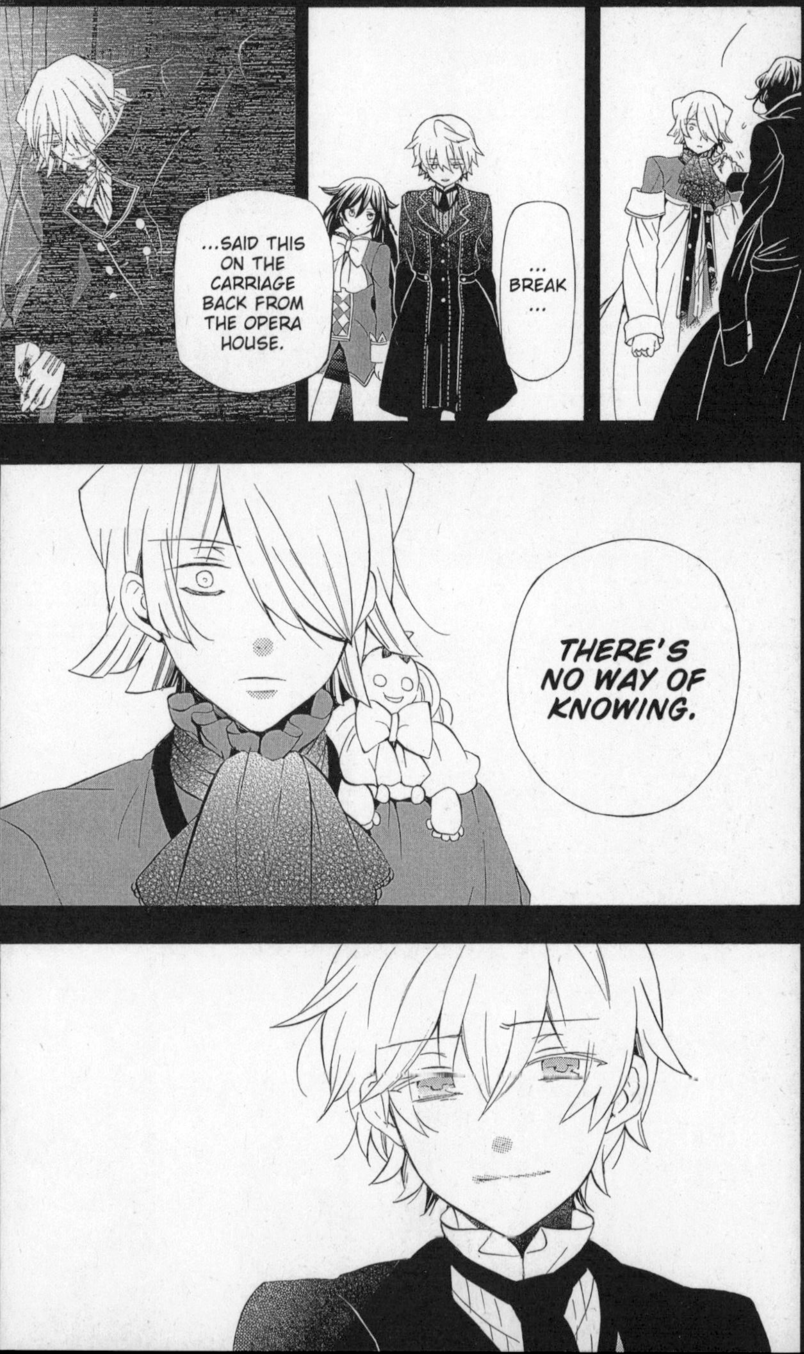
... BREAK ...
...SAID THIS ON THE CARRIAGE BACK FROM THE OPERA HOUSE.
THERE'S NO WAY OF KNOWING.

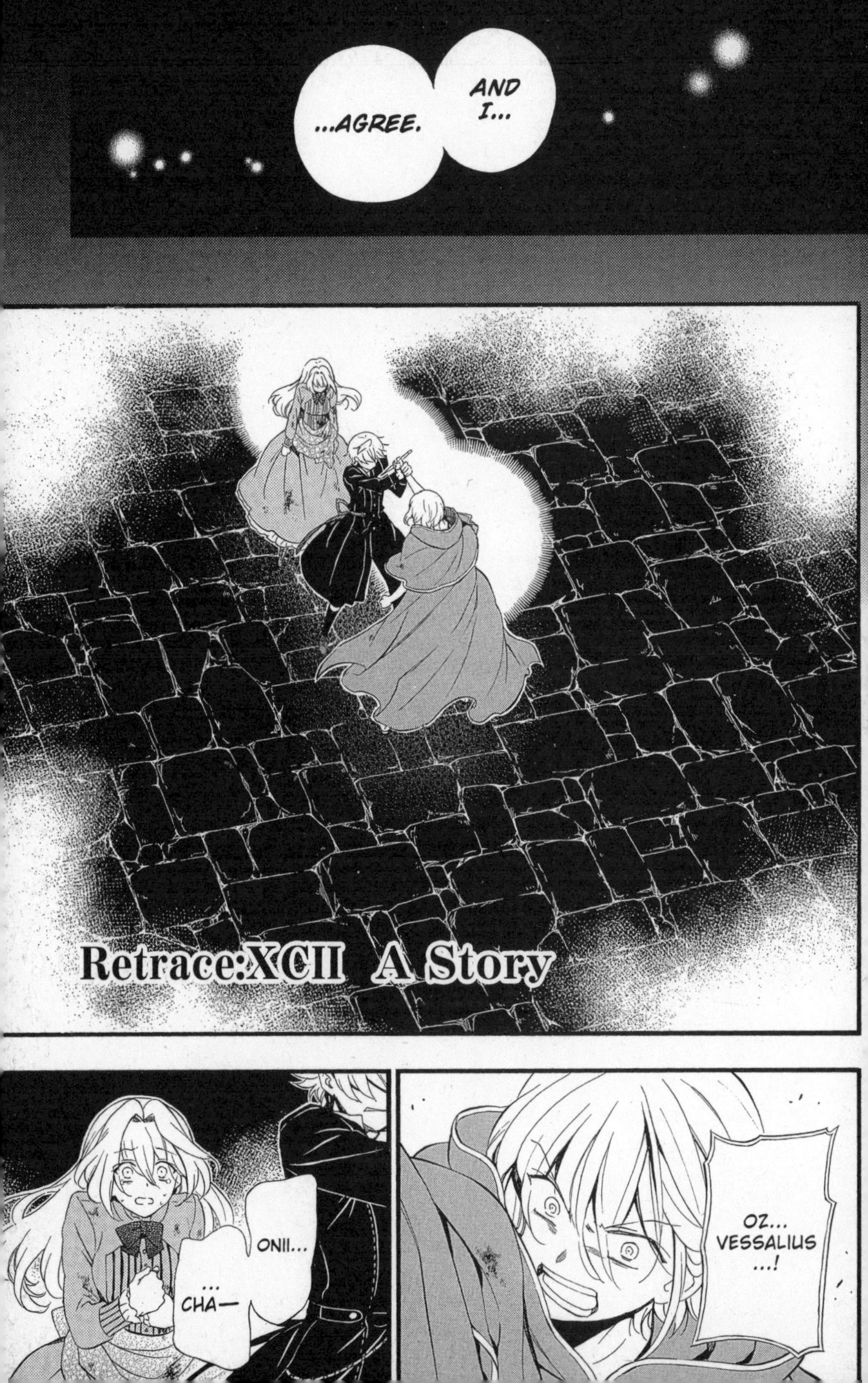
AND I...
...AGREE.
Retrace:XCII A Story
OZ... VESSALIUS ...!
ONII... ...CHA—

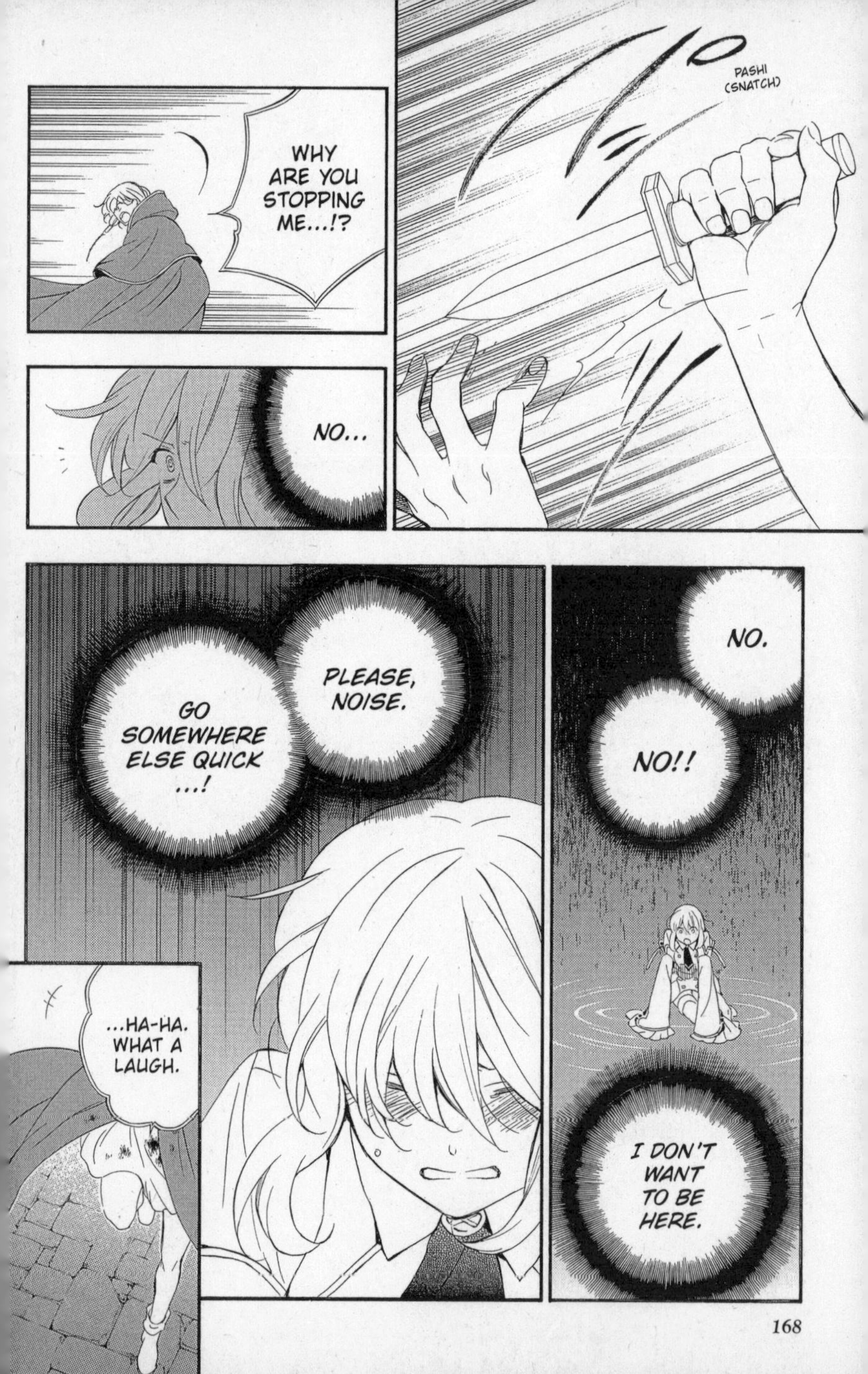
PASHI (SNATCH)
WHY ARE YOU STOPPING ME...!?
NO...
NO.
NO!!
I DON'T WANT TO BE HERE.
PLEASE, NOISE.
GO SOMEWHERE ELSE QUICK ...!
...HA-HA. WHAT A LAUGH.

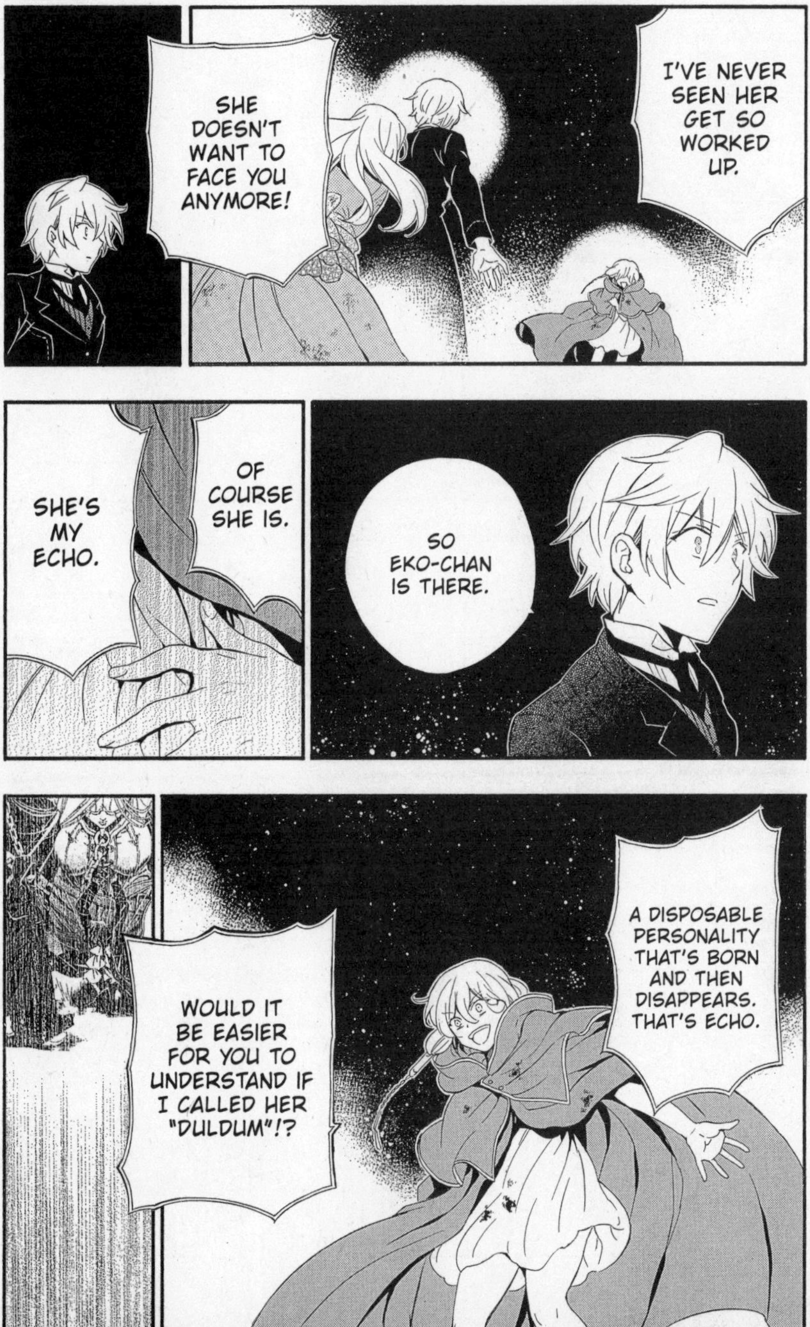
I'VE NEVER SEEN HER GET SO WORKED UP.
SHE DOESN'T WANT TO FACE YOU ANYMORE!
SO EKO-CHAN IS THERE.
OF COURSE SHE IS.
SHE'S MY ECHO.
A DISPOSABLE PERSONALITY THAT'S BORN AND THEN DISAPPEARS. THAT'S ECHO.
WOULD IT BE EASIER FOR YOU TO UNDERSTAND IF I CALLED HER "DULDUM"!?

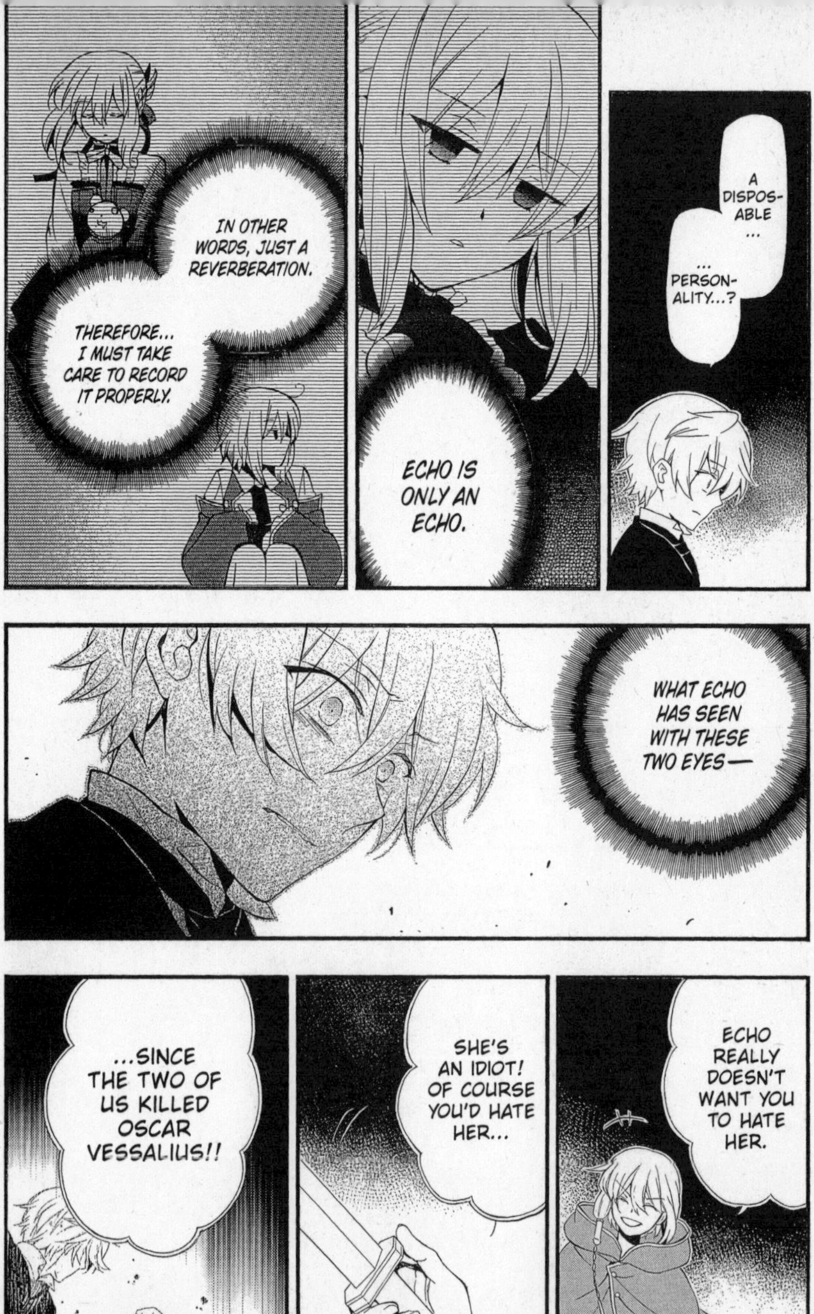
A DISPOSABLE...
...PERSONALITY...?
ECHO IS ONLY AN ECHO.
IN OTHER WORDS, JUST A REVERBERATION.
THEREFORE... I MUST TAKE CARE TO RECORD IT PROPERLY.
WHAT ECHO HAS SEEN WITH THESE TWO EYES—
ECHO REALLY DOESN'T WANT YOU TO HATE HER.
SHE'S AN IDIOT! OF COURSE YOU'D HATE HER...
...SINCE THE TWO OF US KILLED OSCAR VESSALIUS!!

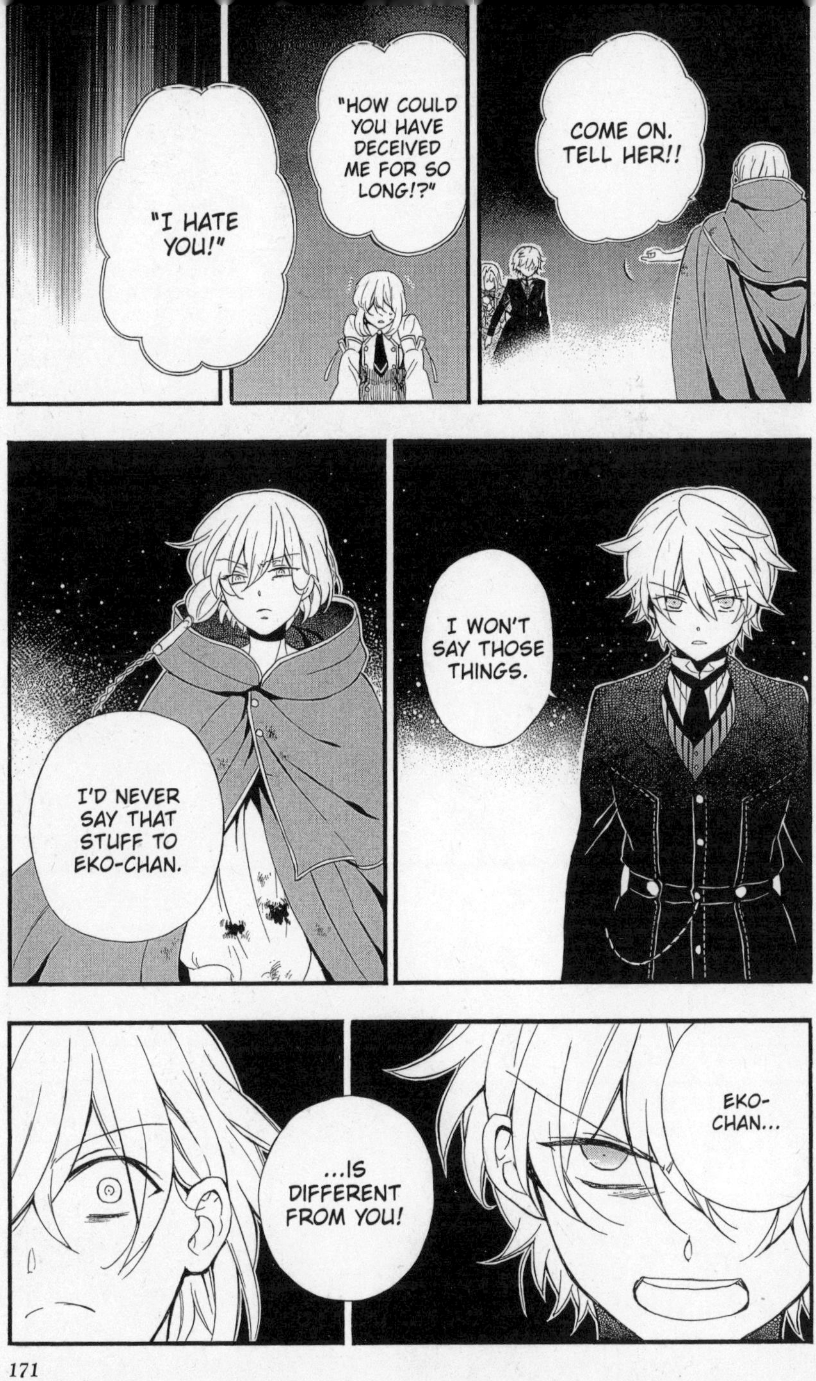
COME ON. TELL HER!!
"HOW COULD YOU HAVE DECEIVED ME FOR SO LONG!?"
"I HATE YOU!"
I WON'T SAY THOSE THINGS.
I'D NEVER SAY THAT STUFF TO EKO-CHAN.
EKO-CHAN...
...IS DIFFERENT FROM YOU!

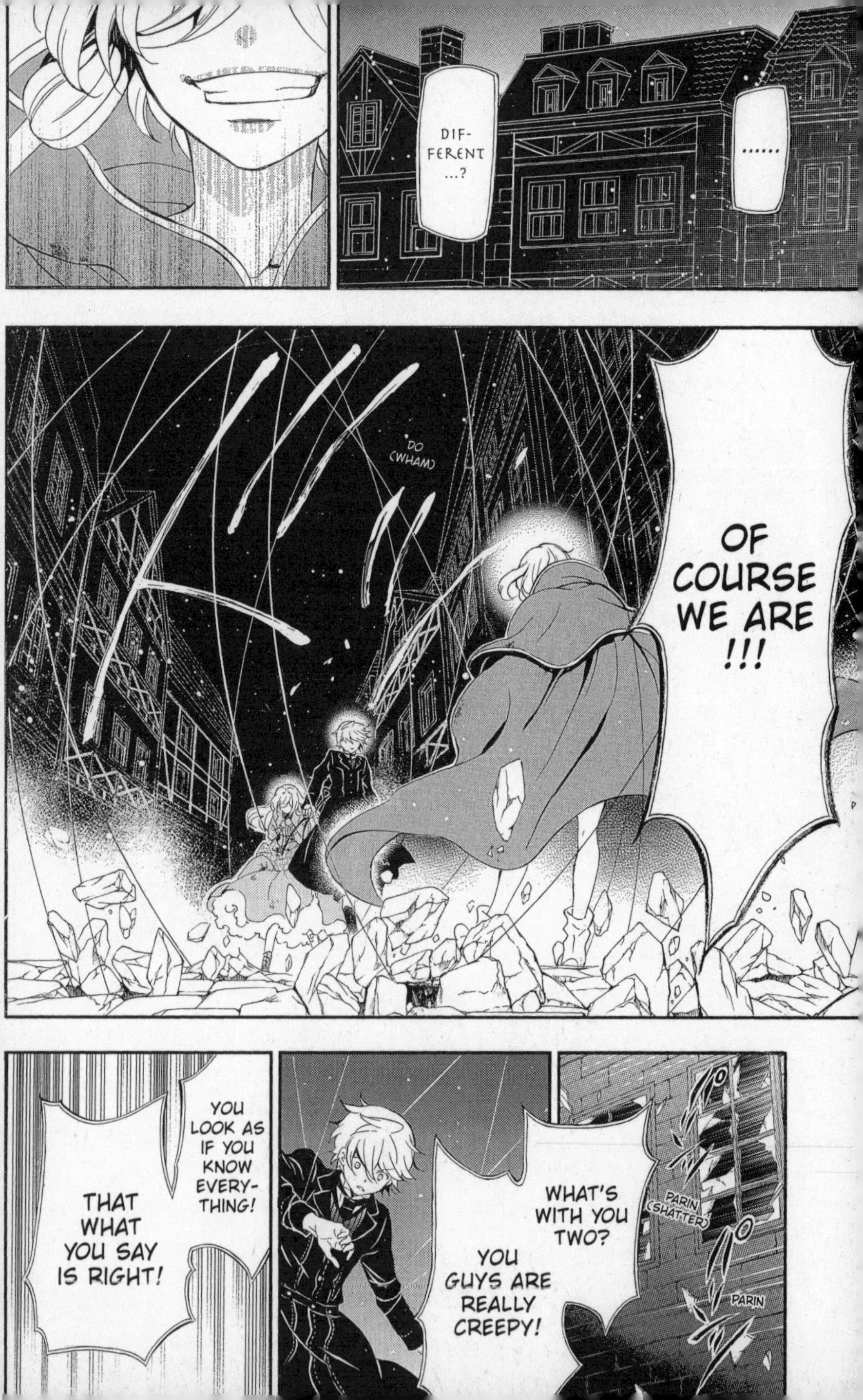
......
DIF-FERENT ...?
OF COURSE WE ARE !!!
DO (WHAM)
PARIN (SHATTER)
PARIN
WHAT'S WITH YOU TWO?
YOU GUYS ARE REALLY CREEPY!
YOU LOOK AS IF YOU KNOW EVERY-THING!
THAT WHAT YOU SAY IS RIGHT!

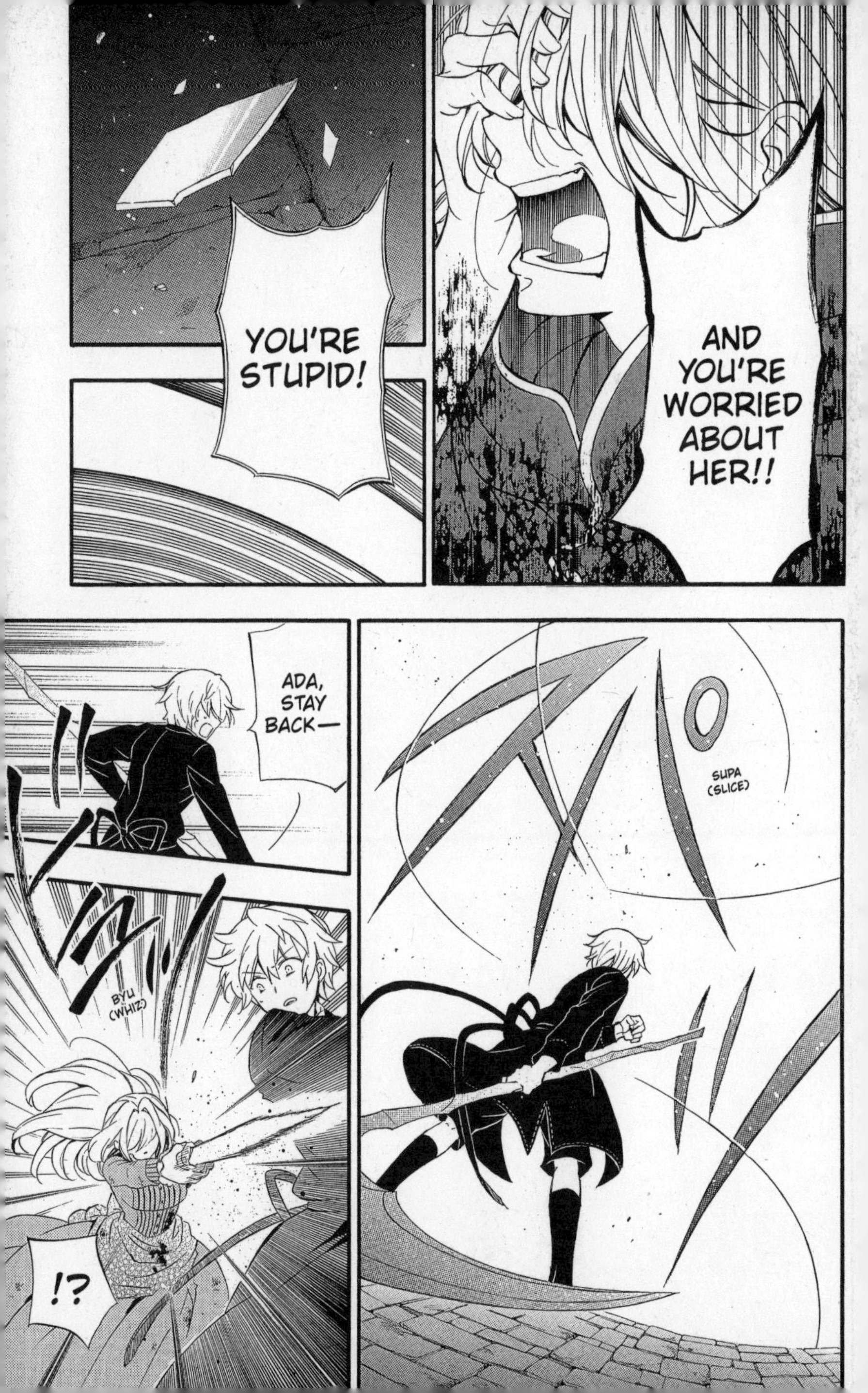

AND YOU'RE WORRIED ABOUT HER!!
YOU'RE STUPID!
SUPA (SLICE)
ADA, STAY BACK—
BYU (WHIZ)
!?

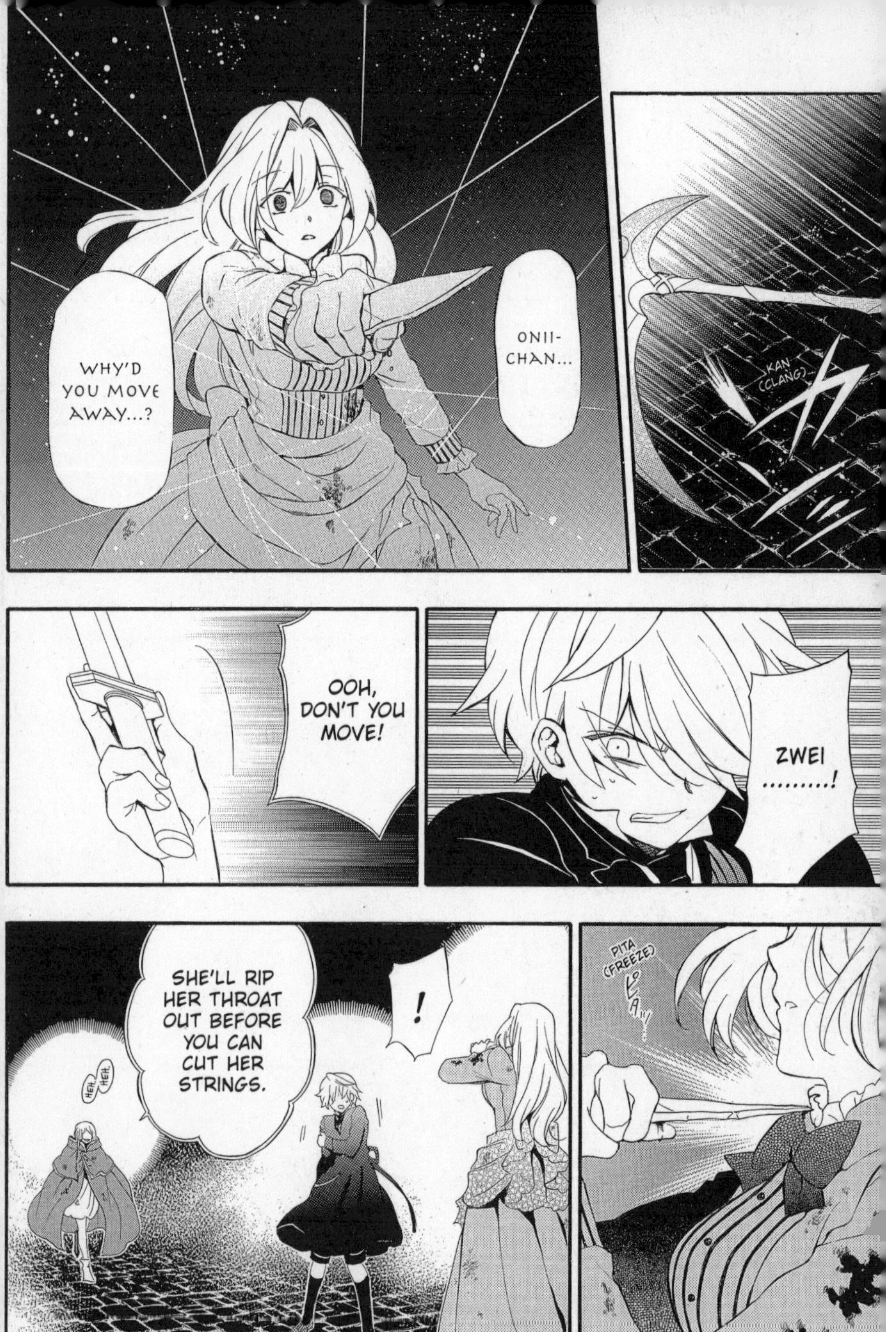
KAN (CLANG)
ONII-CHAN...
WHY'D YOU MOVE AWAY...?
ZWEI ....!
OOH, DON'T YOU MOVE!
PITA (FREEZE)
!
SHE'LL RIP HER THROAT OUT BEFORE YOU CAN CUT HER STRINGS.
HEH. HEH.

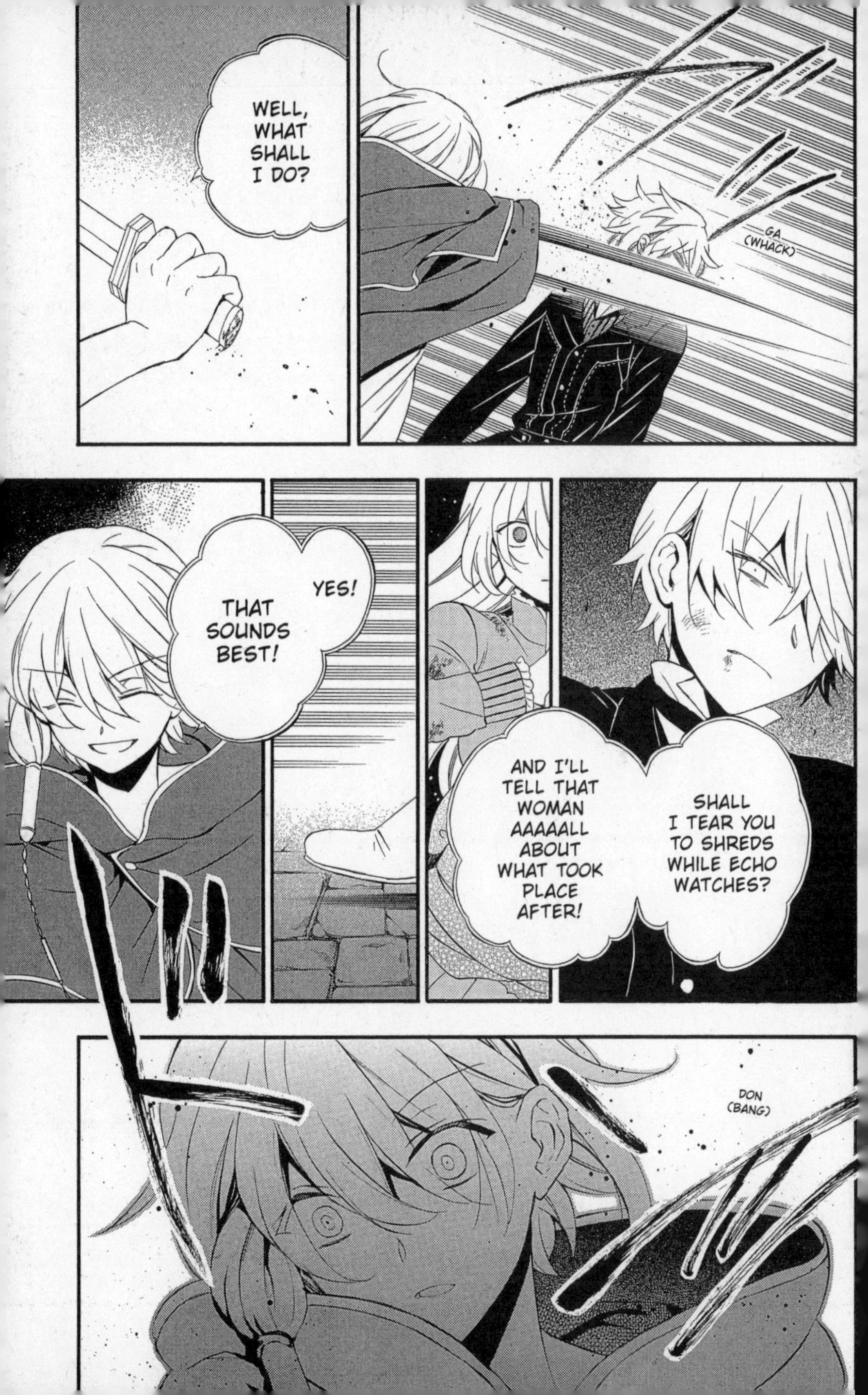
GA (WHACK)
WELL, WHAT SHALL I DO?
SHALL I TEAR YOU TO SHREDS WHILE ECHO WATCHES?
AND I'LL TELL THAT WOMAN AAAAALL ABOUT WHAT TOOK PLACE AFTER!
YES!
THAT SOUNDS BEST!
DON (BANG)

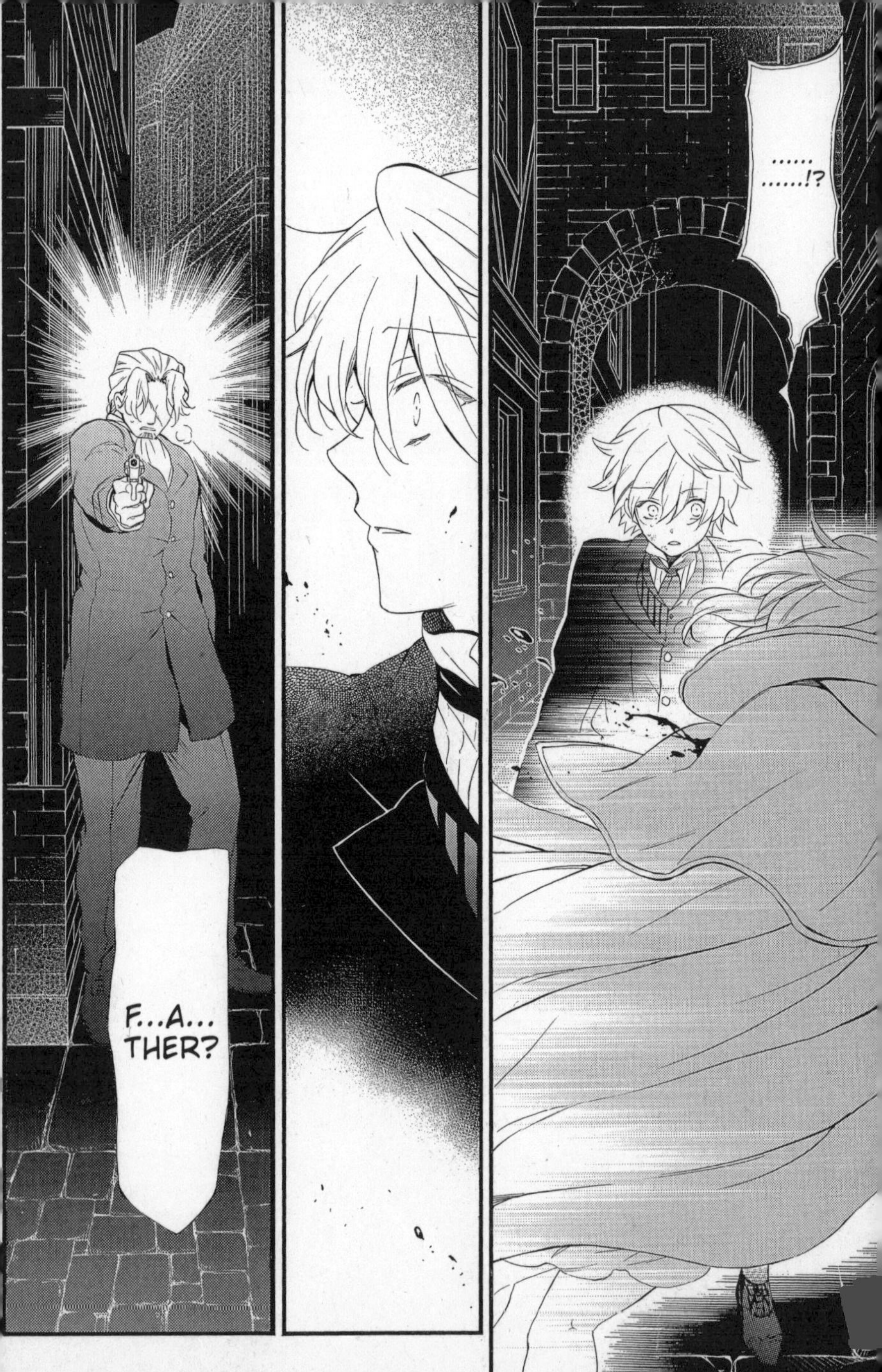
....!?
F...A... THER?

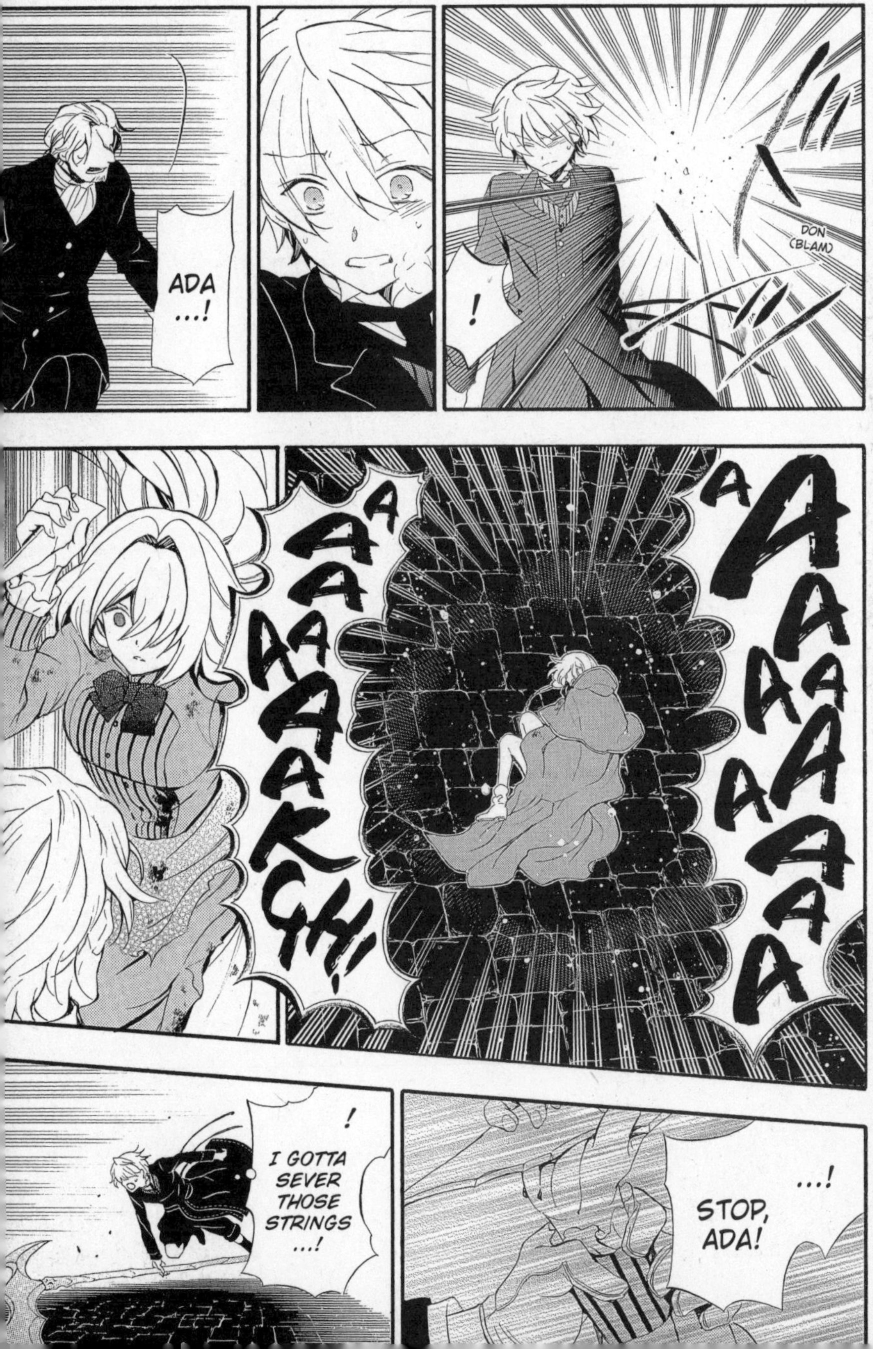

DON (BLAM)
!
ADA ...!
AAAAAAAAAAA
AAAAAAAAARGH!
...!
STOP, ADA!
!
I GOTTA SEVER THOSE STRINGS ...!

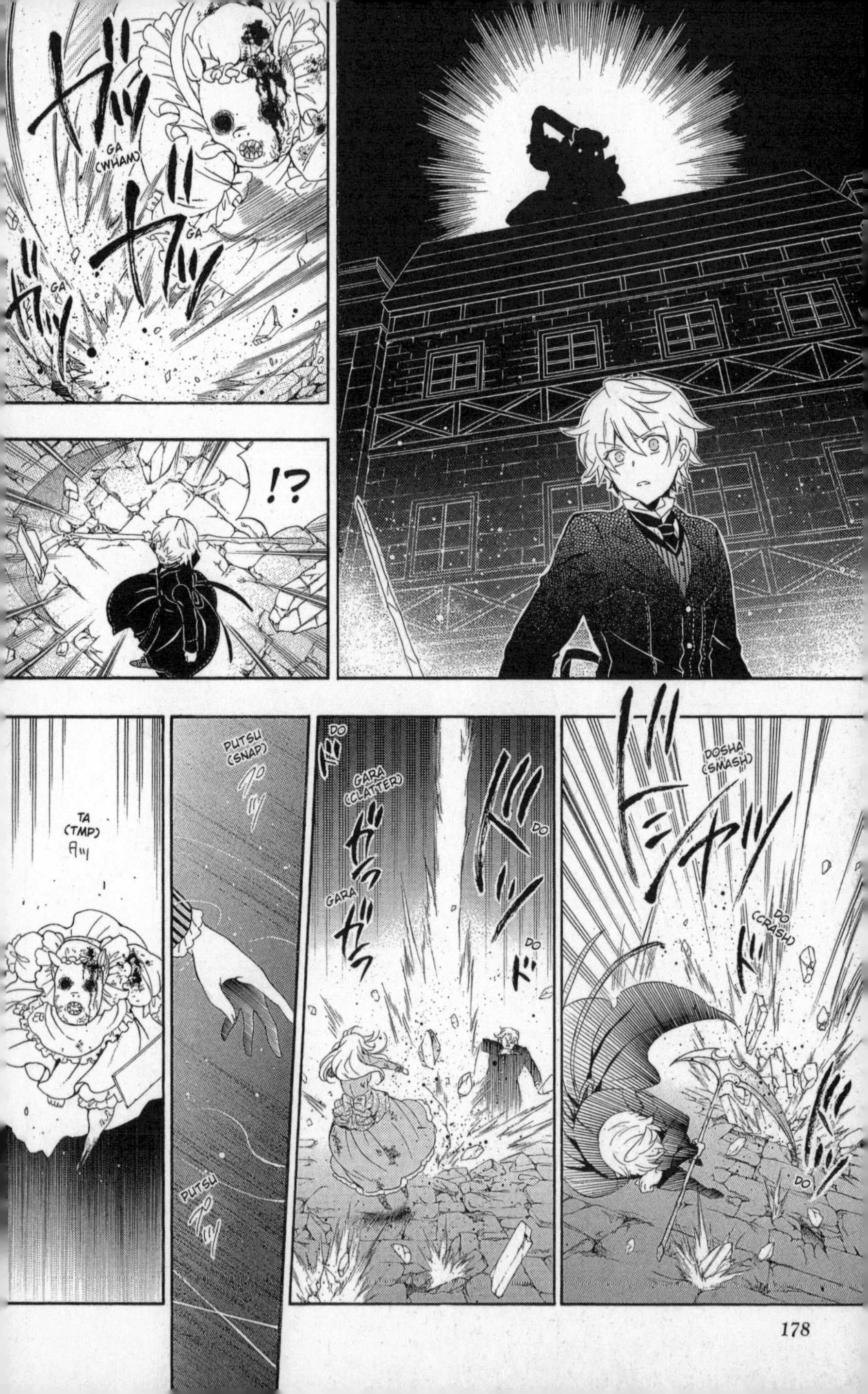
GA (WHAM)
GA
GA
!?
DOSHA (SMASH)
DO (CRASH)
DO
DO
GARA (CLATTER)
GARA
DO
DO
PUTSU (SNAP)
PUTSU
TA (TMP)

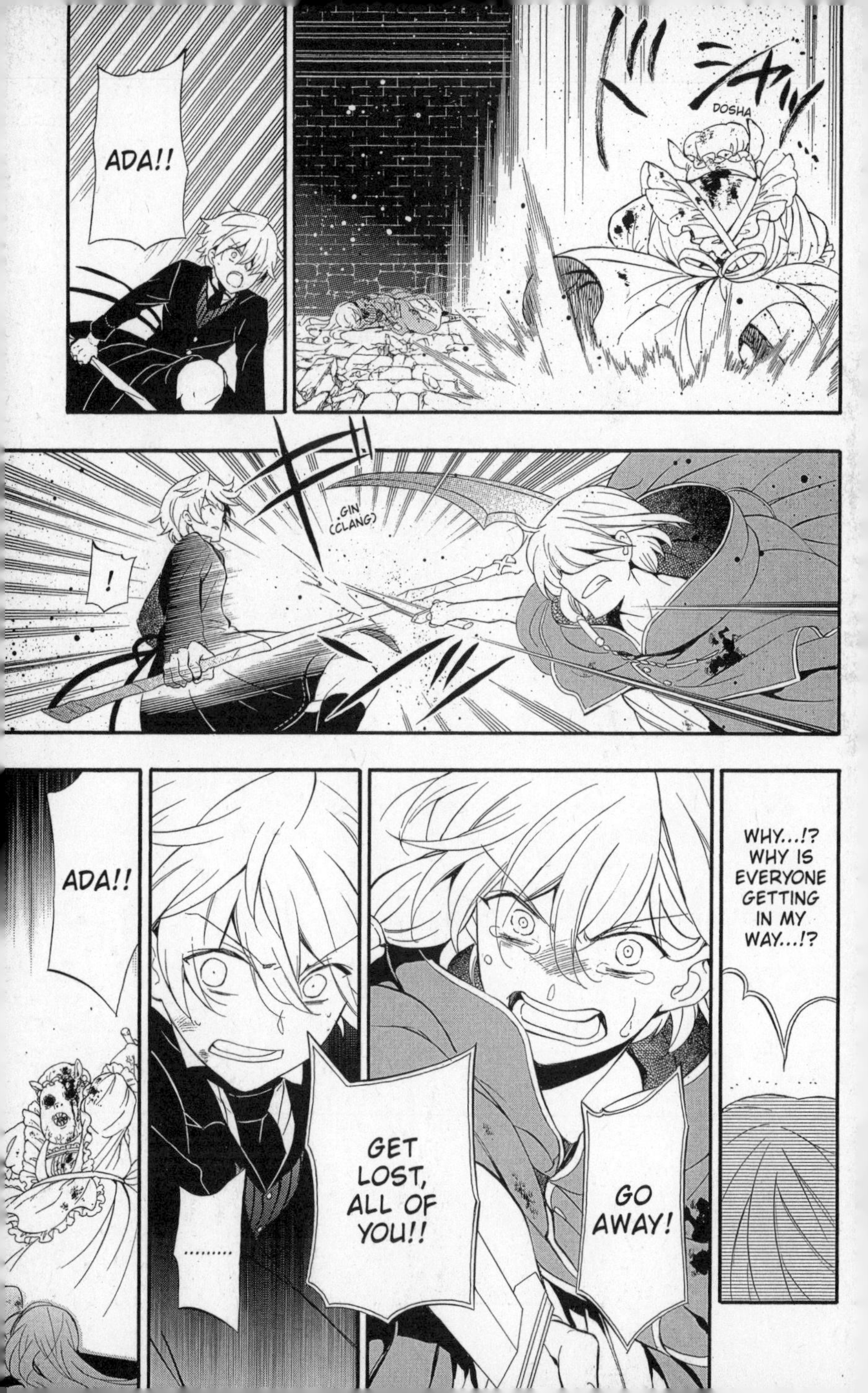

ドシャッ
DOSHA
ADA!!
ギン
GIN (CLANG)
!
WHY...!? WHY IS EVERYONE GETTING IN MY WAY...!?
GO AWAY!
GET LOST, ALL OF YOU!!
....
ADA!!

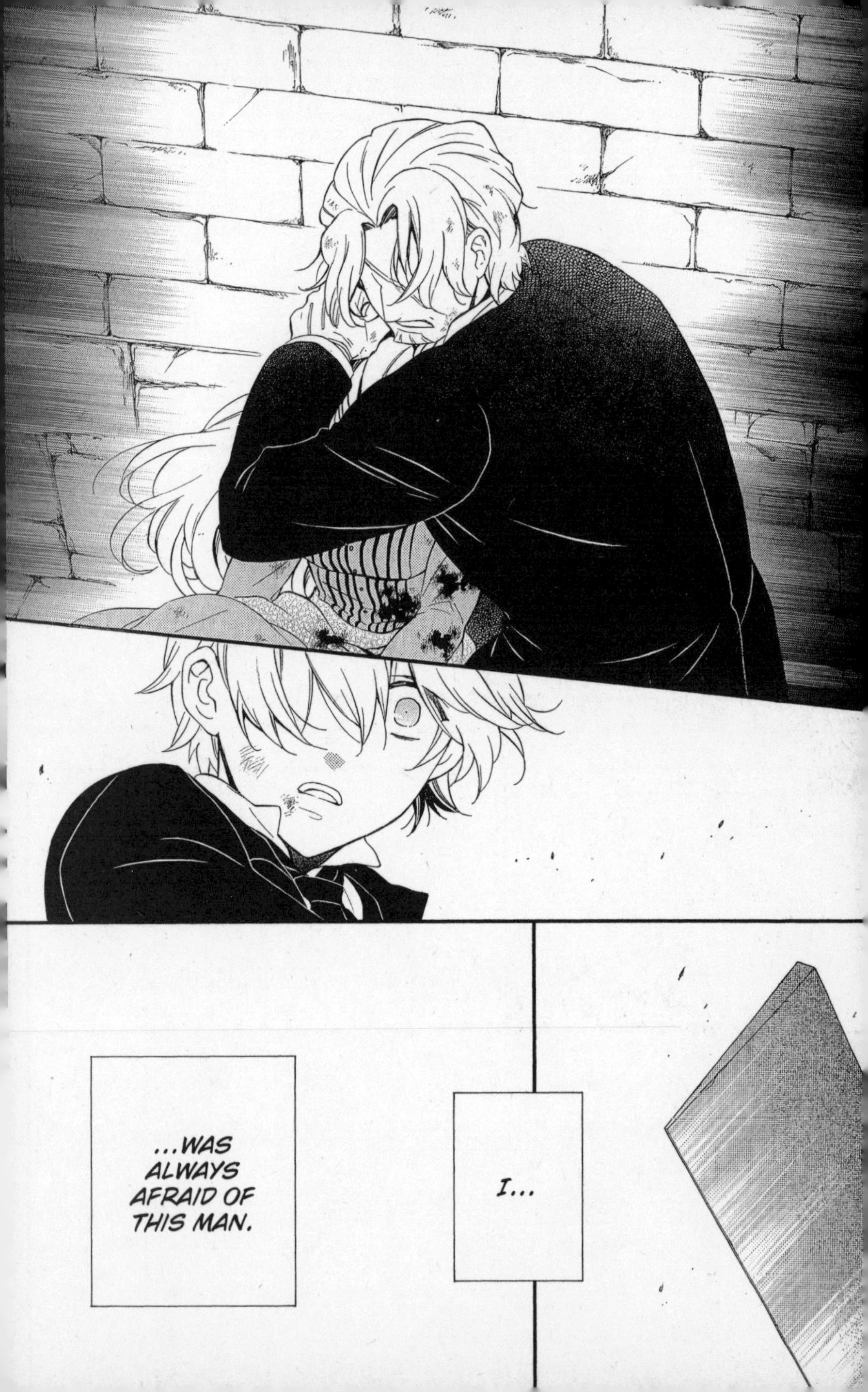
I...
...WAS ALWAYS AFRAID OF THIS MAN.

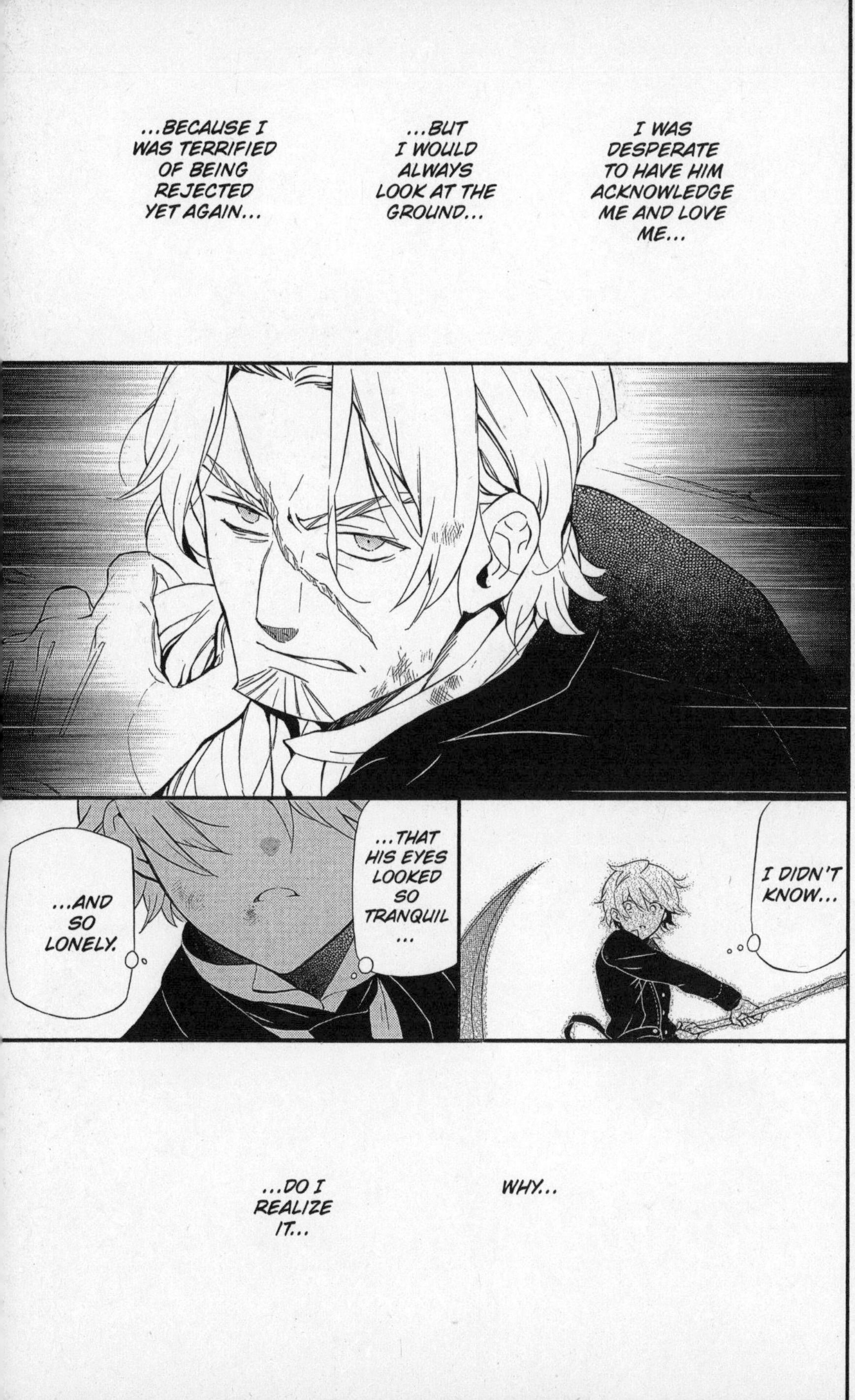
I WAS DESPERATE TO HAVE HIM ACKNOWLEDGE ME AND LOVE ME...
...BUT I WOULD ALWAYS LOOK AT THE GROUND...
...BECAUSE I WAS TERRIFIED OF BEING REJECTED YET AGAIN...
I DIDN'T KNOW...
...THAT HIS EYES LOOKED SO TRANQUIL ...
...AND SO LONELY.
WHY...
...DO I REALIZE IT...

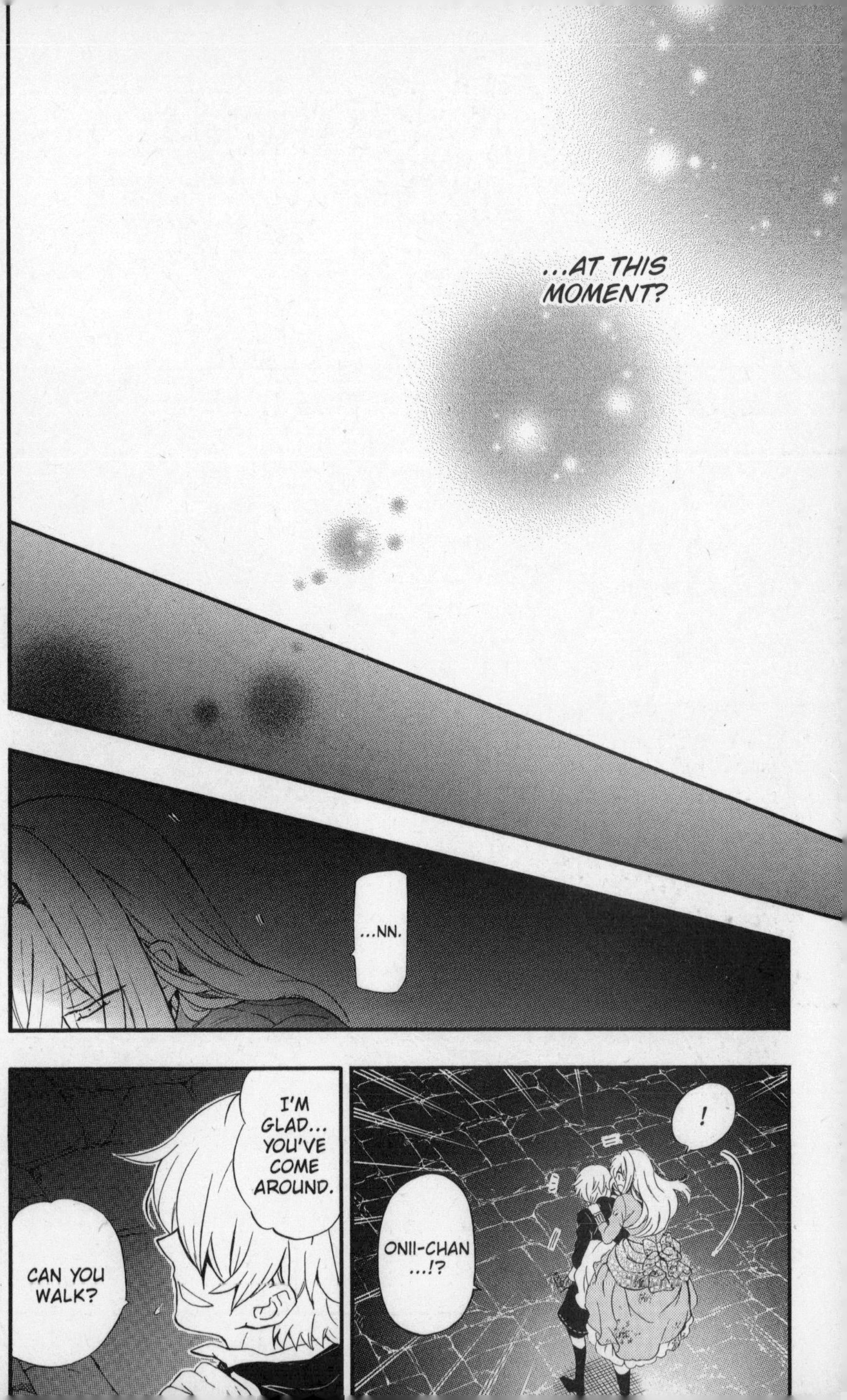
...AT THIS MOMENT?
...NN.
!
ONII-CHAN ...!?
I'M GLAD... YOU'VE COME AROUND.
CAN YOU WALK?

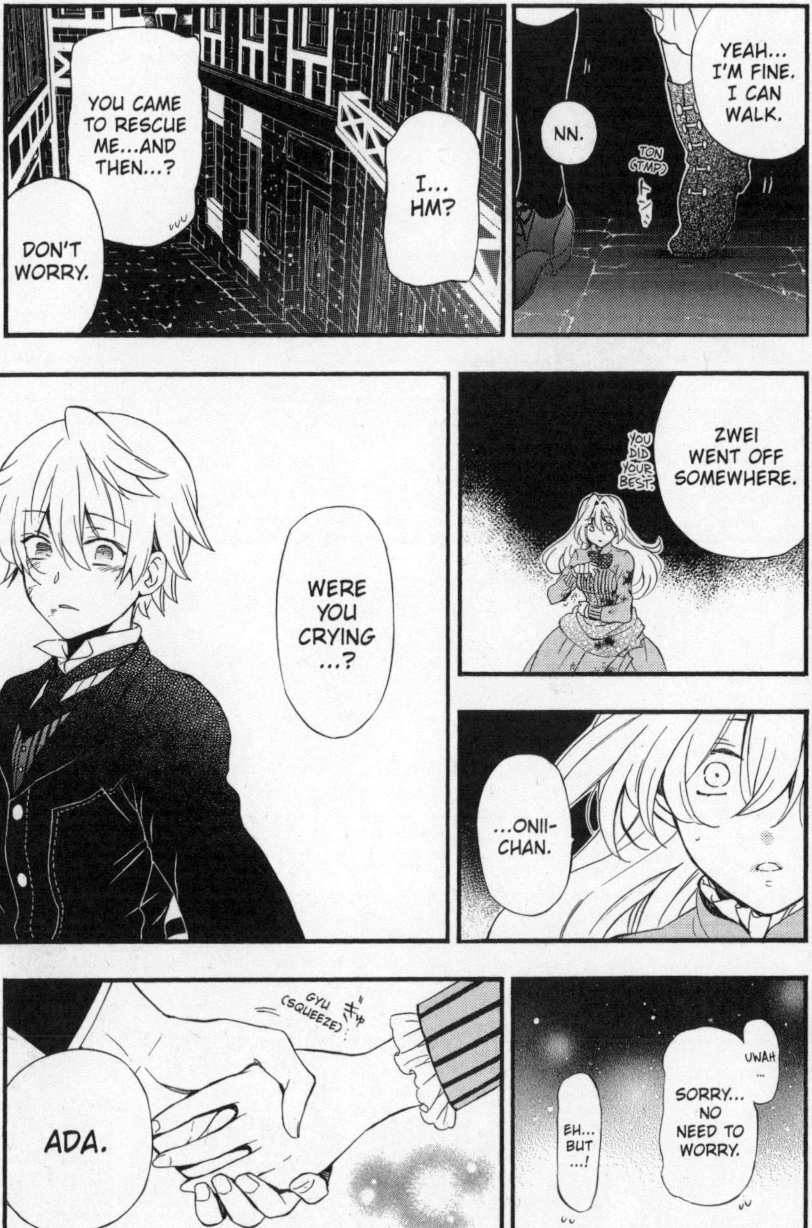
YEAH... I'M FINE. I CAN WALK.
NN.
TON (STMP)
I... HM?
YOU CAME TO RESCUE ME...AND THEN...?
DON'T WORRY.
ZWEI WENT OFF SOMEWHERE.
YOU DID YOUR BEST.
...ONII-CHAN.
WERE YOU CRYING ...?
UWAH ...
SORRY... NO NEED TO WORRY.
EH... BUT ...!
GYU (SQUEEZE)
ADA.

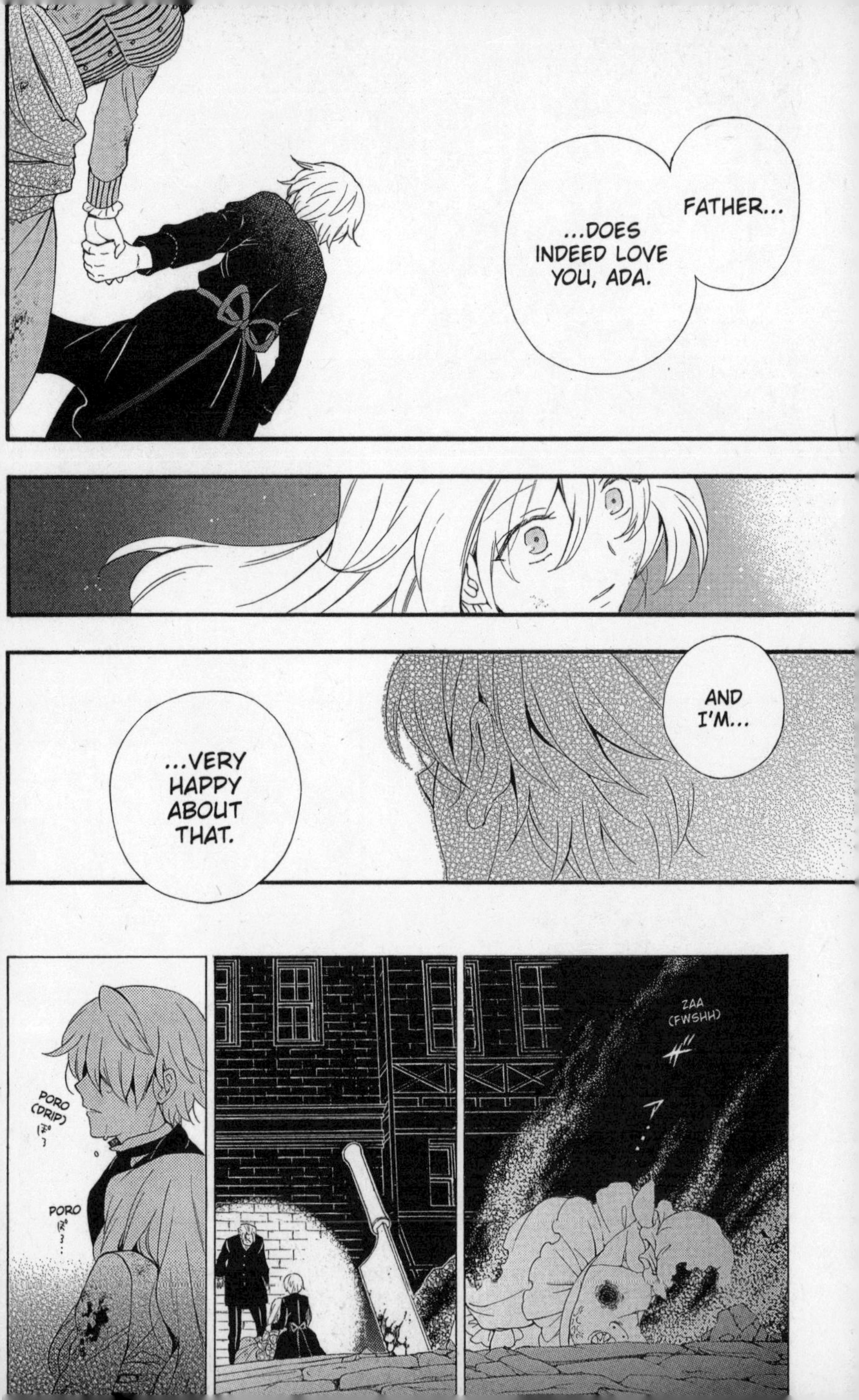
FATHER...
...DOES INDEED LOVE YOU, ADA.
AND I'M...
...VERY HAPPY ABOUT THAT.
ZAA (FWSHH)
PORO (DRIP)
PORO

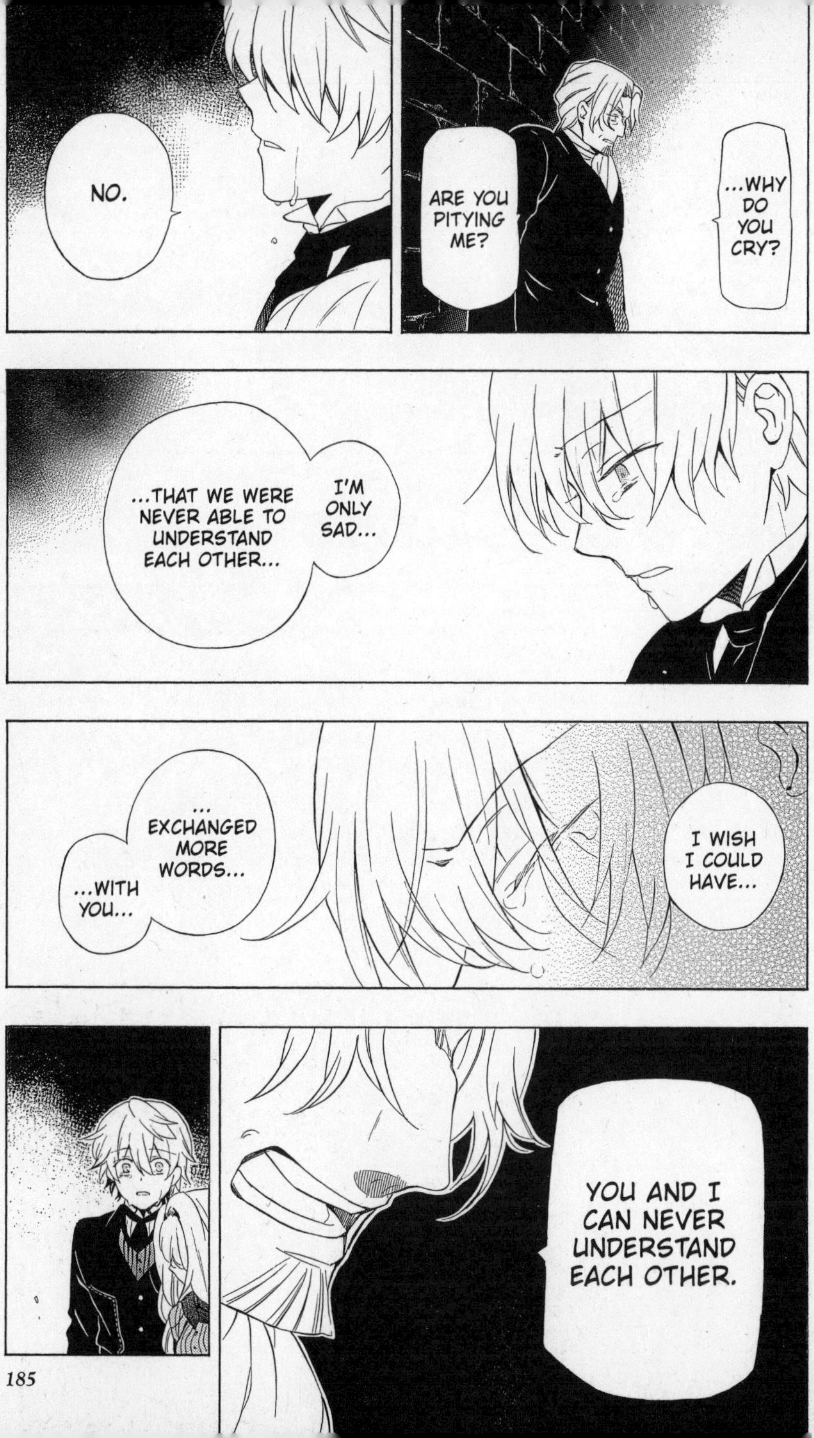
...WHY DO YOU CRY?
ARE YOU PITYING ME?
NO.
I'M ONLY SAD...
...THAT WE WERE NEVER ABLE TO UNDERSTAND EACH OTHER...
I WISH I COULD HAVE...
...EXCHANGED MORE WORDS...
...WITH YOU...
YOU AND I CAN NEVER UNDERSTAND EACH OTHER.

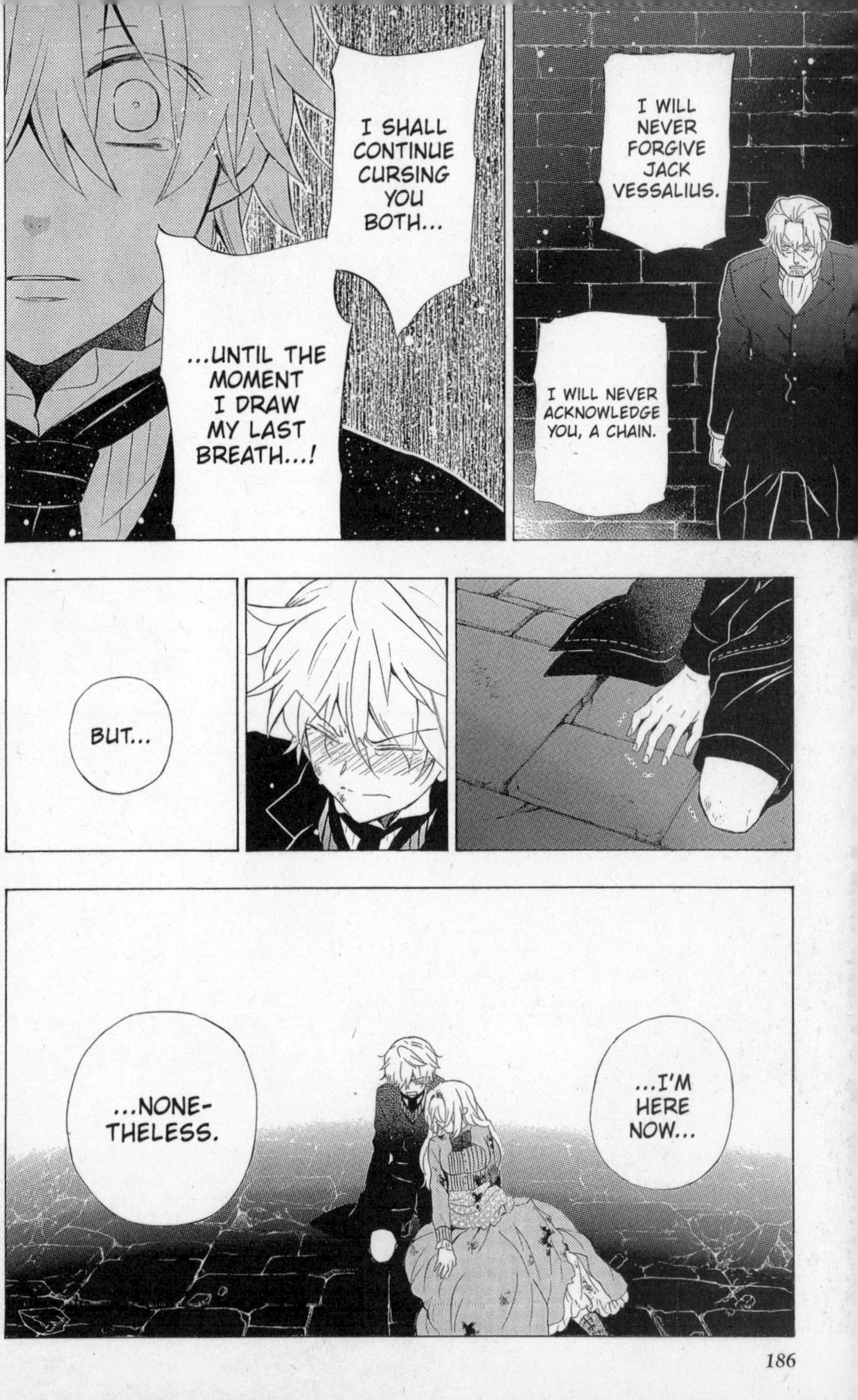

I WILL NEVER FORGIVE JACK VESSALIUS.
I WILL NEVER ACKNOWLEDGE YOU, A CHAIN.
I SHALL CONTINUE CURSING YOU BOTH...
...UNTIL THE MOMENT I DRAW MY LAST BREATH...!
BUT...
...I'M HERE NOW...
...NONE-THELESS.

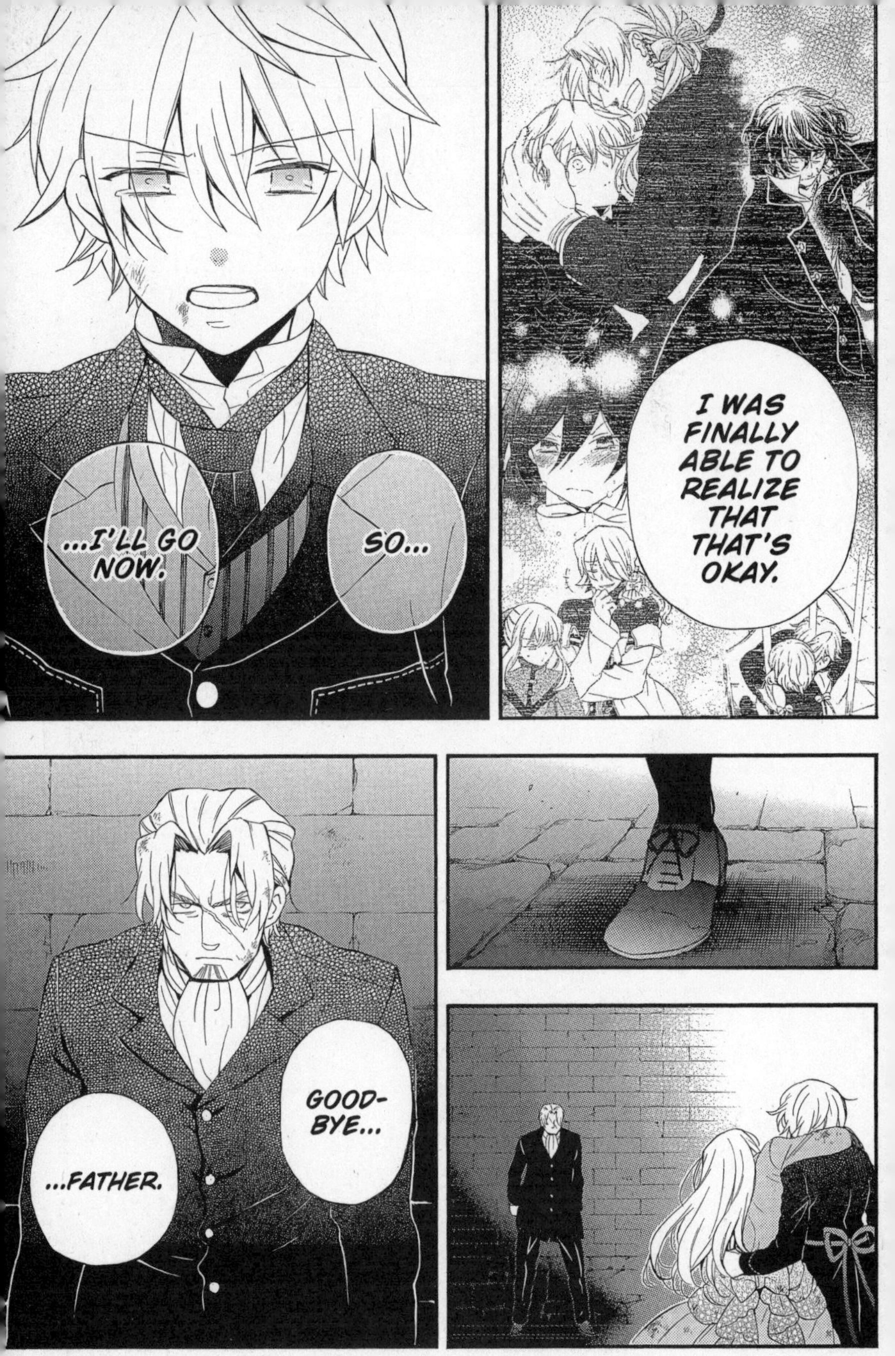
I WAS FINALLY ABLE TO REALIZE THAT THAT'S OKAY.
SO...
...I'LL GO NOW.
GOOD-BYE...
...FATHER.

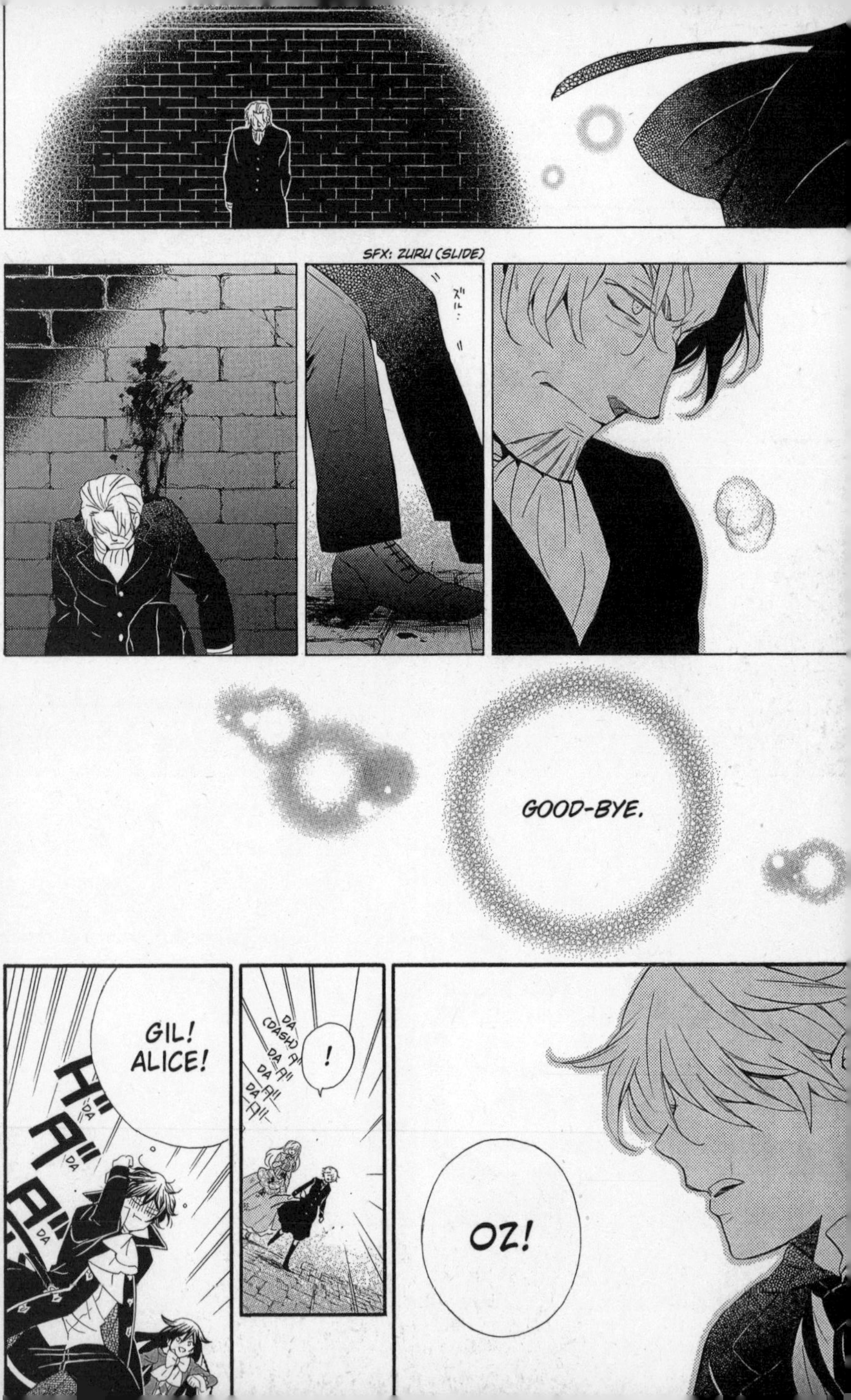
SFX: ZURU (SLIDE)
GOOD-BYE.
OZ!
!
DA (DASH) DA DA DA
GIL! ALICE!

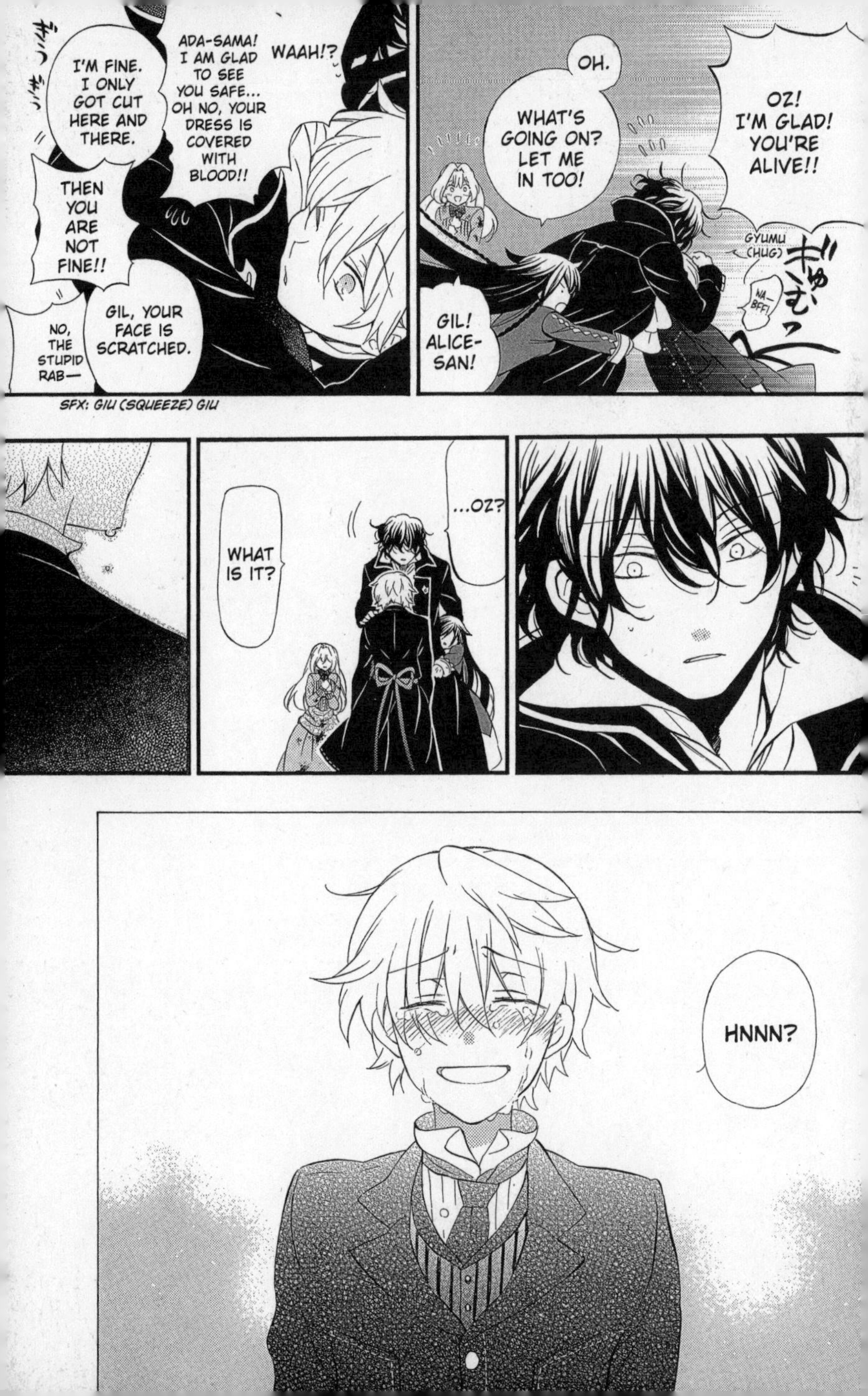
OZ! I'M GLAD! YOU'RE ALIVE!!
GYUMU (HUG)
NA-BFF!
OH.
WHAT'S GOING ON? LET ME IN TOO!
GIL! ALICE-SAN!
WAAH!?
ADA-SAMA! I AM GLAD TO SEE YOU SAFE... OH NO, YOUR DRESS IS COVERED WITH BLOOD!!
I'M FINE. I ONLY GOT CUT HERE AND THERE.
THEN YOU ARE NOT FINE!!
GIL, YOUR FACE IS SCRATCHED.
NO, THE STUPID RAB—
SFX: GIU (SQUEEZE) GIU
...OZ?
WHAT IS IT?
HNNN?

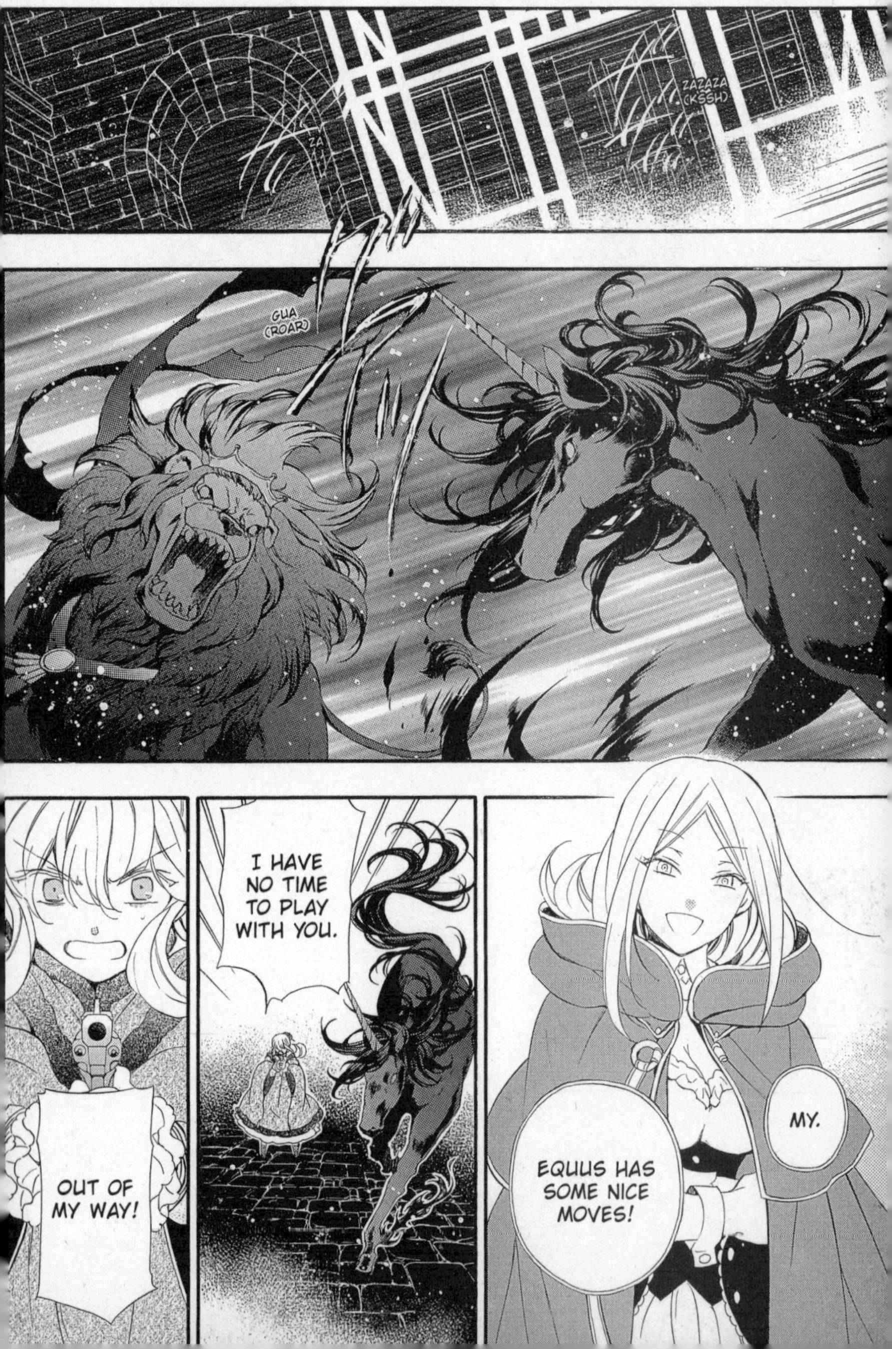
ZAZAZA (KSSH)
ZA
GUA (ROAR)
MY.
EQUUS HAS SOME NICE MOVES!
I HAVE NO TIME TO PLAY WITH YOU.
OUT OF MY WAY!

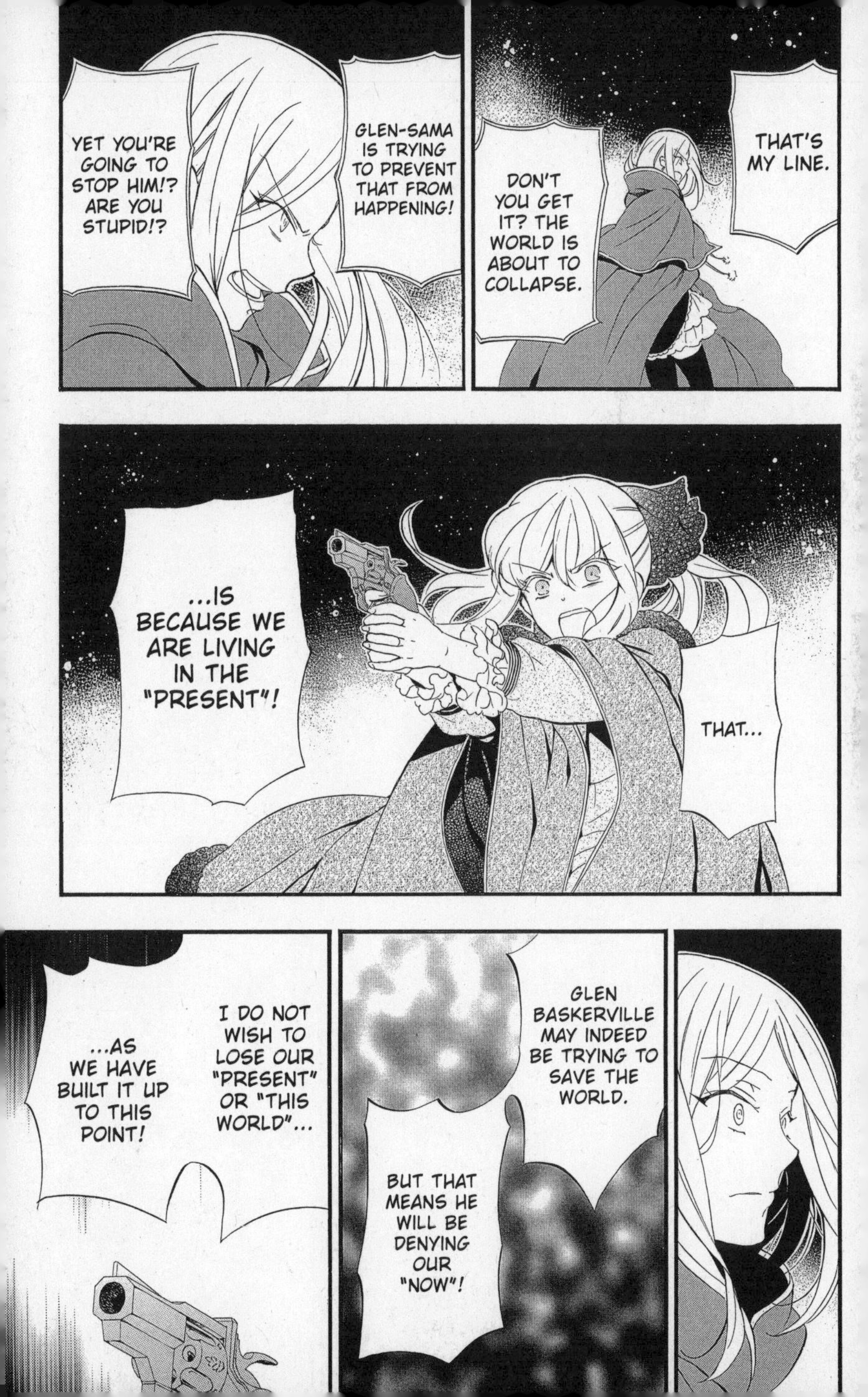
THAT'S MY LINE.
DON'T YOU GET IT? THE WORLD IS ABOUT TO COLLAPSE.
GLEN-SAMA IS TRYING TO PREVENT THAT FROM HAPPENING!
YET YOU'RE GOING TO STOP HIM!? ARE YOU STUPID!?
THAT...
...IS BECAUSE WE ARE LIVING IN THE "PRESENT"!
GLEN BASKERVILLE MAY INDEED BE TRYING TO SAVE THE WORLD.
BUT THAT MEANS HE WILL BE DENYING OUR "NOW"!
I DO NOT WISH TO LOSE OUR "PRESENT" OR "THIS WORLD"...
...AS WE HAVE BUILT IT UP TO THIS POINT!

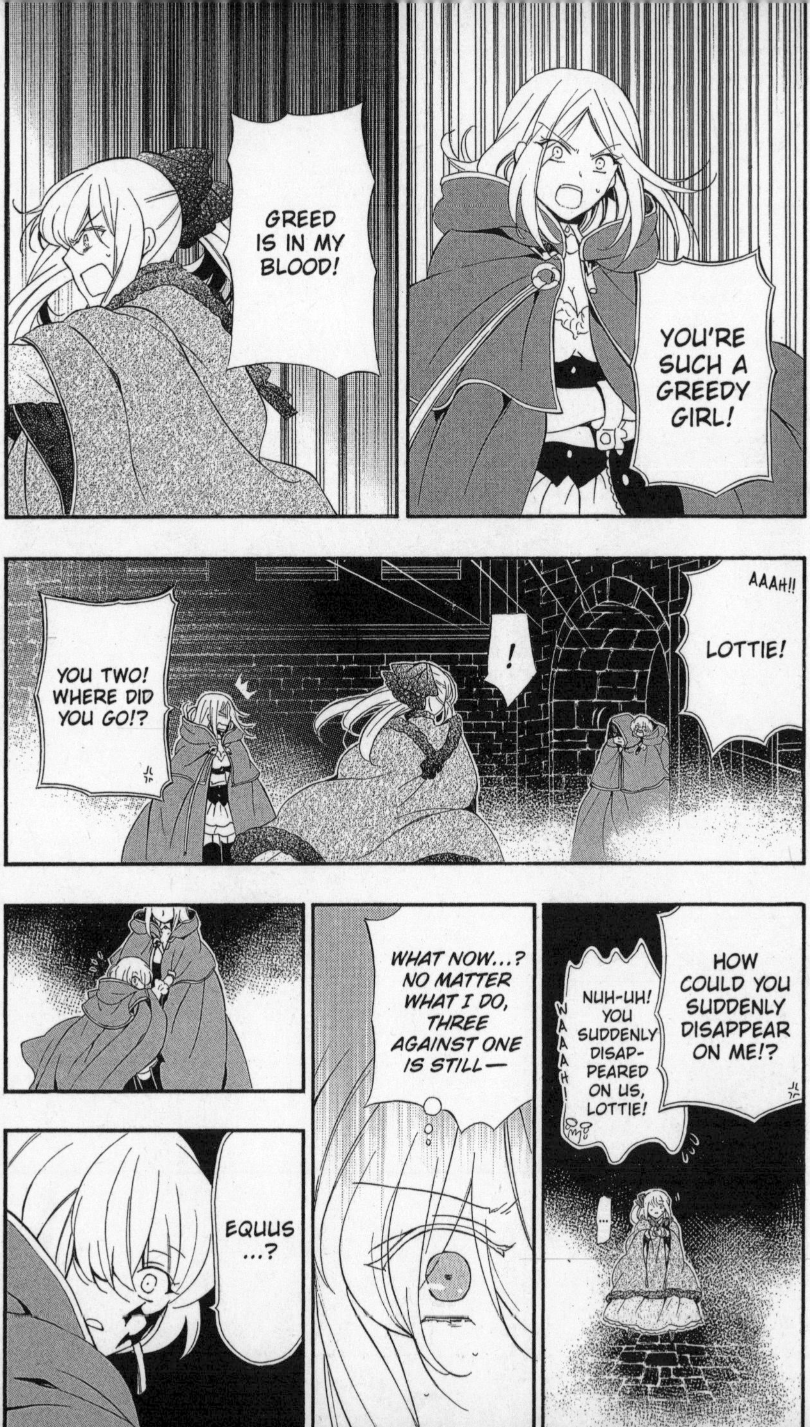
YOU'RE SUCH A GREEDY GIRL!
GREED IS IN MY BLOOD!
AAAH!!
LOTTIE!
!
YOU TWO! WHERE DID YOU GO!?
HOW COULD YOU SUDDENLY DISAPPEAR ON ME!?
NUH-UH! YOU SUDDENLY DISAP-PEARED ON US, LOTTIE!
WAAAAH!
...
WHAT NOW...? NO MATTER WHAT I DO, THREE AGAINST ONE IS STILL—
EQUUS ...?

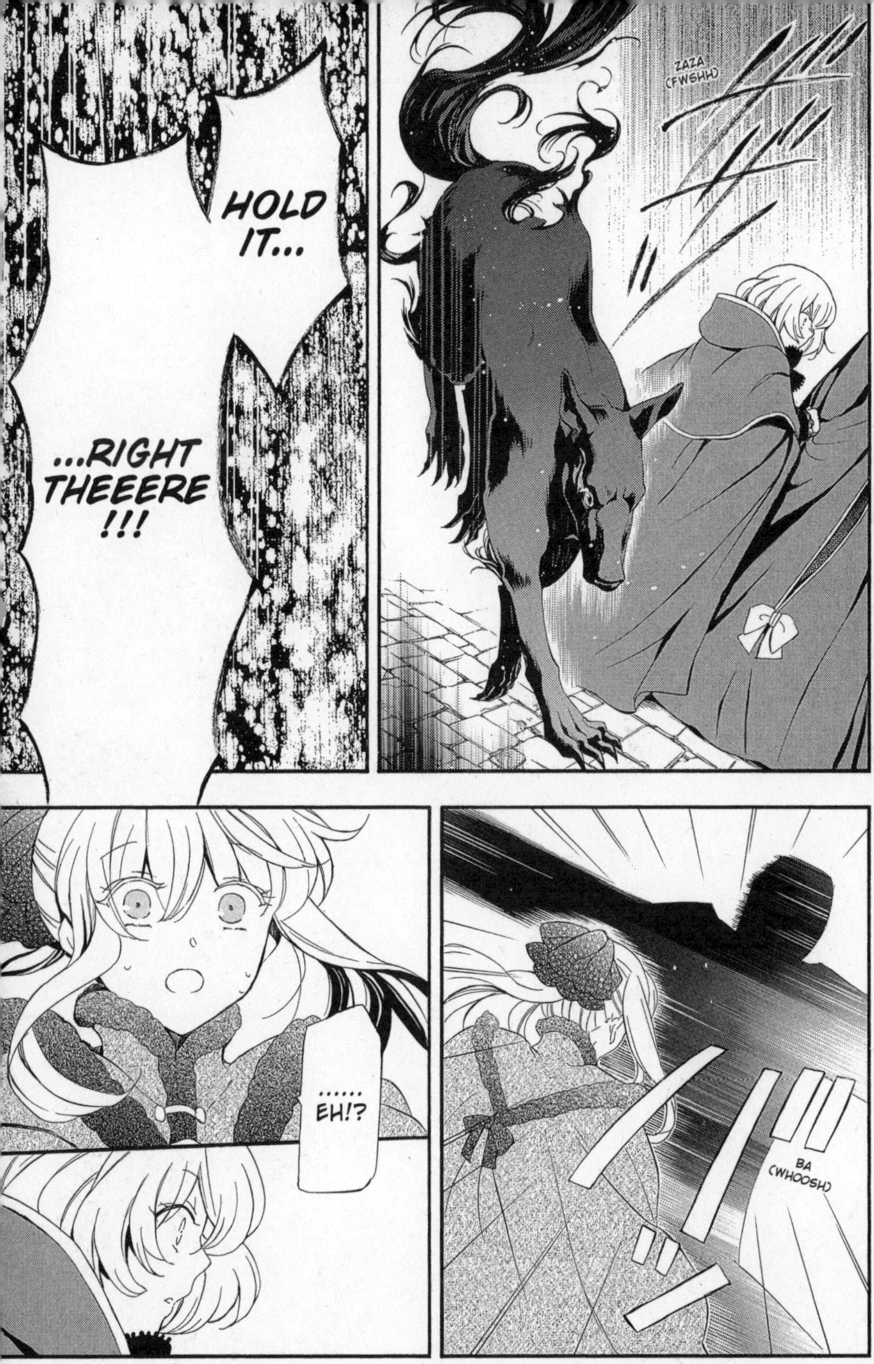
ZAZA (FWSHH)
HOLD IT...
...RIGHT THEEERE !!!
BA (WHOOSH)
......EH!?

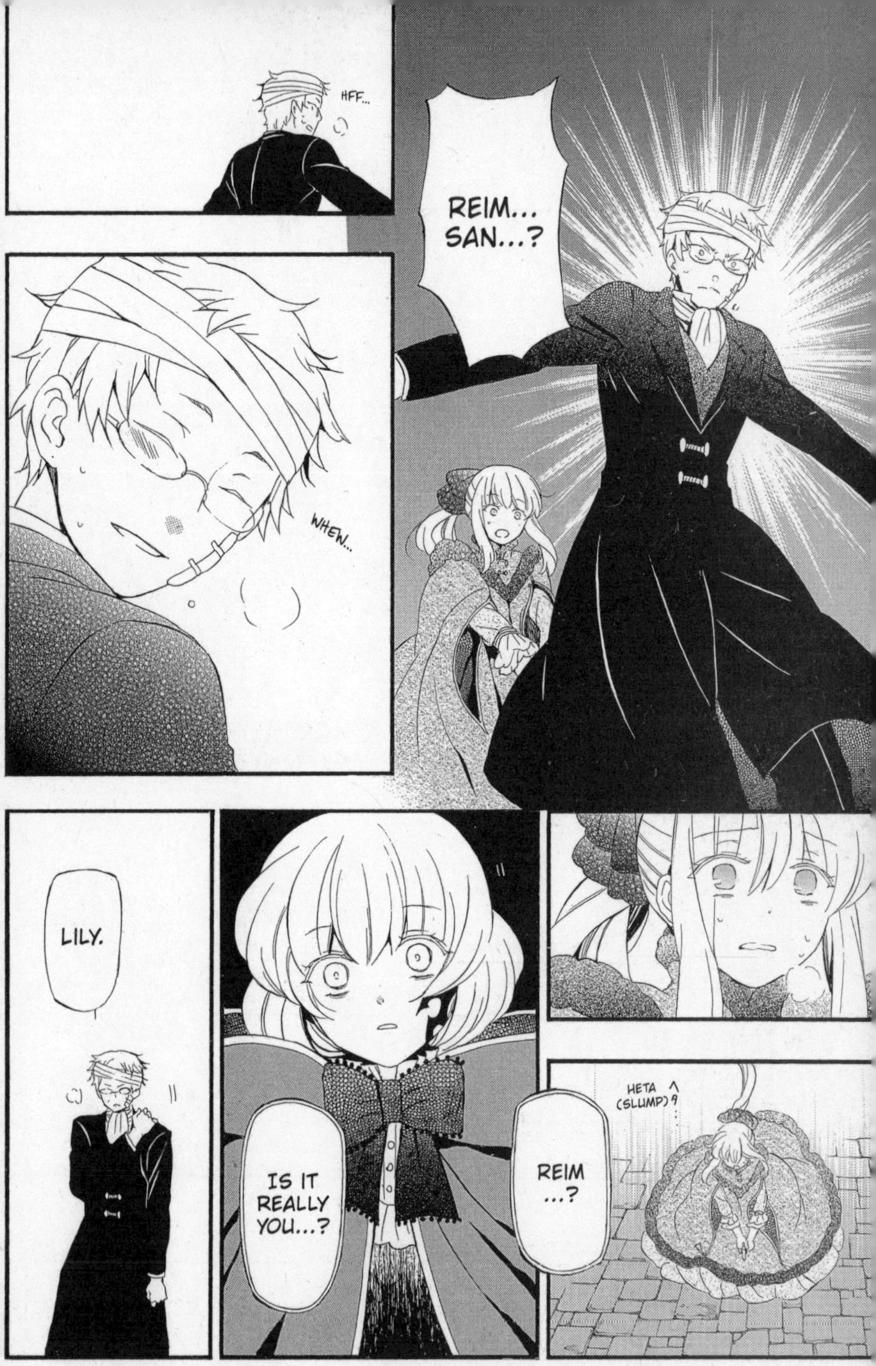
REIM... SAN...?
HFF...
WHEW...
HETA (SLUMP)
REIM ...?
IS IT REALLY YOU...?
LILY.

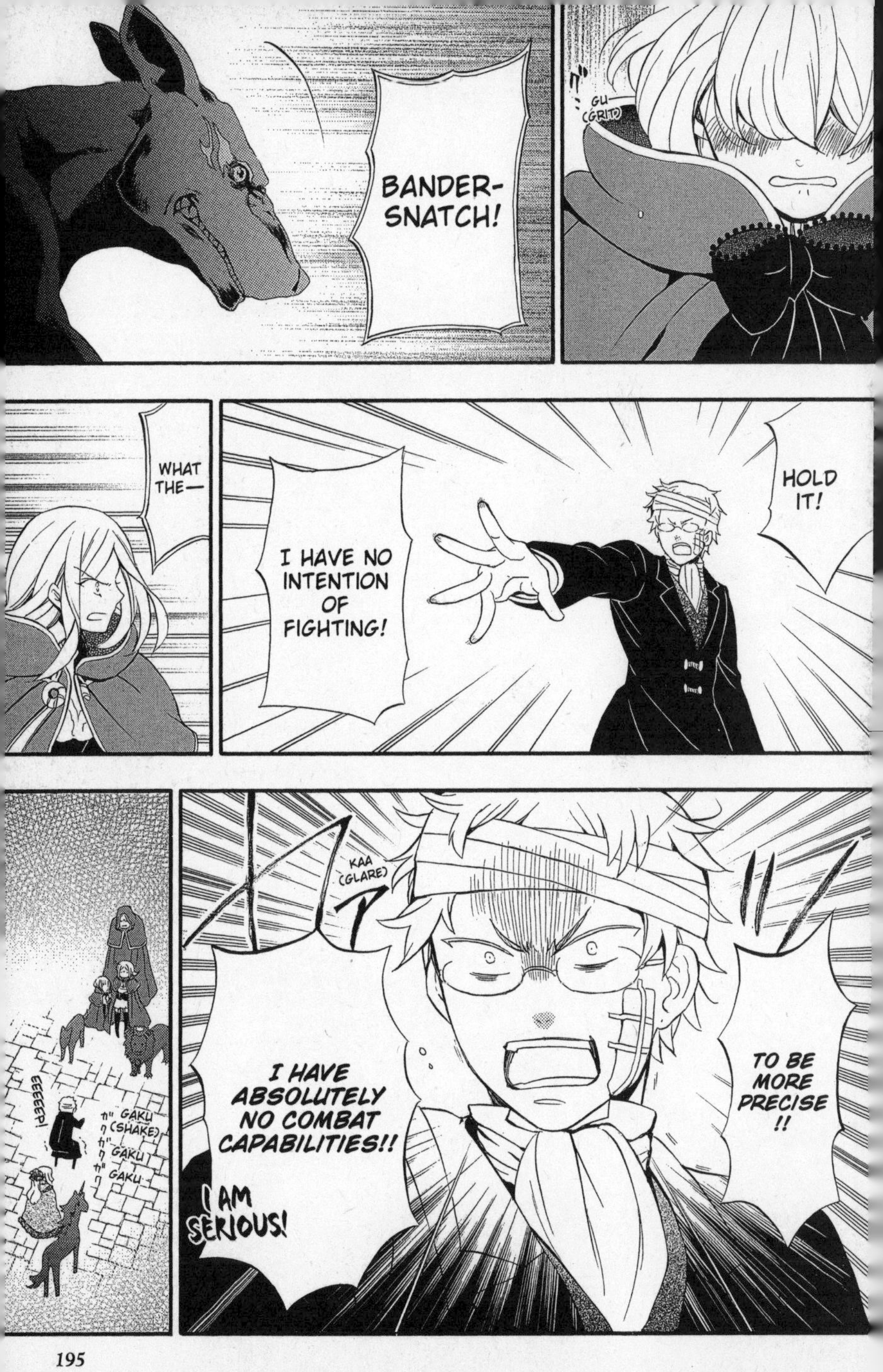
GU (GRIT)
BANDER-SNATCH!
HOLD IT!
I HAVE NO INTENTION OF FIGHTING!
WHAT THE—
KAA (GLARE)
TO BE MORE PRECISE!!
I HAVE ABSOLUTELY NO COMBAT CAPABILITIES!!
I AM SERIOUS!
EEEEEP!
GAKU (SHAKE)
GAKU
GAKU

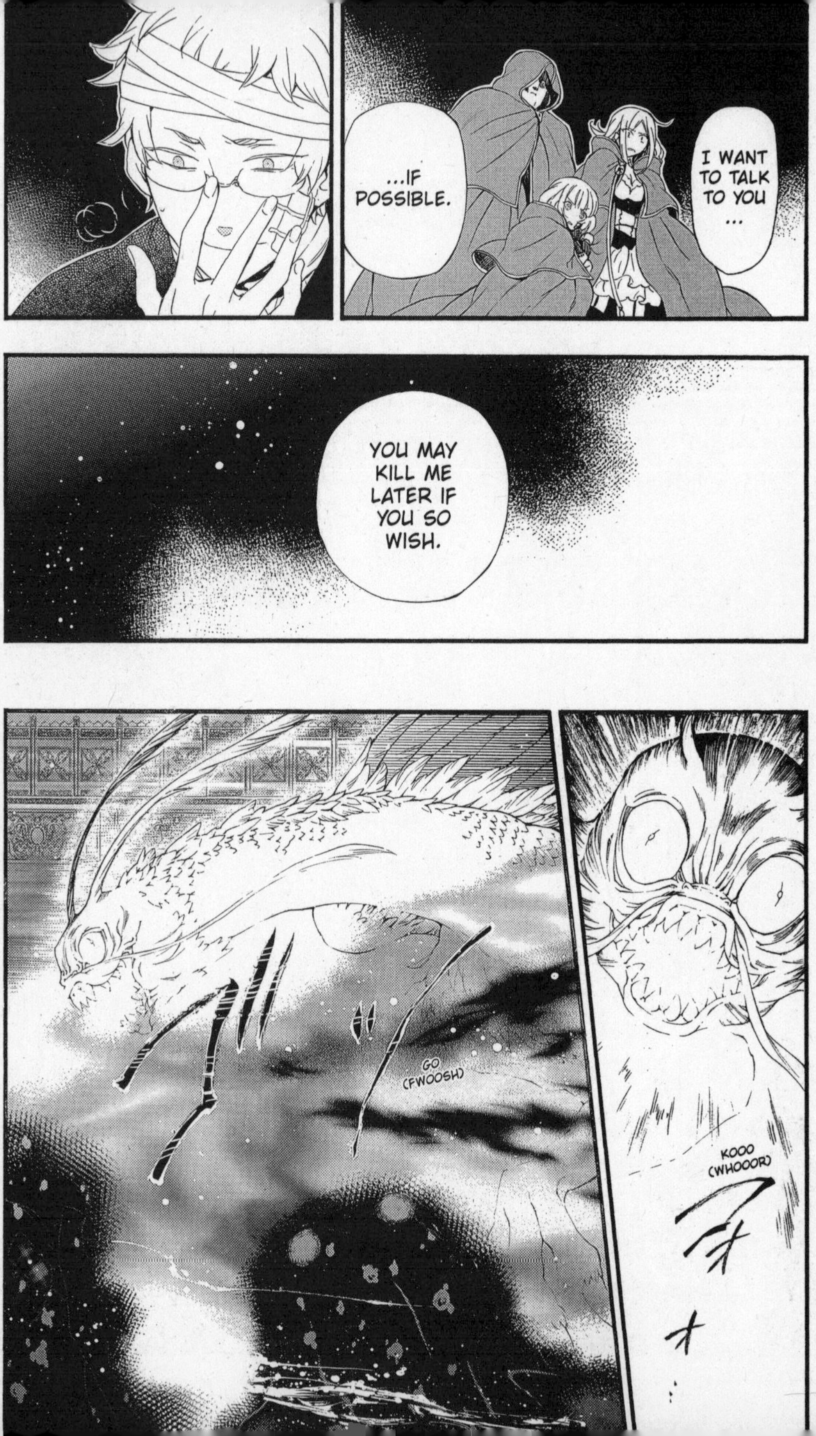
I WANT TO TALK TO YOU ...
...IF POSSIBLE.
YOU MAY KILL ME LATER IF YOU SO WISH.
KOOO (WHOOOR)
GO (FWOOSH)

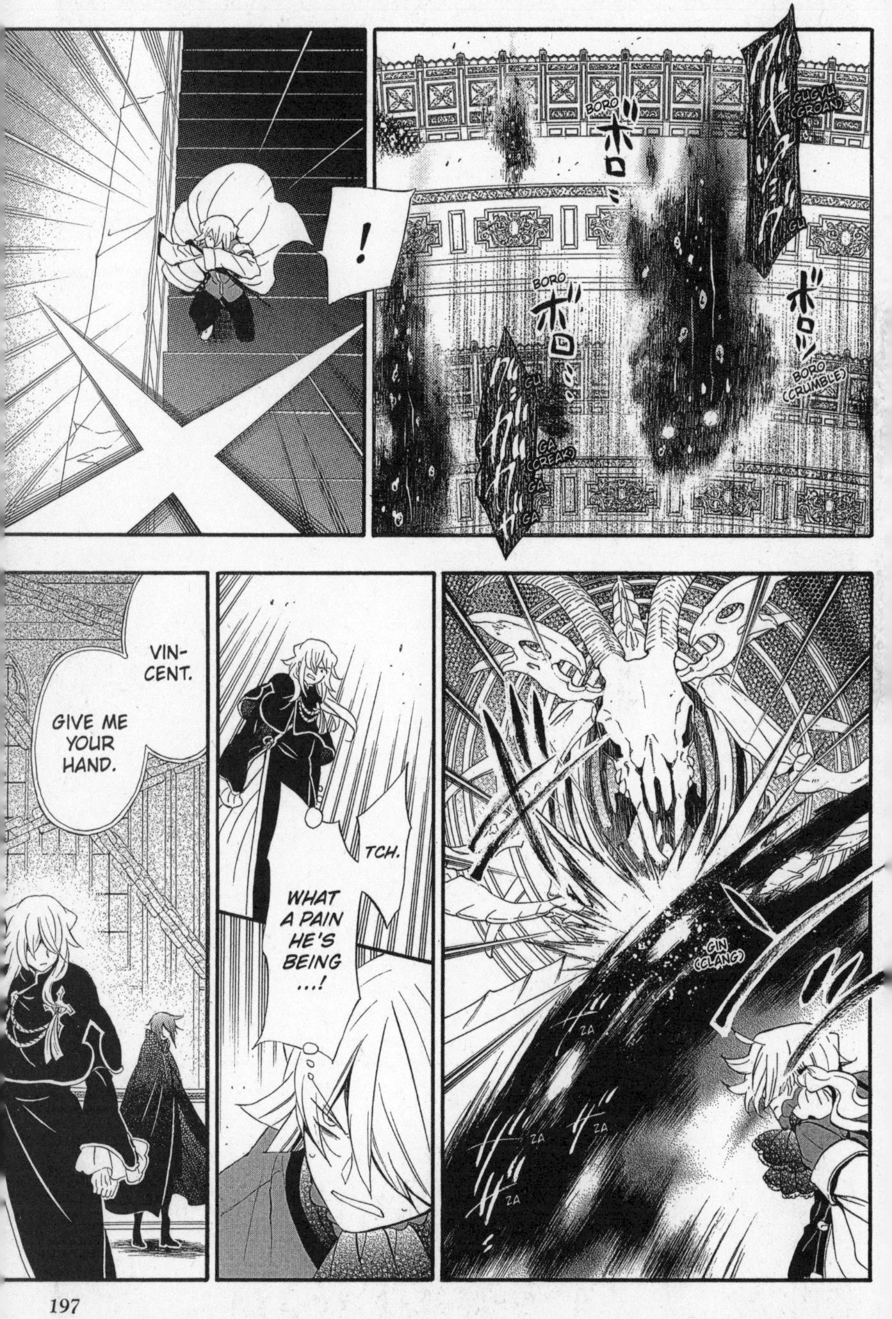
GUGYU (GROAN)
GU
BORO
BORO (CRUMBLE)
BORO
GU
GA (CREAK)
GA
GA
!
GIN (CLANG)
ZA
ZA
ZA
ZA
TCH.
WHAT A PAIN HE'S BEING ...!
VIN-CENT.
GIVE ME YOUR HAND.

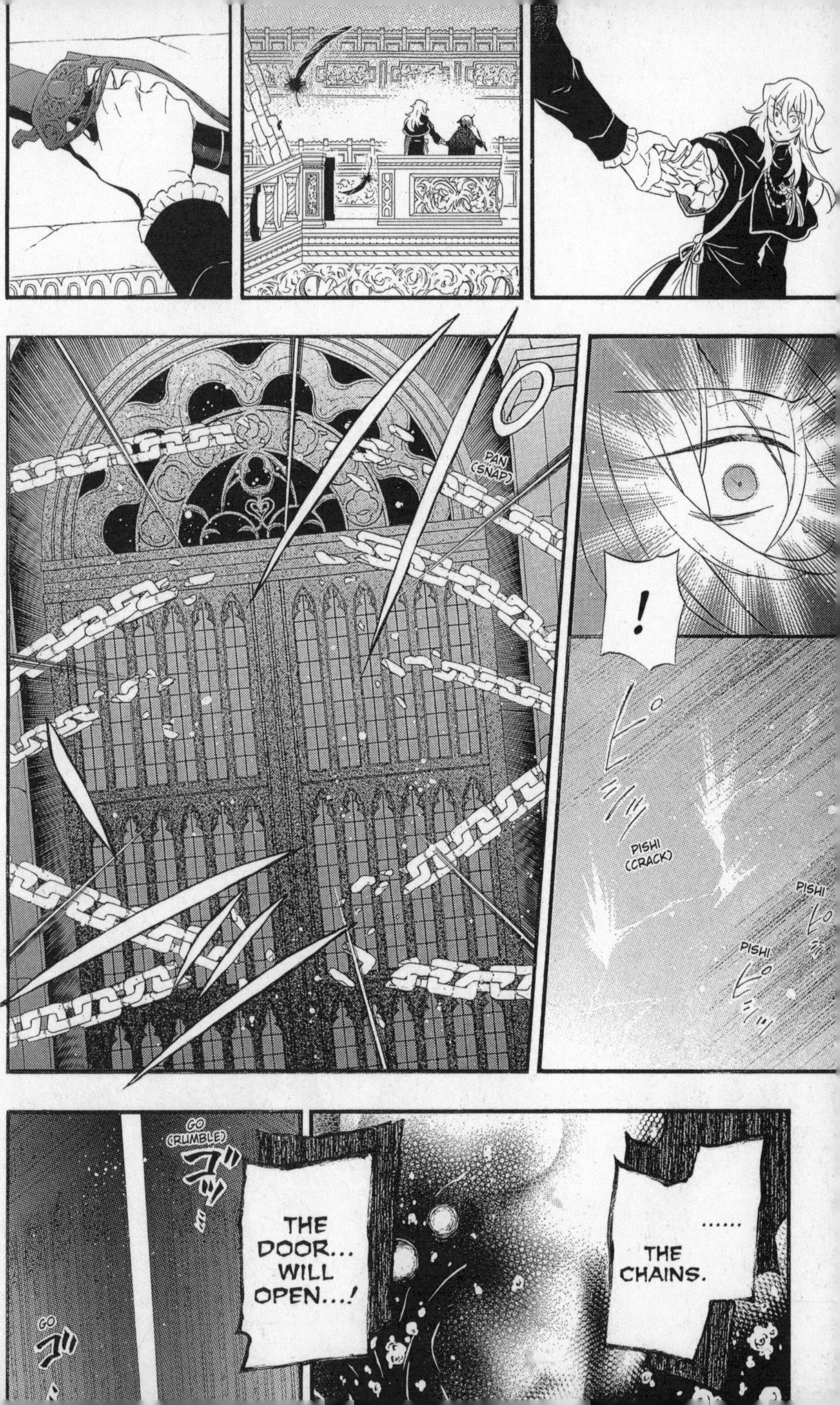
PAN (SNAP)
!
PISHI (CRACK)
PISHI
PISHI
THE DOOR... WILL OPEN...!
......
THE CHAINS.
GO (RUMBLE)
GO

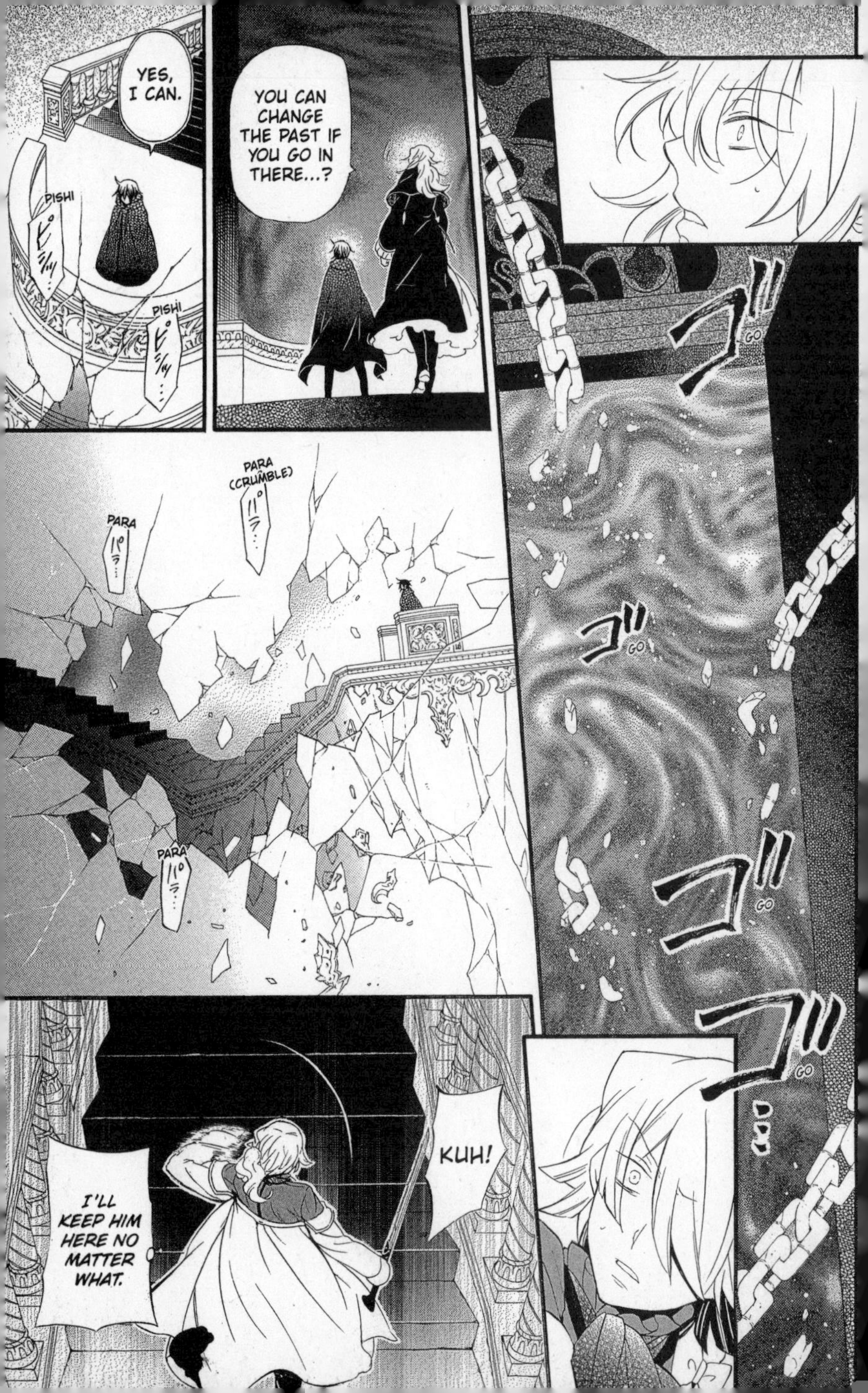
YOU CAN CHANGE THE PAST IF YOU GO IN THERE...?
YES, I CAN.
PISHI
PISHI
GO
GO
PARA (CRUMBLE)
PARA
PARA
GO
GO
KUH!
I'LL KEEP HIM HERE NO MATTER WHAT.

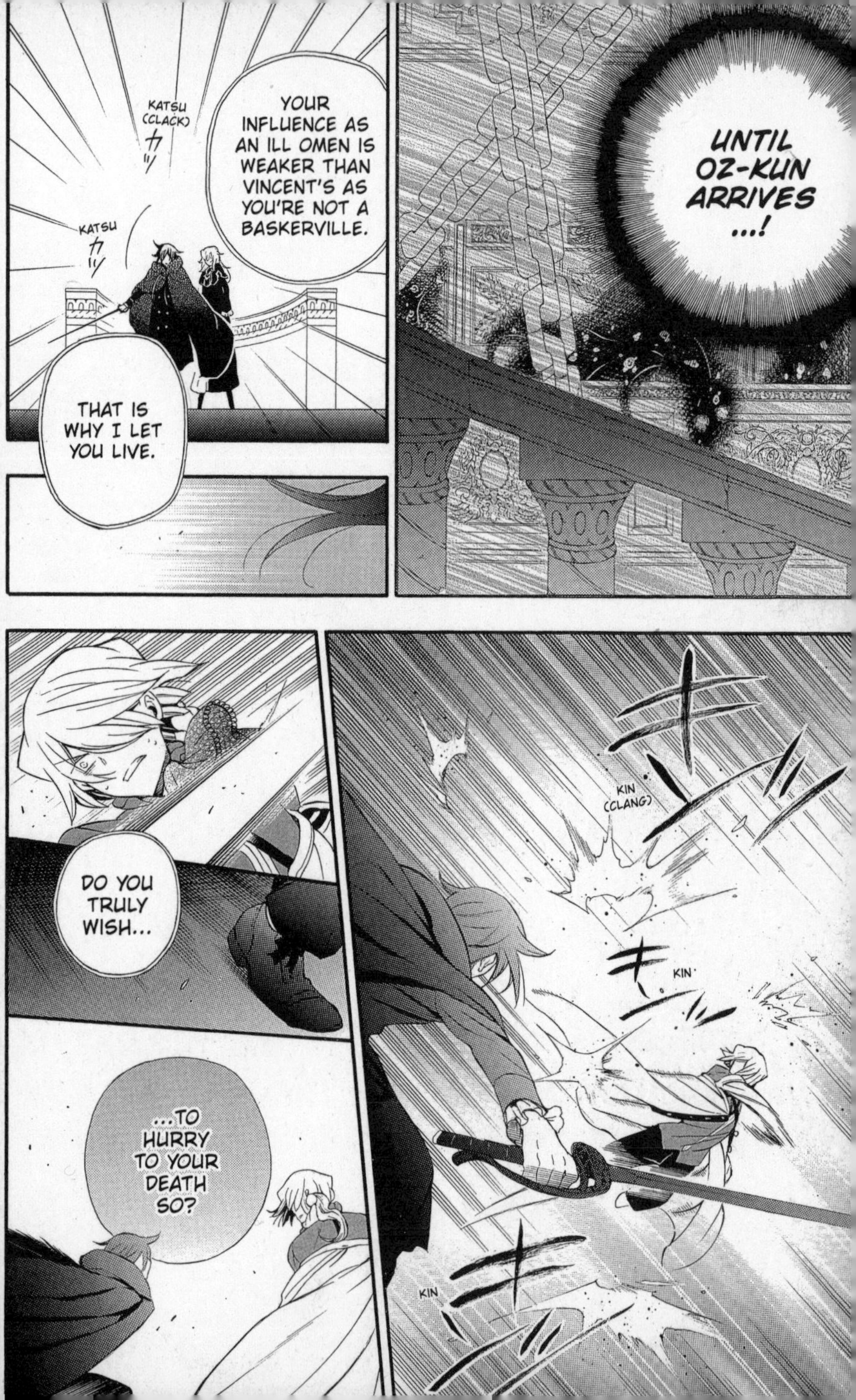
UNTIL OZ-KUN ARRIVES ...!
YOUR INFLUENCE AS AN ILL OMEN IS WEAKER THAN VINCENT'S AS YOU'RE NOT A BASKERVILLE.
KATSU (CLACK)
KATSU
THAT IS WHY I LET YOU LIVE.
KIN (CLANG)
KIN
KIN
DO YOU TRULY WISH...
...TO HURRY TO YOUR DEATH SO?

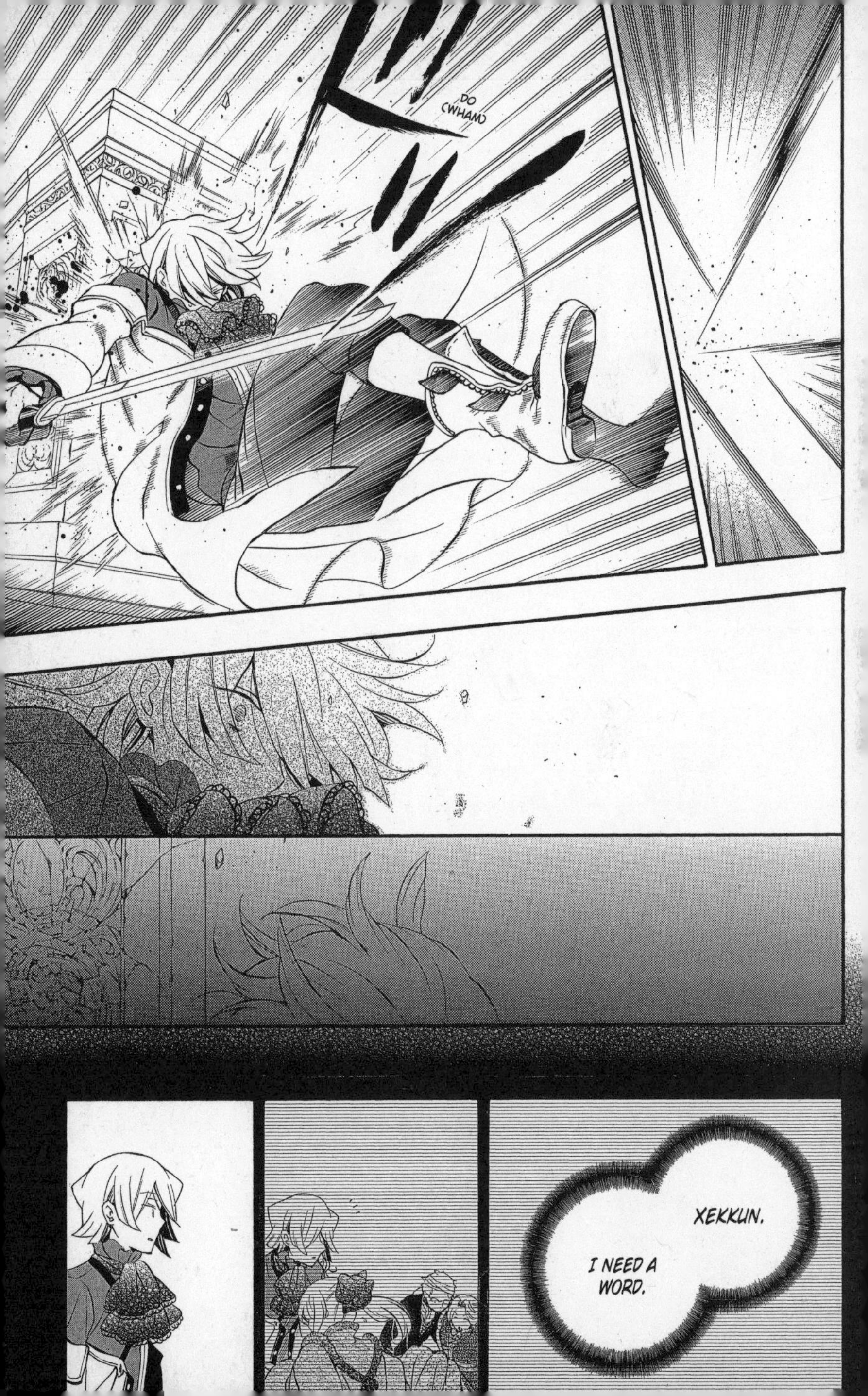
DO
(WHAM)
XEKKUN.
I NEED A WORD.

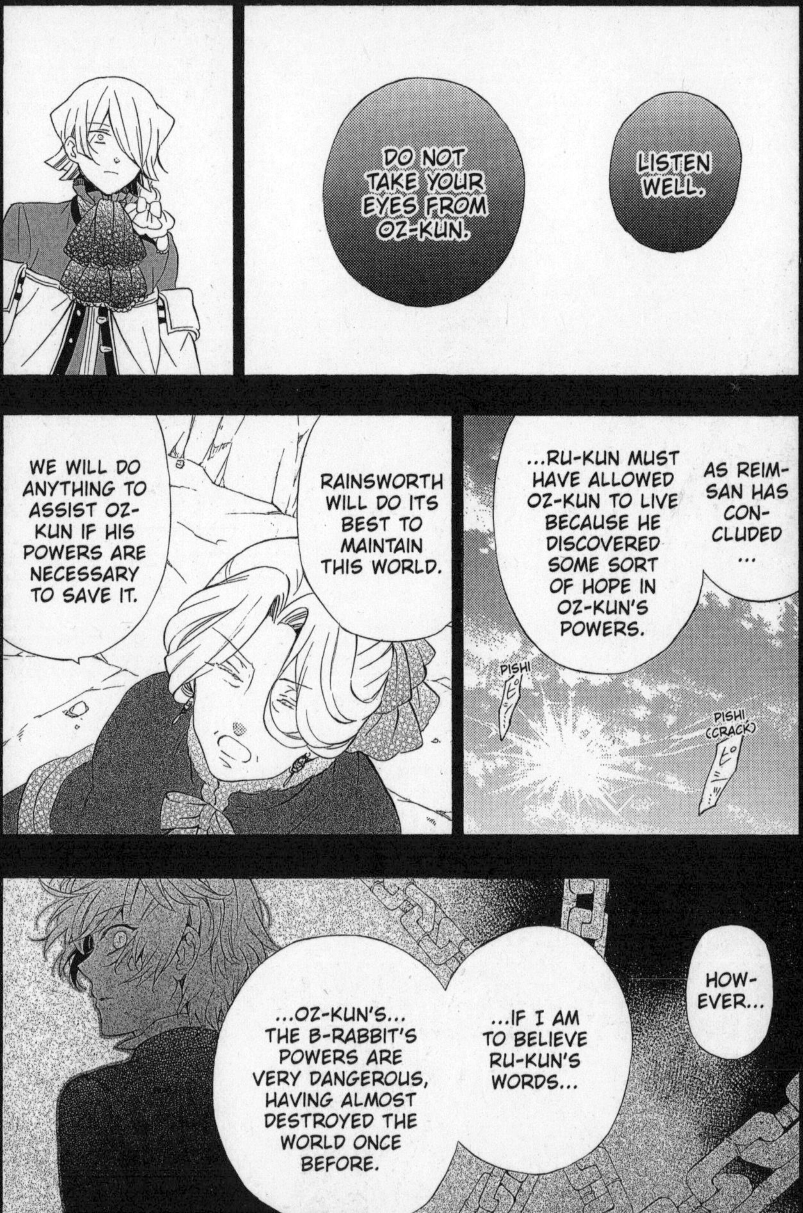
LISTEN WELL.
DO NOT TAKE YOUR EYES FROM OZ-KUN.
AS REIM-SAN HAS CON-CLUDED ...
...RU-KUN MUST HAVE ALLOWED OZ-KUN TO LIVE BECAUSE HE DISCOVERED SOME SORT OF HOPE IN OZ-KUN'S POWERS.
PISHI
PISHI (CRACK)
RAINSWORTH WILL DO ITS BEST TO MAINTAIN THIS WORLD.
WE WILL DO ANYTHING TO ASSIST OZ-KUN IF HIS POWERS ARE NECESSARY TO SAVE IT.
HOW-EVER...
...IF I AM TO BELIEVE RU-KUN'S WORDS...
...OZ-KUN'S... THE B-RABBIT'S POWERS ARE VERY DANGEROUS, HAVING ALMOST DESTROYED THE WORLD ONCE BEFORE.

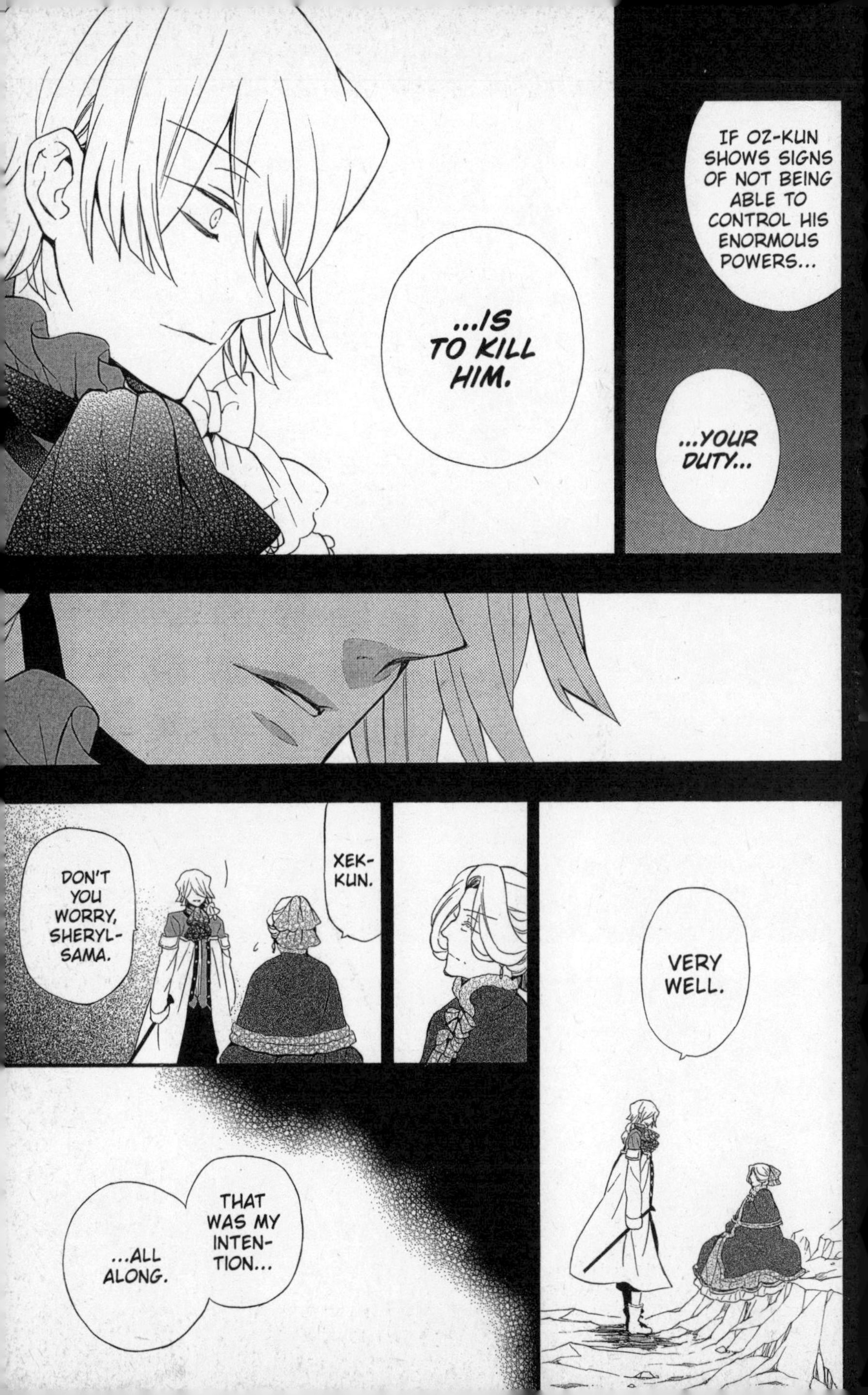
IF OZ-KUN SHOWS SIGNS OF NOT BEING ABLE TO CONTROL HIS ENORMOUS POWERS...
...YOUR DUTY...
...IS TO KILL HIM.
VERY WELL.
XEK-KUN.
DON'T YOU WORRY, SHERYL-SAMA.
THAT WAS MY INTENTION...
...ALL ALONG.

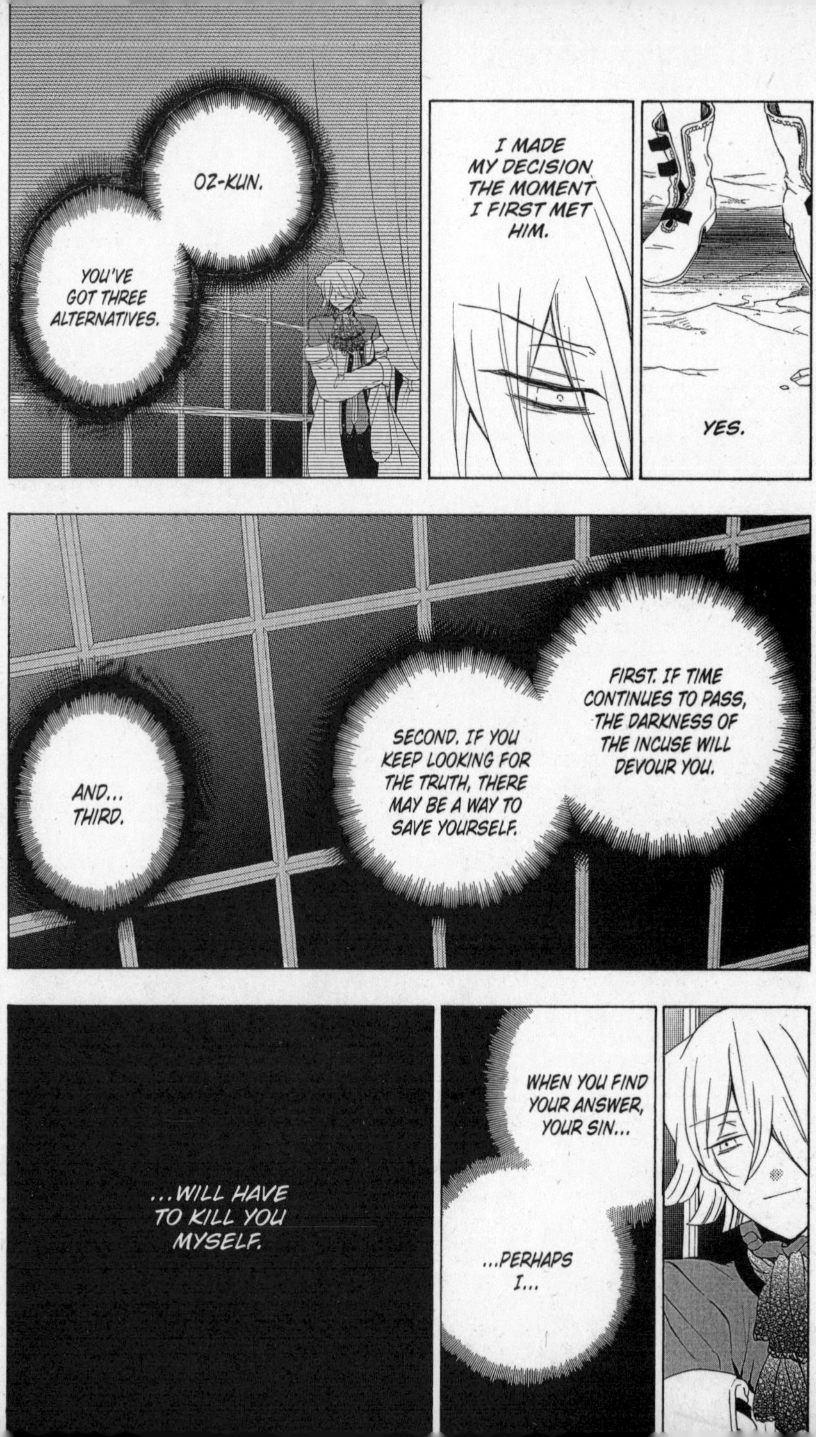
YES.
I MADE MY DECISION THE MOMENT I FIRST MET HIM.
OZ-KUN.
YOU'VE GOT THREE ALTERNATIVES.
FIRST. IF TIME CONTINUES TO PASS, THE DARKNESS OF THE INCUSE WILL DEVOUR YOU.
SECOND. IF YOU KEEP LOOKING FOR THE TRUTH, THERE MAY BE A WAY TO SAVE YOURSELF.
AND... THIRD.
WHEN YOU FIND YOUR ANSWER, YOUR SIN...
...PERHAPS I...
...WILL HAVE TO KILL YOU MYSELF.

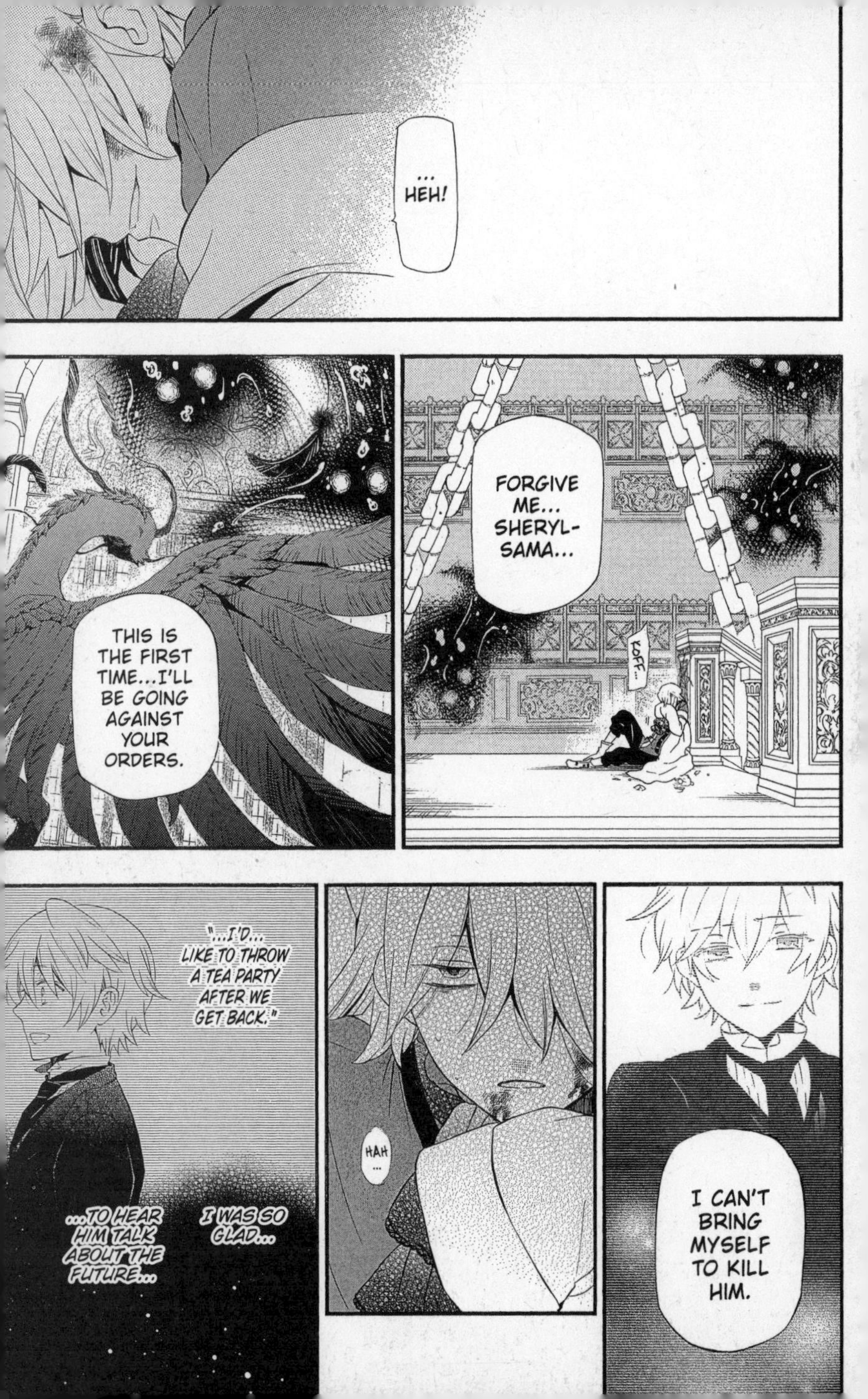
...HEH!
FORGIVE ME... SHERYL-SAMA...
KOFF...
THIS IS THE FIRST TIME...I'LL BE GOING AGAINST YOUR ORDERS.
I CAN'T BRING MYSELF TO KILL HIM.
HAH ...
"...I'D... LIKE TO THROW A TEA PARTY AFTER WE GET BACK."
I WAS SO GLAD...
...TO HEAR HIM TALK ABOUT THE FUTURE...

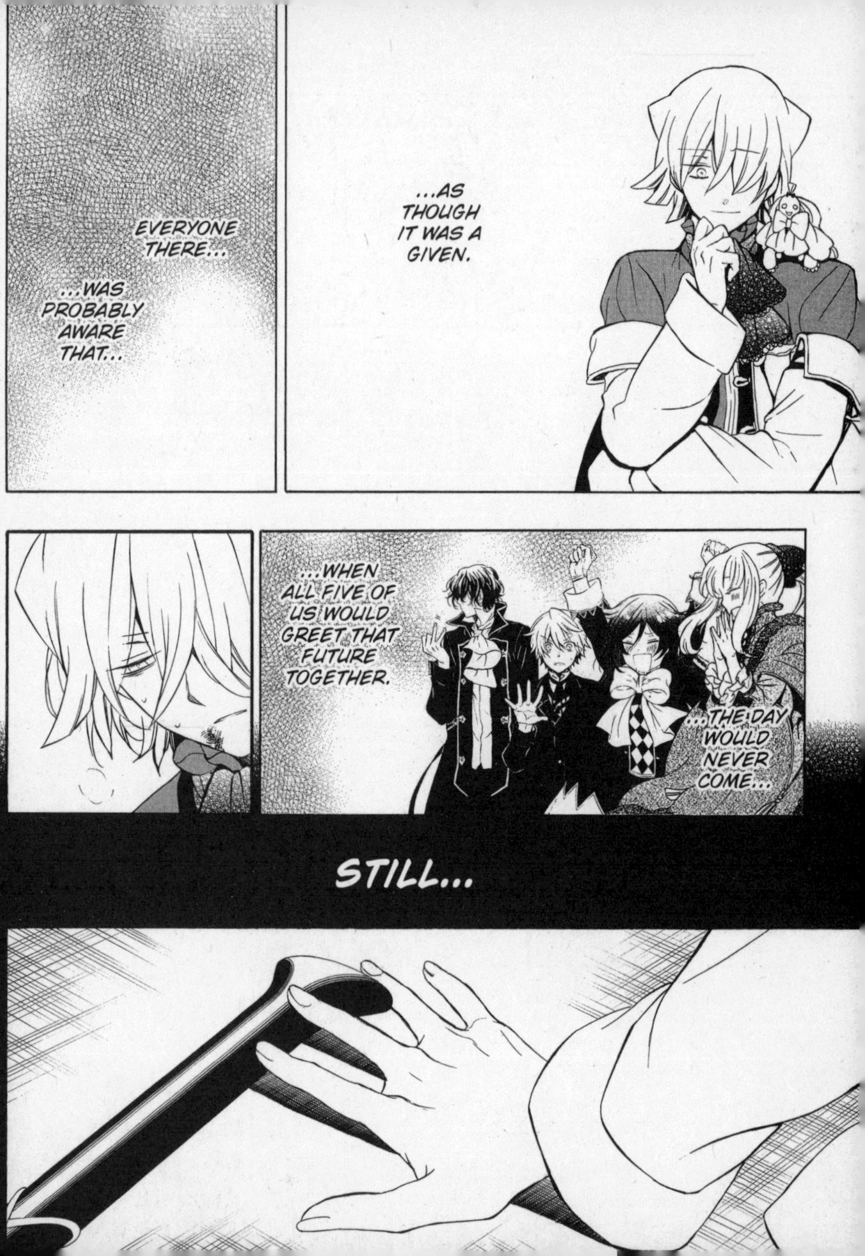
...AS THOUGH IT WAS A GIVEN.
EVERYONE THERE...
...WAS PROBABLY AWARE THAT...
...THE DAY WOULD NEVER COME...
...WHEN ALL FIVE OF US WOULD GREET THAT FUTURE TOGETHER.
STILL...

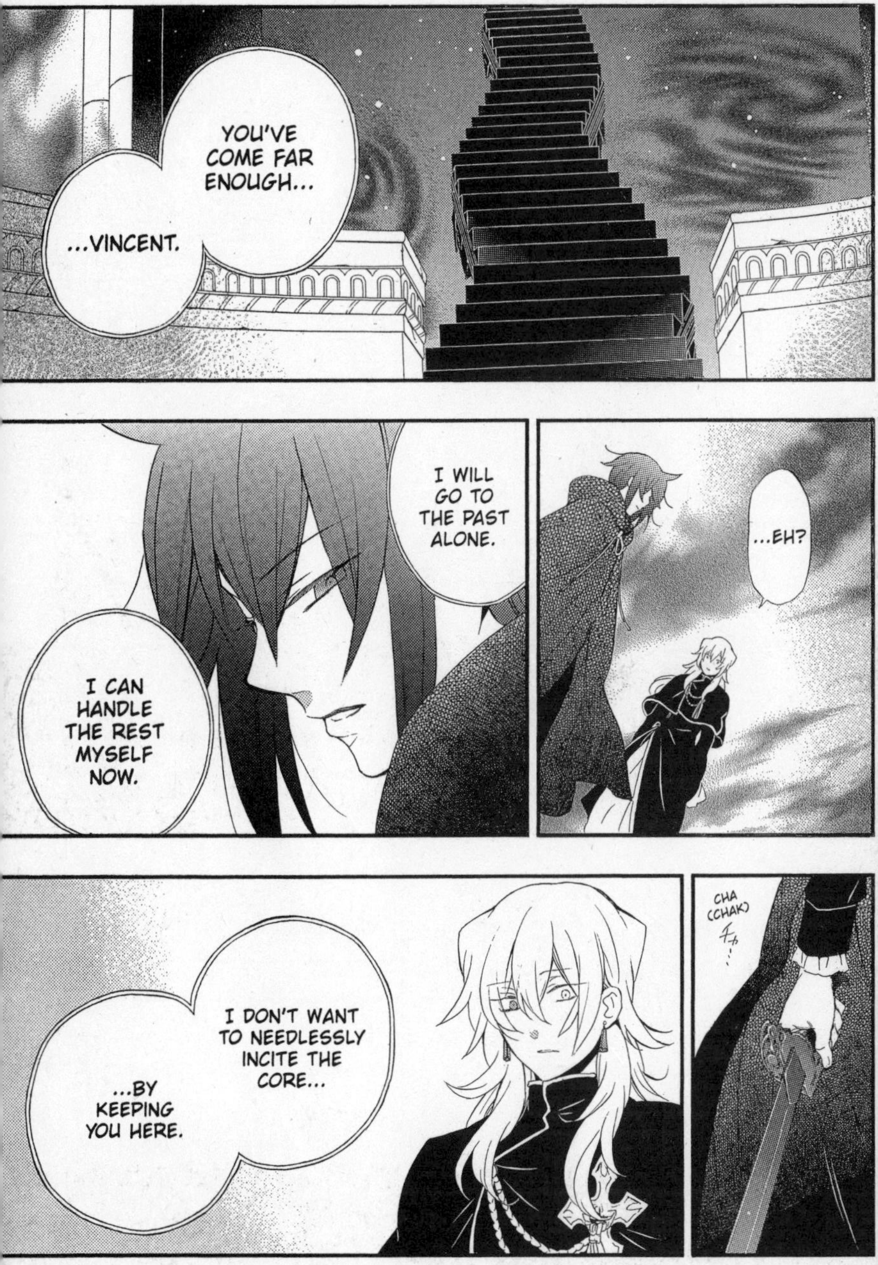
YOU'VE COME FAR ENOUGH...
...VINCENT.
...EH?
I WILL GO TO THE PAST ALONE.
I CAN HANDLE THE REST MYSELF NOW.
CHA (CHAK)
I DON'T WANT TO NEEDLESSLY INCITE THE CORE...
...BY KEEPING YOU HERE.

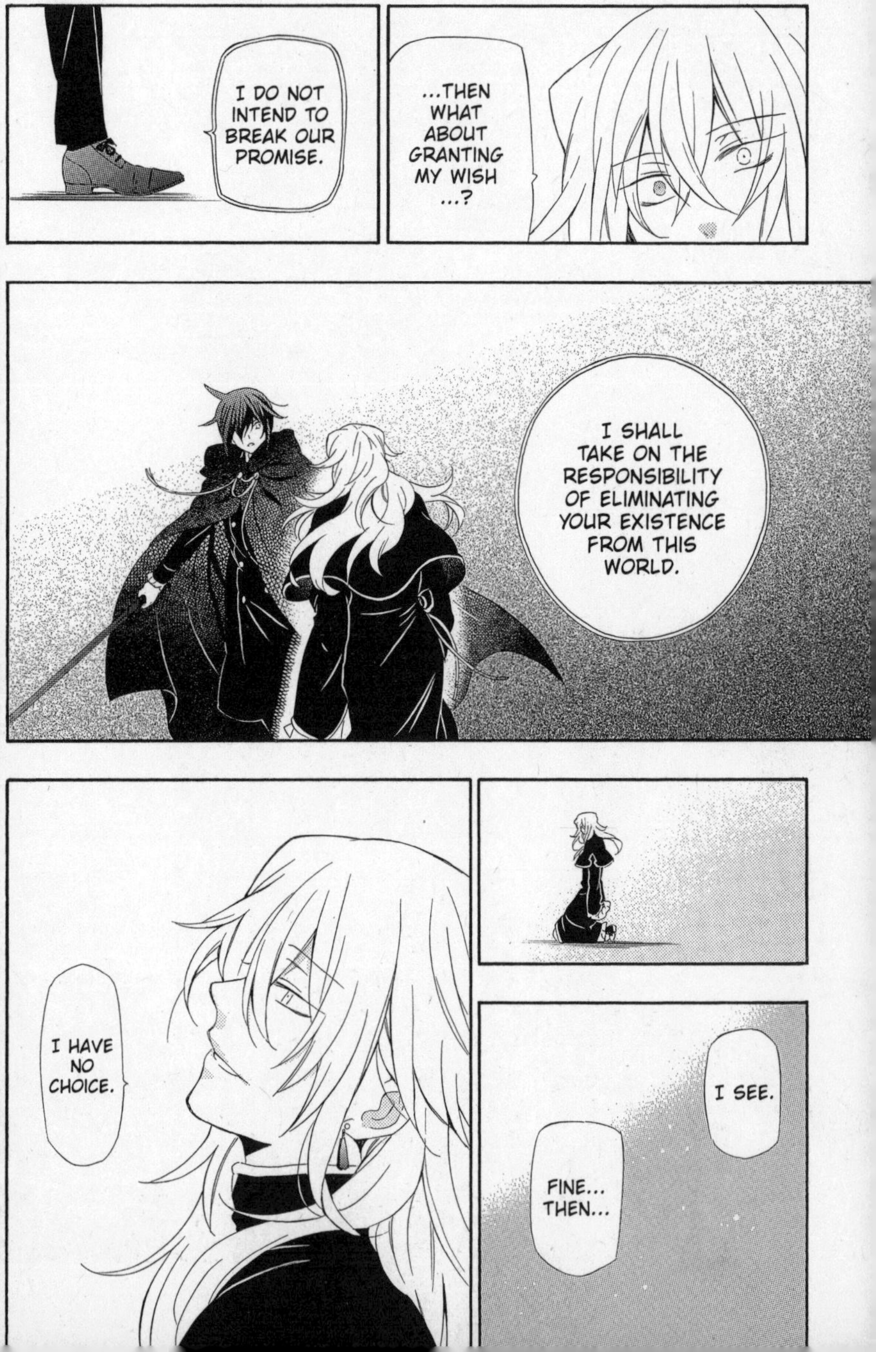
...THEN WHAT ABOUT GRANTING MY WISH ...?
I DO NOT INTEND TO BREAK OUR PROMISE.
I SHALL TAKE ON THE RESPONSIBILITY OF ELIMINATING YOUR EXISTENCE FROM THIS WORLD.
I SEE.
FINE... THEN...
I HAVE NO CHOICE.

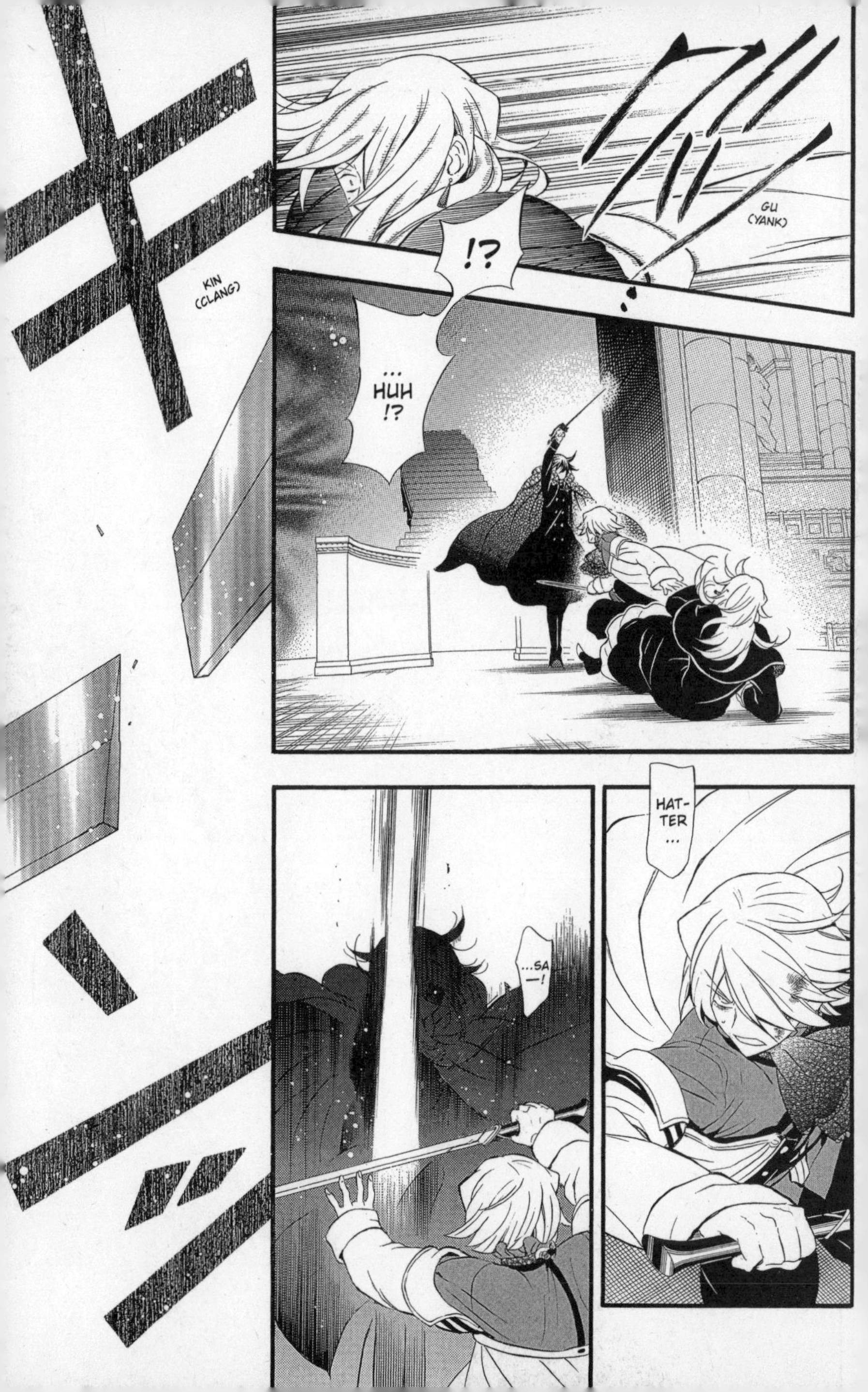
GU (YANK)
!?
KIN (CLANG)
... HUH !?
HAT-TER ...
...SA —!

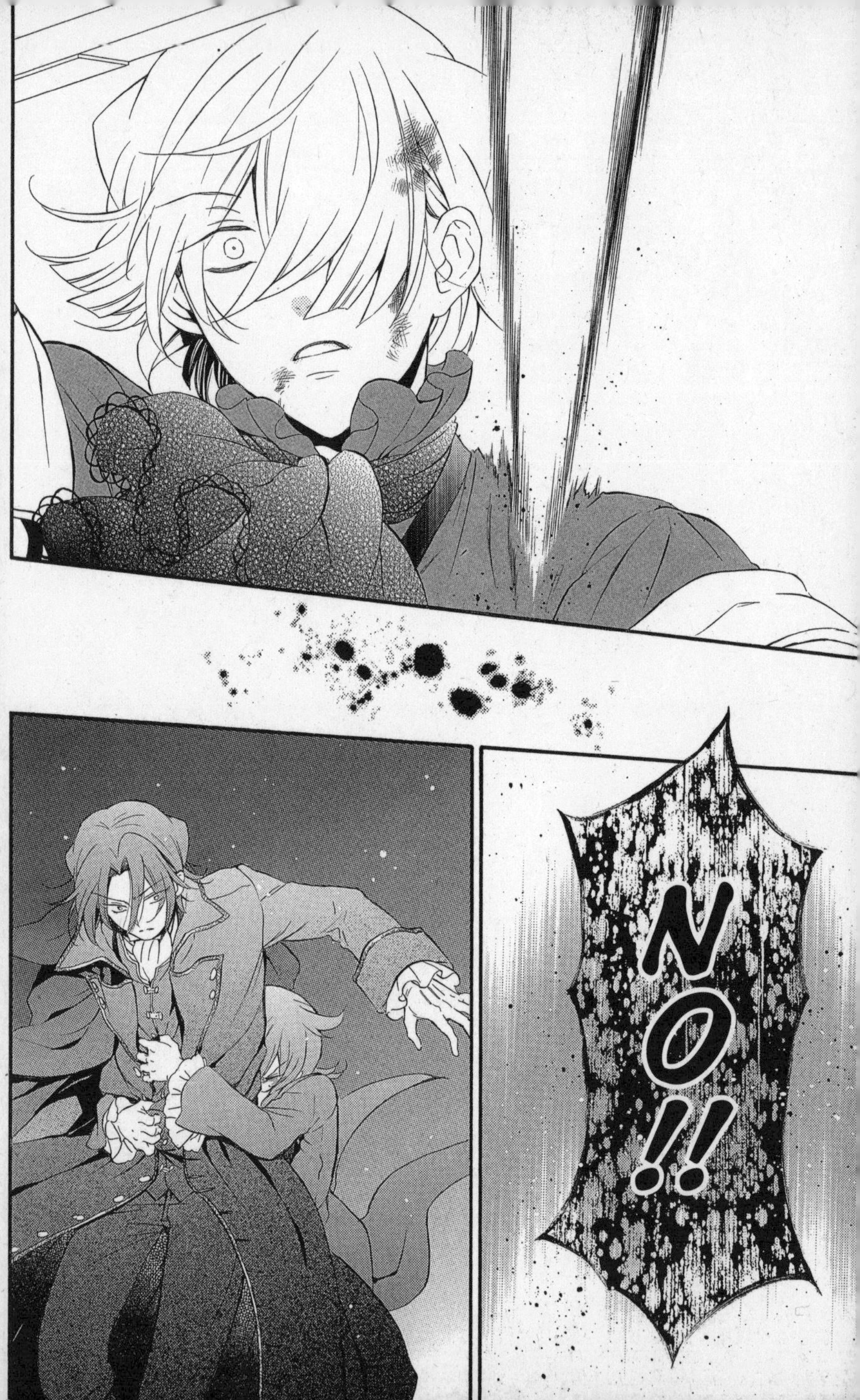
NO!!

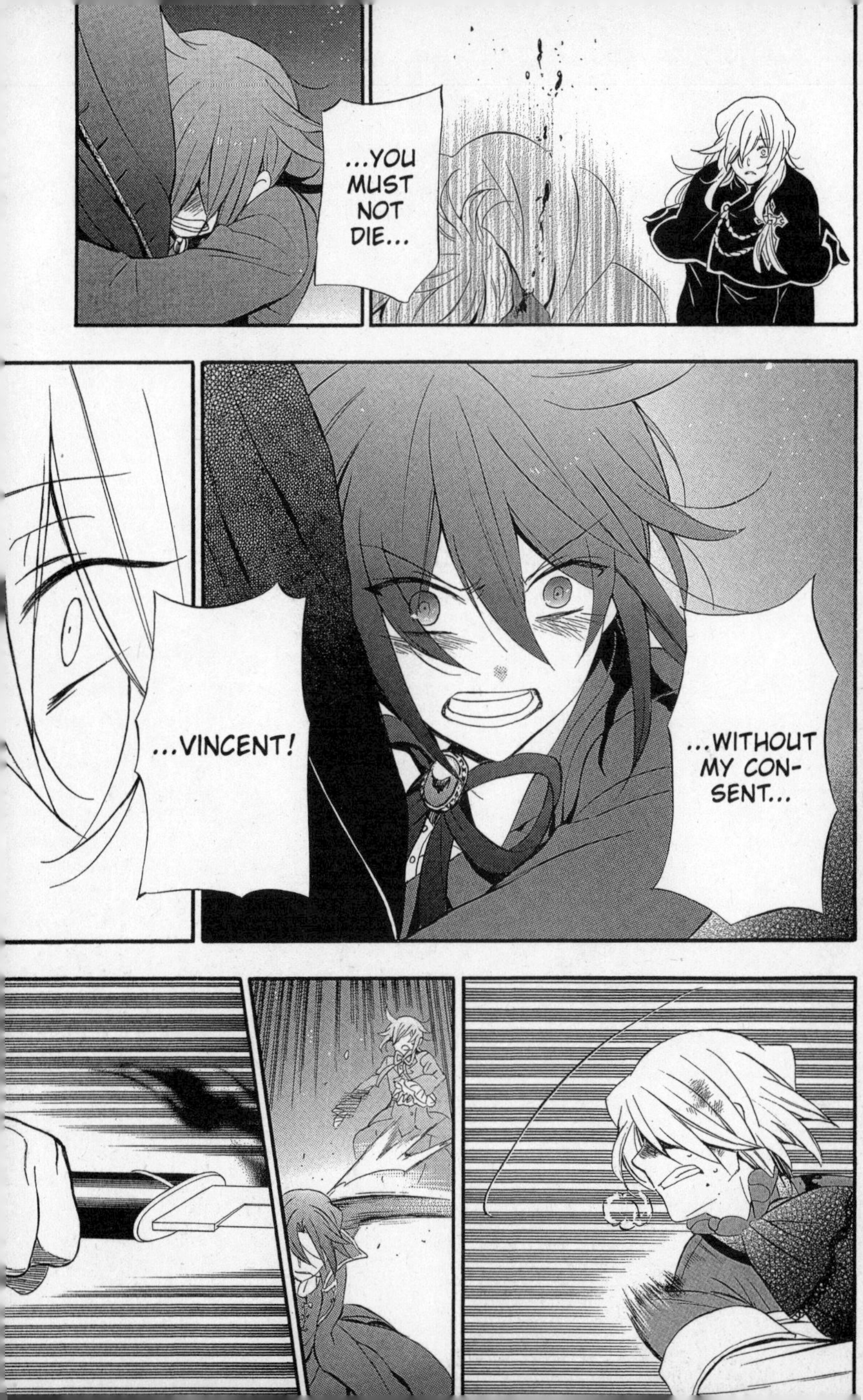
...YOU MUST NOT DIE...
...WITHOUT MY CON-SENT...
...VINCENT!

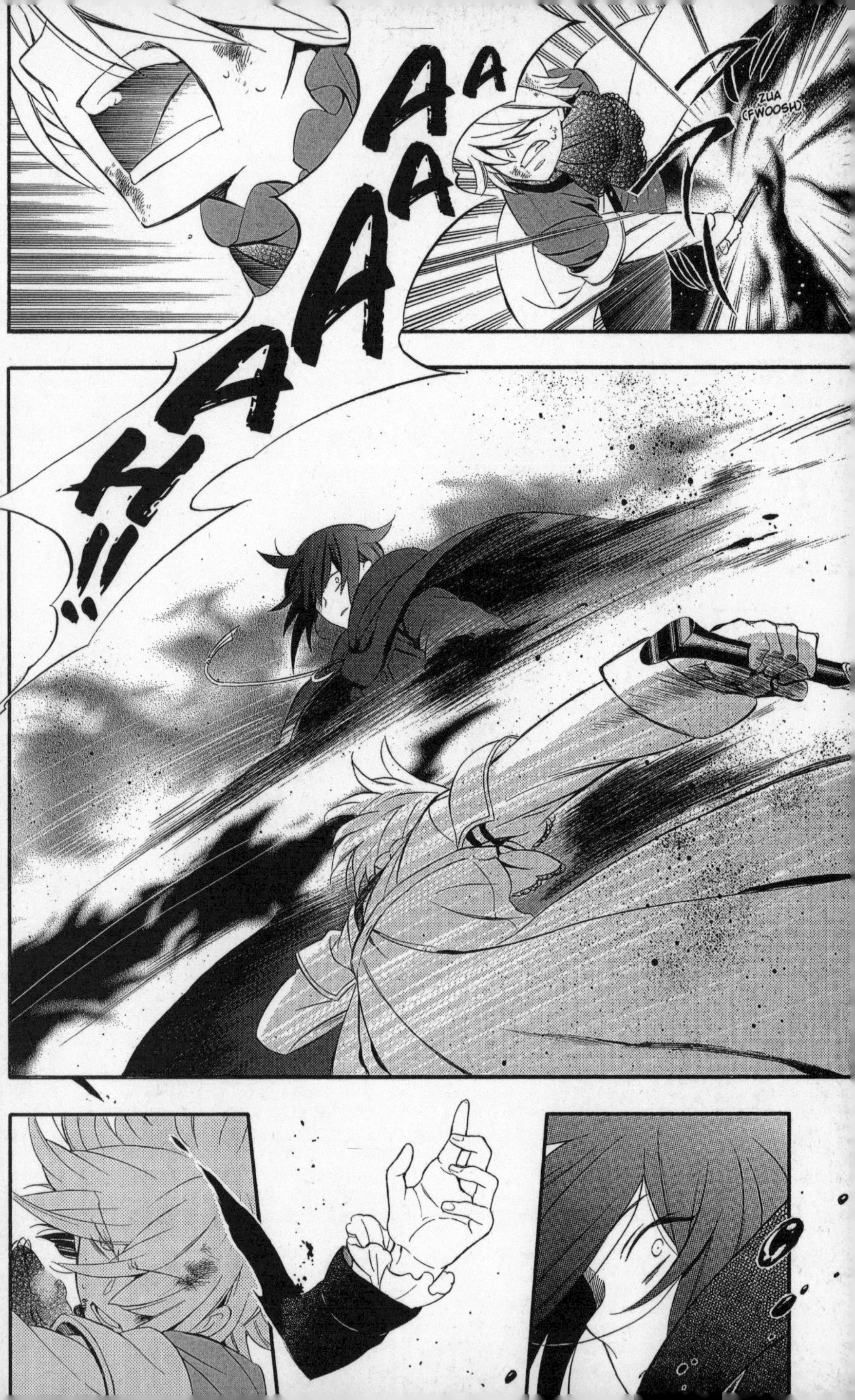
ZUA (FWOOSH)
AAAAAAH!!

GASHI
(GRAB)

DO
(THUD)

I WILL NOT.

...I...

...LET GO.

I WAS FINE...

...WITH DYING RIGHT THERE!

HAH...

HAH...

...WHY...

...DID YOU STOP HIM?

...WHA
—!?

GA
(WHACK)

YOU...

IT'S
ABOUT
TIME YOU
REALIZE...

...KEEP
LOOKING
TO THE
PAST FOR
SALVA-
TION.

THAT'S
WHY YOU
CAN'T MOVE
FORWARD!

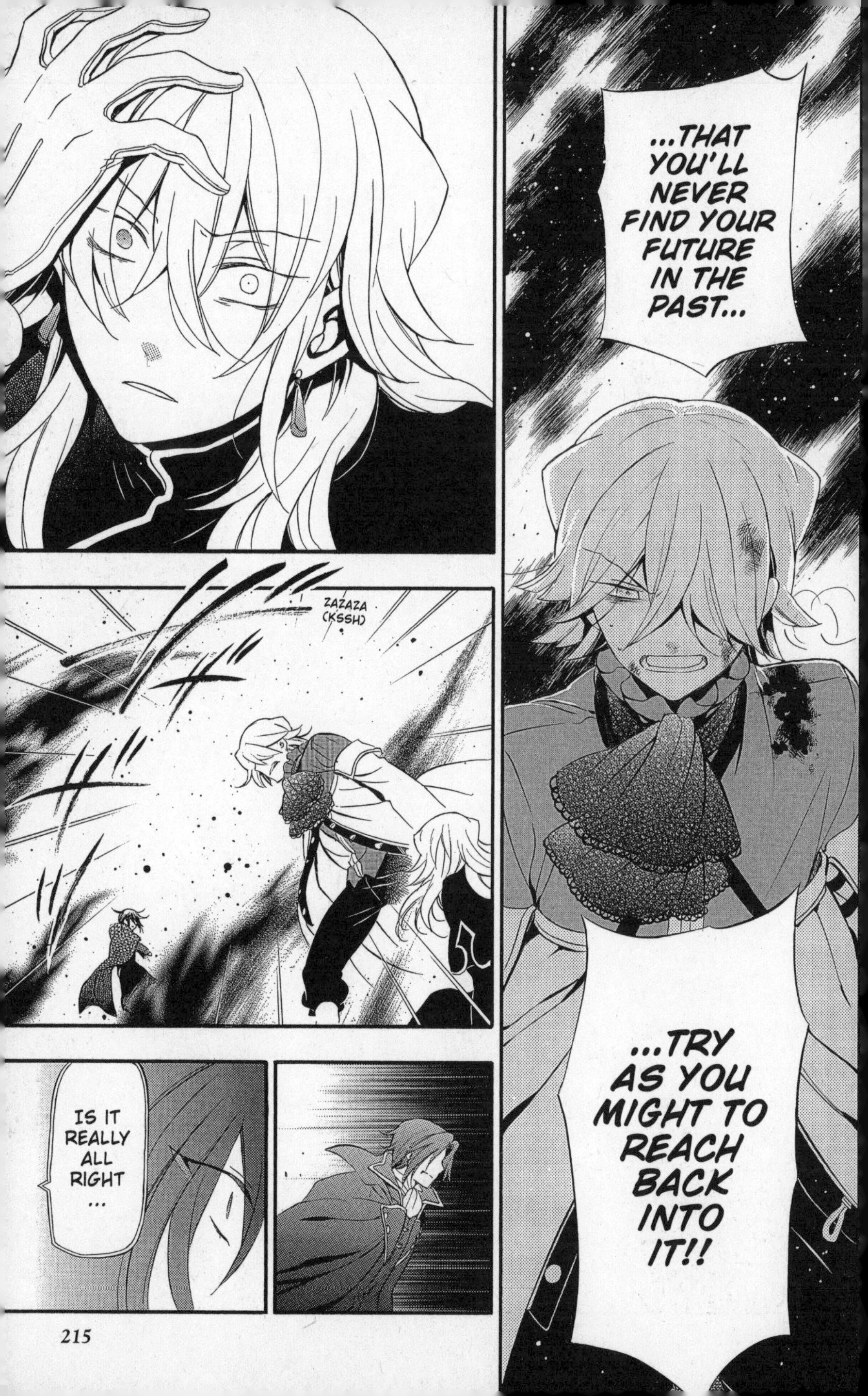
...THAT YOU'LL NEVER FIND YOUR FUTURE IN THE PAST...
...TRY AS YOU MIGHT TO REACH BACK INTO IT!!
ZAZAZA (KSSH)
IS IT REALLY ALL RIGHT ...

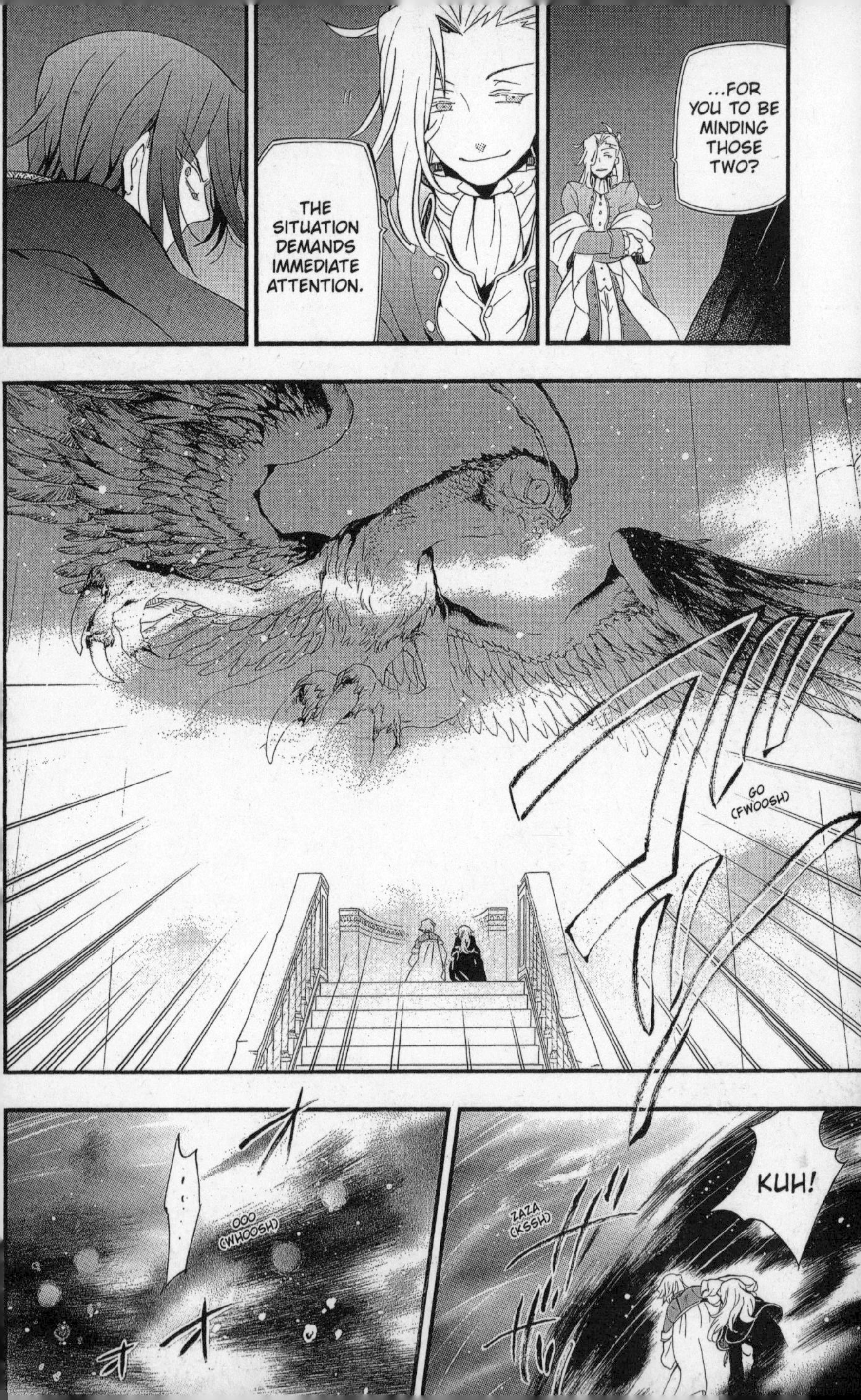
...FOR YOU TO BE MINDING THOSE TWO?
THE SITUATION DEMANDS IMMEDIATE ATTENTION.
GO (FWOOSH)
KUH!
ZAZA (KSSH)
...
OOO (WHOOSH)

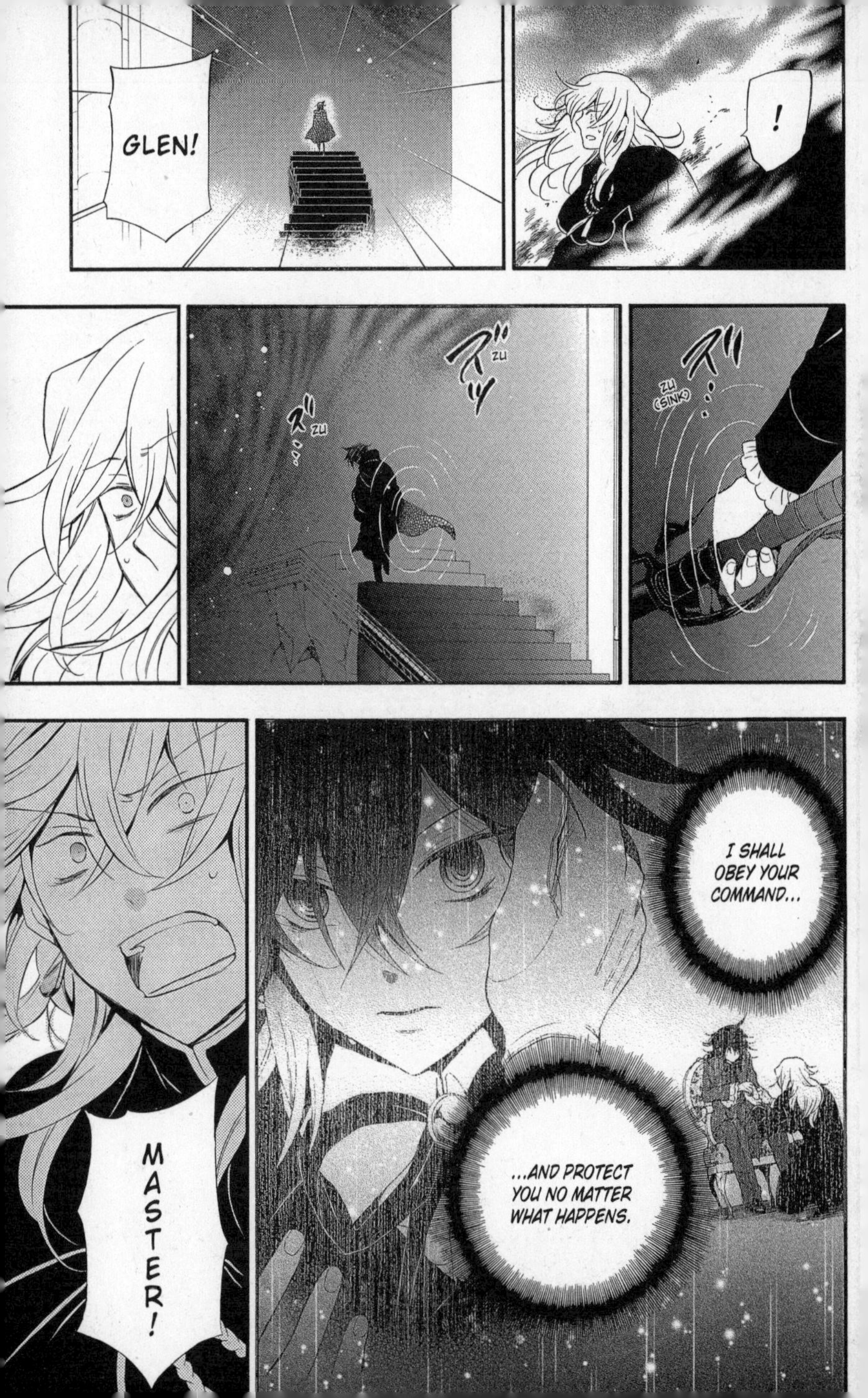
!
GLEN!
ZU (SINK)
ZU
ZU
I SHALL OBEY YOUR COMMAND...
...AND PROTECT YOU NO MATTER WHAT HAPPENS.
MASTER!

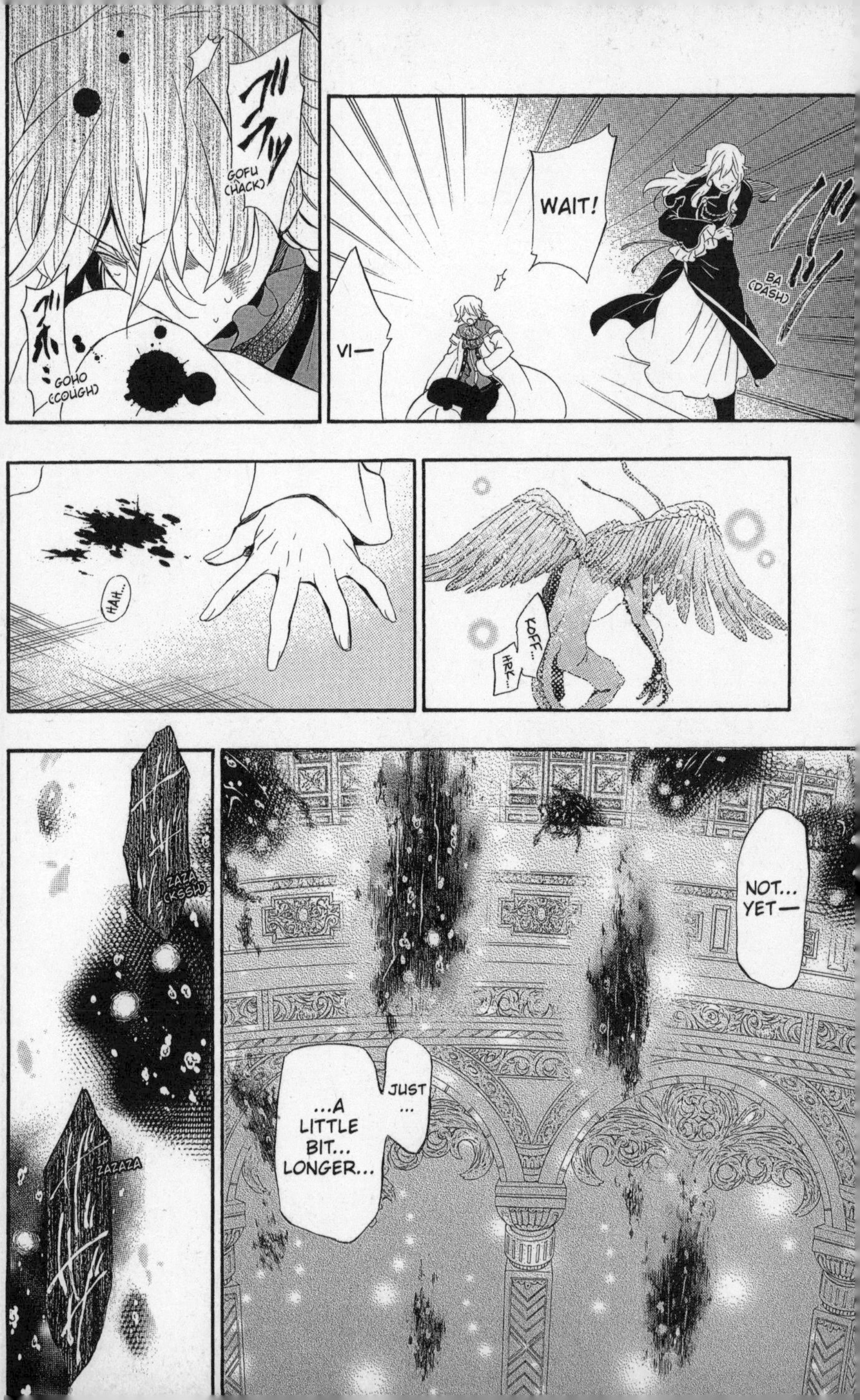
WAIT!
BA (DASH)
VI—
GOFU (HACK)
GOHO (COUGH)
KOFF...
HRK...
HAH...
NOT... YET—
JUST...
...A LITTLE BIT... LONGER...
ZAZA (KSSH)
ZAZAZA

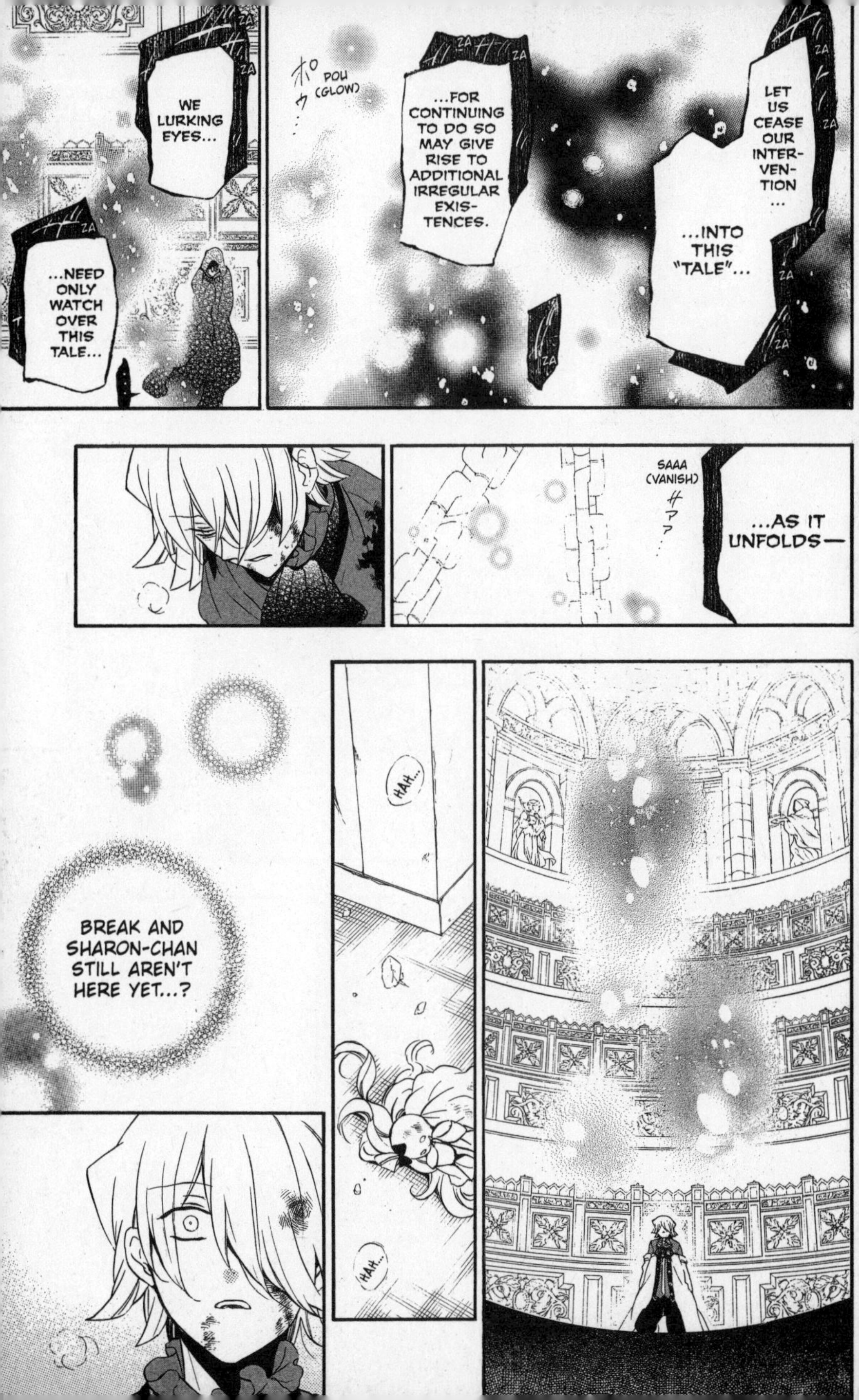
LET US CEASE OUR INTERVENTION...
...INTO THIS "TALE"...
POU (GLOW)
...FOR CONTINUING TO DO SO MAY GIVE RISE TO ADDITIONAL IRREGULAR EXISTENCES.
WE LURKING EYES...
...NEED ONLY WATCH OVER THIS TALE...
SAAA (VANISH)
...AS IT UNFOLDS—
HAH...
HAH...
BREAK AND SHARON-CHAN STILL AREN'T HERE YET...?

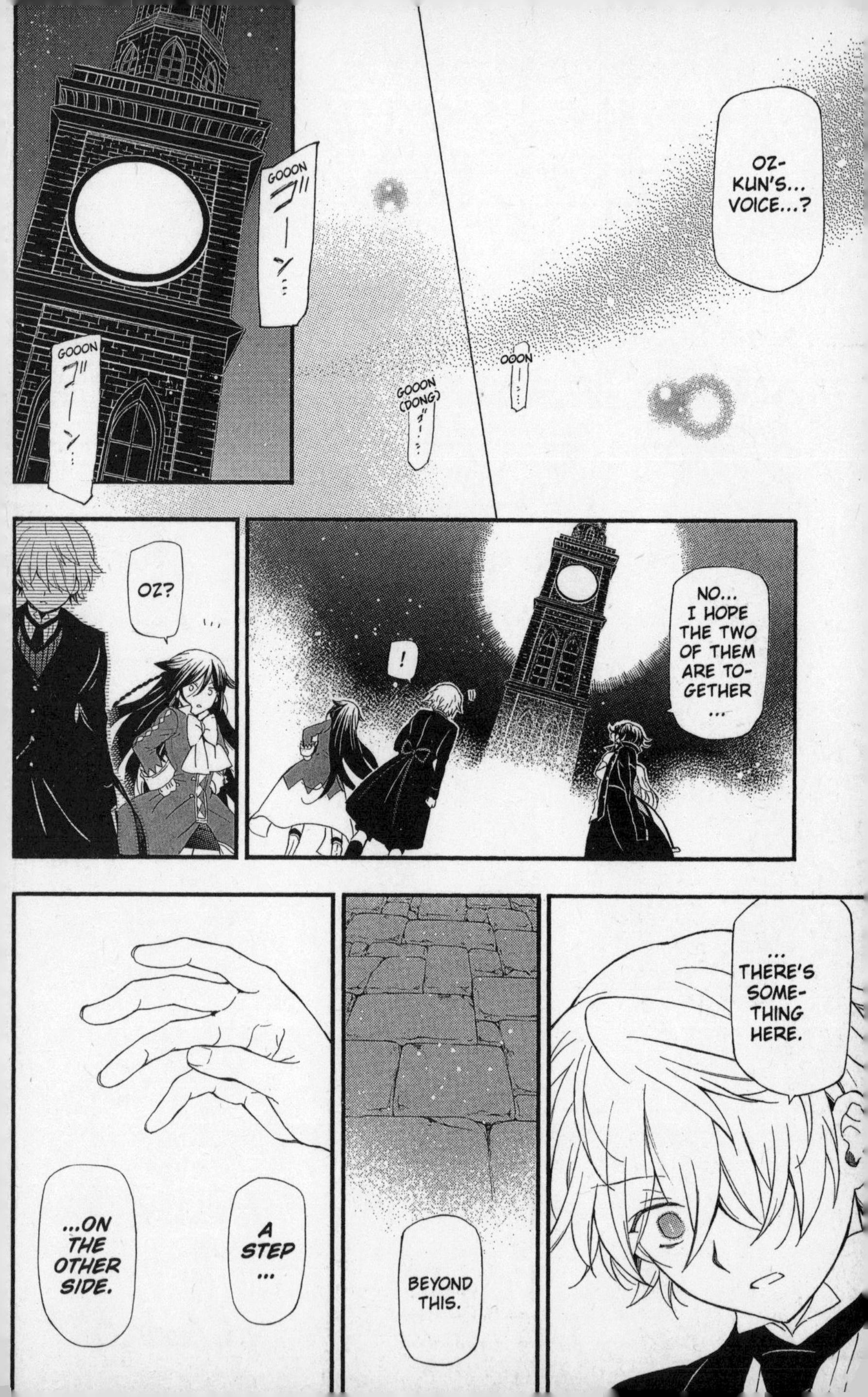
OZ-KUN'S... VOICE...?
OOON
GOOON (DONG)
GOOON
GOOON
NO... I HOPE THE TWO OF THEM ARE TOGETHER...
!
OZ?
...THERE'S SOMETHING HERE.
BEYOND THIS.
A STEP...
...ON THE OTHER SIDE.

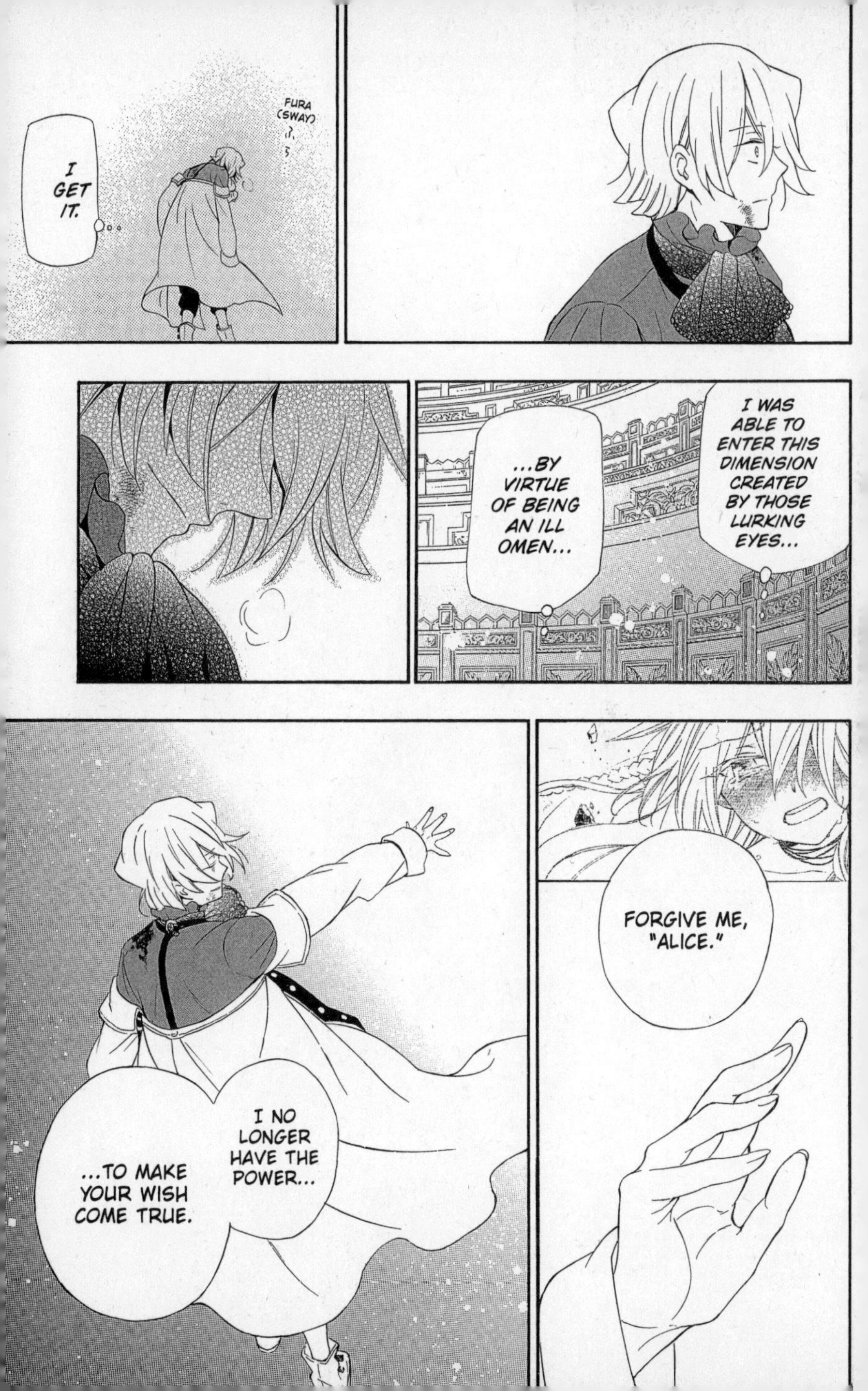
FURA (SWAY)
I GET IT.
I WAS ABLE TO ENTER THIS DIMENSION CREATED BY THOSE LURKING EYES...
...BY VIRTUE OF BEING AN ILL OMEN...
FORGIVE ME, "ALICE."
I NO LONGER HAVE THE POWER...
...TO MAKE YOUR WISH COME TRUE.

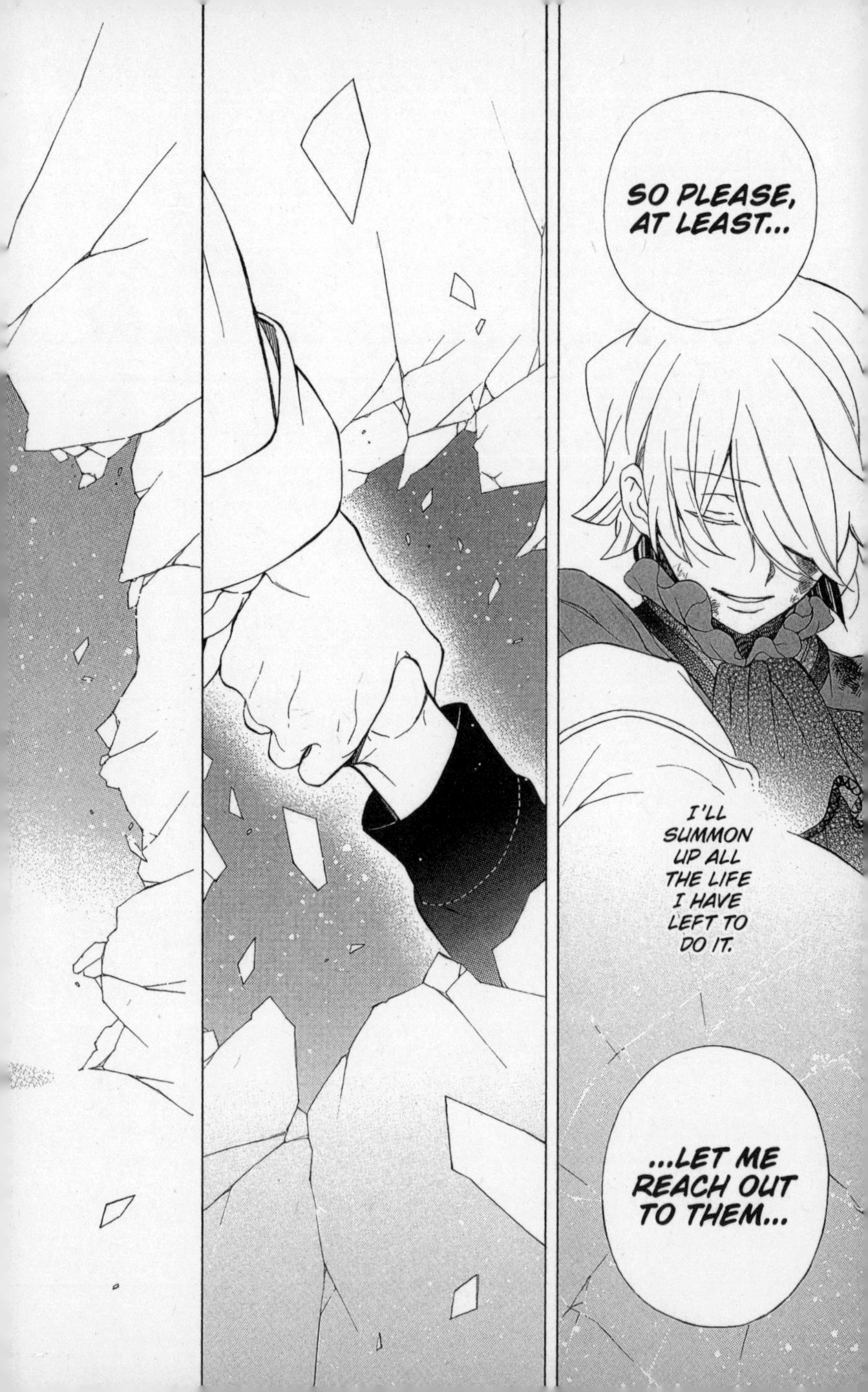
SO PLEASE, AT LEAST...
I'LL SUMMON UP ALL THE LIFE I HAVE LEFT TO DO IT.
...LET ME REACH OUT TO THEM...

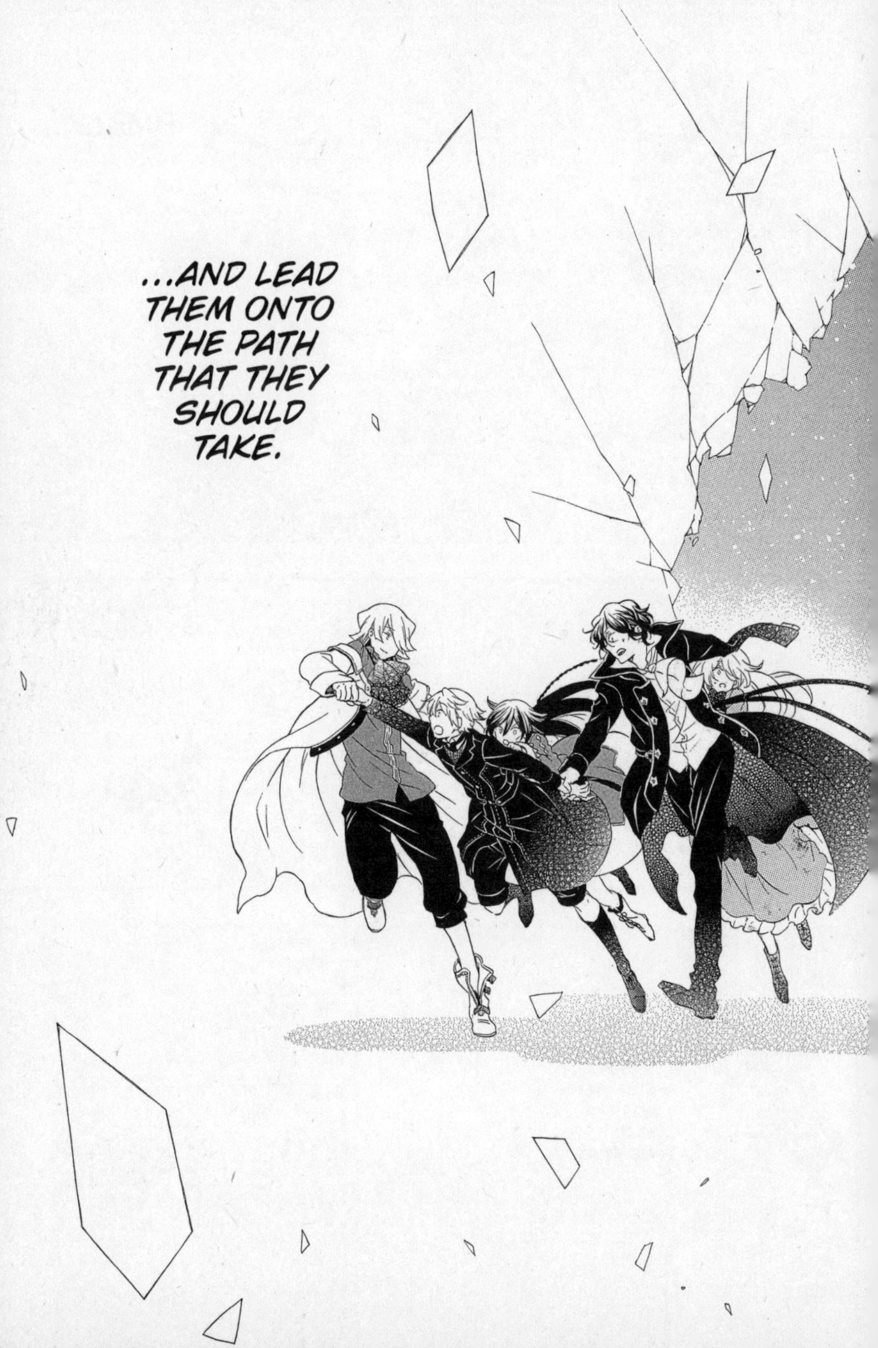
...AND LEAD THEM ONTO THE PATH THAT THEY SHOULD TAKE.

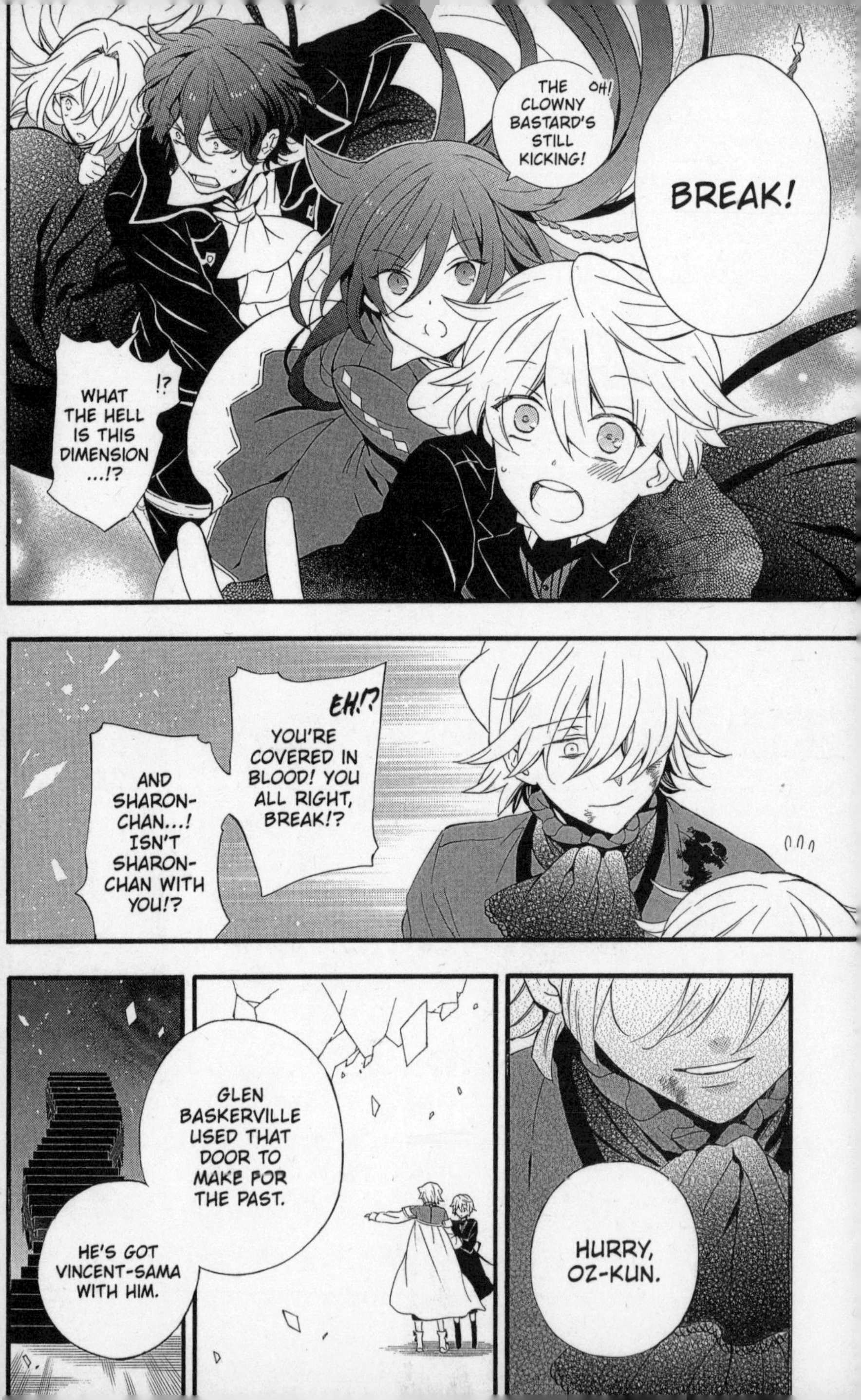
BREAK!
OH!
THE CLOWNY BASTARD'S STILL KICKING!
!?
WHAT THE HELL IS THIS DIMENSION ...!?
EH!?
YOU'RE COVERED IN BLOOD! YOU ALL RIGHT, BREAK!?
AND SHARON-CHAN...! ISN'T SHARON-CHAN WITH YOU!?
HURRY, OZ-KUN.
GLEN BASKERVILLE USED THAT DOOR TO MAKE FOR THE PAST.
HE'S GOT VINCENT-SAMA WITH HIM.

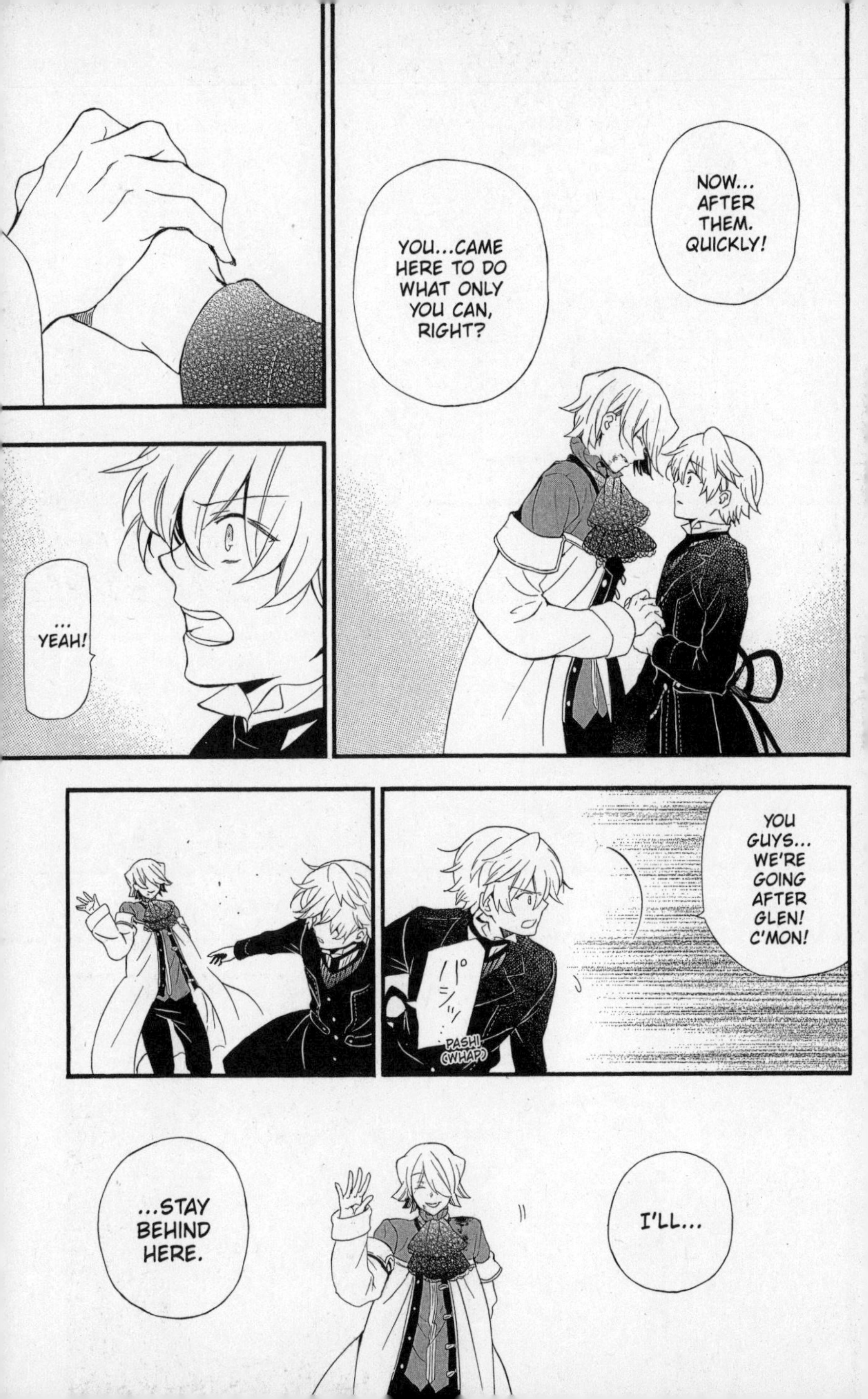
NOW... AFTER THEM. QUICKLY!
YOU...CAME HERE TO DO WHAT ONLY YOU CAN, RIGHT?
...YEAH!
YOU GUYS... WE'RE GOING AFTER GLEN! C'MON!
PASH! (WHAP)
I'LL...
...STAY BEHIND HERE.

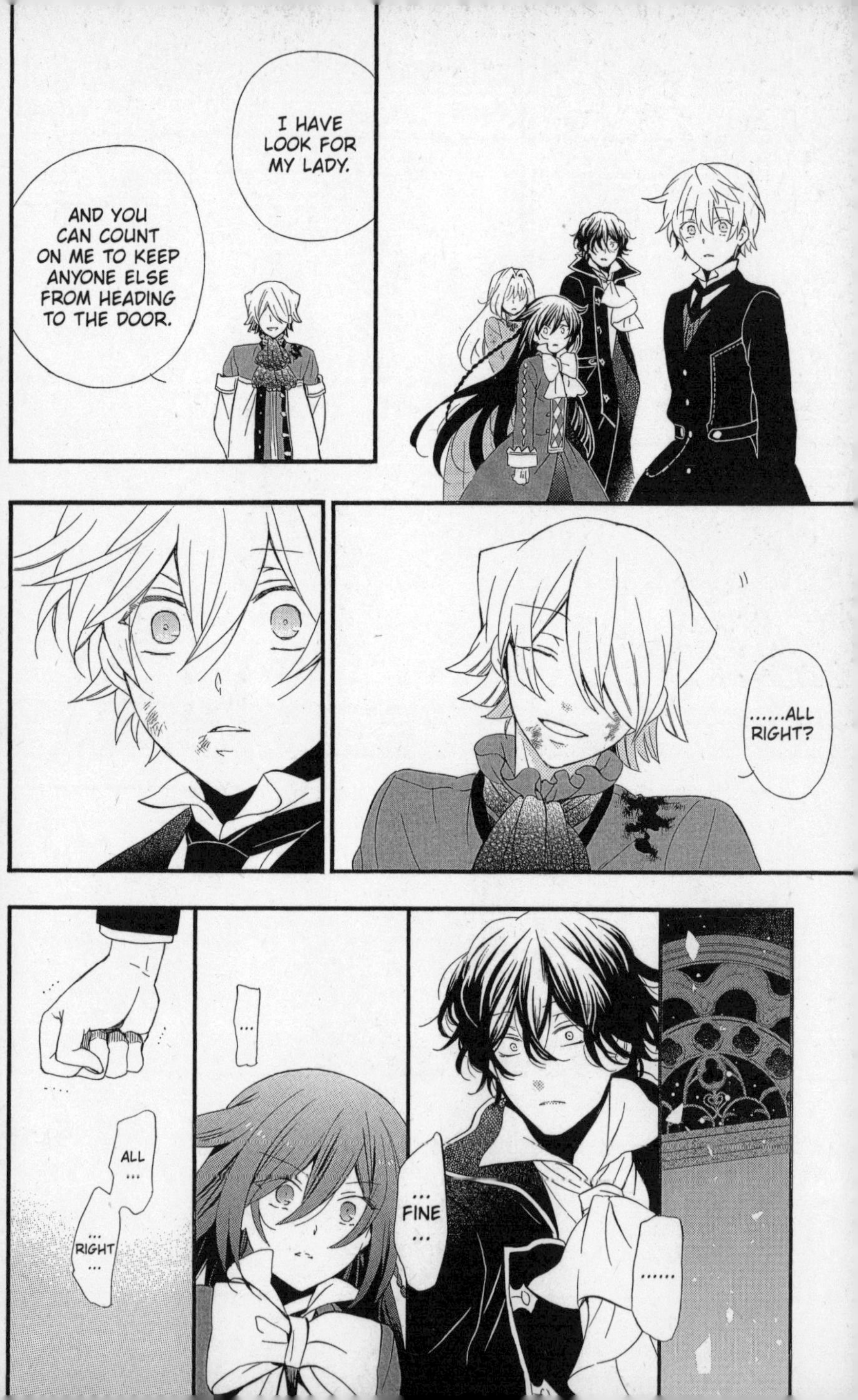
I HAVE LOOK FOR MY LADY.
AND YOU CAN COUNT ON ME TO KEEP ANYONE ELSE FROM HEADING TO THE DOOR.
......ALL RIGHT?
....
... FINE ...
...
ALL ...
... RIGHT ...

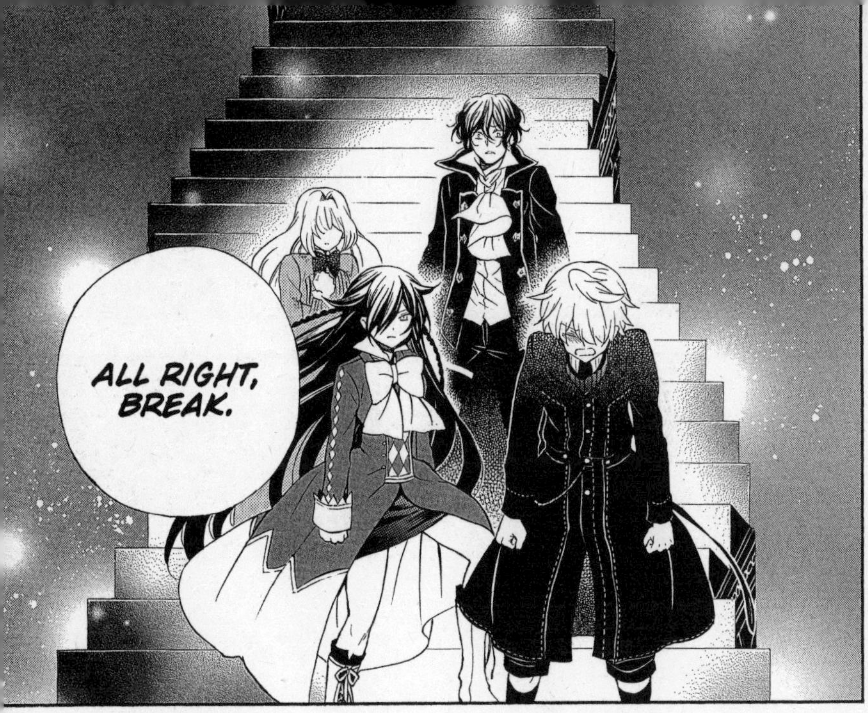
ALL RIGHT, BREAK.
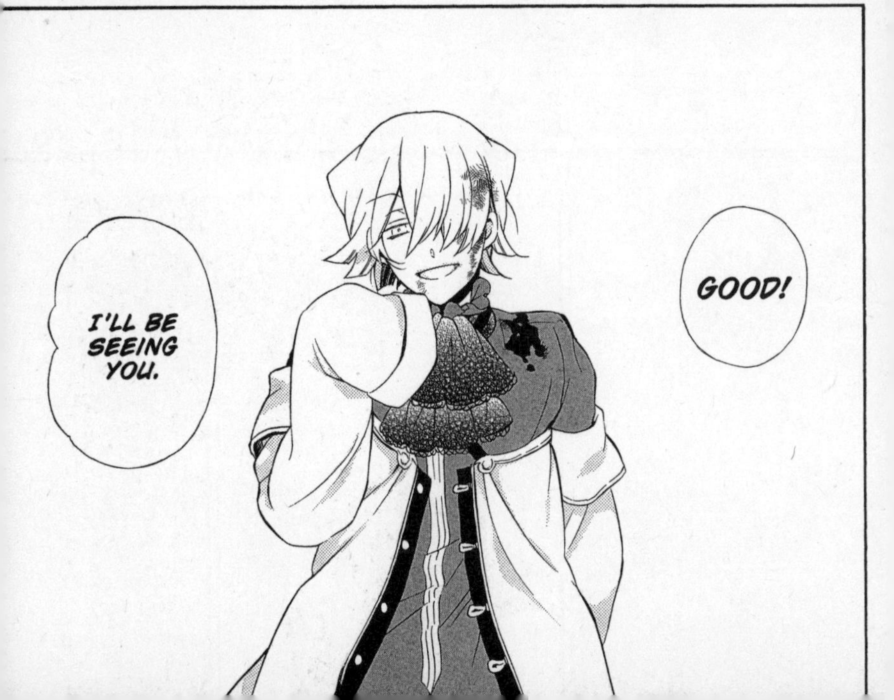
GOOD!
I'LL BE SEEING YOU.

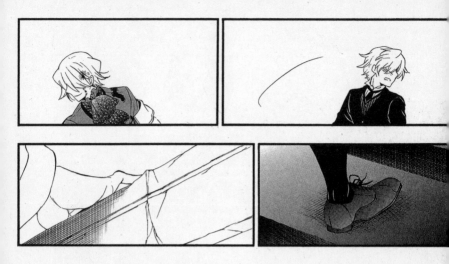

...IS ENOUGH.

THIS...

I'VE...

THIS...
IS AN
END...

...I
DON'T...

...DE-
SERVE
...

...BEEN
ALLOWED
TO LIVE
PLENTY.

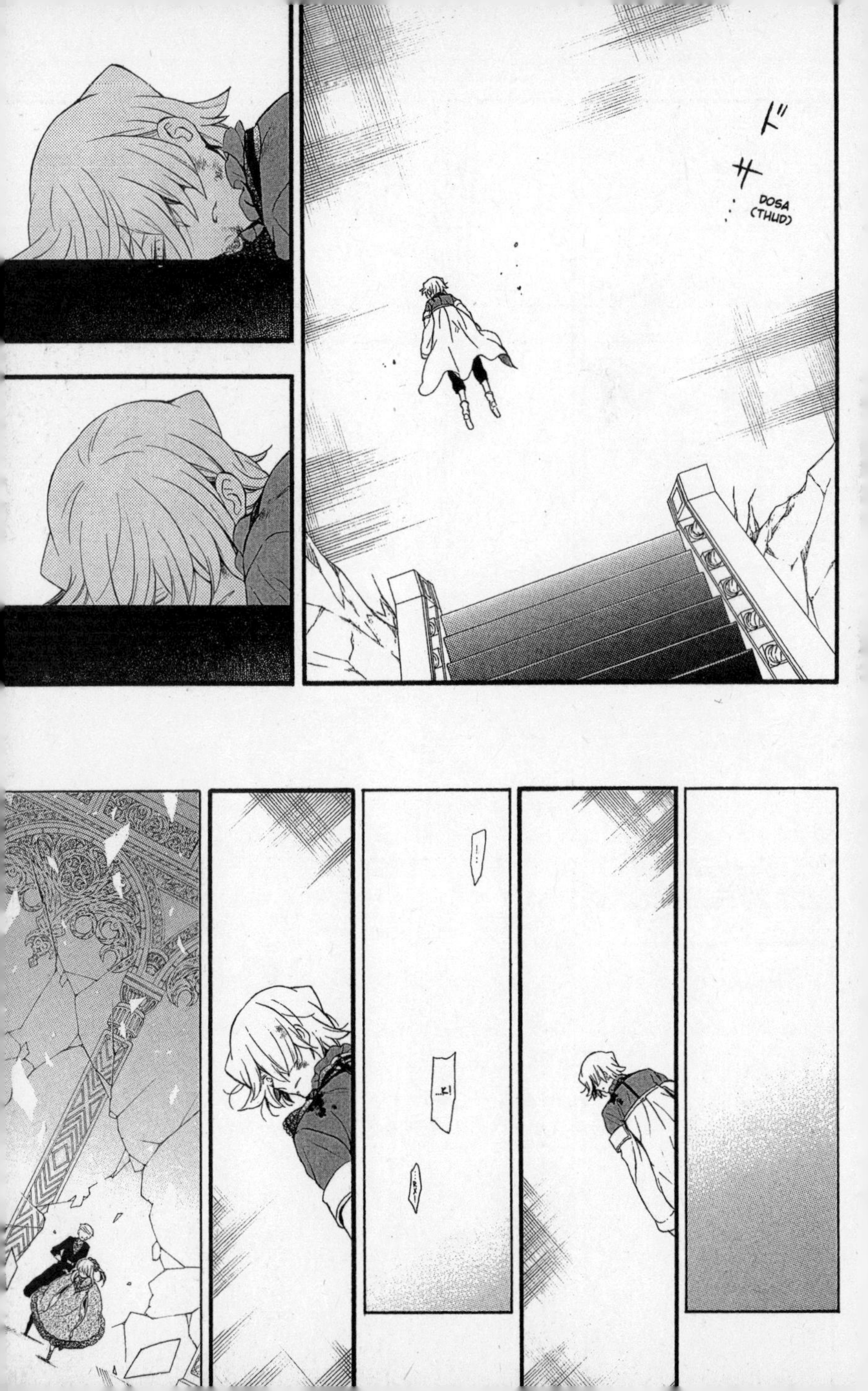
ドサ
DOSA
(THUD)
...!
...K!
...RX!

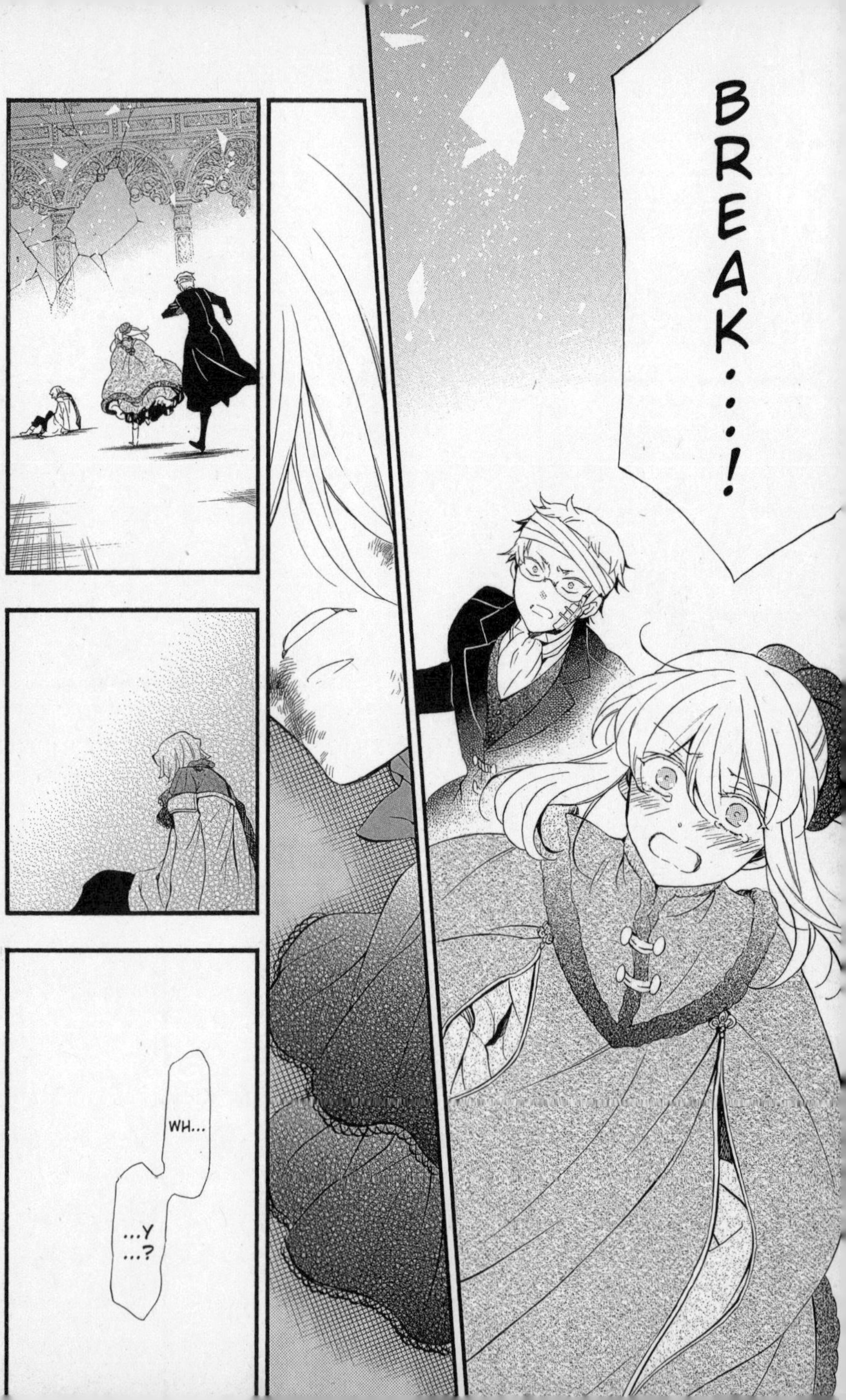
BREAK...!
WH...
...Y ...?

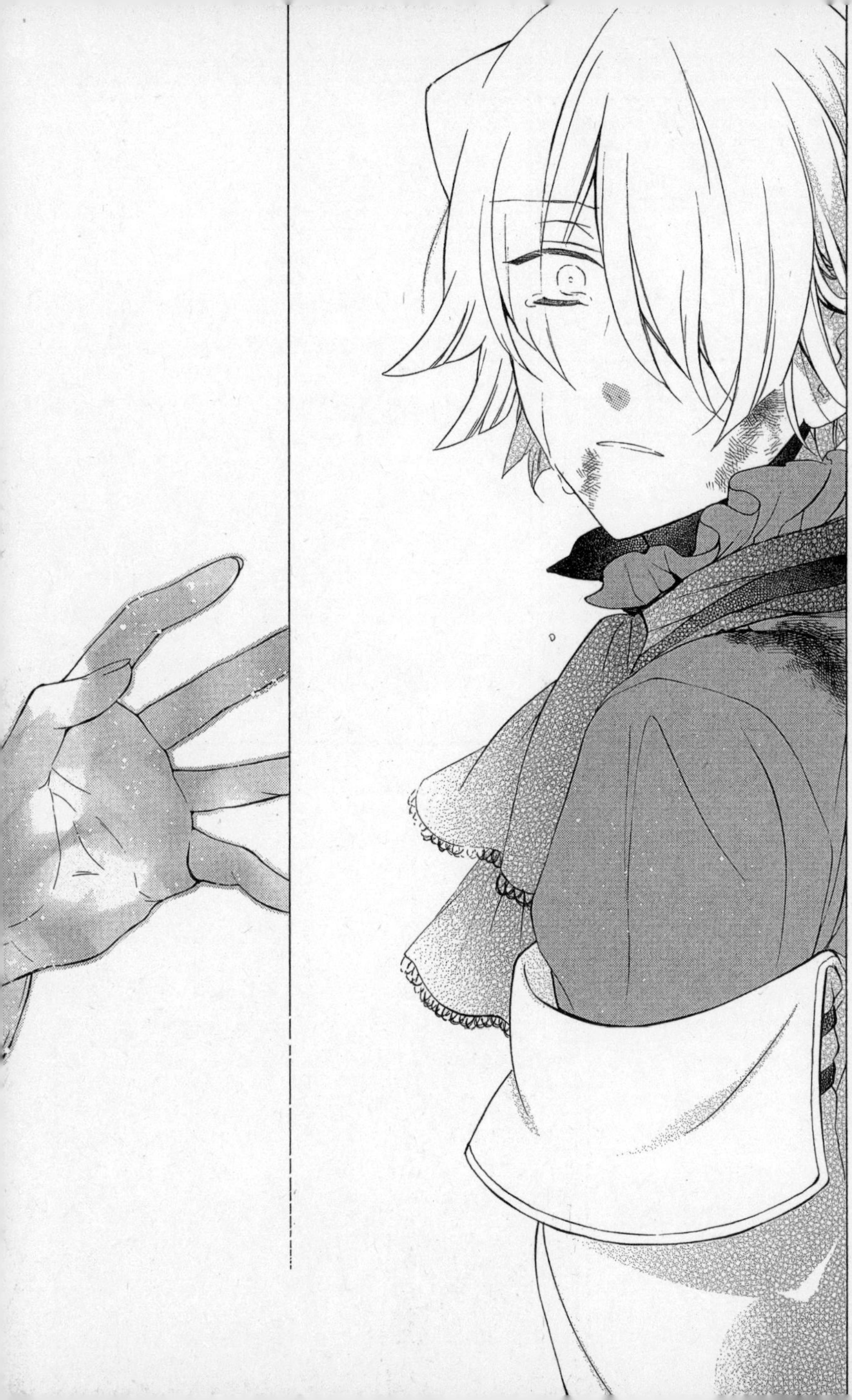

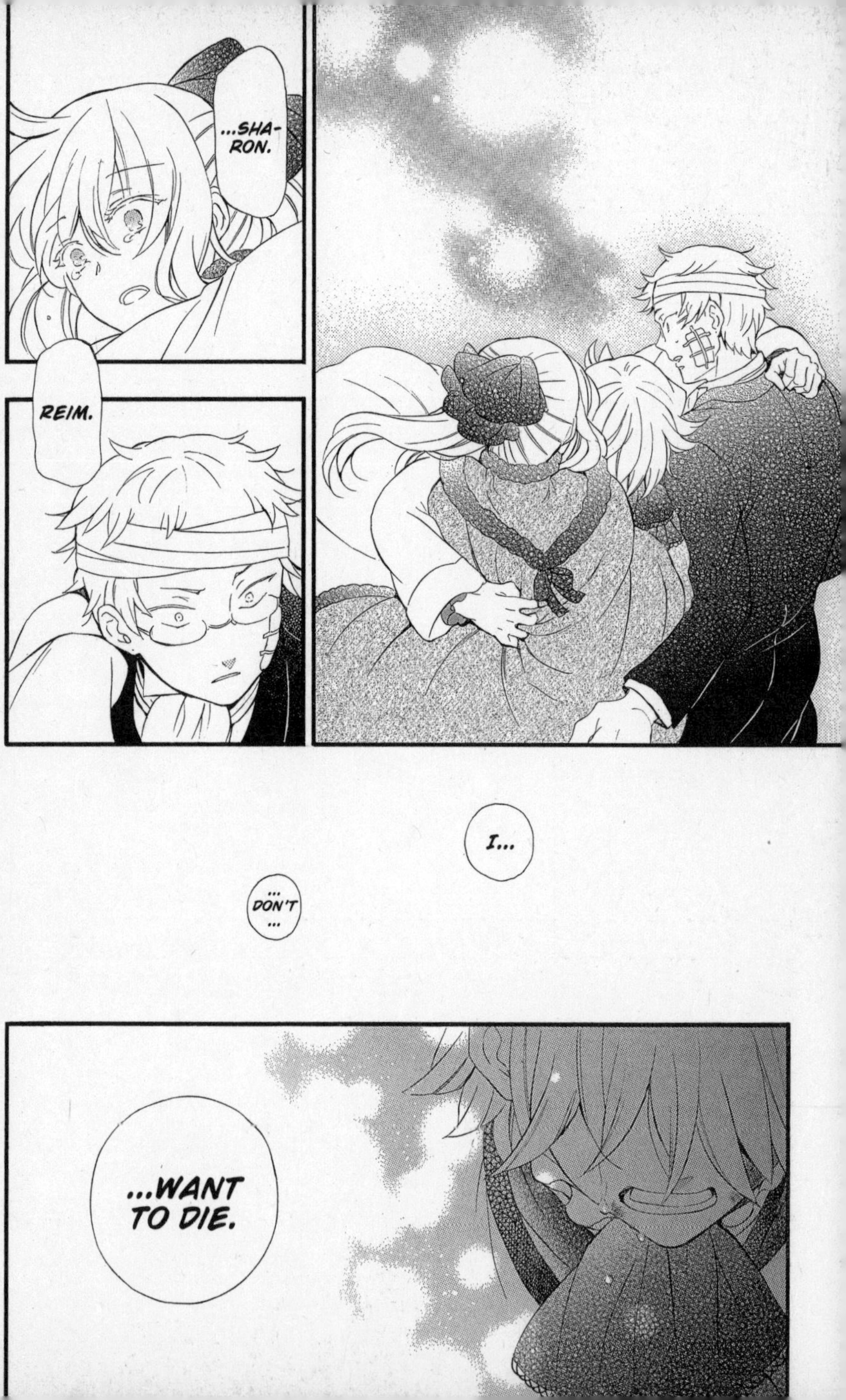
...SHA-RON.
REIM.
I...
...DON'T...
...WANT TO DIE.

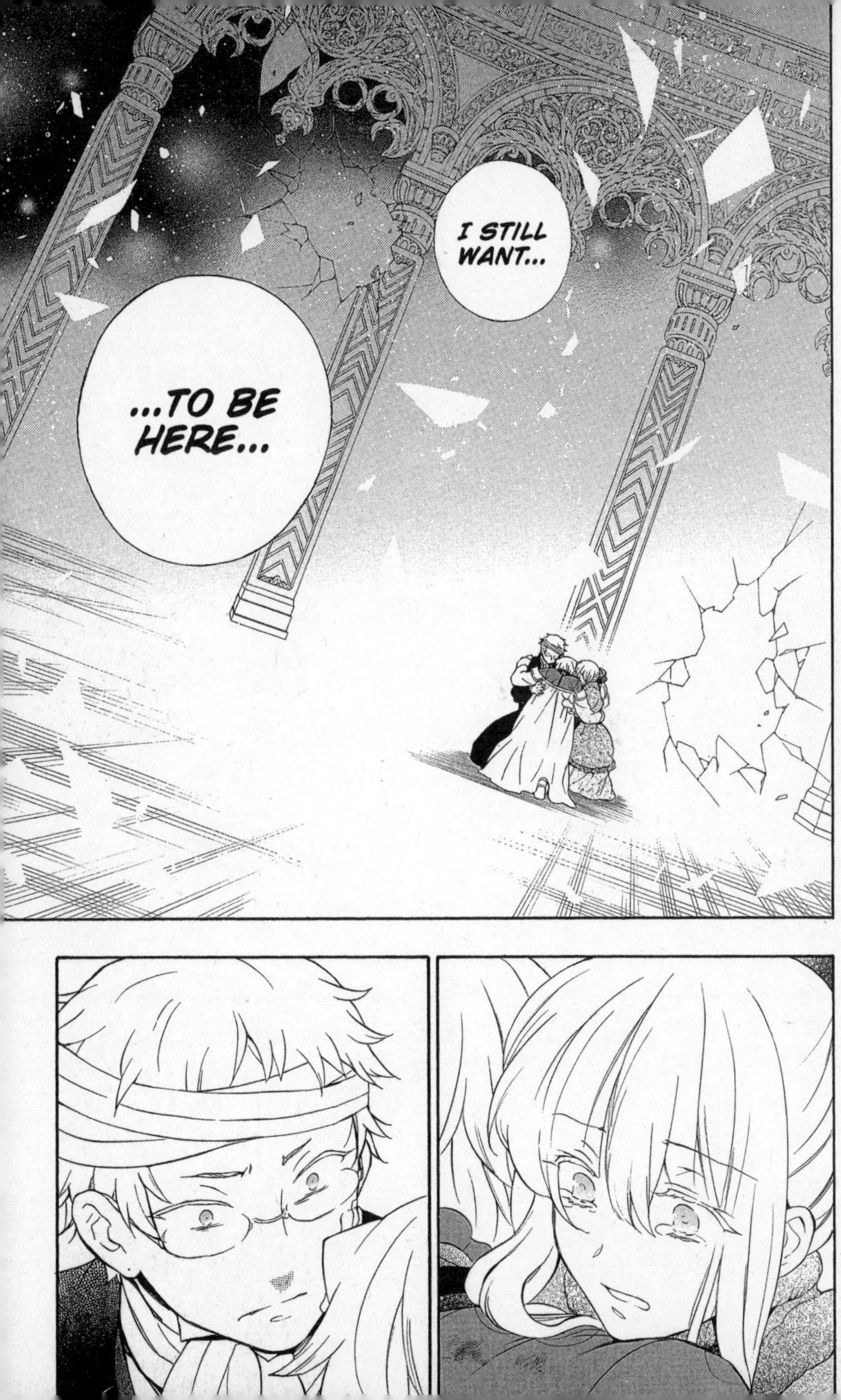
I STILL WANT...
...TO BE HERE...

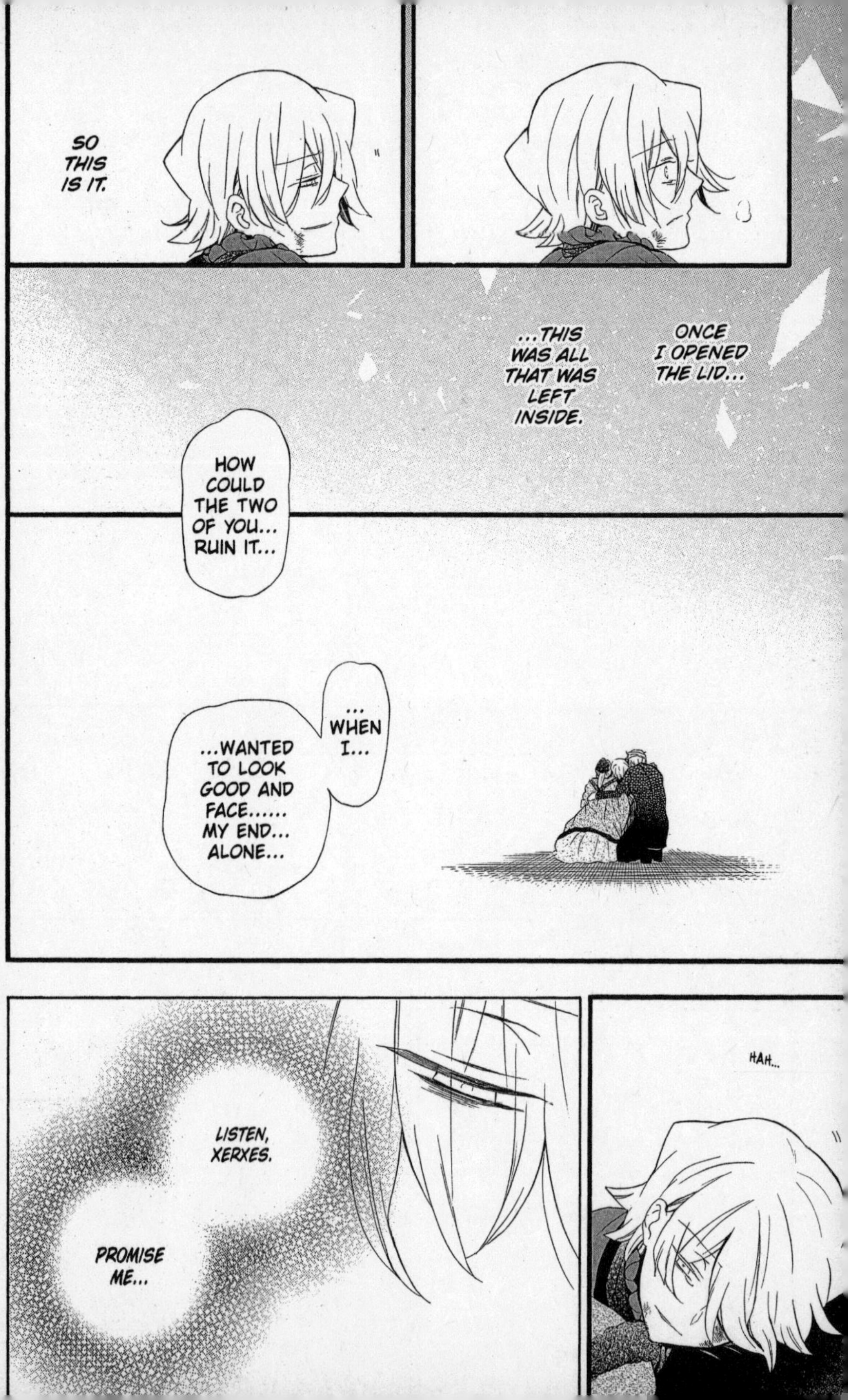
SO THIS IS IT.
ONCE I OPENED THE LID...
...THIS WAS ALL THAT WAS LEFT INSIDE.
HOW COULD THE TWO OF YOU... RUIN IT...
...WHEN I...
...WANTED TO LOOK GOOD AND FACE...... MY END... ALONE...
HAH...
LISTEN, XERXES.
PROMISE ME...

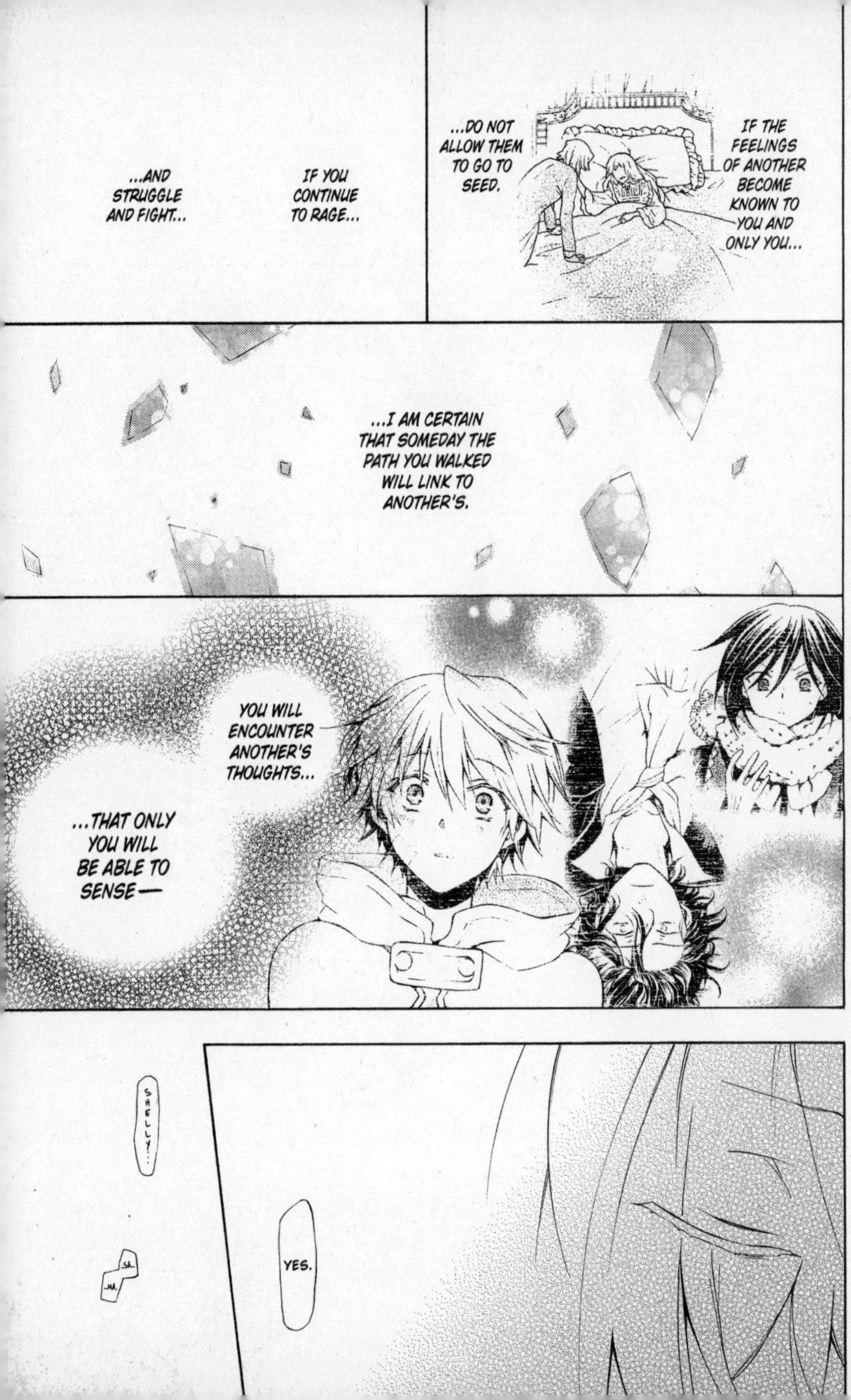
IF THE FEELINGS OF ANOTHER BECOME KNOWN TO YOU AND ONLY YOU...
...DO NOT ALLOW THEM TO GO TO SEED.
IF YOU CONTINUE TO RAGE...
...AND STRUGGLE AND FIGHT...
...I AM CERTAIN THAT SOMEDAY THE PATH YOU WALKED WILL LINK TO ANOTHER'S.
YOU WILL ENCOUNTER ANOTHER'S THOUGHTS...
...THAT ONLY YOU WILL BE ABLE TO SENSE—
SHELLY...
YES.
SA-MA.

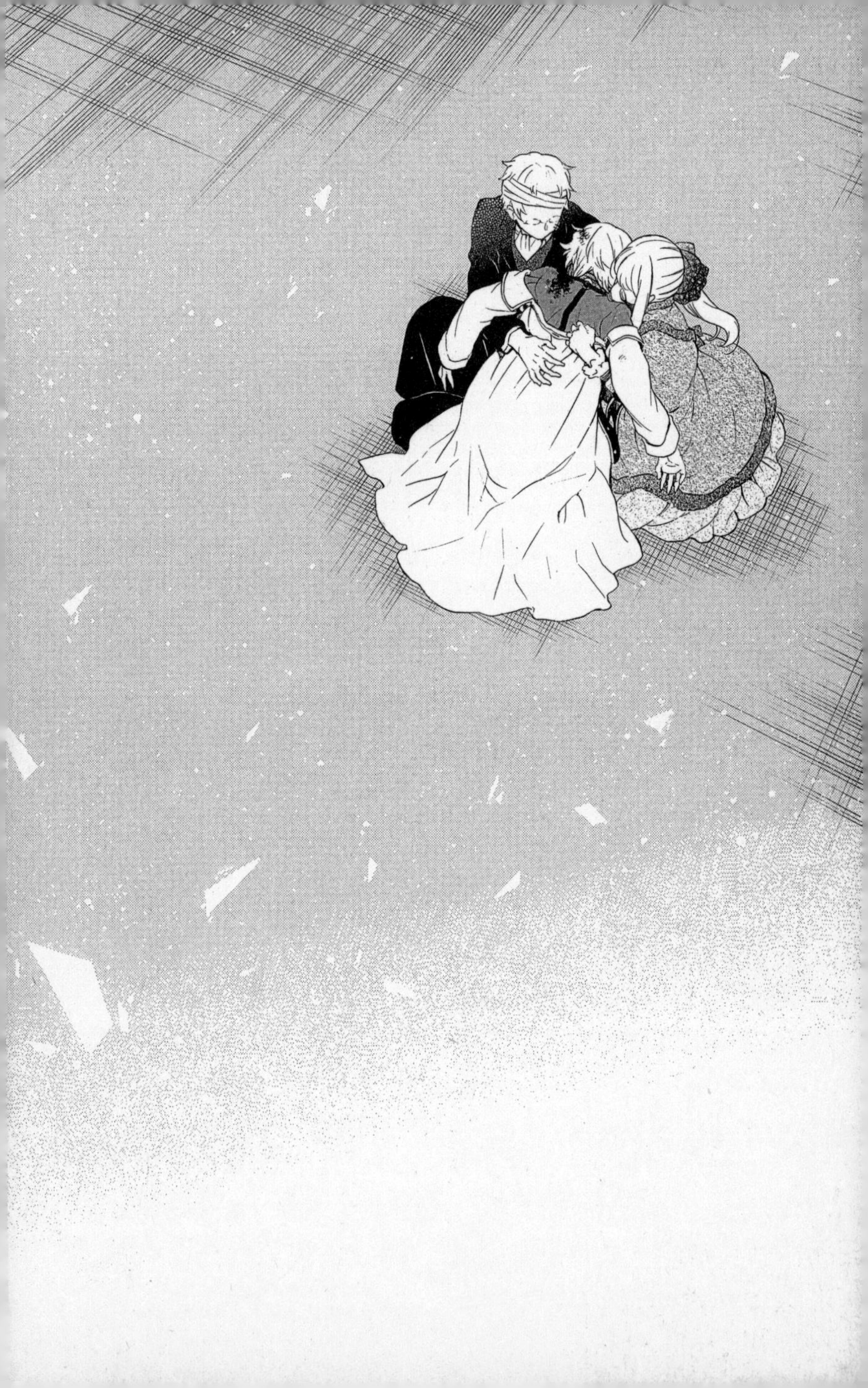

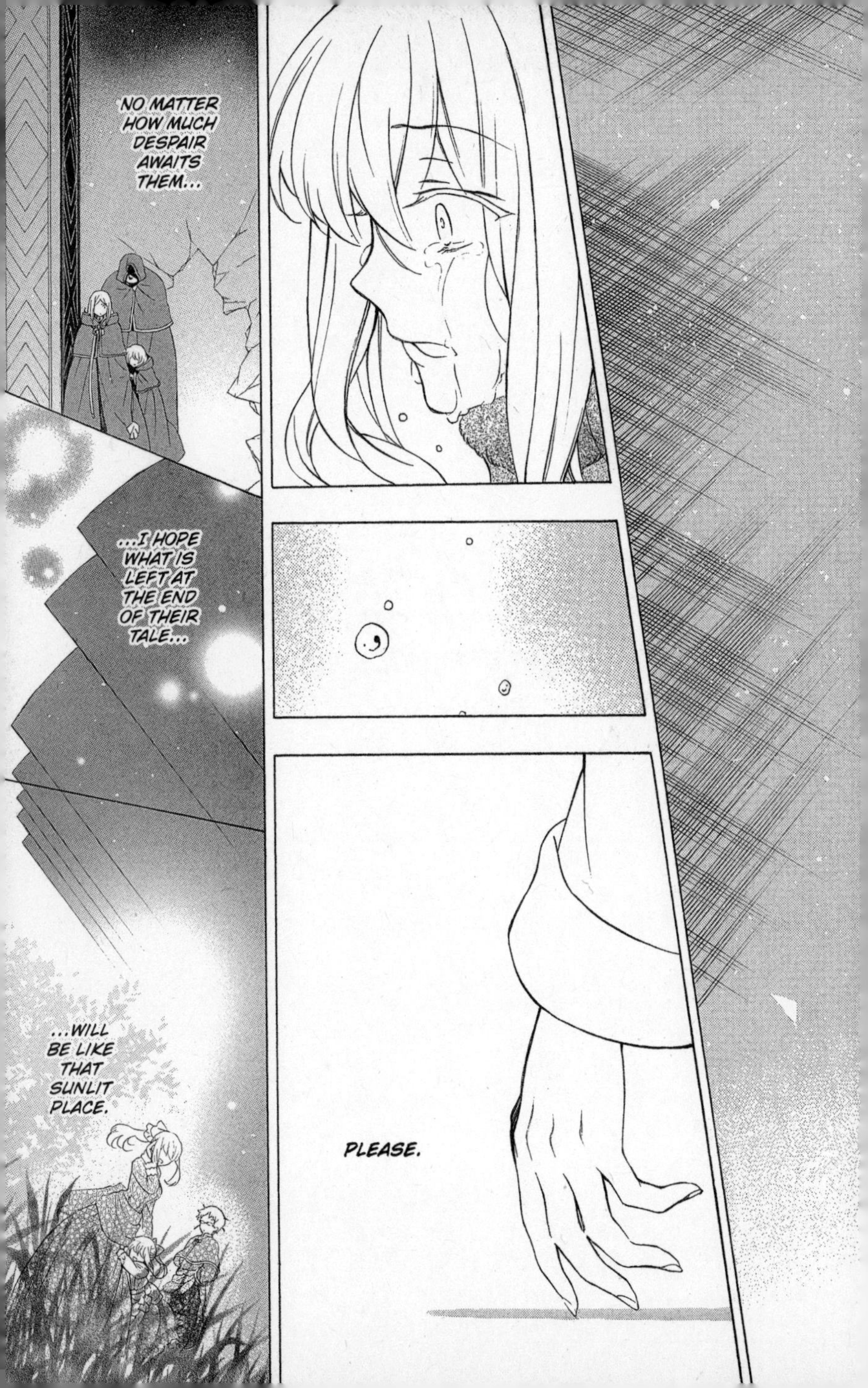
PLEASE.
NO MATTER HOW MUCH DESPAIR AWAITS THEM...
...I HOPE WHAT IS LEFT AT THE END OF THEIR TALE...
...WILL BE LIKE THAT SUNLIT PLACE.

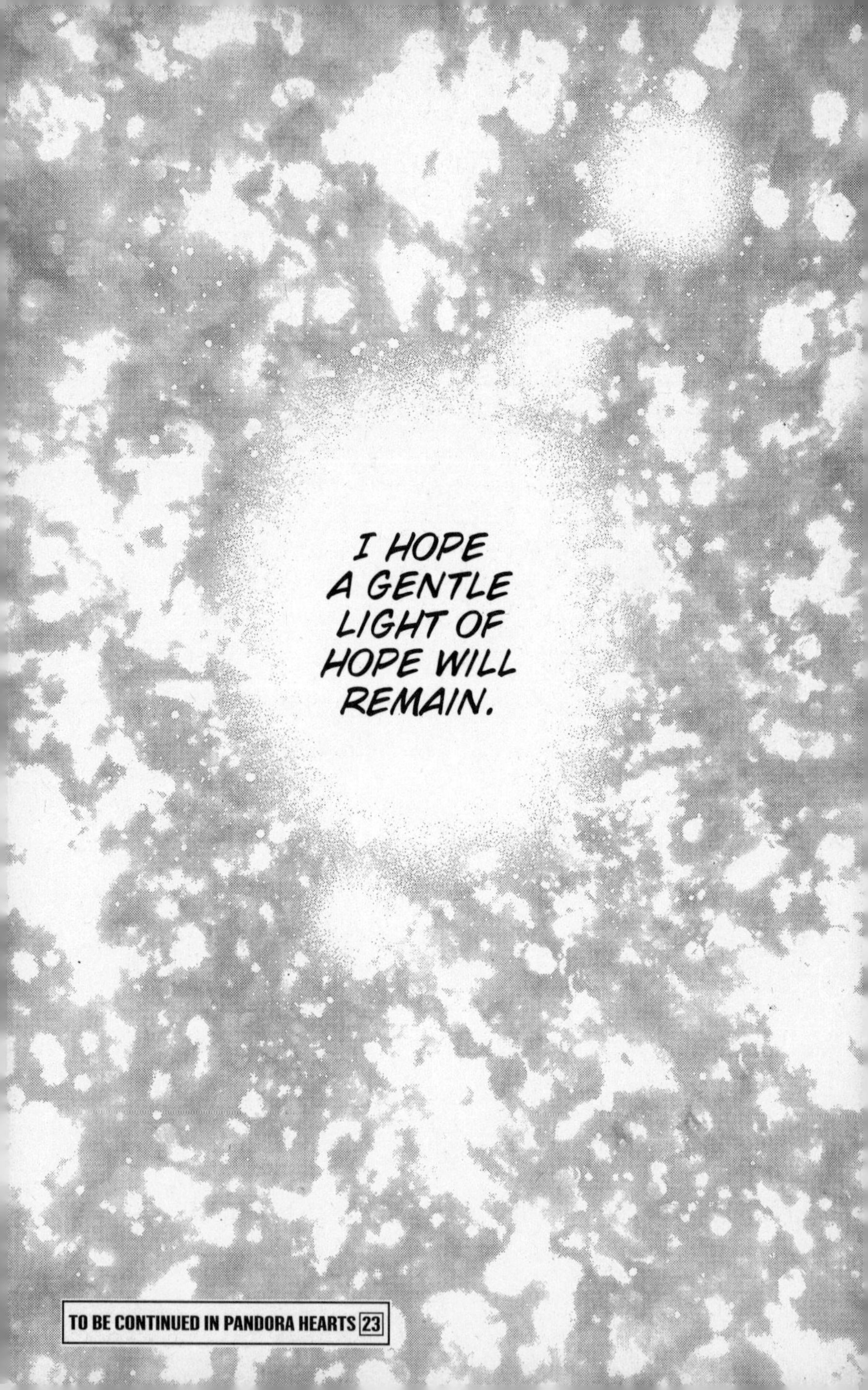
I HOPE A GENTLE LIGHT OF HOPE WILL REMAIN.
TO BE CONTINUED IN PANDORA HEARTS 23

Special thanks

FUMITO YAMAZAKI
IN MOURNING.

SAEKO TAKIGAWA-SAN
YOU GO TO THE HOSPITAL!!

KANATA MINAZUKI-SAN
GIMME A CAT A CAT!

YUKINO-SAN
I LOVE YOUR RUDE ATTITUDE TOWARDS TADUU.

RYO-CHAN
WEAR SOME LOUNGEWEAR!

MIZU KING-SAN
MIZU KING'S LOUNGEWEAR ARE MAGNUM-FORCE

TADUU-SAN
HUNTS FOR KANJI ERRORS AND TYPOS.

SAYA AYAHAMA-SAN
THE WOMAN WHO INVERTS THE WORLD

YOYA MAKOTO-SAN
FROM SMALL ITEMS TO LARGE ONES...

MIYUU-SAAAAAN!
NOTHING OTHER THAN MY MESSIAH.

MY FAMILY
YOUR BENTO ARE DELICIOUS!

MY EDITOR TAKEGASA-SAN SCARY.
HOSHI-SAN FUNNY.

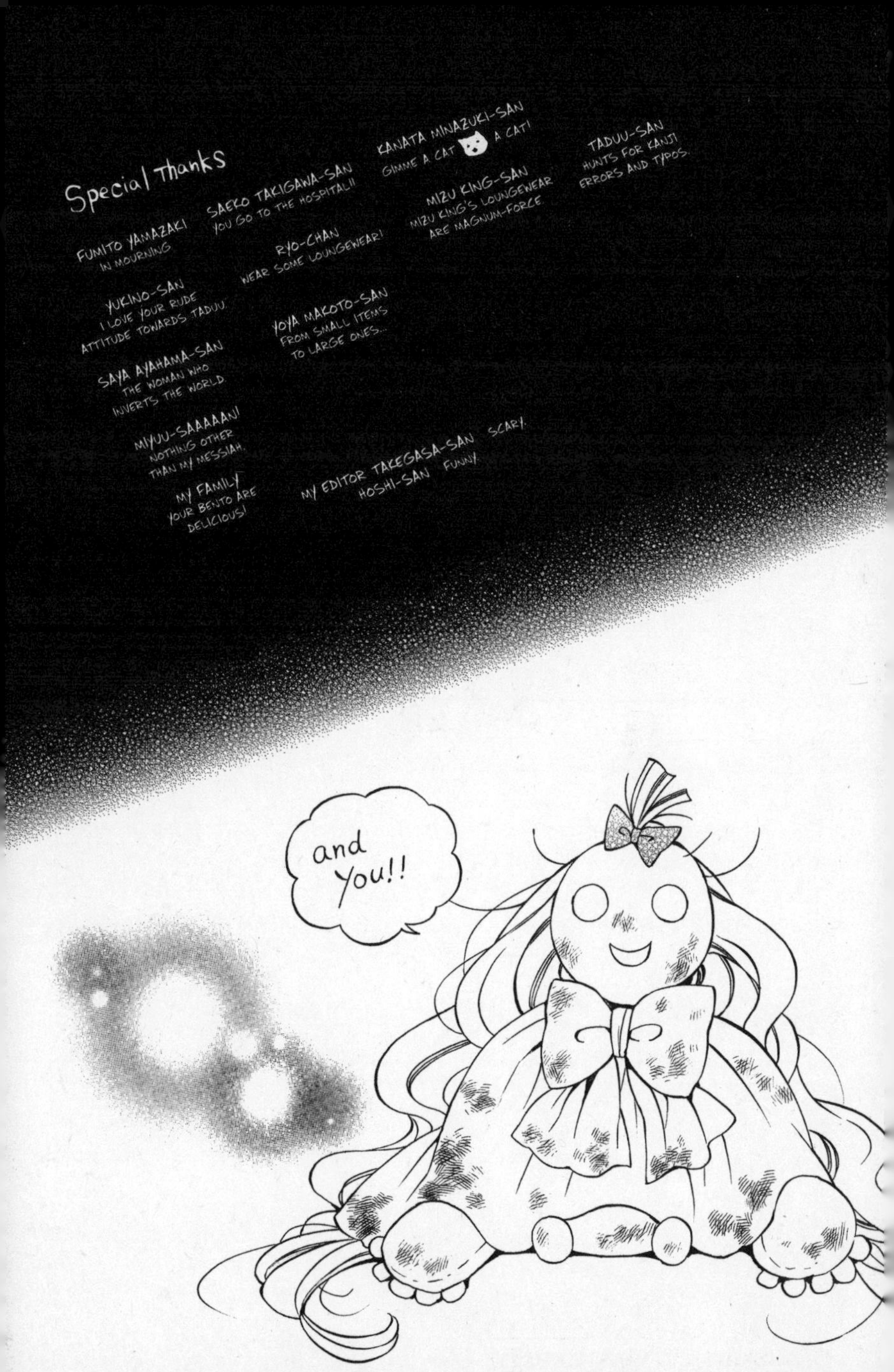
and You!!

NEXT
TIME—

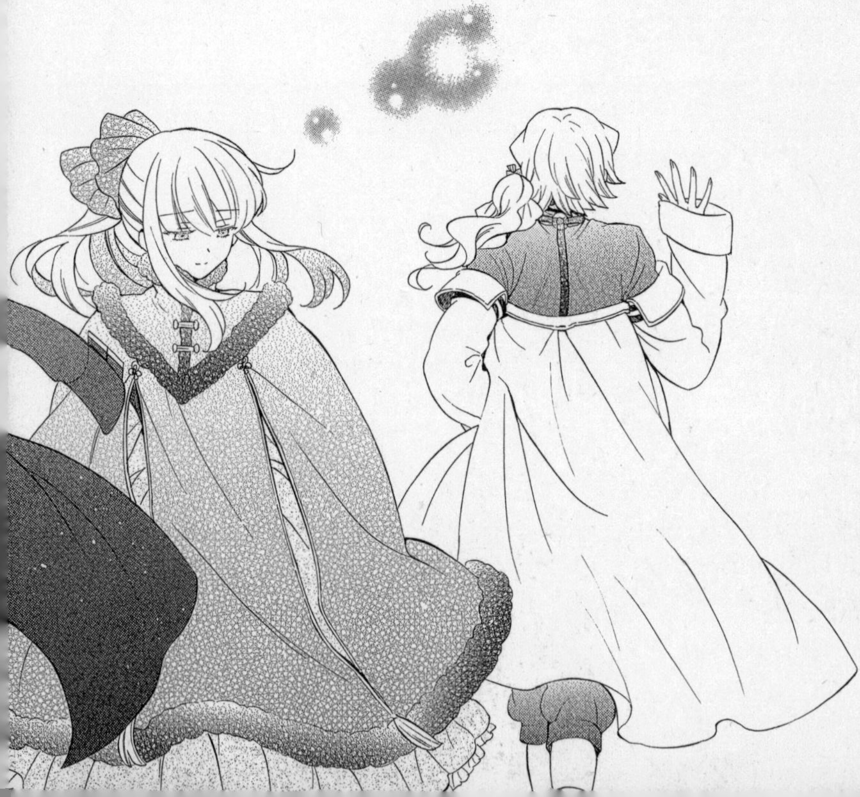

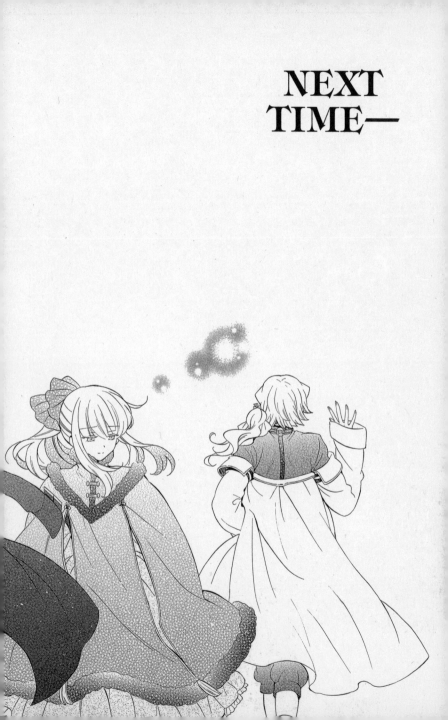

THE FINAL CHAPTER.

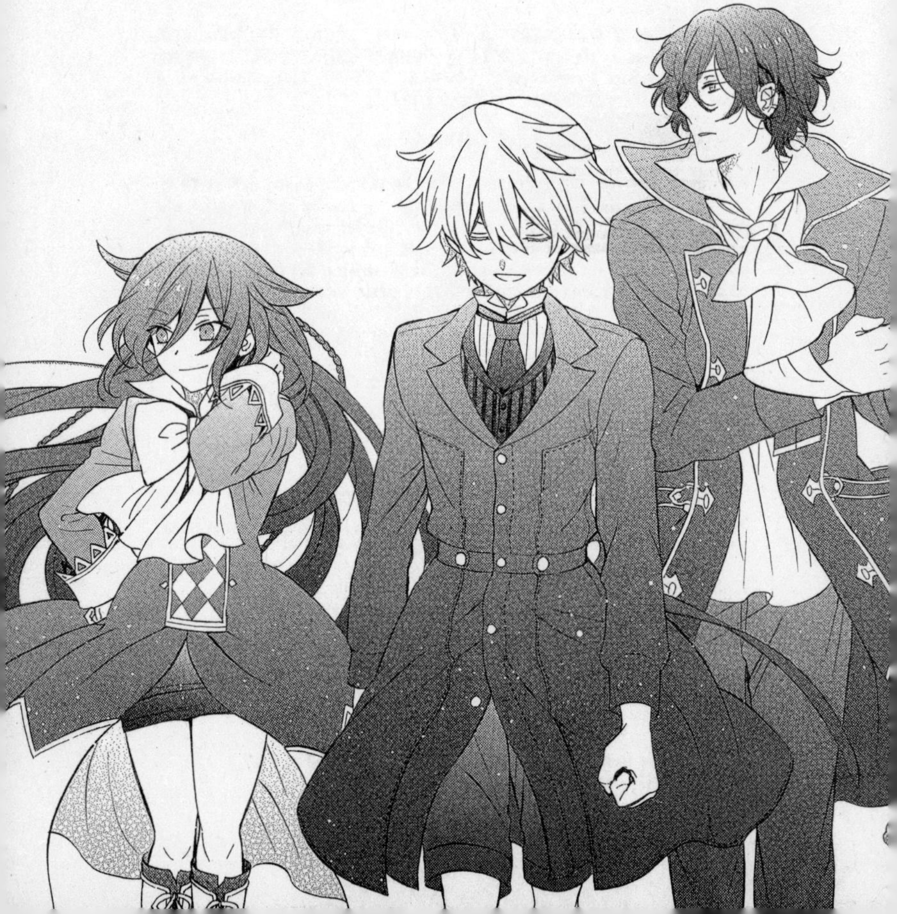

593720887652

PandoraHear

WITHDRAWN

Translation: Tomo Kimura • Lettering: Alexis Eckerman

This book is a work of fiction. Names, characters, places, and incidents are the product of the author's imagination or are used fictitiously. Any resemblance to actual events, locales, or persons, living or dead, is coincidental.

PandoraHearts Vol. 22 © 2014 Jun Mochizuki / SQUARE ENIX CO., LTD. First published in Japan in 2014 by SQUARE ENIX CO., LTD. English translation rights arranged with SQUARE ENIX CO., LTD. and Hachette Book Group through Tuttle-Mori Agency, Inc.

Translation © 2014 by SQUARE ENIX CO., LTD.

Yen Press
Hachette Book Group
1290 Avenue of the Americas,
New York, NY 10104

www.HachetteBookGroup.com
www.YenPress.com

Yen Press is an imprint of Hachette Book Group, Inc. The Yen Press name and logo are trademarks of Hachette Book Group, Inc.

First Yen Press Edition: November 2014

ISBN: 978-0-316-29813-1

10 9 8 7 6 5 4 3 2

BVG

Printed in the United States of America